Fodor's®

Prague and Budapest

The complete guide, thoroughly up-to-date

Packed with details that will make your trip

The must-see sights, off and on the beaten path

What to see, what to skip

Mix-and-match vacation itineraries

City strolls, countryside adventures

Smart lodging and dining options

Essential local do's and taboos

Transportation tips, distances, and directions

Key contacts, savvy travel tips

When to go, what to pack

Clear, accurate, easy-to-use maps

Books to read, helpful vocabulary

Excerpted from *Fodor's Eastern and Central Europe*

Fodor's Travel Publications, Inc.
New York • Toronto • London • Sydney • Auckland
www.fodors.com

II

Fodor's Prague and Budapest

EDITOR: Jennifer J. Paull

Editorial Contributors: David Brown, Christina Knight, Ky Krauthamer, Martha Lagace, Matthew Lore, Robert Rigney, Helayne Schiff, Julie Tomasz, Matt Welch

Editorial Production: Tom Holton

Maps: David Lindroth, *cartographer*; Steven Amsterdam, *map editor*

Design: Fabrizio La Rocca, *creative director*; Guido Caroti, *associate art director*; Jolie Novak, *photo editor*

Production/Manufacturing: Bob Shields

Cover Photograph: Sylvain Grandadam/Tony Stone Images

Copyright

Copyright © 1998 by Fodor's Travel Publications, Inc.

Fodor's is a registered trademark of Fodor's Travel Publications, Inc.

First Edition

ISBN 0-679-00096-8

Special Sales

CONTENTS

Maps and Charts

ON THE ROAD WITH FODOR'S

WHEN I PLAN A VACATION, the first thing I do is cast around among my friends and colleagues to find someone who's just been where I'm going. That's because there's no substitute for a recommendation from a good friend who knows your tastes, your budget, and your circumstances, someone who's just been there. Unfortunately, such friends are few and far between. So it's nice to know that there's *Fodor's Prague and Budapest.*

In the first place, this book won't stay home when you hit the road. It will accompany you every step of the way, steering you away from wrong turns and wrong choices and never expecting a thing in return. Most important of all, it's written and assiduously updated by the kind of people you *would* hit up for travel tips if you knew them. They're as choosy as your pickiest friend, and they have a wealth of insider's knowledge. In these pages, they don't send you chasing down every sight in the two capitals but have instead selected the best ones, the ones that are worthy of your time and money. To make it easy for you to put it all together in the time you have, they've created short, medium, and long itineraries and neighborhood walks that you can mix and match in a snap. Will this be the vacation of your dreams? We hope so.

About Our Writers

Our success in helping to make your trip the best of all possible vacations is a credit to the hard work of our extraordinary writers.

Ky Krauthamer and **Martha Lagace** contributed to the Prague chapter. A resident of Prague since 1992, Ky is the assistant features editor of the weekly *Prague Post*; he has also contributed to *Fodor's Pocket Prague, Fodor's Europe,* and *Fodor's Eastern and Central Europe.* Martha is an editor on the arts and entertainment desk of the *Prague Post.* She grew up in New England, Montana, and Canada, and was a freelance journalist in New York City and Paris before moving to Prague in the spring of 1991. She has also contributed to

Fodor's Pocket Prague, Fodor's Europe, and *Fodor's Eastern and Central Europe.*

Robert Rigney is a freelance writer from West Berlin who has been living in Prague since 1996. He writes about art, culture, and travel for American and European publications. Lately he has become something of a Prague shopping connoisseur.

Julie Tomasz, a travel and fiction writer of Hungarian descent, updated the Budapest chapter. She lived in Budapest for three years working as a founding editor of the *Budapest Sun,* and has been writing and editing for Fodor's for nine years, covering primarily Hungary but also making a foray farther east to write parts of Fodor's India guide. Julie's extensive off-duty travels have taken her to less-trodden areas, such as Albania and Transylvania. Hopelessly in love with Budapest and having acquired Hungarian citizenship, Julie plans to divide her time between the United States and Hungary.

Los Angeles–based writer **Matt Welch** was the founder of *Prognosis* (1991–1995), the first independent English-language newspaper in the former Soviet bloc. He was also manager for the *Budapest Business Journal* from 1995 to 1997 and served as UPI's Bratislava correspondent during Slovakia's first year of independence. He is currently the news editor of the Internet newspaper *Tabloid* and a contributor to the *Online Journalism Review.* He is also a musician, with three cassettes to his credit.

Editor **Jennifer J. Paull** would like to thank the national and local tourist offices for their help with questions great and small. She would also like to thank the updating team for their tremendous efforts.

We gratefully acknowledge **Malév Hungarian Airlines** for its help with realizing the Hungary chapter.

Connections

We're pleased that the American Society of Travel Agents continues to endorse Fodor's as its guidebook of choice. ASTA is the world's largest and most influential travel trade association, operating in more than 170 countries, with 27,000 members pledged to adhere to a strict code of ethics reflecting the Society's motto, "Integrity in Travel." ASTA shares Fodor's devotion to providing smart, honest travel information and advice to travelers, and we've long recommended that our readers—even those who have guidebooks and traveling friends—consult ASTA member agents for the experience and professionalism they bring to your vacation planning.

On Fodor's Web site (www.fodors.com), check out the new Resource Center, an online companion to the Gold Guide section of this book, complete with useful hot links to related sites. In our forums, you can also get lively advice from other travelers and more great tips from Fodor's experts worldwide.

How to Use This Book

Organization

Up front is the **Gold Guide,** an easy-to-use section arranged alphabetically by topic. Under each listing you'll find tips and information that will help you accomplish what you need to in Prague and Budapest. You'll also find addresses and telephone numbers of organizations and companies that offer destination-related services and detailed information and publications.

The first chapter in the guide, Destination: Prague and Budapest, helps get you in the mood for your trip. What's Where gets you oriented, New and Noteworthy cues you in on trends and happenings, Fodor's Choice showcases our top picks, and Festivals and Seasonal Events alerts you to special events you'll want to seek out.

Each city chapter begins with an Exploring section subdivided by neighborhood; each subsection recommends a walking tour and lists sights in alphabetical order. The remainder of the chapter is arranged in alphabetical order by subject—dining, lodging, nightlife and the arts, outdoor activities and sports, shopping. A side trip section is included in each chapter, covering day and overnight possibilities near Prague and Budapest; dining and lodging options are grouped together within each town description. Throughout, Off the Beaten Path sights appear after the places from which they are most easily accessible.

To help you decide what to visit in the time you have, all chapters begin with our recommended itineraries. The A to Z section that ends all chapters covers getting there and getting around. It also provides helpful contacts and resources.

At the end of the book you'll find Portraits, including suggestions for recommended reading and helpful vocabulary charts.

Icons and Symbols

★   Our special recommendations
✕   Restaurant
🏠   Lodging establishment
✕🏠 Lodging establishment whose restaurant warrants a special trip
🦆   Good for kids (rubber duck)
☞   Sends you to another section of the guide for more information
✉   Address
☎   Telephone number
🕗   Opening and closing times
💰   Admission prices (those we give apply to adults; substantially reduced fees are almost always available for children, students, and senior citizens)

Numbers in white and black circles (e.g., ③ ❸) that appear on the maps, in the margins, and within the tours correspond to one another.

Dining and Lodging

The restaurants and lodgings we list are the cream of the crop in each price range. Price charts appear in the Pleasures and Pastimes section that follows each chapter introduction.

Hotel Facilities

We always list the facilities that are available—but we don't specify whether you'll be charged extra to use them: When pricing accommodations, always ask what's included. In addition, assume that all rooms have private baths unless noted otherwise. In addition, when you book a room, be sure to mention if you have a disability or are traveling with children, if you prefer a private bath or a certain type of bed, or if you have specific dietary needs or other concerns.

Restaurant Reservations and Dress Codes

Reservations are always a good idea; we mention them only when they're essential or are not accepted. Book as far ahead as you can, and reconfirm as soon as you arrive. Unless otherwise noted, the restaurants listed are open daily for lunch and dinner. We mention dress only when men are required to wear a jacket or a jacket and tie. Look for an overview of local dining-out habits in the Pleasures and Pastimes section that follows each chapter introduction.

Credit Cards

The following abbreviations are used: **AE,** American Express; **DC,** Diners Club; **MC,** MasterCard; and **V,** Visa.

Don't Forget to Write

You can use this book in the confidence that all prices and opening times are based on information supplied to us at press time; Fodor's cannot accept responsibility for any errors. Time inevitably brings changes, so always confirm information when it matters—especially if you're making a detour to visit a specific place.

Were the restaurants we recommended as described? Did our hotel picks exceed your expectations? Did you find a museum we recommended a waste of time? Keeping a travel guide fresh and up-to-date is a big job, and we welcome your feedback, positive *and* negative. If you have complaints, we'll look into them and revise our entries when the facts warrant it. If you've discovered a special place that we haven't included, we'll pass the information along to our correspondents and have them check it out. So send us your thoughts via e-mail at editors@fodors.com (specifying the name of the book on the subject line) or on paper in care of the Prague and Budapest editor at Fodor's, 201 East 50th Street, New York, New York 10022. In the meantime, have a wonderful trip!

Karen Cure
Editorial Director

Eastern and Central Europe

RUSSIA

LITHUANIA

Minsk

BELARUS

Białystok

Warsaw

RUSSIA

Radom   Lublin

Kiev

Rzeszów
Przemyśl   L'vov   UKRAINE

Suceava   MOLDOVA

ROMANIA   Piatra-
Neamț   Iași

Oradea   Chișinău

Tîrgu
Mureș   Bacău   Odessa

Cluj-
Napoca

Arad   Alba Iulia   Bîrlad

Timișoara   Brașov   Galați

Reșița   Sibiu   Buzău   Brăila

Turnu   Pitești   Ploiești   Hîrșova
Severin   Urziceni

Craiova   Bucharest   Constanța   *Black Sea*

AVIA   Giurgiu

Belogradčik   Ruse

N

Pleven   Šumen   Varna

Veliko Tărnovo
Kazanlăk

Sofia   BULGARIA   Jambol   Burgas

Rila   Plovdiv
Pazardžik   Bačkovo

KEY
—— Rail Lines

Skopje

ACEDONIA   TURKEY

0   180 miles

0   270 km

Istanbul

SMART TRAVEL TIPS A TO Z

Basic Information on Traveling in Eastern and Central Europe, Savvy Tips to Make Your Trip a Breeze, and Companies and Organizations to Contact

AIR TRAVEL

BOOKING YOUR FLIGHT

Price is just one factor to consider when booking a flight: frequency of service and even a carrier's safety record are often just as important. Major airlines offer the greatest number of departures. Smaller airlines—including regional and no-frills airlines—usually have a limited number of flights daily. On the other hand, so-called low-cost airlines usually are cheaper, and their fares impose fewer restrictions, such as advance-purchase requirements. Safety-wise, low-cost carriers as a group have a good history—about equal to that of major carriers.

When you book, **look for nonstop flights** and **remember that "direct" flights stop at least once.** Try to **avoid connecting flights,** which require a change of plane. Two airlines may jointly operate a connecting flight, so ask if your airline operates every segment—you may find that your preferred carrier flies you only part of the way. International flights on a country's flag carrier are almost always nonstop; U.S. airlines often fly direct.

Ask your airline if it offers electronic ticketing, which eliminates all paperwork. There's no ticket to pick up or misplace. You go directly to the gate and give the agent your confirmation number. There's no worry about waiting in line at the airport while precious minutes tick by.

CARRIERS

When flying internationally, you must usually choose between a domestic carrier, the national flag carrier of the country you are visiting, and a foreign carrier from a third country. National flag carriers have the greatest number of nonstops. Domestic carriers may have better connections to your hometown and serve a greater number of gateway cities. Third-party carriers may have a price advantage.

➤ MAJOR AIRLINES: **Continental** (☎ 800/231–0856). **Delta** (☎ 800/241–4141). **Northwest** (☎ 800/447–4747). **United** (☎ 800/538–2929). In most cases, a European co-carrier provides a connecting flight from a gateway in Europe. The Czech and Hungarian national airlines offer nonstop service from the United States to their own countries and connecting flights to others. **Czech Air** (CSA; ☎ 212/765–6022). The most convenient way to fly between Hungary and the United States is with **Malév Hungarian Airlines** (☎ 212/757–6446) nonstop direct service between JFK International Airport in New York and Budapest's Ferihegy Airport—the only nonstop flight that exists. All are on roomy Boeing 767-200s and the service runs daily most of the year.

➤ FROM THE U.K.: **British Airways** (✉ 156 Regent St., London W1R 5TA, ☎ 0181/897–4000; 0345/222–111 outside London; 1/266–7790 or 1/318–3299 in Budapest). **British Midland** (☎ 0345/554–554) flies daily to Prague.

➤ REGIONAL CARRIERS: **Czech Air** (☞ above; ☎ 02/2010–4310 in Prague) offers flights within Eastern and Central Europe from Prague. **Malév Hungarian Airlines** (☞ above; in Budapest, ☎ 1/235–3535 or 06/80–212–121 toll free; 1/235–3804 [ticketing]; 1/296–9696 [after-hours flight information]) has regular nonstop flights between Budapest and major Eastern and Central European cities.

CHARTERS

Charters usually have the lowest fares but are the least dependable. Departures are infrequent and seldom on

time, flights can be delayed for up to
48 hours or can be canceled for any
reason up to 10 days before you're
scheduled to leave. Itineraries and
prices can change after you've booked
your flight.

In the U.S., the Department of Transportation's Aviation Consumer Protection Division has jurisdiction over
charters and provides a certain degree
of protection. The DOT requires that
money paid to charter operators be
held in escrow, so if you can't pay
with a credit card, **always make your
check payable to a charter carrier's
escrow account.** The name of the
bank should be in the charter contract. If you have any problems with a
charter operator, contact the DOT
(☞ Airline Complaints, *below*). If
you buy a charter package that includes both air and land arrangements, remember that the escrow
requirement applies only to the air
component.

CONSOLIDATORS

Consolidators buy tickets for scheduled international flights at reduced
rates from the airlines, then sell them
at prices that beat the best fare available directly from the airlines, usually
without restrictions. Sometimes you
can even get your money back if you
need to return the ticket. Carefully
read the fine print detailing penalties
for changes and cancellations, and
**confirm your consolidator reservation
with the airline.**

➤ CONSOLIDATORS: **Cheap Tickets**
(☎ 800/377–1000). **Up & Away
Travel** (☎ 212/889–2345). **Discount
Travel Network** (☎ 800/576–1600).
Unitravel (☎ 800/325–2222). **World
Travel Network** (☎ 800/409–6753).

COURIERS

When you fly as a courier, you trade
your checked-luggage space for a
ticket deeply subsidized by a courier
service. It's all perfectly legitimate,
but there are restrictions: You can
usually book your flight only a week
or two in advance, your length of stay
may be set for a certain number of
days, and you probably won't be able
to book a companion on the same
flight.

CUTTING COSTS

The least-expensive airfares to Prague
and Budapest are priced for round-
trip travel and usually must be purchased in advance. It's smart to **call a
number of airlines, and when you are
quoted a good price, book it on the
spot**—the same fare may not be
available the next day. Airlines generally allow you to change your return
date for a fee. If you don't use your
ticket, you can apply the cost toward
the purchase of a new ticket, again
for a small charge. However, most
low-fare tickets are nonrefundable.
To get the lowest airfare, **check different routings.** Compare prices of
flights to and from different airports
if your destination or home city has
more than one gateway. Also price
off-peak flights, which may be significantly less expensive.

Travel agents, especially those who
specialize in finding the lowest fares
(☞ Discounts & Deals, *below*), can
be especially helpful when booking a
plane ticket. When you're quoted a
price, **ask your agent if the price is
likely to get any lower.** Good agents
know the seasonal fluctuations of
airfares and can usually anticipate a
sale or fare war. However, waiting
can be risky: The fare could go *up* as
seats become scarce, and you may
wait so long that your preferred flight
sells out. A wait-and-see strategy
works best if your plans are flexible.
If you must arrive and depart on
certain dates, don't delay.

CHECK IN & BOARDING

Airlines routinely overbook planes,
assuming that not everyone with a
ticket will show up, but sometimes
everyone does. When that happens,
airlines ask for volunteers to give up
their seats. In return these volunteers
usually get a certificate for a free
flight and are rebooked on the next
flight out. If there are not enough
volunteers, the airline must choose
who will be denied boarding. The
first to get bumped are passengers
who checked in late and those flying
on discounted tickets, so **get to the
gate and check in as early as possible,** especially during peak periods.

Although the trend on international
flights is to drop reconfirmation

requirements, many airlines still ask you to reconfirm each leg of your international itinerary. Failure to do so may result in your reservation being canceled.

Always **bring a government-issued photo ID to the airport.** You may be asked to show it before you are allowed to check in.

ENJOYING THE FLIGHT

For more legroom, **request an emergency-aisle seat.** Don't sit in the row in front of the emergency aisle or in front of a bulkhead, where seats may not recline.

If you don't like airline food, **ask for special meals when booking.** These can be vegetarian, low-cholesterol, or kosher, for example.

When flying internationally, try to maintain a normal routine, to help fight jet-lag. At night, **get some sleep.** By day, **eat light meals, drink water (not alcohol), and move around the cabin** to stretch your legs.

Many carriers have prohibited smoking on all of their international flights; others allow smoking only on certain routes or certain departures, so **contact your carrier regarding its smoking policy.**

FLYING TIMES

Nonstop flying times to either Prague or Budapest are: nearly 9 hours from New York, about 15 hours from Los Angeles, and 2½ hours from London.

HOW TO COMPLAIN

If your baggage goes astray or your flight goes awry, complain right away. Most carriers require that you **file a claim immediately.**

➤ AIRLINE COMPLAINTS: U.S. Department of Transportation **Aviation Consumer Protection Division** (✉ C-75, Room 4107, Washington, DC 20590, ☎ 202/366–2220). **Federal Aviation Administration Consumer Hotline** (☎ 800/322–7873).

AIRPORTS

For the best way to get between the airport and your destination, *see* Arriving and Departing in the A to Z section at the end of each city's chapter.

➤ BUDAPEST: **Budapest Ferihegy Repülőtér** (Budapest Ferihegy Airport; ☎ 1/296–9696) is about 22 km (14 mi) southeast of Budapest. All Lufthansa and Malév flights operate from the newer Terminal 2, 4 km (2½ mi) farther from the city; other airlines use Terminal 1. For same-day flight information, call 1/296–7155; operators theoretically speak some English.

➤ PRAGUE: **Ruzyně Airport** (☎ 4202/367814 for arrival and departure times) is 20 km (12 mi) northwest of the downtown area; it's small but easily negotiated. Allow yourself plenty of time when departing because the airport is still too small to handle the large numbers of travelers who move through it. You may well encounter long lines at customs and check-in.

BIKE TRAVEL

BIKES IN FLIGHT

Most airlines will accommodate bikes as luggage, provided they are dismantled and put into a box. Call to see if your airline sells bike boxes (about $5; bike bags are at least $100) although you can often pick them up free at bike shops. International travelers can sometimes substitute a bike for a piece of checked luggage for free; otherwise, it will cost about $100. Domestic and Canadian airlines charge a $25–$50 fee.

BUS TRAVEL

Bus travel is generally more costly than travel by train, although this varies by country. In some instances, especially where trains are largely local (and stop seemingly every 100 feet), buses are actually speedier than rail travel. Comfort is minimal, though; roads tend to be bumpy and seats lumpy. Buses are generally tidier; train bathrooms are notoriously rank. It's a bit of a gamble; seats on buses are a rarity during prime traveling hours, and drivers don't always stop where they should, although most leave promptly on time (especially when you're still waiting in line for a ticket). Comfort and fares vary drastically by nation.

See Arriving and Departing by Bus *and* Getting Around by Bus and Tram in the A to Z section at the end of each city's chapter.

FROM THE U.K.

Unless you latch onto a real deal on airfare, a bus ticket from London's Victoria Terminal (☎ 0171/730–0202) is probably the cheapest transit from the United Kingdom to Eastern and Central Europe, although it may take a little research, as regularly scheduled routes to all cities except Berlin and Warsaw are practically nonexistent. Check newspaper ads for eastbound passage.

BUSINESS HOURS

In **Budapest,** banks are generally open weekdays 8–2 or 3, often with a one-hour lunch break at around noon; most close at 1 on Fridays. Museums are generally open Tuesday through Sunday from 10 to 6 and are closed on Mondays; most stop admitting people 30 minutes before closing time. Many have a free-admission day; see individual listings in tours below, but double-check, as the days tend to change. Department stores are open weekdays 10–5 or 6, Saturdays until 1. Grocery stores are generally open weekdays from 7 AM to 6 or 7 PM, Saturdays until 1 PM; "nonstops," or *éjjeli-nappali,* are (theoretically) open 24 hours.

In **Prague,** though hours vary, most banks are open weekdays 8–5. Private exchange offices usually have longer hours. Museums are usually open daily except Monday (or Tuesday) 9–5; they tend to stop selling tickets an hour before closing time. Stores are open weekdays 9–6; some grocery stores open at 6 AM. Department stores often stay open until 7 PM. On Saturday, most stores close at noon. Nearly all stores are closed on Sunday.

CAMERAS & COMPUTERS

EQUIPMENT PRECAUTIONS

Always **keep your film, tape, or computer disks out of the sun.** Carry an extra supply of batteries, and **be prepared to turn on your camera, camcorder, or laptop** to prove to security personnel that the device is real. Always **ask for hand inspection of film,** which becomes clouded after

successive exposure to airport X-ray machines, and **keep videotapes and computer disks away from metal detectors.**

➤ PHOTO HELP: **Kodak Information Center** (☎ 800/242–2424). *Kodak Guide to Shooting Great Travel Pictures,* available in bookstores or from Fodor's Travel Publications (☎ 800/533–6478; $16.50 plus $4 shipping).

CAR RENTAL

The big drawback here is price—rentals can rival airfare for the most expensive transport alternative. The pluses are a freewheeling itinerary and lots of luggage space. One restriction to keep in mind: Many rental companies have stipulations about picking up a car in Western Europe and dropping it off in Eastern or Central Europe. Such one-way rentals are usually prohibited (or prohibitively expensive).

➤ MAJOR AGENCIES: **Avis** (☎ 800/331–1084, 800/879–2847 in Canada, 008/225–533 in Australia). **Budget** (☎ 800/527–0700, 0800/181181 in the U.K.). **Dollar** (☎ 800/800–4000; 0990/565656 in the U.K., where it is known as Eurodollar). **Hertz** (☎ 800/654–3001, 800/263–0600 in Canada, 0345/555888 in the U.K., 03/9222–2523 in Australia, 03/358–6777 in New Zealand). **National InterRent** (☎ 800/227–3876; 0345/222525 in the U.K., where it is known as Europcar InterRent).

For local car rental companies, *see* Contacts and Resources in the A to Z section at the end of each city's chapter.

CUTTING COSTS

To get the best deal, **book through a travel agent who is willing to shop around.**

Also **ask your travel agent about a company's customer-service record.** How has the company responded to late plane arrivals and vehicle mishaps? Are there often lines at the rental counter? If you're traveling during a holiday period, does a confirmed reservation guarantee you a car?

Be sure to **look into wholesalers,** companies that do not own fleets but rent in bulk from those that do and often offer better rates than traditional car-rental operations. Prices are best during off-peak periods. Rentals booked through wholesalers must be paid for before you leave the United States.

➤ RENTAL WHOLESALERS: **Auto Europe** (☎ 207/842−2000 or 800/223−5555, FAX 800−235−6321). **DER Travel Services** (✉ 9501 W. Devon Ave., Rosemont, IL 60018, ☎ 800/782−2424, FAX 800/282−7474 for information or 800/860−9944 for brochures). **Kemwel Holiday Autos** (☎ 914/835−5555 or 800/678−0678, FAX 914/835−5126).

INSURANCE

When driving a rented car you are generally responsible for any damage to or loss of the vehicle. Before you rent, **see what coverage you already have** under the terms of your personal auto-insurance policy and credit cards.

Collision policies that car-rental companies sell for European rentals typically do not cover stolen vehicles. Before you buy additional coverage for theft, check with your credit-card company and personal auto insurance—you may already be covered.

REQUIREMENTS

In most Eastern and Central European countries, visitors need an International Driver's Permit; U.S. and Canadian citizens can obtain one from the American or Canadian Automobile Association, respectively. In some countries, including Hungary and the Czech Republic, many car rental agencies will accept an international license, but the formal permit is technically required. British visitors may use their own domestic licenses.

SURCHARGES

Before you pick up a car in one city and leave it in another, **ask about drop-off charges or one-way service fees,** which can be substantial. Note, too, that some rental agencies charge extra if you return the car before the time specified in your contract. To avoid a hefty refueling fee, **fill the tank just before you turn in the car,** but be aware that gas stations near the rental outlet may overcharge.

CAR TRAVEL

The plus side of driving is an itinerary free from the constraints of bus and train schedules and lots of trunk room for extra baggage. The negatives are many, however, not the least of which are shabbily maintained secondary roads, the risk of theft and vandalism, and difficulty finding gas. Crowded roads and fast and/or careless drivers add to the danger element. However, car travel does make it much easier to get to out-of-the-way monasteries and other sights not easily accessible by public transportation. Good road maps are usually available.

For specific information on driving to Prague and Budapest *see* Arriving and Departing by Car and Getting Around by Car in the A to Z section at the end of each city's chapter. Driving *in* the cities can be quite problematic, especially in Prague, where cars are not allowed in much of the city center.

A word of caution: If you have any alcohol whatsoever in your body, do not drive after drinking. Penalties are fierce, and the blood-alcohol limit is practically zero. (In Hungary, it *is* zero.)

AUTO CLUBS

➤ IN THE CZECH REPUBLIC AND HUNGARY: Czech Republic: **Autoturist** (✉ Na Rybníčku 16, Prague, ☎ 02/2491−1830). Hungary: **Hungarian Automobile Club** (✉ Budapest XIV, Francia út 38/B, ☎ 088).

➤ IN AUSTRALIA: **Australian Automobile Association** (☎ 06/247−7311).

➤ IN CANADA: **Canadian Automobile Association** (CAA, ☎ 613/247−0117).

➤ IN NEW ZEALAND: **New Zealand Automobile Association** (☎ 09/377−4660).

➤ IN THE U.K.: **Automobile Association** (AA, ☎ 0990/500−600), **Royal Automobile Club** (RAC, ☎ 0990/722−722 for membership, 0345/121−345 for insurance).

➤ IN THE U.S.: **American Automobile Association** (☎ 800/564−6222).

FROM THE U.K.

Theoretically it's possible to travel by car from the United Kingdom to the Czech Republic and Hungary, although it's really not recommended— if you have trouble with the car, you may well have difficulty getting parts or even finding a competent mechanic. However, if you do choose to drive your own vehicle, don't leave home without the car registration, third-party insurance, driver's license, and (if you're not the car's owner) a notarized letter of permission from the owner. The vehicle must bear a country ID sticker.

The best ferry ports for Prague and Budapest are Rotterdam, Holland, or Ostende, Belgium, from which you drive to Cologne (Köln), Germany, and then through either Dresden or Frankfurt and on to Prague.

ROADS & GASOLINE

The main roads in the Czech Republic and Hungary are built to a fairly high standard. There are now quite substantial stretches of highway on main routes, and a lot of rebuilding is being done. Gas stations are fewer than in the West, sited at intervals of about 48 kilometers (30 miles) along main routes and on the outskirts of large towns. Very few stations remain open after 9:30 PM. At least two grades of gasoline are sold, usually 90–93 octane (regular) and 94–98 octane (super). Lead-free gasoline is now available in most gas stations in both countries.

For additional information relating to driving, see Getting Around by Car in the A to Z section at the end of each city's chapter.

ROAD MAPS

In the **Czech Republic**, Čedok, the ubiquitous travel agency, is a good first stop for city maps. In Prague, the downstairs level of the Jan Kanzelsberger bookshop on Wenceslas Square (✉ Václavské nám. 42, ☎ 02/2421–7335) has a good selection of hiking maps and auto atlases. In **Hungary**, good maps are sold at most large gas stations. In Budapest, the Globe Térképbolt (Globe Map Store; ✉ VI, Bajcsy-Zsilinszky út 37, ☎ 1/312–6001) has an excellent

supply of domestic and foreign maps.

CHILDREN & TRAVEL

CHILDREN IN PRAGUE AND BUDAPEST

Be sure to plan ahead and **involve your youngsters** as you outline your trip. When packing, include things to keep them busy en route. On sightseeing days try to schedule activities of special interest to your children. If you are renting a car don't forget to **arrange for a car seat** when you reserve.

➤ SUGGESTED READING: *The Adventures of Mickey, Taggy, Pupo, and Cica and How They Discover Budapest,* by Kati Rekai (Canadian Stage Arts Publications, Toronto), is an animal fantasy story set in Budapest, written by a Hungarian-born author. Intricate illustrations of Prague fill Czech-American Peter Sis's *The Three Golden Keys* (Doubleday); aimed at young readers, it evokes the city of the author's childhood.

FLYING

If your children are two or older, **ask about children's airfares.** As a general rule, infants under two not occupying a seat fly at greatly reduced fares or even for free.

In general the adult baggage allowance applies to children paying half or more of the adult fare. When booking, **ask about carry-on allowances for those traveling with infants.** In general, for babies charged 10% of the adult fare you are allowed one carry-on bag and a collapsible stroller, which may have to be checked; you may be limited to less if the flight is full.

Experts agree that it's a good idea to use safety seats aloft for children weighing less than 40 pounds. Airlines, however, can set their own policies: U.S. carriers allow FAA-approved models but usually require that you buy a ticket, even if your child would otherwise ride free, since the seats must be strapped into regular seats. Airline rules vary, so it's important to **check your airline's policy about using safety seats during takeoff and landing.** Safety seats cannot obstruct the movement of other passengers in the row, so get an appropriate seat assignment as early as possible.

When making your reservation, **request children's meals or a free-standing bassinet** if you need them; the latter are available only to those seated at the bulkhead, where there's enough legroom. Remember, however, that bulkhead seats may not have their own overhead bins, and there's no storage space in front of you—a major inconvenience.

GROUP TRAVEL

When planning to take your kids on a tour, look for companies that specialize in family travel.

➤ FAMILY-FRIENDLY TOUR OPERATORS: Grandtravel (✉ 6900 Wisconsin Ave., Suite 706, Chevy Chase, MD 20815, ☎ 301/986–0790 or 800/247–7651) for people traveling with grandchildren ages 7–17. Families Welcome! (✉ 92 N. Main St., Ashland, OR 97520, ☎ 541/482–6121 or 800/326–0724, FAX 541/482–0660).

HOTELS

Most hotels in Prague and Budapest allow children under a certain age to stay in their parents' room at no extra charge, but others charge them as extra adults; be sure to **ask about the cutoff age for children's discounts.**

The **Novotel** chain (☎ 800/221–4542), which has hotels in Budapest, allows up to two children under 12 to stay free in their parents' room. The **Budapest Hilton** (☎ 1/214–3000 in Budapest) has an unusual policy allowing children of any age—even middle-aged adults—to stay for free in their parents' room.

Young visitors to Prague may enjoy staying in one of the city's picturesque floating **"botels."** For further information contact Čedok (☞ Visitor Information, *in* Prague A to Z).

CONSUMER PROTECTION

Whenever possible, **pay with a major credit card** so you can cancel payment or get reimbursed if there's a problem, provided that you can provide documentation. This is the best way to pay, whether you're buying travel

arrangements before your trip or shopping at your destination.

If you're doing business with a particular company for the first time, **contact your local Better Business Bureau and the attorney general's offices** in your state and the company's home state, as well. Have any complaints been filed?

Finally, if you're buying a package or tour, always **consider travel insurance** that includes default coverage (☞ Insurance, *below*).

➤ LOCAL BBBs: Council of Better Business Bureaus (✉ 4200 Wilson Blvd., Suite 800, Arlington, VA 22203, ☎ 703/276–0100, FAX 703/525–8277).

CUSTOMS & DUTIES

When shopping, **keep receipts** for all of your purchases. Upon reentering the country, **be ready to show customs officials what you've bought.** If you feel a duty is incorrect, appeal the assessment. If you object to the way your clearance was handled, get the inspector's badge number. In either case, first ask to see a supervisor, then write to the appropriate authorities, beginning with the port director at your point of entry.

IN THE CZECH REPUBLIC AND HUNGARY

➤ ON ARRIVAL: You may import duty-free into Hungary 250 cigarettes or the equivalent in tobacco, 1 liter of spirits, and 2 liters of wine. In addition to the above, you are permitted to import gifts valued up to 27,000 Ft. You may import duty-free into the Czech Republic 200 cigarettes, 100 cigarillos, 250 grams of tobacco, or 50 cigars, 1 liter of spirits, and 2 liters of wine, as well as gifts and personal items valued at up to 3,000 Kč (about $85).

If you are bringing into either of these countries any valuables or foreign-made equipment from home, such as cameras, it's wise to carry the original receipts with you or register the items with U.S. Customs before you leave (Form 4457). Otherwise you could end up paying duty upon your return. Be aware that leaving the country without expensive items declared upon entering can present a huge hassle with airport police.

➤ ON DEPARTURE: The export of items considered to have historical value from the Czech Republic is not allowed. Antiques, rare craft items, and the like must have an export certificate. Reputable shops should be willing to advise customers on how to comply with the regulations. If the shop can't provide proof of the item's suitability for export, be suspicious—if you aren't, the customs agent at the border will be. Theft of antiques—particularly Baroque religious pieces—is big business.

Take care when you leave Hungary that you have the right documentation for exporting goods. Keep receipts of any items bought from Konsumtourist, Intertourist, or Képcsarnok Vállalat. A special permit is needed for works of art, antiques, or objects of museum value. Upon leaving, you are entitled to a value-added tax (VAT) refund on new goods (i.e., not works of art, antiques, or objects of museum value) valued at more than 25,000 Ft. (VAT inclusive). But applying for the refund may rack up more frustration than money: Cash refunds are given only in forints, and you may find yourself in the airport minutes before boarding with a handful of soft currency, of which no more than 10,000 Ft. may be taken out of the country. If you made your purchases by credit card you can file for a credit to your card or to your bank account (again in forints), but don't expect it to come through in a hurry. If you intend to apply for the credit, make sure you get customs to stamp the original purchase invoice before you leave the country. For more information, pick up a tax refund brochure from any tourist office or hotel, or contact **Intel Trade Rt.** (⊠ I, Csalogány u. 6-10, ☎ 1/201–8120 or 1/356–9800) in Budapest. For further Hungarian customs information, inquire at the **National Customs and Revenue Office** (⊠ IX, Mester u. 7, Budapest, ☎ 1/218–0017). If you have trouble communicating, ask **Tourinform** (☎ 1/317–9800) for help.

IN AUSTRALIA

Australia residents who are 18 or older may bring back A$400 worth of souvenirs and gifts (including jewelry), 250 cigarettes or 250 grams of tobacco, and 1,125 ml of alcohol (including wine, beer, and spirits). Residents under 18 may bring back A$200 worth of goods.

➤ INFORMATION: **Australian Customs Service** (Regional Director, ⊠ Box 8, Sydney, NSW 2001, ☎ 02/9213–2000, ℻ 02/9213–4000).

IN CANADA

Canadian residents who have been out of Canada for at least 7 days may bring in C$500 worth of goods duty-free. If you've been away less than 7 days but more than 48 hours, the duty-free allowance drops to C$200; if your trip lasts 24–48 hours, the allowance is C$50. You may not pool allowances with family members. Goods claimed under the C$500 exemption may follow you by mail; those claimed under the lesser exemptions must accompany you. Alcohol and tobacco products may be included in the 7-day and 48-hour exemptions but not in the 24-hour exemption. If you meet the age requirements of the province or territory through which you reenter Canada, you may bring in, duty-free, 1.14 liters (40 imperial ounces) of wine or liquor *or* 24 12-ounce cans or bottles of beer or ale. If you are 16 or older you may bring in, duty-free, 200 cigarettes and 50 cigars.

You may send an unlimited number of gifts worth up to C$60 each duty-free to Canada. Label the package UNSOLICITED GIFT—VALUE UNDER $60. Alcohol and tobacco are excluded.

➤ INFORMATION: **Revenue Canada** (⊠ 2265 St. Laurent Blvd. S, Ottawa, Ontario K1G 4K3, ☎ 613/993–0534, 800/461–9999 in Canada).

IN NEW ZEALAND

Although greeted with a "Haere Mai" ("Welcome to New Zealand"), homeward-bound residents with goods to declare must present themselves for inspection. If you're 17 or older, you may bring back $700 worth of souvenirs and gifts. Your duty-free al-

THE GOLD GUIDE / SMART TRAVEL TIPS

lowance also includes 4.5 liters of wine or beer; one 1,125-ml bottle of spirits; and either 200 cigarettes, 250 grams of tobacco, 50 cigars, or a combo of all three up to 250 grams.

➤ INFORMATION: **New Zealand Customs** (✉ Custom House, 50 Anzac Ave., Box 29, Auckland, New Zealand, ☎ 09/359–6655, ☎ 09/309–2978).

IN THE U.K.

From countries outside the EU, including those covered in this book, you may import, duty-free, 200 cigarettes or 50 cigars; 1 liter of spirits or 2 liters of fortified or sparkling wine or liqueurs; 2 liters of still table wine; 60 milliliters of perfume; 250 milliliters of toilet water; plus £136 worth of other goods, including gifts and souvenirs.

➤ INFORMATION: **HM Customs and Excise** (✉ Dorset House, Stamford St., London SE1 9NG, ☎ 0171/202–4227).

IN THE U.S.

U.S. residents may bring home $400 worth of foreign goods duty-free if they've been out of the country for at least 48 hours (and if they haven't used the $400 allowance or any part of it in the past 30 days).

U.S. residents 21 and older may bring back 1 liter of alcohol duty-free. In addition, regardless of your age, you are allowed 200 cigarettes and 100 non-Cuban cigars. Antiques, which the U.S. Customs Service defines as objects more than 100 years old, enter duty-free, as do original works of art done entirely by hand, including paintings, drawings, and sculptures.

You may also send packages home duty-free: up to $200 worth of goods for personal use, with a limit of one parcel per addressee per day (and no alcohol or tobacco products or perfume worth more than $5); label the package PERSONAL USE, and attach a list of its contents and their retail value. Do not label the package UNSOLICITED GIFT, or your duty-free exemption will drop to $100. Mailed items do not affect your duty-free allowance on your return.

➤ INFORMATION: **U.S. Customs Service** (inquiries, ✉ Box 7407, Washington, DC 20044, ☎ 202/927–6724; complaints, ✉ Office of Regulations and Rulings, 1301 Constitution Ave. NW, Washington, DC 20229; registration of equipment, ✉ Resource Management, 1301 Constitution Ave. NW, Washington DC 20229, ☎ 202/927–0540).

DINING

For specific dining information, including price charts, *see* Dining *in* Pleasures and Pastimes at the beginning of each city chapter.

DISABILITIES & ACCESSIBILITY

ACCESS

Provisions for travelers with disabilities are extremely limited; probably the best solution is to travel with a nondisabled companion. While many hotels, especially large American or international chains, offer some wheelchair-accessible rooms, special facilities at museums, restaurants, and on public transportation are difficult to find.

➤ LOCAL RESOURCES: Visitors to Prague may contact **Sdružení zdravotné postižených** (Association of Disabled Persons; ✉ Karlínské nám. 12, Prague 8, ☎ 02/2481–5915). In Budapest, contact the **Mozgáskorláto-zottak Egyesületeinek Országos Szövetsége** (National Association of People with Mobility Impairments, or MEOSZ; ✉ 1032 Budapest, San Marco u. 76, ☎ 1/388–8951) for information on special services and accommodations.

MAKING RESERVATIONS

When discussing accessibility with an operator or reservations agent, **ask hard questions.** Are there any stairs, inside *or* out? Are there grab bars next to the toilet *and* in the shower/tub? How wide is the doorway to the room? To the bathroom? For the most extensive facilities meeting the latest legal specifications, **opt for newer accommodations,** which are more likely to have been designed with access in mind. Older buildings or ships may have more limited facilities. Be sure to **discuss your needs before booking.**

TRANSPORTATION

➤ COMPLAINTS: **Disability Rights Section** (✉ U.S. Department of Justice, Civil Rights Division, Box 66738, Washington, DC 20035–6738, ☎ 202/514–0301 or 800/514–0301, TTY 202/514–0383 or 800/514–0383, FAX 202/307–1198) for general complaints. **Aviation Consumer Protection Division** (☞ Air Travel, *above*) for airline-related problems. **Civil Rights Office** (✉ U.S. Department of Transportation, Departmental Office of Civil Rights, S-30, 400 7th St. SW, Room 10215, Washington, DC, 20590, ☎ 202/366–4648, FAX 202/366–9371) for problems with surface transportation.

TRAVEL AGENCIES & TOUR OPERATORS

As a whole, the travel industry has become more aware of the needs of travelers with disabilities. In the U.S., the Americans with Disabilities Act requires that travel firms serve the needs of all travelers. Note, though, that some agencies and operators specialize in making travel arrangements for individuals and groups with disabilities.

➤ TRAVELERS WITH MOBILITY PROBLEMS: **Access Adventures** (✉ 206 Chestnut Ridge Rd., Rochester, NY 14624, ☎ 716/889–9096), run by a former physical-rehabilitation counselor. **Flying Wheels Travel** (✉ 143 W. Bridge St., Box 382, Owatonna, MN 55060, ☎ 507/451–5005 or 800/535–6790, FAX 507/451–1685), a travel agency specializing in customized tours and itineraries worldwide. **Hinsdale Travel Service** (✉ 201 E. Ogden Ave., Suite 100, Hinsdale, IL 60521, ☎ 630/325–1335), a travel agency that benefits from the advice of wheelchair traveler Janice Perkins.

DISCOUNTS & DEALS

Be a smart shopper and **compare all your options** before making any choice. A plane ticket bought with a promotional coupon may not be cheaper than the least expensive fare from a discount ticket agency. For high-price travel purchases, such as packages or tours, keep in mind that what you get is just as important as what you save. Just because something is cheap doesn't mean it's a bargain.

CLUBS & COUPONS

Many companies sell discounts in the form of travel clubs and coupon books, but these cost money. You must use participating advertisers to get a deal, and only after you recoup the initial membership cost or book price do you begin to save. If you plan to use the club or coupons frequently, you may save considerably. Before signing up, find out what discounts you get for free.

➤ DISCOUNT CLUBS: **Entertainment Travel Editions** (✉ 2125 Butterfield Rd., Troy, MI 48084, ☎ 800/445–4137; $20–$51, depending on destination). **Great American Traveler** (✉ Box 27965, Salt Lake City, UT 84127, ☎ 801/974–3033 or 800/548–2812; $49.95 per year). **Moment's Notice Discount Travel Club** (✉ 7301 New Utrecht Ave., Brooklyn, NY 11204, ☎ 718/234–6295; $25 per year, single or family). **Privilege Card International** (✉ 237 E. Front St., Youngstown, OH 44503, ☎ 330/746–5211 or 800/236–9732; $74.95 per year). **Sears's Mature Outlook** (✉ Box 9390, Des Moines, IA 50306, ☎ 800/336–6330; $19.95 per year). **Travelers Advantage** (✉ CUC Travel Service, 3033 S. Parker Rd., Suite 1000, Aurora, CO 80014, ☎ 800/548–1116 or 800/648–4037; $59.95 per year, single or family). **Worldwide Discount Travel Club** (✉ 1674 Meridian Ave., Miami Beach, FL 33139, ☎ 305/534–2082; $50 per year family, $40 single).

CREDIT-CARD BENEFITS

When you use your credit card to make travel purchases you may get free travel-accident insurance, collision-damage insurance, and medical or legal assistance, depending on the card and the bank that issued it. American Express, MasterCard, and Visa provide one or more of these services, so **get a copy of your credit card's travel-benefits policy.** If you are a member of an auto club, always **ask hotel and car-rental reservations agents about auto-club discounts.** Some clubs offer additional discounts on tours, cruises, and admission to attractions.

DISCOUNT RESERVATIONS

To save money, **look into discount-reservations services** with toll-free numbers, which use their buying power to get a better price on hotels, airline tickets, even car rentals. When booking a room, always **call the hotel's local toll-free number** (if one is available) rather than the central reservations number—you'll often get a better price. Always ask about special packages or corporate rates.

When shopping for the best deal on hotels and car rentals, **look for guaranteed exchange rates,** which protect you against a falling dollar. With your rate locked in, you won't pay more, even if the price goes up in the local currency.

➤ AIRLINE TICKETS: ☎ 800/FLY–4–LESS.

➤ HOTEL ROOMS: **Hotels Plus** (☎ 800/235–0909). **International Marketing & Travel Concepts** (☎ 800/790–4682). **Steigenberger Reservation Service** (☎ 800/223–5652). **Travel Interlink** (☎ 800/888–5898).

PACKAGE DEALS

Packages and guided tours can save you money, but don't confuse the two. When you buy a package, your travel remains independent, just as though you had planned and booked the trip yourself. Fly/drive packages, which combine airfare and car rental, are often a good deal. If you **buy a rail/drive pass,** you'll save on train tickets and car rentals. All Eurail- and Europass holders get a discount on Eurostar fares through the Channel Tunnel.

ELECTRICITY

To use your U.S.-purchased electric-powered equipment, **bring a converter and adapter.** The electrical current in Prague and Budapest is 220 volts, 50 cycles alternating current (AC); wall outlets generally take plugs with two round prongs.

If your appliances are dual-voltage, you'll need only an adapter. Don't use 110-volt outlets, marked FOR SHAVERS ONLY, for high-wattage appliances such as blow-dryers. Most laptops operate equally well on 110 and 220 volts and so require only an adapter.

EMERGENCIES

For city-specific emergency information, *see* Emergencies *in* the A to Z section at the end of each city's chapter.

GAY & LESBIAN TRAVEL

Throughout Eastern and Central Europe, gay and lesbian resources are thin on the ground, if not underground. While the level of tolerance varies, the region is generally conservative; strongly Catholic countries are the most intolerant.

The Czech Republic is one of the most liberal countries. **Prague** fosters a growing gay and lesbian scene; the English-language *Prague Post* includes gay and lesbian clubs in its regular club listings. Hungary is also relatively open-minded, though even in **Budapest**, the gay population keeps a fairly low profile. Budapest's thermal baths are popular meeting places, as are the city's several gay bars and clubs, which you can find listed in English-language newspapers and the monthly magazine, *Mások*.

➤ GAY- AND LESBIAN-FRIENDLY TRAVEL AGENCIES: **Corniche Travel** (✉ 8721 Sunset Blvd., Suite 200, West Hollywood, CA 90069, ☎ 310/854–6000 or 800/429–8747, FAX 310/659–7441). **Islanders Kennedy Travel** (✉ 183 W. 10th St., New York, NY 10014, ☎ 212/242–3222 or 800/988–1181, FAX 212/929–8530). **Now Voyager** (✉ 4406 18th St., San Francisco, CA 94114, ☎ 415/626–1169 or 800/255–6951, FAX 415/626–8626). **Yellowbrick Road** (✉ 1500 W. Balmoral Ave., Chicago, IL 60640, ☎ 773/561–1800 or 800/642–2488, FAX 773/561–4497). **Skylink Travel and Tour** (✉ 3577 Moorland Ave., Santa Rosa, CA 95407, ☎ 707/585–8355 or 800/225–5759, FAX 707/584–5637), serving lesbian travelers.

HEALTH

You may gain weight, but there are few other serious health hazards to consider if you're traveling to Prague or Budapest. Tap water tastes bad but is generally drinkable; when it runs rusty out of the tap or the aroma of chlorine is overpowering, it might help to have some iodine tablets or bottled water handy. Vegetarians and those on special diets may have a problem with the heavy local cuisine, which is based almost exclusively on pork and beef. To keep your vitamin intake from falling to danger levels, buy fresh fruits and vegetables at seasonal street markets—regular grocery stores often don't sell them.

No vaccinations are required for entry into the Czech Republic or Hungary, but selective vaccinations are recommended. If you plan to visit forested areas of the countryside outside of the capitals, you should consider vaccinating yourself against Central European, or tick-borne, encephalitis. Tick-borne Lyme disease is also a risk in the Czech Republic. Schedule vaccinations well in advance of departure because some require several doses, and others may cause uncomfortable side effects.

To avoid problems clearing customs, diabetic travelers carrying needles and syringes should have on hand a letter from their physician confirming their need for insulin injections.

MEDICAL PLANS

No one plans to get sick while traveling, but it happens, so **consider signing up with a medical-assistance company.** Members get doctor referrals, emergency evacuation or repatriation, 24-hour telephone hot lines for medical consultation, cash for emergencies, and other personal and legal assistance. Coverage varies by plan, so **review the benefits of each carefully.**

➤ MEDICAL-ASSISTANCE COMPANIES: **International SOS Assistance** (✉ 8 Neshaminy Interplex, Suite 207, Trevose, PA 19053, ☎ 215/245–4707 or 800/523–6586, FAX 215/244–9617; ✉ 12 Chemin Riantbosson, 1217 Meyrin 1, Geneva, Switzerland, ☎ 4122/785–6464, FAX 4122/785–6424; ✉ 10 Anson Rd., 14-07/08 International Plaza, Singapore, 079903, ☎ 65/226–3936, FAX 65/226–3937).

HOLIDAYS

National holidays in the **Czech Republic** are: January 1; Easter Monday; May 1 (Labor Day); May 8 (Liberation Day); July 5 (Sts. Cyril and Methodius); July 6 (Jan Hus); October

28 (Czech National Day); and December 24, 25, and 26.

Hungary's national holidays are: January 1; March 15 (Anniversary of 1848 Revolution); April 4–5, 1999, April 22–23, 2000 (Easter and Easter Monday); May 1 (Labor Day); May 23–24, 1999 (Pentecost); August 20 (St. Stephen's and Constitution Day); October 23 (1956 Revolution Day); December 24–26.

INSURANCE

Travel insurance is the best way to **protect yourself against financial loss.** The most useful plan is a comprehensive policy that includes coverage for trip cancellation and interruption, default, trip delay, and medical expenses (with a waiver for preexisting conditions).

Without insurance, you will lose all or most of your money if you cancel your trip, regardless of the reason. Default insurance covers you if your tour operator, airline, or cruise line goes out of business. Trip-delay covers unforeseen expenses that you may incur due to bad weather or mechanical delays. It's important to compare the fine print regarding trip-delay coverage when comparing policies.

For overseas travel, one of the most important components of travel insurance is its medical coverage. Supplemental health insurance will pick up the cost of your medical bills should you get sick or injured while traveling. U.S. residents should note that Medicare generally does not cover health-care costs outside the United States, nor do many privately issued policies. Residents of the United Kingdom can buy an annual travel-insurance policy valid for most vacations taken during the year in which the coverage is purchased. If you are pregnant or have a preexisting condition, make sure you're covered. British citizens should buy extra medical coverage when traveling overseas, according to the Association of British Insurers. Australian travelers should buy travel insurance, including extra medical coverage, whenever they go abroad, according to the Insurance Council of Australia.

THE GOLD GUIDE / SMART TRAVEL TIPS

Always **buy travel insurance directly from the insurance company**; if you buy it from a cruise line, airline, or tour operator that goes out of business you probably will not be covered for the agency or operator's default, a major risk. Before you make any purchase, **review your existing health and home-owner's policies** to find out whether they cover expenses incurred while traveling.

➤ TRAVEL INSURERS: In the U.S., **Access America** (✉ 6600 W. Broad St., Richmond, VA 23230, ☎ 804/285–3300 or 800/284–8300). **Travel Guard International** (✉ 1145 Clark St., Stevens Point, WI 54481, ☎ 715/345–0505 or 800/826–1300). In Canada, **Mutual of Omaha** (✉ Travel Division, 500 University Ave., Toronto, Ontario M5G 1V8, ☎ 416/598–4083, 800/268–8825 in Canada).

➤ INSURANCE INFORMATION: In the U.K., **Association of British Insurers** (✉ 51 Gresham St., London EC2V 7HQ, ☎ 0171/600–3333). In Australia, the **Insurance Council of Australia** (☎ 613/9614–1077, FAX 613/9614–7924).

LANGUAGE

Czech, a Slavic language closely related to Slovak and Polish, is the official language of the Czech Republic. Learning English is popular among young people, but German is still the most useful language for tourists.

Hungarian (*Magyar*) tends to look and sound intimidating at first because it is not an Indo-European language. Generally, older people speak some German, and many younger people speak at least rudimentary English, which has become the most popular language to learn. It's a safe bet that anyone in the tourist trade will speak at least one of the two languages. Also note that when giving names, Hungarians put the family name before the given name.

LODGING

For city-specific lodging information, including price charts, *see* Lodging *in* Pleasures and Pastimes at the beginning of each city's chapter.

APARTMENT & VILLA RENTALS

If you want a home base that's roomy enough for a family and comes with cooking facilities, **consider a furnished rental.** These can save you money, especially if you're traveling with a large group of people. Home-exchange directories list rentals (often second homes owned by prospective house swappers), and some services search for a house or apartment for you (even a castle if that's your fancy) and handle the paperwork. Some send an illustrated catalog; others send photographs only of specific properties, sometimes at a charge. Up-front registration fees may apply.

➤ RENTAL AGENTS: **Europa-Let/Tropical Inn-Let** (✉ 92 N. Main St., Ashland, OR 97520, ☎ 541/482–5806 or 800/462–4486, FAX 541/482–0660). **Interhome** (✉ 124 Little Falls Rd., Fairfield, NJ 07004, ☎ 973/882–6864 or 800/882–6864, FAX 973/808–1742). **Property Rentals International** (✉ 1008 Mansfield Crossing Rd., Richmond, VA 23236, ☎ 804/378–6054 or 800/220–3332, FAX 804/379–2073). **Rent-a-Home International** (✉ 7200 34th Ave. NW, Seattle, WA 98117, ☎ 206/789–9377 or 800/488–7368, FAX 206/789–9379).

HOSTELS

No matter what your age, you can **save on lodging costs by staying at hostels.** In some 5,000 locations in more than 70 countries around the world, Hostelling International (HI), the umbrella group for a number of national youth hostel associations, offers single-sex, dorm-style beds and, at many hostels, "couples" rooms and family accommodations. Membership in any HI national hostel association, open to travelers of all ages, allows you to stay in HI-affiliated hostels at member rates (one-year membership is about $25 for adults; hostels run about $10–$25 per night). Members also have priority if the hostel is full; they're eligible for discounts around the world, even on rail and bus travel in some countries.

➤ HOSTEL ORGANIZATIONS: **Hostelling International—American Youth Hostels** (✉ 733 15th St. NW, Suite 840, Washington, DC 20005, ☎ 202/783–6161, FAX 202/783–6171). **Hostelling**

International—Canada (✉ 400-205
Catherine St., Ottawa, Ontario K2P
1C3, ☎ 613/237–7884, FAX 613/237–
7868). **Youth Hostel Association of
England and Wales** (✉ Trevelyan
House, 8 St. Stephen's Hill, St. Albans,
Hertfordshire AL1 2DY, ☎ 01727/
855215 or 01727/845047, FAX 01727/
844126); membership in the U.S. $25,
in Canada C$26.75, in the U.K. £9.30.

MAIL

For specific mail information, *see*
Mail *in* the A to Z section at the end
of each city's chapter.

MONEY

COSTS & CURRENCY

For specific money information, *see*
Money and Expenses *in* the A to Z
section at the end of each city's
chapter.

CREDIT & DEBIT CARDS

Should you use a credit card or a
debit card when traveling? Both have
benefits. A credit card allows you to
delay payment and gives you certain
rights as a consumer (☞ Consumer
Protection, *above*). A debit card, also
known as a check card, deducts funds
directly from your checking account
and helps you stay within your budget. When you want to rent a car,
though, you may still need an old-
fashioned credit card. Although you
can always *pay* for your car with a
debit card, some agencies will not
allow you to *reserve* a car with a
debit card.

Otherwise, the two types of plastic
are virtually the same. Both will get
you cash advances at ATMs worldwide if your card is properly pro-
grammed with your personal
identification number (PIN). For use
in the Czech Republic or Hungary,
your PIN must be four digits long.
Both offer excellent, wholesale exchange rates. And both protect you
against unauthorized use if the card is
lost or stolen. Your liability is limited
to $50, as long as you report the card
missing.

➤ ATM LOCATIONS: **Cirrus** (☎ 800/
424–7787). **Plus** (☎ 800/843–7587)
for locations in the U.S. and Canada,
or visit your local bank.

EXCHANGING MONEY

In general, you should **change money
at banks** for the most favorable
exchange rate. Although fees charged
for ATM transactions may be higher
abroad than at home, Cirrus and Plus
exchange rates are excellent, because
they are based on wholesale rates
offered only by major banks. You
often won't do as well at exchange
booths in airports or rail and bus
stations, in hotels, in restaurants, or
in stores, although you may find their
hours more convenient. To avoid lines
at airport exchange booths, **get a bit
of local currency before you leave
home.**

➤ EXCHANGE SERVICES: **Chase *Currency To Go*** (☎ 800/935–9935;
935–9935 in NY, NJ, and CT).
International Currency Express
(☎ 888/842–0880 on the East Coast,
888/278–6628 on the West Coast).
Thomas Cook Currency Services
(☎ 800/287–7362 for telephone
orders and retail locations).

TRAVELER'S CHECKS

Do you need traveler's checks? It
depends on where you're headed. The
general rule is: If you're going to rural
areas and small towns, go with cash;
traveler's checks are best used in
cities.

Lost or stolen checks can usually be
replaced within 24 hours. To ensure a
speedy refund, buy your own traveler's checks—don't let someone else
pay for them: irregularities like this
can cause delays. The person who
bought the checks should make the
call to request a refund.

PACKING

LUGGAGE

How many carry-on bags you can
bring with you is up to the airline.
Most allow two, but the limit is often
reduced to one on certain flights.
Gate agents will take excess baggage—including bags they deem
oversize—from you as you board and
add it to checked luggage. To avoid
this situation, make sure that everything you carry aboard will fit under
your seat. Also, get to the gate early,
and request a seat at the back of the
plane; you'll probably board first,

while the overhead bins are still empty. Since big, bulky baggage attracts the attention of gate agents and flight attendants on a busy flight, make sure your carry-on is really a carry-on. Finally, a carry-on that's long and narrow is more likely to remain unnoticed than one that's wide and squarish.

If you are flying internationally, note that baggage allowances may be determined not by piece but by weight—generally 88 pounds (40 kilograms) in first class, 66 pounds (30 kilograms) in business class, and 44 pounds (20 kilograms) in economy.

Airline liability for baggage is limited to $1,250 per person on flights within the United States. On international flights it amounts to $9.07 per pound or $20 per kilogram for checked baggage (roughly $640 per 70-pound bag) and $400 per passenger for unchecked baggage. You can buy additional coverage at check-in for about $10 per $1,000 of coverage, but it excludes a rather extensive list of items, shown on your airline ticket.

Before departure, **itemize your bags' contents** and their worth, and label the bags with your name, address, and phone number. (If you use your home address, cover it so that potential thieves can't see it readily.) Inside each bag, **pack a copy of your itinerary.** At check-in, **make sure that each bag is correctly tagged** with the destination airport's three-letter code. If your bags arrive damaged or fail to arrive at all, file a written report with the airline before leaving the airport.

PACKING LIST

Don't worry about packing lots of formal clothing. Fashion was all but nonexistent under 40 years of Communist rule, but residents of Prague and Budapest have quickly caught up to Western trends. A sports jacket for men and a dress or pants for women are appropriate for an evening out. Everywhere else, you'll feel comfortable in casual pants or jeans. Many areas are best seen on foot, so take a pair of sturdy walking shoes and be prepared to use them. High heels will present considerable problems on the cobblestone streets of Prague.

In both cities, toiletries and personal-hygiene products are quite easy to find, although if you are devoted to a particular Western brand you may want to bring your own supply. It's always a good idea to bring necessities if you make a side trip to rural areas.

In your carry-on luggage **bring an extra pair of eyeglasses or contact lenses** and **enough of any medication you take** to last the entire trip. You may also want your doctor to write a spare prescription using the drug's generic name, since brand names may vary from country to country. **Never put prescription drugs or valuables in luggage to be checked.** To avoid customs delays, carry medications in their original packaging. And don't forget to copy down and carry addresses of offices that handle refunds of lost traveler's checks.

PASSPORTS & VISAS

When traveling internationally, **carry a passport even if you don't need one** (it's always the best form of I.D.), and make **two photocopies of the data page** (one for someone at home and another for you, carried separately from your passport). If you lose your passport, promptly call the nearest embassy or consulate and the local police.

ENTERING THE CZECH REPUBLIC AND HUNGARY

➤ AUSTRALIANS: Australian citizens need a visa and a valid passport to visit the Czech Republic and Hungary.

➤ CANADIANS: You need a valid passport to enter Hungary for stays of up to 90 days, and to enter the Czech Republic for stays up to six months.

➤ U.K. CITIZENS: Citizens of the United Kingdom need a valid passport to enter Hungary for stays of up to 90 days, and to enter the Czech Republic for stays up to six months.

➤ NEW ZEALAND CITIZENS: New Zealand citizens need a valid passport to enter the Czech Republic for stays of up to one month; for travel to Hungary you must have both a visa and a passport.

➤ U.S. CITIZENS: All U.S. citizens, even infants, need a valid passport to enter the Czech Republic for stays of up to 30 days, and to enter Hungary for stays of up to 90 days.

PASSPORT OFFICES

The best time to apply for a passport or to renew is during the fall and winter. Before any trip, be sure to check your passport's expiration date and, if necessary, renew it as soon as possible. (Some countries won't allow you to enter on a passport that's due to expire in six months or less.)

➤ AUSTRALIAN CITIZENS: **Australian Passport Office** (☎ 13/1232).

➤ CANADIAN CITIZENS: **Passport Office** (☎ 819/994–3500 or 800/567–6868).

➤ NEW ZEALAND CITIZENS: **New Zealand Passport Office** (☎ 04/494–0700 for information on how to apply, 0800/727–776 for information on applications already submitted).

➤ U.K. CITIZENS: **London Passport Office** (☎ 0990/21010), for fees and documentation requirements and to request an emergency passport.

➤ U.S. CITIZENS: **National Passport Information Center** (☎ 900/225–5674; calls are charged at 35¢ per minute for automated service, $1.05 per minute for operator service).

SAFETY

Crime rates are still relatively low in Prague and Budapest, but travelers should beware of pickpockets in crowded areas, especially on public transportation, at railway stations, and in big hotels. In general, always keep your valuables with you—in open bars and restaurants, purses hung on or placed next to chairs are easy targets. Make sure your wallet is safe in a buttoned pocket, or watch your handbag.

In Hungary, pickpocketing and car theft are the main concerns. While a typical rental car is less likely to be stolen, expensive German makes such as Audi, BMW, and Mercedes are hot targets for car thieves. An unusual program recently started in Budapest; beginning in summer 1998, multilingual students have been posted in the city's most touristed areas to help visitors communicate with the police.

At press time, translators were expected to be stationed in the Lake Balaton region as well.

In the Czech Republic, there has been a small but worrying trend of attacks against people of color.

SENIOR-CITIZEN TRAVEL

To qualify for age-related discounts, **mention your senior-citizen status up front** when booking hotel reservations (not when checking out) and before you're seated in restaurants (not when paying the bill). Note that discounts may be limited to certain menus, days, or hours. When renting a car, **ask about promotional car-rental discounts,** which can be cheaper than senior-citizen rates.

➤ LOCAL DISCOUNTS: In Hungary, non-Hungarian senior citizens (men over 60, women over 55) are eligible for a 20% discount on rail travel. Contact or visit **MÁV Passenger Service** (⊠ Andrassy út 35, Budapest VI, ☎ 1/322–8275) for information.

➤ EDUCATIONAL PROGRAMS: **Elderhostel** (⊠ 75 Federal St., 3rd floor, Boston, MA 02110, ☎ 617/426–8056). **Interhostel** (⊠ University of New Hampshire, 6 Garrison Ave., Durham, NH 03824, ☎ 603/862–1147 or 800/733–9753, FAX 603/862–1113).

STUDENT TRAVEL

For city-specific student and youth travel information, *see* Student and Youth Travel *in* the A to Z section at the end of each city's chapter.

TRAVEL AGENCIES

To save money, **look into deals available through student-oriented travel agencies.** To qualify you'll need a bona fide student I.D. card. Members of international student groups are also eligible.

➤ STUDENT I.D.S & SERVICES: **Council on International Educational Exchange** (⊠ CIEE, 205 E. 42nd St., 14th floor, New York, NY 10017, ☎ 212/822–2600 or 888/268–6245, FAX 212/822–2699), for mail orders only, in the United States. **Travel Cuts** (⊠ 187 College St., Toronto, Ontario M5T 1P7, ☎ 416/979–2406 or 800/667–2887) in Canada.

➤ STUDENT TOURS: **Contiki Holidays** (✉ 300 Plaza Alicante, Suite 900, Garden Grove, CA 92840, ☎ 714/740–0808 or 800/266–8454, FAX 714/740–2034).

TAXES

For country-specific tax and VAT information, *see* Customs and Duties *above* and Money and Expenses *in* the A to Z section at the end of each city's chapter.

TELEPHONES

COUNTRY CODES

Country and select city codes are as follows: Czech Republic (420), Prague (2); Hungary (36), Budapest (1).

For additional telephone information, *see* Telephones *in* the A to Z section at the end of each city's chapter.

INTERNATIONAL CALLS

AT&T, MCI, and Sprint international access codes make calling the United States relatively convenient, but you may find the local access number blocked in many hotel rooms. First ask the hotel operator to connect you. If the hotel operator balks, ask for an international operator, or dial the international operator yourself. One way to improve your odds of getting connected to your long-distance carrier is to travel with more than one company's calling card (a hotel may block Sprint, for example, but not MCI). If all else fails, call from a pay phone in the hotel lobby.

➤ ACCESS CODES: **AT&T Direct** (☎ 0042000101 in the Czech Republic; 0080001111 in Hungary; 800/435–0812 for other areas). **MCI World-Phone** (☎ 0042000112 in the Czech Republic; 0080001411 in Hungary; 800/444–4141 for other areas). **Sprint International Access** (☎ 0042087187 in the Czech Republic; 0080001877 in Hungary; 800/877–4646 for other areas).

TOUR OPERATORS

Buying a prepackaged tour or independent vacation can make your trip to Prague or Budapest less expensive and more hassle-free. Because everything is prearranged, you'll spend less time planning.

Operators that handle several hundred thousand travelers per year can use their purchasing power to give you a good price. Their high volume may also indicate financial stability. But some small companies provide more personalized service; because they tend to specialize, they may also be more knowledgeable about a given area.

BOOKING WITH AN AGENT

Travel agents are excellent resources. In fact, large operators accept bookings made only through travel agents. But it's a good idea to **collect brochures from several agencies,** because some agents' suggestions may be influenced by relationships with tour and package firms that reward them for volume sales. If you have a special interest, **find an agent with expertise in that area**; ASTA (☞ Travel Agencies, *below*) has a database of specialists worldwide.

Make sure your travel agent knows the accommodations and other services. Ask about the hotel's location, room size, beds, and whether it has a pool, room service, or programs for children, if you care about these. Has your agent been there in person or sent others you can contact?

Do some homework on your own, too: Local tourism boards can provide information about lesser-known and small-niche operators, some of which may sell only direct.

BUYER BEWARE

Each year consumers are stranded or lose their money when tour operators—even very large ones with excellent reputations—go out of business. So **check out the operator.** Find out how long the company has been in business, and ask several travel agents about its reputation. If the package or tour you are considering is priced lower than in your wildest dreams, **be skeptical.** Try to **book with a company that has a consumer-protection program.** If the operator has such a program, you'll find information about it in the company's brochure. If the operator you are considering does not offer some kind of consumer protection, then ask for references from satisfied customers.

In the U.S., members of the National Tour Association and United States Tour Operators Association are required to set aside funds to cover your payments and travel arrangements in case the company defaults. It's also a good idea to choose a company that participates in the American Society of Travel Agent's Tour Operator Program (TOP). This gives you a forum if there are any disputes between you and your tour operator; ASTA will act as mediator.

➤ TOUR-OPERATOR RECOMMENDATIONS: **American Society of Travel Agents** (☞ Travel Agencies, *below*). **National Tour Association** (✉ NTA, 546 E. Main St., Lexington, KY 40508, ☎ 606/226–4444 or 800/755–8687). **United States Tour Operators Association** (✉ USTOA, 342 Madison Ave., Suite 1522, New York, NY 10173, ☎ 212/599–6599 or 800/468–7862, FAX 212/599–6744).

COSTS

Prices for packages and tours are usually quoted per person, based on two sharing a room. If traveling solo, you may be required to pay the full double-occupancy rate. Some operators eliminate this surcharge if you agree to be matched with a roommate of the same sex, even if one is not found by departure time.

GROUP TOURS

Among companies that sell tours to Prague and Budapest, the following are nationally known, have a proven reputation, and offer plenty of options. The classifications used below represent different price categories, and you'll probably encounter these terms when talking to a travel agent or tour operator. The key difference is usually in accommodations, which run from budget to better, and better-yet to best.

➤ SUPER-DELUXE: **Abercrombie & Kent** (✉ 1520 Kensington Rd., Oak Brook, IL 60521-2141, ☎ 630/954–2944 or 800/323–7308, FAX 630/954–3324). **Travcoa** (✉ Box 2630, 2350 S.E. Bristol St., Newport Beach, CA 92660, ☎ 714/476–2800 or 800/992–2003, FAX 714/476–2538).

➤ DELUXE: **Globus** (✉ 5301 S. Federal Circle, Littleton, CO 80123-2980, ☎ 303/797–2800 or 800/221–

0090, FAX 303/347–2080). **Maupintour** (✉ 1515 St. Andrews Dr., Lawrence, KS 66047, ☎ 785/843–1211 or 800/255–4266, FAX 785/843–8351). **Tauck Tours** (✉ Box 5027, 276 Post Rd. W, Westport, CT 06881-5027, ☎ 203/226–6911 or 800/468–2825, FAX 203/221–6866).

➤ FIRST-CLASS: **Brendan Tours** (✉ 15137 Califa St., Van Nuys, CA 91411, ☎ 818/785–9696 or 800/421–8446, FAX 818/902–9876). **Caravan Tours** (✉ 401 N. Michigan Ave., Chicago, IL 60611, ☎ 312/321–9800 or 800/227–2826, FAX 312/321–9845). **Čedok Travel** (✉ 10 E. 40th St., #3604, New York, NY 10016, ☎ 212/725–0948 or 800/800–8891). **Collette Tours** (✉ 162 Middle St., Pawtucket, RI 02860, ☎ 401/728–3805 or 800/340–5158, FAX 401/728–4745). **DER Tours** (✉ 9501 W. Devon St., Rosemont, IL 60018, ☎ 800/937–1235, FAX 847/692–4141 or 800/282–7474, 800/860–9944 for brochures). **General Tours** (✉ 53 Summer St., Keene, NH 03431, ☎ 603/357–5033 or 800/221–2216, FAX 603/357–4548). **Insight International Tours** (✉ 745 Atlantic Ave., #720, Boston, MA 02111, ☎ 617/482–2000 or 800/582–8380, FAX 617/482–2884 or 800/622–5015). **Trafalgar Tours** (✉ 11 E. 26th St., New York, NY 10010, ☎ 212/689–8977 or 800/854–0103, FAX 800/457–6644).

➤ BUDGET: **Cosmos** (☞ Globus, *above*). **Trafalgar Tours** (☞ *above*).

PACKAGES

Like group tours, independent vacation packages are available from major tour operators and airlines. The companies listed below offer packages in a broad price range.

➤ AIR/HOTEL: **Continental Vacations** (☎ 800/634–5555). **DER Tours** (☞ Group Tours, *above*). **General Tours** (☞ Group Tours, *above*).

THEME TRIPS

➤ BARGE/RIVER CRUISES: **KD River Cruises of Europe** (✉ 2500 Westchester Ave., Purchase, NY 10577, ☎ 914/696–3600 or 800/346–6525, FAX 914/696–0833).

➤ BEER/WINE: **MIR Corporation** (✉ 85 S. Washington St., #210, Seattle,

THE GOLD GUIDE / SMART TRAVEL TIPS

THE GOLD GUIDE / SMART TRAVEL TIPS

WA 98104, ☎ 206/624–7289 or 800/424–7289, FAX 206/624–7360).

➤ CRUISING: **EuroCruises** (✉ 303 W. 13th St., New York, NY 10014-1207, ☎ 800/688–3876, FAX 212/366–4747).

➤ HISTORY & ART: **IST Cultural Tours** (✉ 225 W. 34th St., New York, NY 10122-0913, ☎ 212/563–1202 or 800/833–2111, FAX 212/594–6953). **Smithsonian Study Tours and Seminars** (✉ 1100 Jefferson Dr. SW, Room 3045, MRC 702, Washington, DC 20560, ☎ 202/357–4700, FAX 202/633–9250).

➤ PERFORMING ARTS: **Dailey-Thorp Travel** (✉ 330 W. 58th St., #610, New York, NY 10019-1817, ☎ 212/307–1555 or 800/998–4677, FAX 212/974–1420).

➤ SPAS: **Great Spas of the World** (✉ 55 John St., New York, NY 10038, ☎ 212/267–5500 or 800/772–8463, FAX 212/571–0510). **Spa-Finders** (✉ 91 5th Ave., #301, New York, NY 10003-3039, ☎ 212/924–6800 or 800/255–7727).

TRAIN TRAVEL

Although standards have improved during the past few years, on the whole they are far short of what is acceptable in the West. Trains are very busy, and it is rare to find one running less than full or almost so. Trains in the Czech Republic and Hungary operate their own dining, buffet, and refreshment services. Always crowded, they tend to open and close at the whim of the staff. In Hungary, couchette cars are second class only and can be little more than a hard bunk without springs and adequate bed linen. On Czech trains, there are first-class couchettes and two types of second-class couchettes. The cheapest (*lehatko*) has six hard beds per compartment; the slightly more expensive *lůžko* has three beds and a sink, and is sex-segregated. The most comfortable trains in the Czech Republic and Hungary are the express trains—they're normally less crowded and more comfortable (you should make a reservation).

Although trains in the Czech Republic and Hungary can mean hours of sitting on a hard seat in a smoky car, traveling by rail is very inexpensive (it's much cheaper than renting a car in this part of Europe). Rail networks are very extensive, though trains can be infuriatingly slow. You'll invariably enjoy interesting and friendly traveling company, however; most Czechs and Hungarians are eager to hear about the West and to discuss the changes in their own countries.

DISCOUNT PASSES

To save money, **look into rail passes.** But be aware that if you don't plan to cover many miles, you may come out ahead by buying individual tickets.

You can use the **European East Pass** on the national rail networks of Austria, the Czech Republic, Hungary, Poland, and Slovakia. The pass covers five days of unlimited first-class travel within a one-month period for $199. Additional travel days may be purchased.

You can also combine the East Pass with a national rail pass. A pass for the Czech Republic costs $69 for five days of train travel within a 15-day period. The Hungarian Flexipass costs $55 for five days of unlimited first-class train travel within a 15-day period or $69 for 10 days within a one-month period.

Hungary is one of 17 countries in which you can use **Eurailpasses,** which provide unlimited first-class rail travel, in all of the participating countries. If you plan to rack up the miles, get a standard pass. These are available for 15 days ($538), 21 days ($698), one month ($864), two months ($1,224), and three months ($1,512).

In addition to standard Eurailpasses, **ask about special rail-pass plans.** Among these are the Eurail Youthpass (for those under age 26), the Eurail Saverpass (which gives a discount for two or more people traveling together), a Eurail Flexipass (which allows a certain number of travel days within a set period), the Euraildrive Pass and the Europass Drive (which combine travel by train and rental car). Whichever pass you choose, remember that you must **purchase your pass before you leave** for Europe.

Many travelers assume that rail passes guarantee them seats on the trains they wish to ride. Not so. You need to **book seats ahead even if you are using a rail pass**; seat reservations are required on some European trains, particularly high-speed trains, and are a good idea on trains that may be crowded—particularly in summer on popular routes. You will also need a reservation if you purchase sleeping accommodations.

➤ INFORMATION AND PASSES: **Rail Europe** (⊠ 500 Mamaroneck Ave., Harrison, NY 10528, ☎ 914/682–5172 or 800/438–7245, FAX 800/432–1329; ⊠ 2087 Dundas E, Suite 106, Mississauga, Ontario L4X 1M2, ☎ 800/361–7245, FAX 905/602–4198). **DER Travel Services** (⊠ 9501 W. Devon Ave., Rosemont, IL 60018, ☎ 800/782–2424, FAX 800/282–7474 for information or 800/860–9944 for brochures). **CIT Tours Corp.** (⊠ 15 West 44th Street, 10th Floor, New York, NY 10036, ☎ 212/730–2400 or 800/248–7245 in the U.S., 800/387–0711 or 800/361–7799 in Canada).

FROM THE U.K.

There are no direct trains from London. You can take a direct train from Paris via Frankfurt to Prague (daily) or from Berlin via Dresden to Prague (six times a day). Vienna is a good starting point for Prague; there are three trains a day to Prague from Vienna's Südbahnhof (South Station) via Brno (5 hours).

TRAVEL AGENCIES

A good travel agent puts your needs first. Look for an agency that has been in business at least five years, emphasizes customer service, and has someone on staff who specializes in your destination. In addition, **make sure the agency belongs to a professional trade organization,** such as ASTA in the United States. If your travel agency is also acting as your tour operator, see Buyer Beware in Tour Operators, above).

➤ LOCAL AGENT REFERRALS: **American Society of Travel Agents** (ASTA; ☎ 800/965–2782 24-hr hot line, FAX 703/684–8319). **Association of Canadian Travel Agents** (⊠ Suite 201, 1729 Bank St., Ottawa, Ontario K1V 7Z5, ☎ 613/521–0474, FAX 613/521–0805). **Association of British Travel Agents** (⊠ 55–57 Newman St., London W1P 4AH, ☎ 0171/637–2444, FAX 0171/637–0713). **Australian Federation of Travel Agents** (☎ 02/9264–3299). **Travel Agents' Association of New Zealand** (☎ 04/499–0104).

TRAVEL GEAR

Travel catalogs specialize in useful items, such as compact alarm clocks and travel irons, that can **save space when packing.**

➤ CATALOGS: **Magellan's** (☎ 800/962–4943, FAX 805/568–5406). **Orvis Travel** (☎ 800/541–3541, FAX 540/343–7053). **TravelSmith** (☎ 800/950–1600, FAX 800/950–1656).

VISITOR INFORMATION

For local information bureaus, see Visitor Information in the A to Z section at the end of each city's chapter.

➤ CZECH REPUBLIC: The tourist desk of the **Czech Tourist Authority**, a state-run information service, dispenses brochures, maps, and the like. In the United States: ⊠ 1109–1111 Madison Ave., New York, NY 10028, ☎ 212/288–0830, FAX 212/288–0971. In Canada: ⊠ Box 198, Exchange Tower, 2 First Canadian Place, 14th floor, Toronto, Ontario M5X 1A6, ☎ 416/367–3432, FAX 416/367–3492. In the United Kingdom: (⊠ 95 Great Portland St., London W1N 5RA, ☎ 0171/291–9920, FAX 0171/436–8300).

➤ HUNGARY: **Hungarian National Tourist Office.** In the United States and Canada: IBUSZ, ⊠ 150 E. 58th St., New York, NY 10155, ☎ 212/355–0240, FAX 212/207–4103. In Canada, contact the **Hungarian Consulate General Office** (⊠ 121 Bloor St. E, Suite 1115, Toronto M4W3M5, Ontario, ☎ 416/923–8981, FAX 416/923–2732). In the United Kingdom: **Hungarian National Tourist Board** c/o Embassy of the Republic of Hungary, Commercial Section (⊠ 46 Eaton Pl., London, SW1X 8AL, ☎ 0171/823–1032 or 0171/823–1055, FAX 0171/823–1459).

THE GOLD GUIDE / SMART TRAVEL TIPS

➤ WEB SITES: Do check out the World Wide Web when you're planning your trip. You'll find everything from up-to-date weather forecasts to virtual tours of famous cities. Fodor's Web site, **www.fodors.com**, is a great place to start your on-line travels. For more information specifically on Prague, try the **Prague Information Service** (http://pis.eunet.cz/), which gives you nuts-and-bolts info about the city, posts cultural events, lists tour companies, and more. To get Prague's local scoop before you go, try the *Prague Post*'s site (http://www.praguepost.cz/); it includes a tourist information page. **Website Prague** (http://www.praguesite.cz/) has a good range of tourist essentials. If you find your trip to Prague is lengthening indefinitely, check out the **Prague Expatriate Guide** (http://www.pragueexpatguide.cz/) for information on how to get an apartment, how to get a resident's permit, etc. For more information on Budapest, try *The Budapest Sun* site (http://www.bpsun.hu/).

WHEN TO GO

The tourist season generally runs from April or May through October; spring and fall combine good weather with a more bearable level of tourism.

Prague is beautiful year-round, but avoid midsummer (especially July and August) and the Christmas and Easter holidays, when the city is overrun with tourists. Spring and fall generally combine good weather with a more bearable level of tourism. In winter you'll encounter fewer other visitors and have the opportunity to see Prague breathtakingly covered in snow; but it can get very cold. Most castles are closed November through March.

The ideal times to visit **Budapest** are in the spring (May through June) and end of summer and early fall (late August through September). The months of July and August, peak vacation season for Hungarians as well as foreign tourists, can be extremely hot and humid; Budapest is stuffy and crowded. The entire Lake Balaton region is also overrun with vacationers—and it's the only area that really closes down during the low season, generally from mid- or late September until at least Easter, if not mid-May.

CLIMATE

The following are the average daily maximum and minimum temperatures for Budapest and Prague.

BUDAPEST

Jan.	34F	1C	May	72F	22C	Sept.	73F	23C
	25	– 4		52	11		54	12
Feb.	39F	4C	June	79F	26C	Oct.	61F	16C
	28	– 2		59	15		45	7
Mar.	50F	10C	July	82F	28C	Nov.	46F	8C
	36	2		61	16		37	3
Apr.	63F	17C	Aug.	81F	27C	Dec.	39F	4C
	25	– 4		61	16		30	– 1

PRAGUE

Jan.	36F	2C	May	66F	19C	Sept.	68F	20C
	25	– 4		46	8		50	10
Feb.	37F	3C	June	72F	22C	Oct.	55F	13C
	27	– 3		52	11		41	5
Mar.	46F	8C	July	75F	24C	Nov.	46F	8C
	32	0		55	13		36	2
Apr.	58F	14C	Aug.	73F	23C	Dec.	37F	3C
	39	4		55	13		28	– 2

➤ FORECASTS: **Weather Channel Connection** (☎ 900/932–8437), 95¢ per minute from a Touch-Tone phone.

1 Destination: Prague and Budapest

UNDER THE SPELL

DESPITE OUR MOST LYRICAL fantasies, traveling through Europe has an inescapable element of the predictable. Streams of familiar landmarks and famed artworks are broken by the seemingly endless searches for comfortable hotels, public restrooms, and espressos that cost less than $7. Over a century's worth of tourism industry experience lies behind the glossy brochures and prepackaged souvenirs, and the beaten paths are now beyond well-worn. As the legs tire and the senses numb, the cities themselves begin to take on the look and feel of museums—handsome and well-organized monuments to events that happened long ago.

Then there are Prague and Budapest.

Travelers to these lively, enchanting capitals will be forgiven for wanting to throttle their brothers' friends for steering them toward Vienna or Brussels. Unlike much of Western Europe, Prague and Budapest can easily satiate the castle-and-church set while at the same time inviting adventurous spirits into a whimsical café-and-club party that seems to have been raging since 1878. All this, of course, at prices that still make Germans blush.

Prague and Budapest's intoxicating mixes of beautiful settings, dynamic times, and—not least—cheap and tasty local drink have convinced thousands of visitors since 1989 to stay just one more week, which became one more month, which turned into years. Prague's over-documented expatriates tend toward goatees and tattoos, bookstores and rock bands, while Budapest's lower-profile expats are more likely to work for an ad agency and belong to a wine society. Both communities have produced useful little touches of home, such as vegetarian restaurants and decent newspapers. The two cities are competing, as they have for a thousand years, for the mantle of Capital of Central Europe, and the cosmopolitanism that goes with it. Since both capitals also compete directly for tourist dollars, locals have become accustomed to (and a bit cynical of) loud foreigners asking for directions or occupying the next barstool. Luckily for hospitality's sake, Czechs and Hungarians love to hunker down over beer and brandy shots with strangers, so if you go out for a polite night on the town you can easily wind up, 36 hours later, with a dozen new friends, a smoking habit, and skeleton keys to a downtown apartment.

It has not always been thus. Prague, during the Communist "normalization" period of the 1970s and '80s, was a miserable place. People lived in legitimate fear of imprisonment for listening to bootleg Velvet Underground tapes, and the nameless, soot-stained shops had few edible goods. Hungary, whose "Goulash communism" was a much less repressive strain, nonetheless suffered from the same lack of funds to maintain buildings or modernize foul factories and automobiles. The once-flourishing 19th-century cafés on Budapest's ring boulevard Nagykörút were shuttered in favor of joyless stand-up coffee shacks.

Both nations briefly and gloriously shook off the shackles during the Soviet era, only to be crushed once again by Warsaw Pact tanks—Hungary in 1956 and Czechoslovakia in 1968. After 51 consecutive years of living under failed 20th-century political systems, Czechs and Hungarians threw long and sweet coming-out parties in 1989–90. When the confetti was finally swept away, the two countries took turns playing poster child for post-communist reform, taking great pains to remind visitors with short memories that the nations were taking their rightful, historic place back in the Western family.

Nine years into the process, the cities and people have changed seismically. In Prague, the smothering blanket of gray has given way to birthday-cake pastels. Scaffolding and corrugated tin are being rapidly shed from downtown streets and squares, giving an exhilarating sense of rediscovery and renewal to residents and visitors alike. The radio dial is jammed with good stations, although the excellent Radio One, long an independent-minded mix of international and local music, has come under new American ownership. Budapest has a rash of modern office buildings and spruced-up promenades; it's also starting work on a new metro line. Signs of conspicuous wealth are everywhere, from the new mansions atop the Buda hills to the shiny Mercedes zipping through the crowded streets and the purring of cell phones—in fact, Hungary has more cellular phones per capita than the United States.

For all the cosmetic improvements, Czechs and Hungarians have suffered more this decade than most of us have in a lifetime. Meager pensions have lagged behind the mostly double-digit inflation, factory towns in the countryside have been decimated by unemployment, and the rules and certainties of a half-century of communism have been overturned. Because they enjoyed relative prosperity in the 1980s, Hungarians have had a particularly hard time adjusting; many people find it hard to understand why they need to suffer through the latest austerity program. The pension problem is a bitter example; Hungarian men, on average, die before qualifying for a pension, leaving their widows to struggle with only their own devalued portion. Often these women are reduced to selling bunches of flowers or odd bits of clothing in metro stations.

Crime, too, has gone from nearly nonexistent to pervasive, with Russian thugs setting off pipe bombs in Budapest and corrupt Czech fund managers embezzling investor money from Prague banks to offshore accounts. Ruling parties in both countries were rocked by political corruption scandals before being tossed out in 1998 elections. These issues loom large, but most travelers need not worry about safety beyond keeping their wallets safe from pickpockets and avoiding restaurants that charge foreigners $100 for a drink.

The dramatic pace of change contributes to a sense of action and possibility too often missing in Western capitals, breathing contemporary life to the centuries of drama written on every meandering downtown street. It is here, mere steps off the beaten tourist paths, where the hidden

spirits that seem to govern Prague and Budapest reveal themselves, transcending and even laughing at the political and social shifts of the moment.

Prague's spirit is clever and romantic, with a decidedly dark sense of humor. The easily walkable Malá Strana (Lesser Quarter), Staré Město (Old Town), and Nové Město (New Town) are all haunted alleyways and curves, some leading to hidden 13th-century churches, some coming to abrupt stops, others emptying into exuberant squares or regal gardens. Gaiety and paranoia forge an uneasy truce, neither keeping the upper hand for long. Czechs themselves are just as likely to snarl at you (especially if you set foot inside a restaurant or neighborhood shop) as invite you to their countryside cottage for a week of picking mushrooms and drinking three-day-old wine, called *burčak*.

This duality is crammed side-by-side into ever-smaller living quarters. Just off Wenceslas Square you can find the world's most frivolous Cubist lamp standing next to the solemn Gothic heights of the 14th-century Church of Our Lady of the Snows—and to complete the absurd picture, there's a Japanese bonsai garden in the church's backyard. The spooky St. Vitus Cathedral is a wonderful testament to architectural potluck, with one of its dark 13th-century spires topped by a goofy 18th-century onion dome, while snarling Gothic gargoyles glower above Art Nouveau stained glass.

Because the city has miraculously avoided war damage over the centuries, the streets themselves are a vivid history lesson. Walk through the sad but re-emergent Jewish Quarter, and imagine how Hitler planned on "preserving" this neighborhood as a monument to the "decadent" Jewish culture he was busy annihilating. See the terrific statue of Protestant revolutionary Jan Hus on Old Town Square, imagine how his followers were executed in that very space for insisting that the laity be allowed to take Communion with the same wine reserved for the priests, and then visit any Hussite cathedral and notice the symbolic wine goblet carved above the front door. Go to a performance of *The Bartered Bride* inside the lush, gilded National Theater, and imagine how Bedřich Smetana's opera must have been received here at the height of the 19th-century National Revival, when Czechs flouted their German masters by constructing the theater entirely from private donations. (Note too, the ridiculous juxtaposition of the Communist New Theater monstrosity right next door.)

Visits to the National Gallery, the stunningly restored Art Nouveau Municipal House, and the cavernous new Museum of Modern Art will tell you much of what you need to know about Czech history and art, from the empire years of King Charles IV to the mad alchemy of Rudolf II to the exuberant but unsteady days of the interwar First Republic. You can get a feel for Prague's artistic magnetism—past and present—by catching a film, a reading, or a live band. The city is weird, inhabited by ghosts, tangled with mysterious, narrow streets—a legendary source of inspiration. But for true immersion, nothing beats stepping into any one of a thousand neighborhood pubs, drinking the best beer in the world for 50 cents a pint, watching as the dour locals suddenly spring to life when someone breaks out a guitar, and then stumbling back out into the world to watch the sun rise over a mercifully empty Charles Bridge.

Budapest, unlike Prague, is haunted by memories of more recent grandeur, specifically the Austro-Hungarian empire era of 1867–1918. The streets are grand and broad, suitable for victory marches, and the city's dividing river is the wide, impressive Danube, a stronger presence than Prague's winsome Vltava. The city itself is almost twice as large as Prague, and shares none of the Czech capital's cloying, pastel-frosting cutesiness. Many buildings are still pockmarked with bullet holes from the 1956 uprising and the extensive battles that ripped the city apart in World War II.

The historical wounds seem fresher, more immediate here than in Prague. Besides the tragedy of 1956, residents still invoke the 1918 Treaty of Trianon, which lopped off two-thirds of prewar Hungary's territory. There is an oft-remarked melancholia in the Hungarian people, which pop psychologists attribute to being on the wrong side of seven consecutive wars, or speaking a language everyone else on earth finds incomprehensible.

But visitors expecting a mopey lot grumbling over 19th-century maps are in for a shocker. Hungarians are a hyper-smart, multilingual, and deeply sensual people who enjoy the finer things in life, from Turkish baths to good red wine to coffee cakes drenched in chocolate. Hospitality knows no limits (though one must be careful about scam artists), and people seem to have an uncanny knack for knowing exactly what foreigners want. There is a whiff of decadence and chaos in the air, a happy remnant from the hated 1541–1686 Ottoman occupation. Hungarians seem to have picked up only the nicer of the Balkan habits, such as promenading each afternoon down the riverside *korzo* and other pedestrian zones.

Indeed, the country truly serves as a European crossroads between East and West, North and South. On the streets, it is common to hear Russian, Arabic, Serbo-Croatian, English, and German. Roman ruins lie next to Turkish mosques across the river from the largest synagogue in Europe. There are excellent French, Greek, Italian, Turkish, Mexican, Irish, and Japanese restaurants, and of course the blood-red Hungarian eateries with Gypsy violinists wearing folk vests. But unlike Prague, Budapest's arts and culture scene is still a bit hesitant, trying to weigh the past while incorporating a flood of imported entertainment.

Elegant monuments to Hungary's romanticized failures can be found throughout the city, from the new, understated statue of 1956 leader Imre Nagy looking toward the Parliament building to the riverside memorial to 1848 hero Sándor Petőfi, a young poet who accurately prophesied his own revolutionary death. Many buildings tell long, complicated stories of their own, such as the unheralded Mai Manó Photo Gallery at 20 Nagymezo utca, a street known as the once and future "Hungarian Broadway." This Art Nouveau structure was commissioned in 1894 by court photographer Manó Mai, who used it as a studio for his portrait sittings of luminaries such as Franz Joseph I and composer Béla Bartók. After Mai's death, the building became a decadent cabaret called the Arizona, complete with revolving hydraulic stages and naked girls on chandeliers. The club was a favorite of international royalty and government officials, but during World War II its Jewish owners were murdered by occupying German soldiers. During Communism the building fell into disrepair, but now a small photography gallery has taken root, and the managers have ambitious plans to revamp the entire space, adding a café, exhibition rooms, and a library. The building is taking center stage in the projected rejuvenation of the theaters along the rundown avenue, which itself is a cornerstone of the city's dramatic overhaul.

As post-communism rolls toward its second decade, Prague and Budapest have emerged as the political and cultural epicenters of the former Eastern bloc. Prague has reawakened in its role as capital of Bohemia, becoming the favored European tour date for inventive rock and pop acts (including repeat performers such as Sonic Youth, Bob Dylan, and the Rolling Stones) and inspiring untold thousands of wild young souls to pursue their artistic and entrepreneurial dreams. Budapest attracts multinational companies with equal success, even luring some European headquarters away from nearby Vienna. Hungary is blazing most trails in Central European economic reform, and Budapest's activist mayor is halfway through an ambitious renewal plan aiming to restore the city's salon culture to its pre–World War I splendor.

Hungary and the Czech Republic are quickly distancing themselves from their Communist past; soon they will have their own stars on the European Union flag, and the best Hungarian wines and Czech beers will be sold for prices depressingly familiar to travelers from the West. Before the window closes, though, Prague and Budapest will continue to seduce, infuriate, and even ensnare those daring enough to visit.

— Matt Welch

WHAT'S WHERE

Prague and Environs
Planted firmly in the heart of Central Europe—Prague is some 320 kilometers (200 miles) northwest of Vienna—the Czech Republic is culturally and historically more closely linked to Western, particularly Germanic, culture than any of its former East-bloc brethren. The capital city of

Prague sits on the Vltava (Moldau) River, roughly in the middle of Bohemian territory. A stunning city of human dimensions, Prague offers the traveler a lesson in almost all the major architectural styles of Western European history; relatively unscathed by major wars, most of Prague's buildings are remarkably well preserved. The five main historic districts echo what were once five separate towns: Hradčany (Castle Area), Malá Strana (Lesser Quarter), Staré Město (Old Town), Nové Město (New Town), and Josefov (the Jewish Quarter). The stunning Karlův Most (Charles Bridge) links the Old Town and Lesser Quarter, while the Pražský Hrad (Prague Castle) overlooks the city from its hilltop west of the river.

Prague is planted in the heart of **Bohemia**, an area where the history of internal conflict, invasions, and religious revolts is almost palpable. Southern Bohemia is dotted with several stunning walled towns retaining much of their medieval appearance, many of which played important roles in the Hussite religious wars of the 15th century. The two most notable towns are Tábor and Český Krumlov. Western Bohemia, especially the far western hills near the German border, remains justly famous for its mineral springs and **spa towns,** in particular Karlovy Vary, Mariánské Lázně, and Františkový Lázně. These elegant towns are just a couple of hours away from the capital.

Budapest and Environs
Sandwiched between Slovakia and Romania, Hungary was the Austro-Hungarian Empire's eastern frontier, the geographical link between the Slavic regions of Central Europe and the Black Sea region's amalgam of Orthodox and Islamic cultures. The capital, **Budapest,** crouches on the Danube, just an hour from Bratislava in Slovakia and two hours from Vienna. Like Prague, Budapest is an amalgam of once-separate towns—Óbuda, Buda, and Pest were joined in the 19th century. Buda, on the Danube's western bank, is quite hilly; most of its major sights are clustered on the Várhegy (Castle Hill). Pest, on the eastern side of the river, is flat and laced with wide avenues and circular köröts (ring roads).

Just north of Budapest, the Danube River forms a gentle, heart-shape curve along which lie the romantic and historic towns of the region called the Danube Bend. Southwest of Budapest are the vineyards, historic villages, and popular, developed summer resorts around **Lake Balaton,** the largest lake in Central Europe. The towns along the northern shore of the lake are often less developed and, thus, more attractive—these include the spa town of Balatonfüred and the abbey-crowned village of Tihany.

NEW AND NOTEWORTHY

Prague
One tangible impact of the Czech Republic's recent economic reforms has been an acceleration in the pace of architectural renovations. Many hotels, old private houses, and churches are installing new fixtures and applying a fresh coat of paint. This is most noticeable in Prague, but everywhere, castles, palaces, and dusty old museums are spiffing themselves up and throwing open their doors to visitors. The fiscal shocks of 1997, a year when the Czech crown lost more than 20 percent of its value against the U.S. dollar, could not shut the doors on several **major museum projects** planned for Prague for 1998. These include the private Mucha Museum, the Prague Municipal House's collection of 20th-century Czech art, and the long-awaited reopening of the Prague Castle Picture Gallery.

The number of **hotels and restaurants** keeps pace with the growing number of visitors. Like the number of new large hotels, the number of smaller, privately owned hotels and pensions is also on the rise. The arrival of visitors and long-term residents from all over the world has brought forth new restaurants offering Cajun, Indian, vegetarian, and other exotic fare alongside the traditional ones serving pork and dumplings.

Prague's **cultural life** continues to thrive, and the city in particular is a dream for classical-music lovers and opera fans. The annual mid-May–early June Prague Spring Music Festival, which even before the collapse of the Communist government was one of the great events on the European calendar, is attracting record numbers of music lovers. The less-hyped Prague Autumn festival has begun to bring in equally strong performers and orchestras.

Budapest
Anticipation is running high for the year 2000, especially since it will coincide with the **Magyar Millennium,** the 1,000th anniversary of Hungary's founding as a state. Continuing the celebratory restorations in honor of another recent national anniversary in 1996—the 1,100th anniversary of the Magyar settlement of the Carpathian Basin—restoration work on important sites throughout the country will be finished in the year 2000. A new National Theater will be built in Budapest, and several other new cultural institutions are planned, including a Hungarian literature institute.

The capital is seeing more and more improvements and development, from private restoration of crumbling buildings to city-funded projects, such as the increase in pedestrian-only zones and the construction of a fourth **metro line** through southern Buda, begun in late 1998.

Slowly but surely, Hungary continues to **improve its infrastructure,** helping it fill its increasingly important role as a link between Eastern and Western Europe. Over the next several years, major highways will be upgraded and extended, the airport in Budapest will undergo a major expansion, and the antiquated telephone system will be overhauled. Travelers may witness these changes taking place but should not expect to reap their full benefits for some time to come. An unusual program recently started in Budapest; beginning in summer 1998, multilingual students have been posted in the city's most touristed areas to help visitors communicate with the police. At press time, this arrangement was expected to be extended to the Lake Balaton area.

At press time, Hungary's annual inflation rate had decreased from more than 25% to 16%, and with continued significant devaluation of the forint, exchange rates keep improving for visitors. Yet, while Budapest remains a bargain compared to many Western Europe cities, strictly rock-bottom prices are a thing of the past as restaurant and hotel rates creep upward to compensate for the nation's shrinking currency.

FODOR'S CHOICE

Dining

Prague

★ **V Zátiši.** In one of the city's oldest and calmest squares—the restaurant's name means "still life," or "in a quiet corner"—this refined dining room offers tantalizing international specialties and wonderful service. *$$$$*

★ **Lobkovická.** This atmospheric, 17th-century wine bar has an imaginative menu and an enticing roster of Moravian wines. *$$$*

★ **Dolly Bell.** Informal in spirit, this restaurant has a seriously satisfying Yugoslav menu. *$$*

★ **Rybářský klub.** The "Fishing Club" restaurant shares its building with a real fishing club—it's a great place to try freshwater fish, including the favorite *candát* (pike-perch). *$*

★ **Slávia kavárna.** To lap up some of the artistic scene, come to this Art Deco café; the views of the Prague Castle and the National Theater aren't too shabby either. *$*

Budapest

★ **Gundel.** Established at the turn of the century, Budapest's most famous restaurant continues its legacy of Old World grandeur and elegant cuisine. *$$$$*

★ **Kisbuda Gyöngye.** This intimate setting is the place to look for a *liba lakodalmas* (goose wedding feast)—a roast goose leg, goose liver, and goose cracklings. *$$$*

★ **Lou Lou.** This restaurant has been buzzing for years, having struck a mouthwatering balance between Hungarian and Continental influences. At press time it was about to relocate, so check with the tourist office to track it down. *$$$*

★ **Művészinas.** The chef at this romantic, bustling bistro in downtown Pest has a flair for taking typical Hungarian dishes to new heights. *$$$*

★ **Náncsi Néni.** It's a bit out of the way, but that hasn't deterred the crowds from this warm restaurant—garlic and paprika hang from the ceiling and jars of home-pickled vegetables line the walls. These will hopefully sharpen your appetite, as the plates are loaded with excellent Hungarian home-cooking. *$$*

Lodging

Prague

★ **Dům U Červeného Lva.** Just five minutes from Prague Castle's front gates, this immaculate hotel has striking details, such as the painted-beam ceilings. *$$$$*

★ **Palace.** The soft pinks and greens of the room decor, the classic Continental restaurant, and the location near Wenceslas Square make this a great combination of elegance and convenience. *$$$$*

★ **Savoy.** From the Jugendstil facade to the afternoon tea in the library, this small hotel is all about luxury. *$$$$*

★ **Pension U Raka.** There are just six rooms in this 18th-century building, so plan way ahead to snare a spot. It's just behind the Loreto Church, so you'll have a wonderful base for exploring the city. *$$$*

★ **Pension Louda.** While this pension is a good 20 minutes away from the city center, the south-facing rooms have stunning views of Prague. *$*

Budapest

★ **Danubius Hotel Gellért.** This grand 1918 Art Nouveau hotel on the Danube at the foot of Gellért Hill is the pride of Budapest. Housing an extensive, elegant complex of marble bathing facilities fed by ancient curative springs, it is also one of Europe's most famous Old World spas. *$$$$*

★ **Kempinski Hotel Corvinus Budapest.** Sleek, modern, and luxurious, this hotel oozes solicitousness. The large, sparkling bathrooms are the city's best. *$$$$*

★ **Victoria.** You can see the Parliament building and the twinkling city lights from every room of this small hotel smack on the Danube. *$$*

★ **Kulturinov.** Set on one of historic Castle Hill's most famous cobblestone squares, this neo-Baroque castle houses budget accommodations in a priceless location. *$*

Museums and Religious Buildings

Prague

★ **Chrám svatého Mikuláše (St. Nicholas Church).** With its dynamic curves, dramatic statues, and remarkable dome, this church embodies the height of high Baroque.

★ **Chrám svatého Vita (St. Vitus Cathedral).** Soaring above the castle walls and dominating the city at its feet, St. Vitus Cathedral is among the most beautiful sights in Europe. Its stained-glass windows are particularly brilliant.

★ **Kostel Panny Marie před Týnem (Týn Church).** The exterior of this 15th-century cathedral, with its twin gold-tipped, jet-black spires, is a sterling example of Prague Gothic.

★ **Národní galérie (National Gallery).** Spread among a half-dozen branches around the city, the National Gallery's collections span most major periods of European art, from medieval and Baroque masters to a vast constructivist gallery of 20th-century Czech and European works.

★ **Strahovský klášter (Strahov Monastery).** Now a museum of national literature, this monastery is known for its collection of early Czech manuscripts and the striking fresco on the ceiling of its Philosophical Hall.

★ **Židovské muzeum v Praze (Prague Jewish Museum).** Actually a collection of several must-see sights and exhibits, the Jewish Museum includes the Old Jewish Cemetery, crowded with tombstones, and several historic synagogues.

Budapest

★ **Mátyás Templom (Matthias Church).** Castle Hill's soaring Gothic church is colorfully ornate inside with lavishly frescoed Byzantine pillars.

★ **Nagy Zsinagóga (Great Synagogue).** This giant Byzantine-Moorish beauty (Europe's largest synagogue) underwent a massive restoration after being ravaged by Hungarian and German Nazis during World War II.

★ **Néprajzi Múzeum (Museum of Ethnography).** A majestic 1890s structure across from the Parliament building—the lavish marble entrance hall alone is worth a visit—houses an impressive exhibit on Hungary's historic folk traditions.

★ **Szent István Bazilika (St. Stephen's Basilica).** Inside this massive neo-Renaissance beauty, the capital's biggest church, is a rich collection of mosaics and statuary, as well as the mummified right hand of Hungary's first king and patron saint, St. Stephen.

★ **Szépművészeti Múzeum (Museum of Fine Arts).** Hungary's best collection of fine art includes esteemed works by Dutch and Spanish old masters, as well as exhibits on major Hungarian artists.

FESTIVALS AND SEASONAL EVENTS

Prague
DECEMBER➤ **Christmas fairs and programs** take place in towns and cities throughout the country.

JANUARY➤ Prague hosts the **FebioFest International Film, Television and Video Festival.**

MARCH➤ Prague holds **St. Matthew's Fair,** an annual children's fair in honor of St. Matthew.

APRIL➤ Several international music festivals are held in the capital: **Classical Easter,** and two festivals of sacred music, **Musica Ecumenica** and **Musica Sacra Praga.** Prague is also the site of **Days of European Film.**

MAY➤ Events both athletic and artistic fill the calendar; there's the **Prague Spring International Music Festival** as well as the **Prague Marathon.** Major writers from around the world present readings during the **Prague Writers' Festival.**

JUNE➤ The international dance festival **Tanec Praha** hits the capital.

AUGUST➤ Prague's **Verdi Festival** is staged at the State Opera.

SEPTEMBER➤ Several arts festivals take place: the **Autumn International Music Festival,** the **Bedřich Smetana Festival,** and the **Festival of German-Language Theater.**

OCTOBER➤ The capital continues its run of cultural events, including an **International Jazz Festival,** the **Festival of Progressive Personalities in European Dance Theater, Musica Iudaica,** a festival of Jewish music, and the **Festival of 20th Century Music.** The **Velká Pardubická Steeplechase** is considered one of Europe's toughest racing events.

NOVEMBER➤ Prague focuses on visual arts with the **Festival of Independent Film** and the **Czech Press Photo** annual exhibition.

Budapest
For contact information about most of these festivals, *see* the city's Nightlife and the Arts section or inquire at the Budapest Tourinform office.

DECEMBER➤ Budapest's **New Year's Eve** festivities include a gala in the beautiful, neo-Renaissance Opera House.

MID-MARCH TO EARLY APRIL➤ The season's first and biggest arts festival, the **Budapest Spring Festival,** showcases Hungary's best opera, music, theater, fine arts, and dance, as well as visiting foreign artists. Other towns—including Kecskemét, Szentendre, and Szombathely—also participate.

JUNE➤ The **World Music Festival,** held in early June, has several days of world music concerts by local and international artists.

AUGUST➤ Early in the month, Budapest hosts a **Formula 1** car race, while the weeklong **BudaFest** opera and ballet festival takes place mid-month at the opera house after the opera season ends. **St. Stephen's Day** (August 20) is a major national holiday—there are **fireworks** in the capital. A weeklong, music-oriented **Youth Culture Festival** is held in mid-August on Óbuda Island. Young people swarm over the island, sometimes camping out for the week, to catch performances by bands ranging from international (and aging) heavy-metal groups to folk musicians.

SEPTEMBER➤ A **wine festival** in the capital celebrates the autumn grape harvest.

2 Prague

The "hundred-spired" capital city of Prague—one of the world's best-preserved architectural cityscapes—has come to life with breathtaking speed. The Communist-gray crust is quickly dissolving under a flood of renovations, and the long-admired cultural scene crackles with energy.

By Mark Baker

Updated by Ky
Krauthamer,
Martha
Lagace, and
Robert Rigney

A **VICTIM OF ENFORCED OBSCURITY** throughout much of the 20th century, the Czech Republic, comprising the provinces of Bohemia and Moravia (but no longer Slovakia), is once again in the spotlight. In a world where revolution was synonymous with violence, and in a country where truth was quashed by the tanks of Eastern-bloc socialism, in November 1989 Václav Havel's sonorous voice proclaimed the victory of the "Velvet Revolution" to enthusiastic crowds on Wenceslas Square and preached the value of "living in truth." Recording the dramatic events of the time, television cameras panned across Prague's glorious skyline and fired the world's imagination with the image of political renewal superimposed on somber Gothic and voluptuous Baroque.

Travelers have rediscovered the country, and Czechs and Moravians have rediscovered the world. Not so long ago, the visitor to Prague was unhindered by crowds of tourists but had to struggle with a creeping sensation of melancholy and neglect that threatened to eclipse the capital's beauty. Combined with a truly frustrating lack of services in every branch of the tourist industry, a trip to Prague was always an adventure in the full sense of the word. But after the revolution, the city sprang into action, renovating its buildings, bursting with new restaurants, and crackling with energy.

The arrival of designer boutiques, chain restaurants, and shopping malls—not only in Prague but increasingly in the larger provincial towns—does mean that the country has lost some of the "feel" it had just a few years ago. However, you'll still run into strange, Old World, and at times frustratingly bureaucratic rituals that are actually remnants of the Hapsburg Empire and are also to be found, perhaps to a lesser degree, in Vienna and Budapest. The *šatna* (coatroom), for example, plays a vivid role in any visit to a restaurant or theater at any time of year other than summer. Even in the coldest weather, coats must be given with a few coins to the attendant, usually an old lady with a sharp eye for ignorant or disobedient tourists. The attendant often also plays a role in controlling the rest room; the entrance fee entitles the visitor to a small roll of paper, ceremoniously kept on the attendant's table. Another odd institution associated with this part of the world is the *Tabák-Trafik*, a newsstand that sells two things connected for no apparent reason: tobacco products and public-transportation tickets.

At the same time, the seemingly unstoppable transition of the economy signals an increasing harmonization of Czechs' way of life with that of Western Europe. But the process goes slowly, and the heavy blows of 1997—the fall of the currency, devastating floods, and the scandal-marred end of Prime Minister Václav Klaus's government—may retard it for several years. The good news is that the country is on track to join the NATO alliance in 1999 and to become a European Union member state sometime in the next decade.

In the nine years since Prague's students took to the streets to help bring down the 40-year-old Communist regime, the city has enjoyed an unparalleled cultural renaissance. Much of the energy has come from planeloads of idealistic young foreigners, but the enthusiasm has been shared in near-equal measure by their Czech counterparts. Amid Prague's cobblestone streets and gold-tipped spires, new galleries, cafés, and clubs teem with bright-eyed expatriates and ever more locals.

The arts and theater are also thriving in the "new" Prague. Young playwrights, some writing in English, regularly stage their own works. Weekly poetry readings are standing room only. The city's dozen or so rock

Czech Republic (Česká Republika)

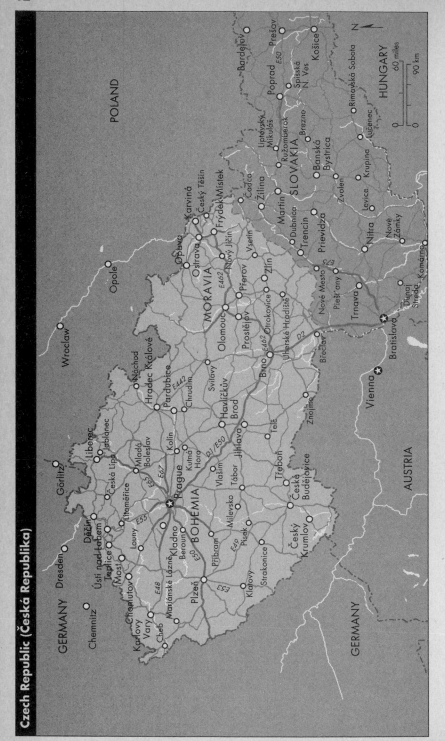

POLAND

GERMANY

Dresden

Chemnitz

Karlovy Vary

Cheb

Chomutov

Mariánské Lázně

Plzeň

Děčín

Ústí nad Labem

Teplice

Most

Louny

Kladno

Beroun

Příbram

Klatovy

Strakonice

Písek

Milevsko

Tábor

Vlašim

Vltava

Litoměřice

Česká Lípa

Liberec

Jablonec

Görlitz

Wrocław

Opole

Náchod

Hradec Králové

Pardubice

Chrudim

Mladá Boleslav

Kolín

Kutná Hora

Prague

BOHEMIA

E55

E65

E67

E50

E48

E53

E49

Svitavy

Havlíčkův Brod

Jihlava

D1/E50

Třeboň

Český Krumlov

České Budějovice

Telč

Znojmo

Brno

D2

Břeclav

Uherské Hradiště

Olomouc

Prostějov

Otrokovice

Přerov

Zlín

Vsetín

Nový Jičín

Ostrava

Opava

Karviná

Český Těšín

Frýdek-Místek

MORAVIA

E462

E462

E50

Čadca

Žilina

Martin

Dubnica

Trenčín

Prievidza

Nové Mesto

Piešťany

Trnava

Bratislava

Vienna

AUSTRIA

GERMANY

SLOVAKIA

Nitra

Nové Zámky

Komárno

Dunaj. Streda

Banská Bystrica

Zvolen

Krupina

Levice

Lučenec

Brezno

Ružomberok

Liptovský Mikuláš

Poprad

Spišská N. Ves

Bardejov

Prešov

Košice

Rimavská Sobota

HUNGARY

E50

E75

N

60 miles

90 km

clubs are jammed nightly; bands play everything from metal and psychedelic to garage and grunge.

All of this frenetic activity plays well against a stunning backdrop of towering churches and centuries-old bridges and alleyways. Prague achieved much of its present glory in the 14th century, during the long reign of Charles IV, king of Bohemia and Moravia and Holy Roman Emperor. It was Charles who established a university in the city and laid out the New Town (Nové Město), charting Prague's growth.

During the 15th century, the city's development was hampered by the Hussite Wars, a series of crusades launched by the Holy Roman Empire to subdue the fiercely independent Czech noblemen. The Czechs were eventually defeated in 1620 at the Battle of White Mountain (Bílá Hora) near Prague and were ruled by the Hapsburg family for the next 300 years. Under the Hapsburgs, Prague became a German-speaking city and an important administrative center, but it was forced to play second fiddle to the monarchy's capital of Vienna. Much of the Lesser Town (Malá Strana), across the river, was built up at this time, becoming home to Austrian nobility and its Baroque tastes.

Prague regained its status as a national capital in 1918, with the creation of the modern Czechoslovak state, and quickly asserted itself in the interwar period as a vital cultural center. Although the city escaped World War II essentially intact, it and the rest of Czechoslovakia fell under the political and cultural domination of the Soviet Union until the 1989 popular uprisings. The election of dissident playwright Václav Havel to the post of national president set the stage for the city's renaissance, which has since proceeded at a dizzying, quite Bohemian rate.

Pleasures and Pastimes

Beer and Wine

Czechs are reputed to drink more beer per capita than any people on earth; small wonder, as many connoisseurs rank Bohemian lager-style beer as the best in the world. This cool, crisp brew was invented in Plzeň (Pilsen) in 1842, although Czech beer had already been brewed for centuries prior to that time. Aside from the world-famous *Plzeňský Prazdroj* (Pilsner Urquell) and milder *Budvar* (the original Budweiser) brands, some typical beers are the slightly bitter *Krušovice,* fruity *Radegast,* and the sweeter, Prague-brewed *Staropramen. Světlé pivo,* or golden beer, is most common, although many pubs also serve *černé* (dark), which is often slightly sweeter than the light variety. Pubs are an indisputable part of Prague's culture and social life—whether you're spending a few days or a few years in the city, you should make their acquaintance. For a rundown on pub etiquette, *see* Pubs, Bars, and Lounges *in* Nightlife and the Arts, *below.*

Czechs also produce quite drinkable wines: peppy, fruity whites and mild, versatile reds. Southern Moravia, with comparatively warm summers and rich soil, grows the bulk of the wine harvest; look for the Mikulov and Znojmo regional designations. Favorite white varietals are *Müller Thurgau,* with a fine muscat bouquet and light flavor, and *Neuburské,* yellow-green in color and with a dry, smoky bouquet. *Rulandské bílé,* a semidry Burgundy-like white, has a flowery bouquet and full-bodied flavor. Belying the notion that northerly climes are more auspicious for white than red grapes, northern Bohemia's scant few hundred acres of vineyards produce reliable reds and the occasional jewel. *Frankovka* is fiery red and slightly acidic, while the cherry-red *Rulandské červené* is an excellent, drier choice. *Vavřinecké* is dark and slightly sweet.

Dining

Dining choices in Prague have increased greatly in the past decade as hundreds of new places have opened to cope with the soaring tourist demand. Quality and price vary widely, though. Be wary of tourist traps, especially on Old Town Square; cross-check prices of foreign-language menus with Czech versions, and even in the better restaurants it's always wise to take a close look at the addition in your bill at the end of a meal before simply paying up. Also ask if there is a *denní lístek* (daily menu). These menus, usually written only in Czech, generally list cheaper and often fresher selections (though many places provide daily menus for the midday meal only). Special local dishes worth making a beeline for include *cibulačka* (onion soup), *kulajda* (potato soup with sour cream), *svíčková* (beef sirloin in cream sauce) and *ovocné knedlíky* (fruit dumplings). The traditional dishes—roast pork or duck with dumplings, or broiled meat with sauce—can be light and tasty when well prepared. An annoying "cover charge" usually makes its way onto restaurant bills, seeming to subsidize the salt and pepper shakers.

Restaurants generally fall into three categories. A *pivnice*, or beer hall, usually offers a simple menu of goulash or pork with dumplings at very low prices. The atmosphere tends to be friendly and casual; you can expect to share a table. More attractive (and more expensive) are the *vinárna* (wine cellars) and *restaurace* (restaurants), which serve a full range of dishes. Wine cellars, some occupying Romanesque basements, can be a real treat, and you should certainly seek them out. A fourth dining option, the *lahůdky* (snack bar or deli), is the quickest and cheapest option.

Lunch, usually eaten between noon and 2, is the main meal for Czechs and offers you the best deal. Dinner is usually served from 5 until 9 or 10, but don't wait too long to eat. First of all, most Czechs eat only a light meal or a cold plate of meat and cheese in the evening. Second, restaurant cooks frequently knock off early on slow nights, and the later you arrive, the more likely it is that the kitchen will be closed. In general, dinner menus do not differ substantially from lunch offerings, except the prices are higher.

The crush of visitors has placed tremendous strain on the more popular restaurants. The upshot: Reservations are nearly always required, especially during peak tourist periods. If you don't have reservations, try arriving a little before standard meal times: 11:30 AM for lunch or 5:30 PM for dinner.

CATEGORY	PRAGUE*	OTHER AREAS*
$$$$	over $40	over $35
$$$	$25–$40	$20–$35
$$	$15–$25	$10–$20
$	under $15	under $10

per person for a three-course meal, excluding wine and tip

Lodging

The number of hotels and pensions has increased dramatically throughout the Czech Republic, in step with the influx of tourists. Finding a suitable room should pose no problem, although it is highly recommended that you book ahead during the peak tourist season (July and August, and the Christmas and Easter holidays). Hotel prices, in general, remain high, especially in Prague.

The Czech Republic's official hotel classification now follows the international star system. These ratings correspond closely to our categories as follows: deluxe or five-star plus four-star ($$$$); three-star ($$$); two-star ($$). The $ category will most often be met by private rooms. Often you can book rooms—both at hotels and in private homes—through Čedok or visitor bureaus. Otherwise, try calling or writing the hotel directly. Keep in mind that in many hotels, except at the deluxe level, a "double" bed means two singles that can be pushed together. (Single-mattress double beds are generally not available.)

A slow rise in lodging standards continues, but at all but the most expensive hotels standards lag behind those of Germany and Austria—as do prices. In most of the $$$$ and $$$ hotels, you can expect to find a restaurant and an exchange bureau on or near the premises. During the summer season reservations are absolutely imperative; for the remainder of the year they are highly recommended. A few hotels in the higher price categories also drop their rates in July to off-season levels.

A cheaper and often more interesting alternative to Prague's generally mediocre hotels are private rooms and apartments (signs for private rooms are often in German: ZIMMER FREI or PRIVAT ZIMMER). Prague is full of travel agencies offering such accommodations; sacrificing a little privacy is the only drawback. Room-finding services flourish at the main train station (Hlavní nádraží), Holešovice station (Nádraží Holešovice), and at Ruzyně Airport. These bureaus normally have employees with a basic level of English and they open between 6 and 9 AM; several stay open until 9 PM or later. Most can book rooms in hotels and pensions as well as private accommodations. Rates for private rooms start at around $15 per person per night and can go much higher for better-quality rooms. In general, there is no fee, but you may need to try several bureaus in search of an accommodation you want. Ask to see a photo of the room before accepting it, and be sure to pinpoint its location on a map. Prague is divided into 10 administrative districts; only Prague 1 and part of Prague 2 lie entirely within the historic center. Other districts have pleasant neighborhoods but can extend out to far-flung suburbs; you don't want to end up in an inconveniently distant location. You may also be approached by (usually) men in the stations hawking rooms; while these deals aren't an automatic ripoff, you should be wary of them. **Prague Information Service** (PIS; ☞ Visitor Information *in* Prague A to Z, *below*) arranges lodging from all of its central-city offices, including the branch in the main train station, in the booth marked TURISTICKÉ INFORMACE by the stairs down to the metro platform, on the left side of the main hall as you exit the station (✉ Hlavní nádraží, ☎ 02/2423–9258). Between April and October, this branch is open weekdays 9–7 and weekends 9–4; between November and March, it's open weekdays 9–6 and Saturday 9–3.

The prices quoted below are for double rooms during high season; generally, breakfast is included in the room rate. At certain periods, such as Easter and during festivals, prices can jump 15%–25%; as a rule, always ask the price before taking a room.

CATEGORY	PRAGUE*	OTHER AREAS*
$$$$	over $200	over $100
$$$	$100–$200	$50–$100
$$	$50–$100	$25–$50
$	under $50	under $25

*All prices are for a standard double room during peak season, including breakfast.

EXPLORING PRAGUE

Numbers in the text correspond to numbers in the margin and on the Exploring Prague and Prague Castle (Pražský hrad) maps.

The spine of the city is the River Vltava (also known by its German name, Moldau), which runs through the city from south to north with a single sharp curve to the east. Prague originally comprised five independent towns, represented today by its main historic districts: **Hradčany** (Castle Area), **Malá Strana** (Lesser Quarter), **Staré Město** (Old Town), **Nové Město** (New Town), and **Josefov** (the Jewish Quarter).

Hradčany, the seat of Czech royalty for hundreds of years, has as its center the **Pražský Hrad** (Prague Castle), which overlooks the city from its hilltop west of the Vltava. Steps lead down from Hradčany to Malá Strana, an area dense with ornate mansions built by 17th- and 18th-century nobility.

Karlův Most (Charles Bridge) connects Malá Strana with Staré Město. Just a few blocks east of the bridge is the focal point of the Old Town, **Staroměstské náměstí** (Old Town Square). Staré Město is bounded by the curving Vltava and three large commercial avenues: **Revoluční** to the east, **Na Příkopě** to the southeast, and **Národní třída** to the south. Josefov is northwest of Staroměstské náměstí, bordered by the streets 17 listopadu, Na Františku, and Kozí.

Beyond lies the Nové Město; several blocks south is **Karlovo náměstí**, the city's largest square. Roughly 1 km (½ mi) farther south is **Vyšehrad**, an ancient castle high above the river.

On a promontory to the east of Wenceslas Square stretches **Vinohrady**, once the favored neighborhood of well-to-do Czechs; below Vinohrady lie the crumbling neighborhoods of **Žižkov** to the north and **Nusle** to the south. On the west bank of the Vltava south and east of Hradčany lie many older residential neighborhoods and enormous parks. About 3 km (2 mi) from the center in every direction, Communist-era housing projects begin their unsightly sprawl.

Great Itineraries

IF YOU HAVE 1–2 DAYS

Even during such a short stay, you can get a strong taste of Prague's historical richness and buzzing energy. Start at the top with the hilltop Pražský hrad (Prague Castle), visiting the soaring, Gothic Chrám svatého Vita (St. Vitus Cathedral) and the Královský palác (Royal Palace) and drinking in views of the city. To get to or from the castle, walk along Nerudova ulice, a steep street lined with burgher's homes— and little restaurants if you need a break. Cross over the river to the Staré Město (Old Town) and the stunning Staroměstské náměstí (Old Town Square). Try to time your visit to coincide with the hourly performance of the astronomical clock on the Staroměstská radnice (Old Town Hall); you can also visit the Gothic-on-the-outside, Baroque-on-the-inside Kostel Panny Marie před Týnem (Týn Church). Stretching southeast of the Old Town is Václavské náměstí (Wenceslas Square), actually a long avenue humming with activity—be sure to duck into some of the arcades that branch off the boulevard. In the evening, go back toward the river for the unforgettable view from the statue-lined Karlův most (Charles Bridge). If you have another morning here, head to the Josefov (Jewish Ghetto) early, before the crowds of tourists pack its tiny streets. You can also dip into the Malá Strana (Lesser Quarter) to see the voluptuous Baroque curves of Chrám svatého Mikuláše (St. Nicholas Church).

With a few extra days, you can devote more time in the historic quarters, spending most of a day in the castle, and later visiting the Strahovský klášter (Strahov Monastery) and Národní galerie (National Gallery) in the castle district. You could also duck into one of the city's beautiful gardens, such as the Vrtbovská zahrada (Vrtba Garden). If you're interested in modern architecture, head to the Nové Město (New Town), where you can see the "Fred and Ginger" building by Frank Gehry and Vlado Milunić as well as several Cubist buildings.

Besides the explorations described above, take a quick trip out to the spa towns in Western Bohemia (☞ Side Trip to the Bohemian Spa Towns, *below*). The rich, famous, and curious flocked here in the 19th century, and you can walk through the colonnades and sip the waters that drew everyone from Chopin to Mark Twain to Karl Marx. The classic resort hotels in Karlovy Vary or Mariánské Lázně are tempting places to overnight.

Staré Město (the Old Town)

A Good Walk

Václavské náměsti ①, marked by the **Statue of St. Wenceslas** ② and convenient to hotels and transportation, is an excellent place to begin a tour of the Old Town. A long, gently sloping boulevard rather than a square in the usual sense, Václavské náměstí is bounded at the top (the southern end) by the **Národní Muzeum** ③ and at the bottom by the pedestrian shopping areas of Národní třída and Na Příkopě. Today Václavské náměstí comprises Prague's liveliest street scene. Don't miss the dense maze of arcades tucked away from the street in buildings that line both sides. You'll find an odd assortment of cafés, discos, ice cream parlors, and movie houses, all seemingly unfazed by the passage of time. At night the square changes character somewhat as dance music pours out from the crowded discos and leather-jacketed cronies crowd around the taxi stands. One eye-catching building on the square is the **Hotel Europa** ④, at No. 25, a riot of Art Nouveau that recalls the glamorous world of turn-of-the-century Prague.

To begin the approach to the Old Town proper, walk past the tall, Art Deco Koruna complex and turn right onto the handsome pedestrian zone of Na Příkopě. Turn left onto Havířská ulice and follow this small alley to the glittering green-and-cream splendor of the 18th-century **Stavovské Divadlo** ⑤.

Return to Na Příkopě, turn left, and continue to the end of the street. On weekdays between 8 AM and 5 PM, it's well worth taking a peek at the stunning interior of the **Živnostenská banka** ⑥, at No. 20.

Na Příkopě ends abruptly at the **Náměstí Republiky** ⑦, an important New Town transportation hub (with a metro stop). The severe depression-era facade of the Česká Národní banka (at Na Příkopě 30) makes the building look more like a fortress than the nation's central bank. Close by stands the stately **Prašná brána,** its festive Gothic spires looming above the square. Adjacent to the dignified Prašná brána, the **Obecní dům** looks decidedly decadent.

Walk through the arch at the base of Prašná brána and down the formal **Celetná ulice,** the first leg of the so-called Royal Way. Monarchs favored this route primarily because it has a stunning entry into Staroměstské náměstí and because the houses along Celetná were among the city's finest, providing a suitable backdrop to the corona-

18

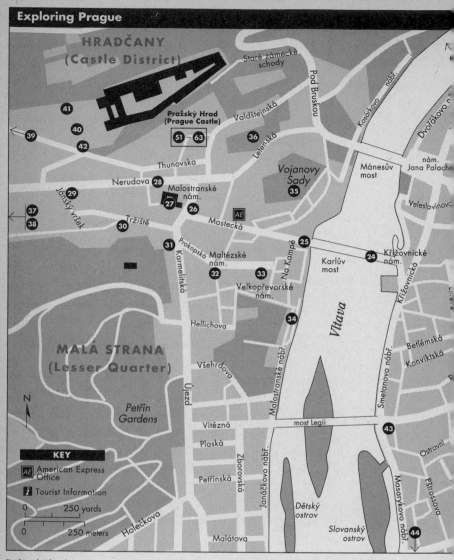

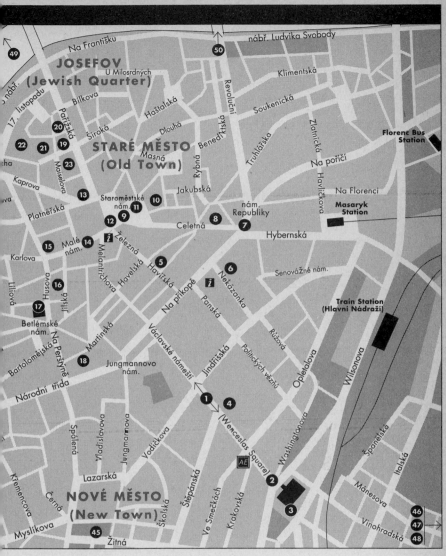

Zahrada Valdštejn-
ského paláca, **36**
Židovská radnice, **19**
Živnostenská banka, **6**

tion procession. The pink **U Sixtu** ⑧, at Celetná 2, sports one of the street's handsomest, if restrained, Baroque facades.

Staroměstské náměstí ⑨, at the end of Celetná, is dazzling, thanks partly to the double-spired **Kostel Panny Marie před Týnem** ⑩, which rises over the square from behind a row of patrician houses. To the immediate left of this church, at No. 13, is **Dům U Kamenného zvonu,** a Baroque structure that has been stripped down to its original Gothic elements.

Next door stands the gorgeous pink-and-ocher **Palác Kinských.** At this end of the square, you can't help noticing the expressive **Jan Hus monument** ⑪. Opposite the Kostel Panny Marie před Týnem is the Gothic **Staroměstská radnice** ⑫, which, with its impressive 200-ft tower, gives the square its sense of importance. As the hour approaches, join the crowds milling below the tower's 15th-century **astronomical clock** for a brief but spooky spectacle taken straight from the Middle Ages, every hour on the hour.

Walk north along the edge of the small park beside Town Hall to reach the Baroque **Kostel svatého Mikuláše** ⑬, not to be confused with the Lesser Town's Chrám svatého Mikuláše on the other side of the river (☞ A Good Walk *in* Karlův Most [Charles Bridge] and Malá Strana [Lesser Quarter], *below*). For a small detour, head down Kaprova street to the **Rudolfinum** concert hall and gallery; across the street is the **Uměleckoprůmyslové muzeum.** Both are notable neo-Renaissance buildings.

Returning to Staroměstské náměstí, you'll find **Výstava Franze Kafky** just to the left of Kostel svatého Mikuláše on U radnice. A small plaque can be found on the side of the house. Continue southwest from Staroměstské náměstí until you come to **Malé náměstí** ⑭, a nearly perfect ensemble of facades dating from the Middle Ages. Look for tiny **Karlova ulice,** which begins in the southwest corner of Malé náměstí, and take another quick right to stay on it (watch the signs—this medieval street seems designed to confound the visitor). Turn left at the T intersection where Karlova seems to end in front of the České muzeum výtvarných umění (Czech Museum of Fine Arts) and continue left down the quieter Husova ulice (veer to the right for the Karlův most and the other side of the river). Pause and inspect the exotic **Clam-Gallas palác** ⑮, at Husova 20. You'll recognize it easily: Look for the Titans in the doorway holding up what must be a very heavy Baroque facade.

Return to the T and continue down Husova. For a glimpse of a less successful Baroque reconstruction, take a close look at the **Kostel svatého Jiljí** ⑯, across from No. 7.

Continue walking along Husova ulice to Na Perštýně and turn right at tiny Betlémská ulice. The alley opens up onto a quiet square of the same name (Betlémská náměstí) and upon the most revered of all Hussite churches in Prague, the **Betlémská kaple** ⑰.

Return to Na Perštýně and continue walking to the right. As you near the back of the buildings of the busy Národní třída (National Boulevard), turn left at Martinská ulice. At the end of the street, the forlorn but majestic church **Kostel svatého Martina ve zdi** ⑱ stands like a postwar ruin. Walk around the church to the left and through a little archway of apartments onto the bustling Národní třída. To the left, a five-minute walk away, lies Václavské náměstí and the starting point of the walk.

TIMING

Václavské náměstí and Staroměstské náměstí are busy with activity around the clock almost all year round. If you're in search of a little peace and quiet, you will find the streets at their most subdued on early weekend mornings or right after a sudden downpour; otherwise, expect to share Prague's pleasures. The streets in this walking tour are reasonably close together and can be covered in half a day, or in a full day if you have more time. Remember to be in the Staroměstské náměstí just before the hour if you want to see the astronomical clock in action.

Sights to See

⑰ Betlémská kaple (Bethlehem Chapel). The church's elegant simplicity is in stark contrast to the diverting Gothic and Baroque of the rest of the city. The original structure dates from the end of the 14th century, and the Czech religious reformer Jan Hus was a regular preacher here from 1402 until his exile in 1412. After the Thirty Years' War the church fell into the hands of the Jesuits and was finally demolished in 1786. Excavations carried out after World War I uncovered the original portal and three windows, and the entire church was reconstructed during the 1950s. Although little remains of the first church, some remnants of Hus's teachings can still be read on the inside walls. ⊠ *Betlémské nám. 5.* ☜ *30 Kč.* ☉ *Apr.–Sept., daily 9–6; Oct.–Mar., daily 9–5.*

Celetná ulice (Celetna Street). Most of the facades indicate the buildings are from the 17th or 18th century, but appearances are deceiving: Many of the houses in fact have foundations dating from the 12th century or earlier. **⑧** U Sixtu (Sixt House), at Celetná 2, dates from the 12th century—its Romanesque vaults are still visible in the wine restaurant in the basement.

⑮ Clam-Gallas palác (Clam-Gallas Palace). The palace dates from 1713 and is the work of Johann Bernhard Fischer von Erlach, the famed Viennese architectural virtuoso of the day. Enter the building (push past the guard as if you know what you're doing) for a glimpse of the finely carved staircase, the work of the master himself, and of the Italian frescoes featuring Apollo that surround it. The Gallas family was prominent during the 18th century but has long since died out. The building now houses the municipal archives and is rarely open to visitors. ⊠ *Husova 20.*

Dům U černé Matky Boží (House of the Black Madonna). This Cubist building adds a decided jolt to the architectural styles along Celetná Street. In the second decade of this century, several leading Czech architects boldly applied Cubism's radical reworking of visual space to structures. The Black Madonna, designed by Josef Gočár, is unflinchingly modern yet topped with an almost Baroque tiled roof. It now houses a permanent exhibit of Czech Cubist design, as well as rotating exhibitions of modern art. ⊠ *Celetná 34 at Ovocný trh,* ☎ *02/2421–1732.* ☜ *35 Kč.* ☉ *Tues.–Sun. 10–6.*

Dům U Kamenného zvonu. (House at the Stone Bell). This Baroque-cum-Gothic structure occasionally hosts concerts and art exhibitions. The exhibitions change frequently, and it's worth stopping by to see what's on. ⊠ *Staroměstské nám. 13.*

④ Hotel Europa. An Art Nouveau gem, it has elegant stained glass and mosaics in the café and restaurant. The terrace is an excellent spot for people-watching. ⊠ *Václavské nám. 25.*

⑪ Jan Hus monument. Few memorials have elicited as much controversy as this one, which was dedicated in July 1915, exactly 500 years after Hus was burned at the stake in Constance, Germany. Some maintain that the monument's Secessionist style (the inscription seems to come right from turn-of-the-century Vienna) clashes with the Gothic and Baroque of the square. Others dispute the romantic depiction of Hus, who appears here in flowing garb as tall and bearded. The real Hus, historians maintain, was short and had a baby face. Still, no one can take issue with the influence of this fiery preacher, whose ability to transform doctrinal disputes, both literally and metaphorically, into the language of the common man made him into a religious and national symbol for the Czechs. ⊠ *Staroměstské nám.*

Karlova ulice. The character of Karlova ulice has changed in recent years to meet the growing number of tourists. Galleries and gift shops now occupy almost every storefront. But the cobblestones, narrow alleys, and crumbling gables still make it easy to imagine what life was like 400 years ago.

★ ⑩ **Kostel Panny Marie před Týnem** (Týn Church). The exterior of Týn Church is one of the best examples of Prague Gothic; it is in part the work of Peter Parler, architect of the Charles Bridge and St. Vitus Cathedral. Construction of its twin jet-black spires, which still jar the eye, was begun by King Jiří of Poděbrad in 1461, during the heyday of the Hussites. Jiří had a gilded chalice, the symbol of the Hussites, proudly displayed on the front gable between the two towers. Following the defeat of the Hussites by the Catholic Hapsburgs, the chalice was removed and eventually replaced by a Madonna. As a final blow, the chalice was melted down and made into the Madonna's glimmering halo (you still can see it by walking into the center of the square and looking up between the spires). The entrance to Týn Church is through the arcades, under the house at No. 604.

Much of the interior, including the tall nave, was rebuilt in the Baroque style in the 17th century. Some Gothic pieces remain, however: Look to the left of the main altar for a beautifully preserved set of early Gothic carvings. The main altar itself was painted by Karel Škréta, a luminary of the Czech Baroque. Before leaving the church, look for the grave marker (tucked away to the right of the main altar) of the great Danish astronomer Tycho Brahe, who came to Prague as "Imperial Mathematicus" in 1599 under Rudolf II. As a scientist, Tycho had a place in history that is assured: Johannes Kepler (another resident of the Prague court) used Tycho's observations to formulate his laws of planetary motion. But it is myth that has endeared Tycho to the hearts of Prague residents: The robust Dane, who was apparently fond of duels, lost part of his nose in one (take a closer look at the marker). He quickly had a wax nose fashioned for everyday use but preferred to parade around on holidays and festive occasions sporting a bright silver one. ⊠ *Celetná 5.* ⊘ *Daily 10–6.*

⑯ **Kostel svatého Jiljí** (Church of St. Giles). This Baroque church was another important outpost of Czech Protestantism in the 16th century. The exterior is a powerful example of Gothic architecture, including the buttresses and a characteristic portal; the interior, surprisingly, is Baroque, dating from the 17th century. The church is only open for evening concerts, held several times a week. ⊠ *Across from Husova 7.*

⑱ **Kostel svatého Martina ve zdi** (St. Martin-in-the-Wall). It was here in 1414 that Holy Communion was first given to the Bohemian laity—with both bread and wine, in defiance of the Catholic custom of the time, which dictated that only bread was to be offered to the masses, with wine reserved for the priests and clergy. From then on, the chalice came to symbolize the Hussite movement. The church is open for evening concerts, held several times each week. ⊠ *Martinská ul.*

⑬ **Kostel svatého Mikuláše** (Church of St. Nicholas). Designed in the 18th century by Prague's own master of late Baroque, Kilian Ignaz Dientzenhofer, this church is probably less successful than its namesake across town, the Chrám svatého Mikuláše, in capturing the style's lyric exuberance. Still, Dientzenhofer utilized the limited space to create a structure that neither dominates nor retreats from the imposing square. The interior is compact, with a beautiful but small chandelier and an enormous black organ that seems to overwhelm the rear of the church. The church often hosts afternoon and evening concerts. ✉ *Staroměstské nám.*

⑭ **Malé náměstí** (Small Square). Note the Renaissance iron fountain dating from 1560 in the center of the square. The sgraffito on the house at No. 3 is not as old (1890) as it looks, but here and there you can find authentic Gothic portals and Renaissance sgraffiti that betray the square's true age.

Mucha Museum. For decades it was almost impossible to find an Alfons Mucha original in the homeland of this famous Czech artist. In February 1998 this museum opened with nearly 100 works from his long career. What you'd expect to see is here—the theater posters of actress Sarah Bernhardt; the magazine covers; the luscious, sinuous Art Nouveau designs—but there are also paintings, photographs taken in Mucha's studio (one shows Paul Gauguin playing the piano in his underwear), childhood drawings, and even Czechoslovak banknotes designed by the artist. ✉ *Panská 7,* ☎ *02/628–4162.* 🎟 *100 Kč.* ☉ *Daily 10–6.*

Na Příkopě. The name means "at the moat," harking back to the time when the street was indeed a moat separating the Old Town on the left from the New Town on the right. Today the pedestrian zone Na Příkopě is prime shopping territory, its boutiques rivaling the often elegant shops on Wenceslas Square. But don't expect much real high fashion here: After 40 years of Communist orthodoxy in the fashion world, it will be many years before the boutiques really can match Western European standards.

⑦ **Náměstí Republiky** (Republic Square). Although an important New Town transportation hub (with a metro stop), the square has never really come together as a vital public space, perhaps because of its jarring architectural eclecticism. Taken one by one, each building is interesting in its own right, but the ensemble is less than the sum of the parts.

⑨ **Národní Muzeum** (Czech National Museum). This imposing structure, designed by Prague architect Josef Schulz and built between 1885 and 1890, does not come into its own until it is bathed in nighttime lighting. By day the grandiose edifice seems an inappropriate venue for a musty collection of stones and bones, minerals, and coins. This museum is only for dedicated fans of the genre. ✉ *Václavské nám. 68,* ☎ *02/2449–7111.* 🎟 *60 Kč.* ☉ *Daily 9–5; closed 1st Tues. of month.*

Obecní dům (Municipal House). After several years of on-again, off-again reconstruction, this building has been reinstated as a center for concerts, rotating art exhibits, and café society. The mature Art Nouveau style recalls the lengths the Czech middle classes went to at the turn of the century to imitate Paris, then the epitome of style and glamour. Much of the interior bears the work of the Art Nouveau master Alfons Mucha and other leading Czech artists. Mucha decorated the main Hall of the Lord Mayor upstairs; his impressive, magical frescoes depict Czech history. The beautiful Smetana Hall, which hosts concerts by the Prague Symphony Orchestra as well as international guests, is on the second floor. The ground-floor café is lovely but overpriced; you should pass on the two restaurants (one French and one Czech) as the food is decidedly disappointing. ✉ *Nám. Republiky 5,* ☎ *02/ 2200–2100.* ☉ *Daily 9–6.*

NEED A
BREAK?

If you prefer subtle elegance, head around the corner to the café at **Hotel Paříž** (✉ U Obecního domu 1, ☎ 02/2422–2151), a Jugendstil jewel tucked away on a relatively quiet street.

Palác Kinských (Kinský Palace). This exhuberant building, built in 1765, is considered one of Prague's finest late-Baroque structures. With its exaggerated pink overlay and numerous statues, the facade looks extreme when contrasted with the more staid Baroque elements of other nearby buildings. (The interior, however, was "modernized" under communism.) The palace once housed a German school—where Franz Kafka was a student for nine misery-laden years—and presently contains the National Gallery's graphics collection. The main exhibition room is on the second floor; exhibits change every few months and are usually worth seeing. It was from this building that Communist leader Klement Gottwald, flanked by his comrade Clementis, first addressed the crowds after seizing power in February 1948—an event recounted in the first chapter of Milan Kundera's novel *The Book of Laughter and Forgetting.* ✉ *Staroměstské nám. 12.* 🎟 *70 Kč.* ☉ *Tues.–Sun. 10–6.*

Prašná brána (Powder Tower). Construction of the tower, one of the city's 13 original gates, was begun by King Vladislav II of Jagiello in 1475. At the time, the kings of Bohemia maintained their royal residence next door (on the site of the current Municipal House; ☞ *above*), and the tower was intended to be the grandest gate of all. But Vladislav was Polish and thus heartily disliked by the rebellious Czech citizens of Prague. Nine years after he assumed power, fearing for his life, he moved the royal court across the river to Prague Castle. Work on the tower was abandoned, and the half-finished structure was used for storing gunpowder—hence its odd name—until the end of the 17th century. The oldest part of the tower is the base; the golden spires were not added until the end of the last century. The climb to the top affords a striking view of the Old Town and Prague Castle in the distance. ✉ *Nám. Republiky.* 🎟 *20 Kč.* ☉ *Apr.–Oct., daily 9–6.*

Rudolfinum. Thanks to a thorough makeover and exterior sandblasting, this neo-Renaissance monument designed by Josef Zítek and Josef Schulz presents the cleanest, brightest stonework in the city. Completed in 1884 and named for then–Hapsburg Crown Prince Rudolf, the rather low-slung sandstone building was meant to be a combination concert hall and exhibition gallery; after 1918 it was converted into the parliament of the newly independent Czechoslovakia. German invaders reinstated the concert hall in 1939; Czech writer Jiří Weil's novel *Mendelssohn Is on the Roof* tells of the cruel farce that ensued when officials ordered the removal of the Jewish composer's statue from the roof balustrade. Now the Czech Philharmonic has its home base here; the 1,200-seat **Dvořakova síň** (Dvořák Hall) has superb acoustics. The box office is on the right-hand side of the building. ✉ *Náměstí Jana Palacha,* ☎ *02/2489–3352.*

Behind Dvořák Hall is a set of large exhibition rooms, the **Galerie Rudolfinum,** an innovative, state-supported gallery for rotating shows of contemporary art. Four or five large shows are mounted here annually, showcasing excellent Czech work along with international artists such as photographer Cindy Sherman. It remains to be seen to what extent the country's fiscal crisis of 1997 will affect this and other public arts institutions. ✉ *Alšovo nábřeží 12,* ☎ *02/2489–3205.* 🎟 *40 Kč.* ☉ *Tues.–Sun. 10–6.*

★ ⑫ **Staroměstská radnice** (Old Town Hall). This is one of Prague's mag-
nets; hundreds of people gravitate to it to see the hour struck by the
mechanical figures of the **astronomical clock**. Just before the hour, look
to the upper part of the clock, where a skeleton begins by tolling a death
knell and turning an hourglass upside down. The Twelve Apostles parade momentarily, and then a cockerel flaps its wings and crows, pierc-
ing the air as the hour finally strikes. To the right of the skeleton, the
dreaded Turk nods his head, seemingly hinting at another invasion like
those of the 16th and 17th centuries.

The Town Hall has served as the center of administration for the Old
Town since 1338, when King Johann of Luxembourg first granted the
city council the right to a permanent location. The impressive 200-ft
Town Hall Tower, where the clock is mounted, was first built in the
14th century and given its current late-Gothic appearance around
1500 by the master Matyáš Rejsek. For a rare view of the Old Town
and its maze of crooked streets and alleyways, climb to the top of the
tower. The climb is not strenuous, but steep stairs at the top unfortunately prevent people with disabilities from enjoying the view. Enter
through the door to the left of the tower.

Just in front of the hall, look for the 27 white crosses on the ground.
These mark the spot where 27 Bohemian noblemen were killed by the
Hapsburgs in 1621 during the dark days following the defeat of the
Czechs at the Battle of White Mountain. The grotesque spectacle, designed to quash any further national or religious opposition, took
some five hours to complete, as the men were put to the sword or hanged
one by one. If you walk around the hall to the left, you'll see it's actually a series of houses jutting into the square; they were purchased
over the years and successively added to the complex. The most interesting is the **U Minuty**, the corner building to the left of the clock
tower, with its 16th-century Renaissance sgraffiti of biblical and classical motifs.

Immediately after the hour, guided tours in English and German (German only in winter) of the Town Hall depart from the main desk inside. However, the only notable features inside are the fine Renaissance
ceilings and the Gothic Council Room. ⊠ *Staroměstské nám.* ☎ *All
sights 40 Kč.* ☉ *Daily 9–6 (until 5 in winter).*

★ ⑨ **Staroměstské náměsti** (Old Town Square). Dazzling. Long the heart
of the Old Town, the square grew to its present proportions when the
city's original marketplace was moved away from the river in the 12th
century. Its shape and appearance have changed little over the years—
during the day the square has a festive atmosphere as musicians vie
for the favor of onlookers, hefty young men in medieval outfits mint
coins, and artists display renditions of Prague street scenes. If you come
back to the square at night, the unlit shadowy towers of the Týn
Church (to your right as you enter the square) rise ominously over the
glowing Baroque facades. The crowds thin out, and the ghosts of the
square's stormy past return.

During the 15th century the square was the focal point of conflict between Czech Hussites and German Catholics. In 1422 the radical Hussite preacher Jan Želevský was executed here for his part in storming
the New Town's town hall. Three Catholic consuls and seven German
citizens were thrown out of the window in the ensuing fray—the first
of Prague's many famous defenestrations. Within a few years, the
Hussites had taken over the town, expelled the Germans, and set up
their own administration.

NEED A
BREAK?
Staroměstské náměstí is a convenient spot for refreshments. **Tchibo**, at No. 6 (☎ 02/2481–1026), has tasty sandwiches and pastries, excellent coffee, and an outdoor terrace in season.

❷ **Statue of St. Wenceslas.** In 1848 citizens protested Hapsburg rule at this statue in front of the National Museum. In 1939 residents gathered to oppose Hitler's takeover of Bohemia and Moravia. It was here also, in 1969, that the student Jan Palach set himself on fire to protest the bloody invasion of his country by the Soviet Union and other Warsaw Pact countries in August of the previous year. The invasion ended the "Prague Spring," a cultural and political movement emphasizing free expression, which was supported by Alexander Dubček, the popular leader at the time. Although Dubček never intended to dismantle Communist authority completely, his political and economic reforms proved too daring for fellow comrades in the rest of Eastern Europe. In the months following the invasion, conservatives loyal to the Soviet Union were installed in all influential positions. The subsequent two decades were a period of cultural stagnation. Thousands of residents left the country or went underground; many more resigned themselves to lives of minimal expectations and small pleasures. ⊠ *Václavské nám.*

❺ **Stavovské Divadlo** (Estates Theater). Built in the 1780s in the classical style and reopened in 1991 after years of renovation, this handsome theater was for many years a beacon of Czech-language culture in a city long dominated by the German variety. It is probably best known as the site of the world premiere of Mozart's opera *Don Giovanni* in October 1787, with the composer himself conducting. Prague audiences were quick to acknowledge Mozart's genius: The opera was an instant hit here, though it flopped nearly everywhere else in Europe. Mozart wrote most of the opera's second act in Prague at the Villa Bertramka (☞ Karlův Most [Charles Bridge] and Malá Strana [Lesser Quarter], *below*), where he was a frequent guest. ⊠ *Ovocný trh.*

Uměleckoprůmyslové muzeum (Museum of Decorative Arts). The best things here are the oldest: the Renaissance furniture and glass from Bohemia and Germany, and the amazing mosaic landscapes inlaid into tabletops. Clothing, metalwork, books, and miniatures from the 16th to the 19th century are also on display. ⊠ *Ulice 17. listopadu 2,* ☎ *02/2481–1241.* ▦ *40 Kč.* ☼ *Tues.–Sun. 10–6.*

❶ **Václavské náměstí** (Wenceslas Square). You may recognize this spot from your television set, for it was here that some 500,000 students and citizens gathered in the heady days of November 1989 to protest the policies of the former Communist regime. The government capitulated after a week of demonstrations, without a shot fired or the loss of a single life, bringing to power the first democratic government in 40 years (under playwright-president Václav Havel). Today this peaceful transfer of power is proudly referred to as the "Velvet" or "Gentle" Revolution (*něžná revolucia*). It was only fitting that the 1989 revolution should take place on Wenceslas Square; throughout much of Czech history, the square has served as the focal point for popular discontent. Although Wenceslas Square was first laid out by Charles IV in 1348 as the center of the New Town (Nové Město), few buildings of architectural merit line the square today.

Výstava Franze Kafky (Franz Kafka's birthplace). For years this memorial to Kafka's birth (July 3, 1883) was the only public acknowledgment of the writer's stature in world literature, reflecting the traditionally ambiguous attitude of the Czech government to his work. The Communists were always too uncomfortable with Kafka's themes of bureaucracy and alienation to sing his praises loudly, if at all. As a

German and a Jew, moreover, Kafka could easily be dismissed as standing outside the mainstream of Czech literature. Following the 1989 revolution, however, Kafka's popularity soared, and his works are now widely available in Czech. Only the portal of the original house remains; inside the building is a fascinating little exhibit (mostly photographs) on Kafka's life, with commentary in English. ⊠ *U radnice 5.* ▣ *50 Kč.* ☉ *Tues.–Fri. 10–6, Sat. 10–5 (until 7 in summer).*

❻ **Živnostenská banka** (Merchants' Bank). The style, a tasteful example of 19th-century exuberance, reflected the city's growing prosperity at the time. Ignore the guards and walk up the decorated stairs to the beautiful main banking room (note, however, that taking photos is forbidden). ⊠ *Na Příkopě 20.*

Josefov (The Jewish Ghetto)

Prague's Jews survived centuries of discrimination, but two unrelated events of modern times have left their historic ghetto little more than a collection of museums. Around 1900, city officials decided for hygienic purposes to raze the ghetto and pave over its crooked streets. Only the synagogues, the town hall, and a few other buildings survived this early attempt at urban renewal. The second event was the Holocaust. Under Nazi occupation, a staggering percentage of the city's Jews were deported or murdered in concentration camps. Of the 35,000 Jews living in the ghetto before World War II, only about 1,200 returned to resettle the neighborhood after the war. The community is still quite small; there are now roughly 5,000 Jews living in the quarter.

A Good Walk

To reach **Josefov,** the Jewish ghetto, leave Old Town Square via the handsome Pařížská and head north toward the river. The festive atmosphere changes suddenly as you enter the area of the ghetto. The buildings are lower here and older; the mood is hushed. Treasures and artifacts of the ghetto are now the property of the **Židovské muzeum v Praze,** a complex comprising the Old Jewish Cemetery and the collections of the remaining individual synagogues. On Maiselova ulice is the **Židovská radnice** ⑲, now home to the Jewish Community Center. The **Staronová synagóga** ⑳ across the street at Červená 2 is the oldest standing synagogue in Europe.

Červená becomes the little U starého hřbitova (At the Old Cemetery Street). The **main museum ticket office** is at the Klausová synagóga (Klaus Synagogue) at No. 3a, which also displays an exhibition of Czech Jewish traditions and occasional art shows. Just to the right is the **Obřadní síň,** which exhibits traditional Jewish funeral objects.

Return to Maiselova and follow it to Široká. Turn right to find the **Pinkasova synagóga** ㉑, a handsome Gothic structure that houses the restored memorial to murdered Czech Jews and a moving exhibition of drawings made by children held at the Nazi concentration camp at Terezín (Theresienstadt), in northern Bohemia. Here also is the entrance to the Jewish ghetto's most astonishing sight, the **Starý židovský hřbitov** ㉒.

Return to Maiselova once more and turn right in the direction of the Old Town, crossing Široká. Look in at the enormous collection of silver articles of worship in the **Maiselova synagóga** ㉓.

TIMING

The Jewish ghetto is one of the most popular visitor destinations in Prague, especially in the height of summer, when its tiny streets are jammed to bursting with tourists almost all the time. The best time to savor any of these sights without any crowds and distractions would be early morning when the museums and cemetery first open. The area itself is very compact, and a basic walk-through should take only half a day. Travelers who'd like to linger in the museums could easily spend two days or more exploring this area.

Sights to See

㉓ Maiselova synagóga (Maisel Synagogue). This houses a huge number of silver articles of worship confiscated by the Nazis from synagogues throughout Central Europe. Here you'll find the Jewish Museum's finest collection of Torah wrappers and mantles, silver pointers, breastplates, spice boxes, candleholders (the eight-branched *Hanukkiah* and the seven-branched menorah), and Levite washing sets. ✉ *Maiselova 10.* 🎫 *For admission information to this and other synagogues,* see *entry under Židovské muzeum v Praze,* below.

Obřadní síň (Ceremony Hall). After reopening in spring 1998, this space focuses on rather grim subjects; there are displays of Jewish funeral paraphernalia, old gravestones, and medical instruments. ✉ *U starého hřbitova 3a.* 🎫 *For admission information,* see *entry under Židovské muzeum v Praze,* below.

Pařížská street. The buildings on this street date from the end of the 19th century, and their elegant facades reflect the prosperity of the Czech middle classes at the time. Here and there you can spot the influence of the Viennese Jugendstil, with its emphasis on mosaics, geometric forms, and gold inlay; there's also a Cubist building on Elišky Krasnohorské street off Parizska. The look is fresh against the busier 19th-century revival facades of most of the other structures.

㉑ Pinkasova synagóga (Pinkas Synagogue). This synagogue has two particularly moving testimonies to the appalling crimes perpetrated against the Jews during World War II. One tribute can astound by sheer numbers; the inside walls are covered with nearly 80,000 names of Bohemian and Moravian Jews murdered by the Nazis. Among them are the names of the paternal grandparents of U.S. Secretary of State Madeleine Albright, who learned of their fate only in 1997. There is also an exhibition of drawings made by children at the Nazi concentration camp Terezín. During the early years of the war the Nazis used the camp for propaganda purposes to demonstrate their "humanity" toward the Jews, and prisoners were given relative freedom to lead "normal" lives. Transports to death camps in Poland began in earnest in the final months of the war, however, and many thousands of Terezín prisoners, including many of these children, eventually perished. Enter the synagogue from Široká Street. ✉ *Široká 3.* 🎫 *For admission information to this and other synagogues,* see *entry under Židovské muzeum v Praze,* below.

⑳ Staronová synagóga (Old-New Synagogue). Dating from the mid-13th century, it is one of the most important works of early Gothic in Prague. The odd name recalls the legend that the synagogue was built on the site of an ancient Jewish temple and that stones from the temple were used to build the present structure. The synagogue has not only survived fires and the razing of the ghetto at the end of the last century but also emerged from the Nazi occupation intact; it is still in active use. The oldest part of the synagogue is the entrance, with its vault supported by two pillars. The grille at the center of the hall dates from the 15th century. Note that men are required to cover their heads inside and that during services men and women sit apart. ✉ *Červená 2.* 🎫 *For admission information,* see *entry under Židovské muzeum v Praze,* below.

★ ㉒ **Starý židovský hřbitov** (Old Jewish Cemetery). This unforgettably melancholy sight not far from the busy city was, from the 14th century to 1787, the final resting place for all Jews living in Prague. Some 12,000 graves in all are piled atop one another in layers. Walk the paths amid the gravestones; the relief symbols you'll see represent the name or profession of the deceased. The oldest marked grave belongs to the poet Avigdor Kara, who died in 1439. The best-known marker is probably that of Jehuda ben Bezalel, the famed Rabbi Loew, who is credited with having created the mythical Golem in 1573. Even today, small scraps of paper bearing wishes are stuffed into the cracks of the rabbi's tomb in the hope he will grant them. Loew's grave lies just a few steps from the entrance, near the western wall of the cemetery. ✆ *For admission information,* see *entry under Židovské muzeum v Praze, below.*

★ ⑲ **Židovská radnice** (Jewish Town Hall). The hall was the creation of Mordecai Maisel, an influential Jewish leader at the end of the 16th century. It was restored in the 18th century and given its clock and bell tower at that time. A second clock, with Hebrew numbers, keeps time counterclockwise. Now home to the Jewish Community Center, the building also houses Prague's only kosher restaurant, Shalom. ✉ *Maiselova 18.*

Židovské muzeum v Praze (Prague Jewish Museum). All the synagogues and the Old Jewish Cemetery are under the auspices of this museum. (The Old-New Synagogue [☞ *above*], which is a functioning house of worship, technically does not belong to the museum, but the Prague Jewish Community oversees both.) In a bit of irony, the holdings' abundance can be credited to Hitler, who had planned to open a museum here documenting the life and practices of what he had hoped would be an "extinct" people. The cemetery and most of the synagogues are open to the public. Each synagogue specializes in certain artifacts, and you can buy tickets for all the buildings at either Maisel Synagogue, Pinkas Synagogue, or Klausova synagóga. ☎ *02/231–7191.* ✆ *Combined ticket to Jewish Museum collections 450 Kč; museum collections only 250 Kč; Old-New Synagogue only 200 Kč. ⊙ Apr.–May, Sun.–Fri. 9–6; June–Oct., Sun.–Fri. 9–6:30; Nov.–Mar., Sun.–Fri. 9–4; closed Sat. and Jewish holidays. Old-New Synagogue closes 2 hrs early on Fri.*

Karlův Most (Charles Bridge) and Malá Strana (Lesser Quarter)

A Good Walk

Prague's Malá Strana (the so-called Lesser Quarter, or Little Town) is not for the methodical traveler. Its charm lies in the tiny lanes, the sudden blasts of bombastic architecture, and the soul-stirring views that emerge for a second before disappearing behind the sloping roofs. The neighborhood dates back to the mid-13th century, and for years it was home to the merchants and craftsmen who served the royal court.

Begin the tour on the Old Town side of **Karlův most** ㉔, which you can reach by foot in about 10 minutes from the Old Town Square. Rising above it is the majestic **Staroměstská mostecká věž**; the climb of 138 steps is worth the effort for the views it affords of the Old Town and, across the river, of the Lesser Quarter and Prague Castle.

It's worth pausing to take a closer look at some of the statues as you walk across the Karlův most toward the Lesser Quarter. Approaching the Lesser Quarter, you'll see the Kampa Island below you, separated from the mainland by an arm of the Vltava known as Čertovka (Devil's Stream).

By now you are almost at the end of the bridge. In front of you is the striking conjunction of the two **Malá Strana bridge towers** ㉕, one Gothic, the other Romanesque. Together they frame the Baroque flamboyance of Chrám svatého Mikuláše in the distance. At night this is an absolutely wondrous sight. If you didn't climb the tower on the Old Town side of the bridge, it's worth scrambling up the wooden stairs inside the Gothic tower Mostecká věž for the views over the roofs of the Lesser Quarter and of the Old Town across the river.

Walk under the gateway of the towers into the little uphill street called Mostecká ulice. You have now entered the **Malá Strana.** Follow Mostecká ulice up to the rectangular **Malostranské náměstí** ㉖, now the district's traffic hub rather than its heart. On the left side of the square stands **Chrám svatého Mikuláše** ㉗.

Nerudova ulice ㉘ runs up from the square toward Prague Castle. Lined with gorgeous houses (and in recent years an ever-larger number of places to spend money), it's sometimes burdened with the moniker "Prague's most beautiful street." A tiny passageway at No. 13, on the left-hand side as you go up, leads to Tržiště ulice and the **Schönbornský palác** ㉚, once Franz Kafka's home, now the embassy of the United States. The street winds down to the quarter's noisy main street, Karmelitská, where the famous "Infant Jesus of Prague" resides in the **Kostel Panny Marie vítězné.** A few doors away, closer to Tržiště ulice, is the **Vrtbovská zahrada** ㉛. Tiny Prokopská ulice leads off of Karmelitská, past the former Church of St. Procopius, now converted, oddly, into an apartment block, and into **Maltézské náměstí** ㉜, a characteristically noble compound. Nearby, **Velkopřevorské náměstí** ㉝ boasts even grander palaces.

A tiny bridge at the cramped square's lower end takes you across a small water channel called Čertovka to **Kampa** ㉞ island and its broad lawns, cafés, and river views. Winding your way underneath the Karlův most and along the street U lužického semináře brings you to a quiet walled garden, **Vojanovy sady** ㉟. Another, more formal garden, with an unbeatable view of Prague Castle looming above, the **Zahrada Valdštejnského paláca** ㊱ hides itself off busy Letenská ulice near the Malostranská metro station.

TIMING

The area is at its best in the evening, when the softer light hides the crumbling facades and brings you into a world of glimmering beauty. The basic walk described here could take as little as half a day—longer if you'd like to explore the area's lovely nooks and crannies.

Sights to See

㉙ **Bretfeld palác** (Bretfeld Palace). It's worth taking a quick look at this rococo house on the corner of Nerudova ulice and Jánský vršek. The relief of St. Nicholas on the facade is the work of Ignaz Platzer, a sculptor known for his classic and rococo work, but the building is valued more for its historical associations than for its architecture: This is where Mozart, his lyricist partner Lorenzo da Ponte, and the aging but still infamous philanderer and music lover Casanova stayed at the time of the world premiere of *Don Giovanni* in 1787. The Lesser Quarter gained a new connection with Mozart when its streets were used to represent 18th-century Vienna in the filming of Miloš Forman's *Amadeus*. The palace is now a residential building and so is not open to the public. ⊠ *Nerudova 33.*

The archway at Nerudova 13, more or less opposite the Santini-designed **Kostel Panny Marie ustavičné pomoci u Kajetánů** (Church of Our Lady of Perpetual Help at the Theatines), hides one of the many winding passageways that give the Lesser Quarter its enchantingly ghostly character at night. Follow the dogleg curve downhill, past two restau-

rants, vine-covered walls, and some broken-down houses. The alleyway really comes into its own only in the dark, the dim lighting hid-
ing the grime and highlighting the mystery. (It's a safe area, as the
neighborhood is quite active.)

★ ㉗ **Chrám svatého Mikuláše** (St. Nicholas Church). With its dynamic
curves, this church is one of the purest and most ambitious examples
of high Baroque. The celebrated architect Christoph Dientzenhofer began
the Jesuit church in 1704 on the site of one of the more active Hussite
churches of 15th-century Prague. Work on the building was taken over
by his son Kilian Ignaz Dientzenhofer, who built the dome and pres-
bytery; Anselmo Lurago completed the whole in 1755 by adding the
bell tower. The juxtaposition of the broad, full-bodied dome with the
slender bell tower is one of the many striking architectural contrasts
that mark the Prague skyline. Inside, the vast pink-and-green space is
impossible to take in with a single glance; every corner bristles with
movement, guiding the eye first to the dramatic statues, then to the hec-
tic frescoes, and on to the shining faux-marble pillars. Many of the statues are the work of Ignaz Platzer; they constitute his last blaze of success.
When the centralizing and secularizing reforms of Joseph II toward the
end of the 18th century brought an end to the flamboyant Baroque
era, Platzer's workshop was forced to declare bankruptcy. ⊠ *Malostranské nám.* ▦ *30 Kč.* ☉ *Daily 9–4 (until 5 or 6 in summer).*

㉞ **Kampa.** Prague's largest island is cut off from the "mainland" by the
narrow Čertovka streamlet. The name Čertovka translates as Devil's
Stream and reputedly refers to a cranky old lady who once lived on
Maltese Square (given the river's present filthy state, however, the
name is ironically appropriate). The unusually well kept lawns of the
Kampa Gardens that occupy much of the island are one of the few places
in Prague where sitting on the grass is openly tolerated. If it's a warm
day, spread out a blanket and bask for a while in the sunshine. The
row of benches that lines the river is also a popular spot from which
to contemplate the city. At night this stretch along the river is especially romantic.

★ ㉔ **Karlův most** (Charles Bridge). The view from the foot of the bridge on
the Old Town side is nothing short of breathtaking, encompassing the
towers and domes of the Lesser Quarter and the soaring spires of St.
Vitus Cathedral to the northwest. This heavenly vision, one of the most
beautiful in Europe, changes subtly in perspective as you walk across
the bridge, attended by the host of Baroque saints that decorate the
bridge's peaceful Gothic stones. At night its drama is spellbinding: St.
Vitus Cathedral lit in a ghostly green, the castle in monumental yellow, and the Church of St. Nicholas in a voluptuous pink, all viewed
through the menacing silhouettes of the bowed statues and the Gothic
towers. If you do nothing else in Prague, you must visit the Charles
Bridge at night. During the day the pedestrian bridge buzzes with activity. Street musicians vie with artisans hawking jewelry, paintings, and
glass for the hearts and wallets of the passing multitude. At night the
crowds thin out a little, the musicians multiply, and the bridge becomes
a long block party—nearly everyone brings a bottle.

When the Přemyslide princes set up residence in Prague in the 10th century, there was a ford across the Vltava at this point, a vital link along
one of Europe's major trading routes. After several wooden bridges
and the first stone bridge had washed away in floods, Charles IV ap-
pointed the 27-year-old German Peter Parler, the architect of St. Vitus
Cathedral, to build a new structure in 1357. After 1620, following the
defeat of Czech Protestants by Catholic Hapsburgs at the Battle of White
Mountain, the bridge and its adornment became caught up in the

Catholic–Hussite (Protestant) conflict. The many Baroque statues that began to appear in the late 17th century, commissioned by Catholics, eventually came to symbolize the totality of the Austrian (hence Catholic) triumph. The Czech writer Milan Kundera sees the statues from this perspective: "The thousands of saints looking out from all sides, threatening you, following you, hypnotizing you, are the raging hordes of occupiers who invaded Bohemia three hundred and fifty years ago to tear the people's faith and language from their hearts."

The religious conflict is less obvious nowadays, leaving only the artistic tension between Baroque and Gothic that gives the bridge its allure. It's worth pausing to take a closer look at some of the statues as you walk toward the Lesser Quarter. The third on the right, a brass crucifix with Hebrew lettering in gold, was mounted on the location of a wooden cross destroyed in the battle with the Swedes. The eighth statue on the right, St. John of Nepomuk, is the oldest of all; it was designed by Johann Brokoff in 1683. On the left-hand side, sticking out from the bridge between the 9th and 10th statues (the latter has a wonderfully expressive vanquished Satan), stands a Roland (Brunvík) statue. This knightly figure, bearing the coat of arms of the Old Town, was once a reminder that this part of the bridge belonged to the Old Town before Prague became a unified city in 1784.

In the eyes of most art historians, the most valuable statue is the 12th, on the left. Mathias Braun's statue of St. Luitgarde depicts the blind saint kissing Christ's wounds. The most compelling grouping, however, is the second from the end on the left, a work of Ferdinand Maximilien Brokoff from 1714. Here the saints are incidental; the main attraction is the Turk, his face expressing extreme boredom while guarding Christians imprisoned in the cage at his side. When the statue was erected, just 29 years after the second Turkish invasion of Vienna, it scandalized the Prague public, who smeared the statue with mud. St. Luitgarde and all but five of the other Baroque sculptures on the bridge are 20th-century copies; in addition, a half dozen of the 30 bridge sculptures are 19th-century replacements for originals damaged in wars or fallen into the river in 1784 during a flood. Most of the surviving Baroque originals have been removed to safer quarters, protected from Prague's acidic air; several can be viewed in the Lapidarium museum at Výstaviště exhibition grounds in Prague 7 and in a man-made cavern at Vyšehrad (☞ Nové město [New Town] and Vyšehrad, *below*).

Kostel Panny Marie vítězné (Church of Our Lady Victorious). Just down the street from the Vrtbovská zahrada (☞ *below*), this comfortably ramshackle church makes the unlikely home of one of Prague's best-known religious artifacts, the *Pražské Jezulátko* (Infant Jesus of Prague). Originally brought to Prague from Spain in the 16th century, this tiny porcelain doll (now bathed in neon lighting straight out of Las Vegas) is renowned worldwide for showering miracles on anyone willing to kneel before it and pray. Nuns from a nearby convent arrive at dawn each day to change the infant's clothes; pieces of the doll's extensive wardrobe have been sent by believers from around the world. ⊠ *Karmelitská 9a.* 🎟 *Free.* ☉ *Mon.–Sat. 10–5:30, Sun. 1–5.*

Ledeburská zahrada (Ledeburg Garden). Among the row of steeply banked Baroque gardens behind the palaces of Valdštejnská ulice, this is the only one presently open to the public. It's a pleasant spot for a rest amid shady arbors and niches. The garden with its frescoes and statuary was restored in 1995 with support from a fund headed by Czech president Václav Havel and Charles, Prince of Wales. ⊠ *Entrance at*

Valdštejnské nám. 3; in summer also from the South Gardens of Prague Castle. ▣ *25 Kč.* ⊘ *Daily 10–6.*

㉕ **Malá Strana bridge towers.** The lower, Romanesque tower formed a part of the earlier wooden and stone bridges, and its present appearance stems from a renovation in 1591; it's not open to the public. The Gothic tower, **Mostecká věž,** was added to the bridge a few decades after its completion; you can climb up it to see the view. ✉ *Mostecká ul.* ▣ *20 Kč.* ⊘ *Apr.–Oct., daily 9–6.*

㉖ **Malostranské náměstí** (Lesser Quarter Square). The arcaded houses on the east and south sides, dating from the 16th and 17th centuries, exhibit a mix of Baroque and Renaissance elements. The Czech Parliament resides partly in the gaudy yellow-and-green palace on the square's north side, partly in the street behind the palace, Sněmovní. From this corner of the square the great fire of 1541 began. Now the square buzzes with restaurants, street vendors, clubs, and shops; the huge bulk of St. Nicholas Church divides the lower, busier section from the quieter upper part. ✉ *Mostecká ul., Letenská ul., and Karmelitská ul. lead into square.*

㉜ **Maltézské náměstí** (Maltese Square). Peaceful and grandiose, this square was named for the Knights of Malta. In the middle is a sculpture depicting John the Baptist. This work, by Ferdinand Brokoff, was erected in 1715 to commemorate the end of a plague. The relief on the far side shows Salome engrossed in her dance of the seven veils while John is being decapitated. There are two intricately decorated palaces on this square: to the right the rococo Turba Palace, now the Japanese Embassy, and at the bottom the Nostitz Palace, the Dutch Embassy. ✉ *Prokopská ul., Harantova ul., and Nebovídská ul. lead into square.*

㉘ **Nerudova ulice.** This steep little street used to be the last leg of the Royal Way, walked by the king before his coronation, and it is still the best way to get to Prague Castle. It was named for the 19th-century Czech journalist and poet Jan Neruda (after whom Chilean poet Pablo Neruda renamed himself). Until Joseph II's administrative reforms in the late 18th century, house numbering was unknown in Prague. Each house bore a name, depicted on the facade, and these are particularly prominent on Nerudova ulice. House No. 6, **U červeného orla** (At the Red Eagle), proudly displays a faded painting of a red eagle. No. 12 is known as **U tří housliček** (At the Three Violins). In the early 18th century, three generations of the Edlinger violin-making family lived here. Joseph II's scheme numbered each house according to its position in Prague's separate "towns" (here the Lesser Quarter) rather than according to its sequence on the street. The red plates record these original house numbers; the blue ones are the numbers used in addresses today—except, oddly enough, in some of the newer suburbs—while, to confuse the tourist, many architectural guides refer to the old, red-number plates.

NEED A
BREAK?
Nerudova ulice is filled with little restaurants and snack bars and offers something for everyone. **U zeleného čaje,** at No. 19, is a fragrant little tearoom, offering fruit and herbal teas as well as light salads and sweets. **U Kocoura,** at No. 2, is a traditional pub that hasn't caved in to touristic niceties.

Two palaces break the unity of the burghers' houses on Nerudova ulice. Both were designed by the adventurous Baroque architect Giovanni Santini, one of the Italian builders most in demand by wealthy nobles of the early 18th century. The **Morzin Palace,** on the left at No. 5, is now the Romanian Embassy. The fascinating facade, with an allegory of night and day, was created in 1713 and is the work of Ferdinand Brokoff of Charles Bridge statue fame. Across the street at No. 20 is the **Thun-Hohenstein Palace,** now the Italian Embassy. The gateway with two enormous eagles (the emblem of the Kolovrat family, who owned the building at the time) is the work of the other great Charles Bridge statue sculptor, Mathias Braun. Santini himself lived at No. 14, the so-called **Valkoun House.**

③⓪ **Schönbornský palác** (Schönborn Palace). Franz Kafka had an apartment in this massive Baroque building at the top of Tržiště ulice from March through August 1917, after moving out from Zlatá ulička (Golden Lane; ☞ Pražský hrad [Prague Castle], *below*). The U.S. Embassy now occupies this prime location. If you look through the gates, you can see the beautiful formal gardens rising up to the Petřín hill; they are unfortunately not open to the public. ⊠ *Tržiště at Vlašská.*

Staroměstská mostecká věž (Old Town Bridge Tower). This was where Peter Parler (the architect of St. Vitus Cathedral) began his bridge building. The carved facades he designed for the sides of the bridge were destroyed by Swedish soldiers in 1648, at the end of the Thirty Years' War. The sculptures facing the square, however, are still intact (although some are recent copies); they depict an old and gout-ridden Charles IV with his son, who later became Wenceslas IV. Above them are two of Bohemia's patron saints: Adalbert (Vojtěch) and Sigismund. Inside the tower is a small exhibit of antique musical instruments. 🖃 *20 Kč.* ⊙ *Daily 9–7.*

U tří pštrosů (The Three Ostriches). The original building stems from the 16th century, when one of the early owners was a supplier of ostrich feathers to the royal court and had the house's three unmistakable emblems painted on the facade. The top floors and curlicue gables were early Baroque additions from the 17th century. The ancient inn functions as a hotel to this day. It was the site of the first coffeehouse in Prague, opened by the Armenian Deodat Damajian in 1714. ⊠ *Dražického nám. 12.*

NEED A   At the corner of Na Kampě, right next to the arches of the Charles
BREAK?   Bridge, the small stand-up café **Bistro Bruncvik** serves hot wine and coffee
                in winter and cold drinks in summer. Its slices of pizza are also satisfying.

---

③③ **Velkopřevorské náměstí** (Grand Priory Square). The palace fronting the square is considered one of the finest Baroque buildings in the Lesser Quarter, though it is now part of the Embassy of the Knights of Malta and no longer open to the public. Opposite is the flamboyant orange-and-white stucco facade of the Buquoy Palace, built in 1719 by Giovanni Santini and the present home of the French Embassy. From the street you can glimpse an enormous twinkling chandelier through the window, but this is about all you'll get to see of the elegant interior. The so-called **John Lennon Peace Wall,** leading to a bridge over the Čertovka stream, was once a kind of monument to youthful rebellion, emblazoned with a large painted head of the former Beatle, lyrics from his songs, and other messages of peace. It has lost much social significance, not to mention attractiveness, since the years around the 1989 revolution when graffiti actually meant something in Prague. ⊠ *Lázeňská ulice leads into square.*

③⑤ **Vojanovy sady** (Vojan Park). Once the gardens of the Monastery of the Discalced Carmelites, later taken over by the Order of the English Virgins, and now part of the Ministry of Finance, this walled garden, with its weeping willows, fruit trees, and benches, makes another peaceful haven in summer. Exhibitions of modern sculptures are often held here, contrasting sharply with the two Baroque chapels and the graceful Ignaz Platzer statue of John of Nepomuk standing on a fish at the entrance. The park is surrounded by the high walls of the old monastery and new Ministry of Finance buildings, with only an occasional glimpse of a tower or spire to remind you that you're in Prague. ⊠ *U lužického semináře, between Letenská and Míšeňská ul.* ⊙ *Nov.–Mar. 8–5, Apr.–Oct. 8–7.*

★ ㉛ **Vrtbovská zahrada** (Vrtba Garden). An unobtrusive door on noisy Karmelitská hides the entranceway to a fascinating oasis, which also affords one of the best views over the Lesser Quarter. The street door opens onto the intimate courtyard of the Vrtbovský palác (Vrtba Palace), which is now private housing. Two Renaissance wings flank the courtyard, the one to the left built in 1575, the one to the right in 1591. The owner of the latter house was one of the 27 Bohemian nobles executed by the Hapsburgs in 1621 before the Old Town Hall. The house was given as confiscated property to Count Sezima of Vrtba, who bought the neighboring property and turned the buildings into a late-Renaissance palace. The Vrtbovská zahrada (Vrtba Garden), created a century later, reopened in summer 1998 after an excruciatingly long renovation. This is the most elegant of the Lesser Quarter's public gardens, built in five levels rising from behind the courtyard in a wave of statuary-bedecked staircases and formal terraces to reach a seashell-decorated pavilion at the top. (The fenced-off garden immediately behind and above belongs to the U.S. Embassy.) The powerful stone figure of Atlas that caps the entranceway in the courtyard, as well as most of the other classically derived statues, are from the workshop of Mathias Braun, perhaps the best of Czech Baroque sculptors. There's a frescoed grotto at the bottom level. ⊠ *Karmelitská ul. 25.* 🕮 *20 Kč.* ⊙ *Garden open Apr.–Oct., daily 10–6.*

OFF THE
BEATEN PATH

VILLA BERTRAMKA – Mozart fans won't want to pass up a visit to this villa, where the great composer lived during a couple of his visits to Prague. The small, well-organized museum is packed with memorabilia, including the program from that exciting night in 1787 when *Don Giovanni* had its world premiere in Prague. Also on hand is one of the master's pianos. Take Tram No. 12 from Karmelitská south to the Anděl metro station (or ride Metro Line B), walk down Plzeňská ulice a few hundred yards, and take a left at Mozartova ulice. ⊠ *Mozartova ul. 169, Prague 5 (Smíchov),* ⊙ *02/543893.* 🕮 *60 Kč.* ⊙ *Daily 10–5.*

★ ㊱ **Zahrada Valdštejnského paláce** (Wallenstein Palace Gardens). Albrecht von Wallenstein, onetime owner of the house and gardens, began a meteoric military career in 1622 when the Austrian emperor Ferdinand II retained him to save the empire from the Swedes and Protestants during the Thirty Years' War. Wallenstein, wealthy by marriage, offered to raise 20,000 men at his own cost and lead them personally. Ferdinand II accepted and showered Wallenstein with confiscated land and titles. Wallenstein's first acquisition was this enormous area. Having knocked down 23 houses, a brick factory, and three gardens, in 1623 he began to build his magnificent palace with its idiosyncratic high-walled gardens and superb, vaulted Renaissance *sala terrena* (room opening onto a garden). Walking around the formal paths, you'll come across numerous statues, an unusual fountain with a woman spouting water from her breasts, and a lava-stone grotto along the wall. Most of the palace itself now serves the Czech Senate as meeting space and offices. The only part open to the public is an exhibition devoted to the 17th-century Mora-

vian Protestant divine and educational philosopher Jan Amos Komen-
ský, known to the world as Comenius. The palace's cavernous former
Jízdárna, or riding school, now hosts occasional art exhibitions. ⊠
*Komenský Museum entrance at Valdštejnská 20. Garden entrance at
Letenská 10.* ✆ *Garden free; museum 6 Kč.* ☉ *Garden May–Sept., daily
9–7; Apr. and Oct, daily 10–6; Nov.–March, daily 10–5. Museum Tues.–
Sun. 10–12:30 and 1–5.*

Hradčany (The Castle District)

To the west of Prague Castle is the residential **Hradčany** (Castle District), the town that during the early 14th century emerged out of a
collection of monasteries and churches. The concentration of history
packed into one small area makes Prague Castle and the Castle District challenging objects for visitors not versed in the ups and downs
of Bohemian kings, religious uprisings, wars, and oppression. The picturesque area surrounding Prague Castle, with its breathtaking vistas
of the Old Town and the Lesser Quarter, is ideal for just wandering;
but the castle itself, with its convoluted history and architecture, is difficult to appreciate fully without investing a little more time.

A Good Walk

Begin on **Nerudova ulice** ㉘, which runs east–west a few hundred
yards south of Prague Castle. At the western (upper) end of the street,
look for a flight of stone steps guarded by two saintly statues. The stairs
lead up to Loretánská ulice, affording panoramic views of St. Nicholas
Church and the Lesser Quarter. At the top of the steps, turn left and
walk a couple hundred yards until you come to a dusty elongated square
named **Pohořelec** ㉟. Go through the inconspicuous gateway at No. 8
and up the steps, and you'll find yourself in the courtyard of one of
the city's richest monasteries, the **Strahovský klášter** ㊳.

Retrace your steps to Loretánské náměstí, the square at the head of
Loretánská ulice, which is flanked by the feminine curves of the Baroque
church, **Loreta** ㊴. Across the road, the 29 half pillars of the **Černínský
palác** now mask the Czech Ministry of Foreign Affairs. At the bottom
of Loretánské náměstí, a little lane trails to the left into the area known
as **Nový Svět**; the name means "new world," though the district is as
Old World as they come. Turn right onto the street Nový Svět. Around
the corner you get a tantalizing view of the cathedral through the
trees. Walk past the Austrian Embassy to Kanovnická ulice, a winding street lined with the dignified but melancholy Kostel svatého Jana
Nepomuckého (Church of St. John of Nepomuk). At the top of the street
on the left, the rounded, Renaissance corner house Martinický palác
catches the eye with its detailed sgraffito decorations. Martinický palác
opens onto **Hradčanské náměstí** ㊵ with its grandiose gathering of Renaissance and Baroque palaces. To the left of the bright yellow
Arcibiskupský palác (Archbishop's Palace) on the square is an alleyway leading down to the **Národní galerie** ㊶ and its collections of European art. Across the square, the handsome sgraffito sweep of
Schwarzenberský palác ㊷ beckons; this is the building you saw from
the back side at the beginning of the tour.

TIMING

Brisk-paced sightseers could zip through Hradčany in an hour, but to
do it justice, allow at least an hour just for ambling and admiring the
passing buildings and views of the city. The Strahovský klášter halls
need about a half hour to take in, more if you tour the small picture
gallery there, and the Loreta and its treasures at least that length of
time. The National Gallery in the Šternberský palác deserves at least
a couple of hours. Keep in mind that several places, including the

Loreta, Národní galerie, and the Strahovský klášter, are not open on Mondays.

Sights to See

Černínský palác (Chernin Palace). While the Loreta represents the softer side of the Counter-Reformation, this ungainly, overbearing structure seems to stand for the harsh political fate that met the Czechs after their defeat at the battle of Bílá Hora in 1620. During World War II it was the seat of the occupying German government.

㊵ Hradčanské náměstí (Hradčany Square). With its fabulous mixture of Baroque and Renaissance housing, topped by the castle itself, the square featured prominently (ironically, disguised as Vienna) in the film *Amadeus,* directed by the then-exiled Czech director Miloš Forman. The house at No. 7 was the set for Mozart's residence, where the composer was haunted by the masked figure he thought was his father. Forman used the flamboyant rococo **Arcibiskupský palác** (Archbishop's Palace), at the top of the square on the left, as the Viennese archbishop's palace. The plush interior, shown off in the film, is open to the public only on Maundy Thursday. ⌧ *Loretánská ul. and Kanovnická ul. lead into square.*

㊴ Loreta (Loreto Church). The church's seductive lines were a conscious move on the part of Counter-Reformation Jesuits in the 17th century who wanted to build up the cult of Mary and attract the largely Protestant Bohemians back to the church. According to legend, angels had carried Mary's house in Nazareth and dropped it in a patch of laurel trees in Ancona, Italy; known as *Loreto* (from the Latin for laurel), it immediately became a center of pilgrimage. The Prague Loreto was one of many symbolic re-enactments of this scene across Europe, and it worked: Pilgrims came in droves. The graceful facade, with its voluptuous tower, was built in 1720 by Kilian Ignaz Dientzenhofer, the architect of the two St. Nicholas churches in Prague. Most spectacular of all is a small exhibition upstairs displaying the religious treasures presented to Mary in thanks for various services, including a monstrance studded with 6,500 diamonds. ⌧ *Loretánské nám. 7.* ▨ *80 Kč (priests, monks, and nuns admitted free).* ⊙ *Tues.–Sun. 9–12:15 and 1–4:30.*

★ **㊶ Národní galerie** (National Gallery). Housed in the 18th-century **Šternberský palác** (Sternberg Palace), this collection is small but impressive. During the time when Berlin, Dresden, and Vienna were building up superlative old-master galleries, Prague languished, neglected by her Viennese rulers—one reason why the city's museums lag behind. On the first floor there's an exhibition of icons and other religious art from the 3rd through the 14th centuries. Up a second flight of steps is an entire room full of Cranachs and an assortment of paintings by Holbein, Dürer, Brueghel, Van Dyck, Canaletto, and Rubens. Other branches of the National Gallery are scattered around town, notably the modern art collections in the Veletržní palác (☞ Letná and Holešovice, *below*). ⌧ *Hradčanské nám. 15,* ☎ *02/2051–4634.* ▨ *70 Kč.* ⊙ *Tues.–Sun. 10–6.*

Nový Svět. This picturesque, winding little alley, with facades from the 17th and 18th centuries, once housed Prague's poorest residents; now many of the homes are used as artists' studios. The last house on the street, No. 1, was the home of the Danish-born astronomer Tycho Brahe. Living so close to the Loreto, so the story goes, Tycho was constantly disturbed during his nightly stargazing by the church bells. He ended up complaining to his patron, Emperor Rudolf II, who instructed the Capuchin monks to finish their services before the first star appeared in the sky.

③⑦ **Pohořelec** (Scene of Fire). This square suffered tragic fires in 1420, 1541, and 1741. The 1541 calamity sparked into life on Malostranské náměstí and spread up the hill to Pohořelec, ravaging much of the Lesser Quarter and the castle as it raged. Many Gothic houses burned down, opening up large plots for the Renaissance and especially the Baroque houses and palaces that dominate the the the architectural face of Hradčany and the hillside sloping down to Malá Strana.

④② **Schwarzenberský palác** (Schwarzenberg Palace). This boxy palace with its extravagant sgraffito facade was built for the Lobkowicz family between 1545 and 1563; today it houses the **Vojenské historické muzeum** (Military History Museum), one of the largest of its kind in Europe. A dim, old-fashioned collection, it concentrates on pre-20th century Czech military history. Of more general interest are the jousting tournaments held in the courtyard in summer. ⊠ *Hradčanské nám. 2.* 🎫 *20 Kč.* ⊙ *Apr.–Oct., Tues.–Sun. 10–6.*

★ ③⑧ **Strahovský klášter** (Strahov Monastery). Founded by the Premonstratensian order in 1140, the monastery remained in their hands until 1952, when the Communists suppressed all religious orders and turned the entire complex into the **Památník národního písemnictví** (Museum of National Literature). The major building of interest is the **Strahov Library,** with its collection of early Czech manuscripts, the 10th-century Strahov New Testament, and the collected works of famed Danish astronomer Tycho Brahe. Also of note is the late-18th-century **Philosophical Hall.** Engulfing its ceilings is a startling sky-blue fresco completed by the Austrian painter Franz Anton Maulbertsch in just six months. The fresco depicts an unusual cast of characters, including Socrates's nagging wife, Xanthippe, Greek astronomer Thales with his trusty telescope, and a collection of Greek philosophers mingling with Descartes, Diderot, and Voltaire. Also on the premises is the order's small art gallery, highlighted by late-Gothic altars and paintings from Rudolf II's time. You can arrange for a tour in English with several days' advance notice. ⊠ *Strahovské nádvoří 1/132,* ☎ *02/2051–6671 for tour arrangements.* 🎫 *Library tour 20 Kč, gallery 25 Kč.* ⊙ *Library daily 9–noon and 1–5; gallery Tues.–Sun. 9–noon and 12:30–5.*

OFF THE
BEATEN PATH

PETŘÍN – For a superb view of the city—from a mostly undiscovered, tourist-free perch—stroll over from the Strahov Monastery along the paths toward Prague's own miniature version of the Eiffel Tower. You'll find yourself in a hilltop park, laced with footpaths, with several buildings clustered together near the tower—just keep going gradually upward till you reach the tower's base. The tower and its breathtaking view, the hall of mirrors, or *bludiště,* in a small structure near the tower's base, and the seemingly abandoned sv. Vavřinec (St. Lawrence) church are beautifully peaceful and well worth an afternoon's wandering. You can also walk up from Karmelitská ulice or Újezd down in the Lesser Quarter or ride the funicular railway from U lanové dráhy ulice, off Újezd. Regular public-transportation tickets are valid. For the descent, take the funicular or meander on foot down through the stations of the cross on the pathways leading back to the Lesser Quarter.

Pražský hrad (Prague Castle)

Despite its monolithic presence, Pražský hrad (Prague Castle) is a collection of buildings dating from the 10th to the 20th century, all linked by internal courtyards. The most important structures are **Chrám svatého Víta** ⑤⑦, clearly visible soaring above the castle walls, and the **Královský palác** ⑤⑧, the official residence of kings and presidents and

39

Prague Castle (Pražský hrad)

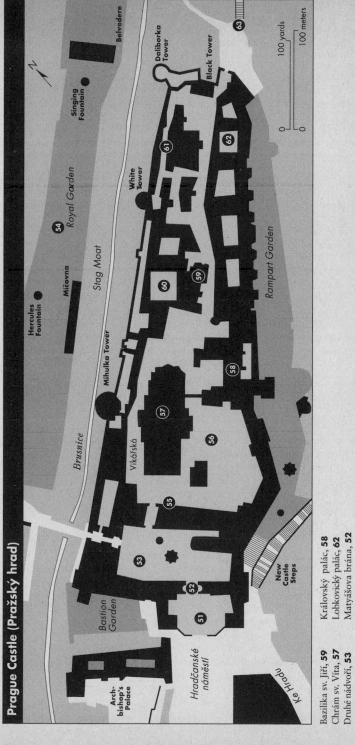

Bazilika sv. Jiří, **59**
Chrám sv. Víta, **57**
Druhé nádvoří, **53**
Informační,
středisko, **55**
Klášter sv. Jiří, **60**
Královská
zahrada, **54**

Královský palác, **58**
Lobkovický palác, **62**
Matyášova brána, **52**
První nádvoří, **51**
Staré zámecké
schody, **63**
Třetí nádvoří, **56**
Zlatá ulička, **61**

still the center of political power in the Czech Republic. The castle is compact and easy to navigate in. You can easily design a walking tour to fit your interests and the time you have for sightseeing. Be forewarned: In summer, Chrám svatého Víta and Zlatá ulička take the brunt of the heavy sightseeing traffic, while all of the castle is hugely popular.

TIMING

The castle is at its mysterious best in early morning and late evening, and it is incomparable when it snows. You can charge through the castle in 10 minutes, but that would be criminal. The cathedral deserves an hour, as does the Královský palác, while you can easily spend an entire day taking in the museums, the architectural details, the views of the city, and the hidden nooks of the castle. Remember that some sights, such as the Lobkovický palác, are not open on Monday.

Sights to See

59 **Bazilika svatého Jiří** (St. George's Basilica). This church was originally built in the 10th century by Prince Vratislav I, the father of Prince (and St.) Wenceslas. It was dedicated to St. George (of dragon fame), who it was believed would be more agreeable to the still largely pagan people. The outside was remodeled during early Baroque times, although the striking rusty-red color is in keeping with the look of the Romanesque edifice. The interior, following substantial renovation in the early 20th century, looks more or less as it did in the 12th century and is the best-preserved Romanesque relic in the country. The effect is at once barnlike and peaceful, the warm golden yellow of the stone walls and the small triplet arched windows exuding a sense of enduring harmony. The house-shaped painted tomb at the front of the church holds the remains of the founder, Vratislav I. Up the steps, in a chapel to the right, is the tomb Peter Parler designed for St. Ludmila, the grandmother of St. Wenceslas. ⊠ *Náměstí U sv. Jiří.* ✆ *For admission information,* see *Informační středisko,* below. ☉ *Apr.–Oct., daily 9–5; Nov.–Mar., daily 9–4.*

★ **57** **Chrám svatého Víta** (St. Vitus Cathedral). With its graceful, soaring towers, this Gothic cathedral—among the most beautiful in Europe—is the spiritual heart of Prague Castle, the city itself, and all of the Czech Republic. It has a long and complicated history, beginning in the 10th century and continuing to its completion in 1929. If you want to hear its history in depth, English-speaking guided tours of the cathedral and the Královský palác (☞ *below*) can be arranged at the information office across from the cathedral entrance (☞ Informační středisko, *below*).

Once you enter the cathedral, pause to take in the vast but delicate beauty of the Gothic and neo-Gothic interior glowing in the colorful light that filters through the startlingly brilliant stained-glass windows. This western third of the structure, including the facade and the two towers you can see from outside, was not completed until 1929, following the initiative of the Union for the Completion of the Cathedral, set up in the last days of the 19th century. Don't let the neo-Gothic delusion keep you from examining this new section. The six stained-glass windows to your left and right and the large rose window behind are modern masterpieces. Take a good look at the third window up on the left. The familiar Art Nouveau flamboyance, depicting the blessing of the 9th-century St. Cyril and St. Methodius (missionaries to the Slavs and creators of the Cyrillic alphabet), is the work of the Czech father of the style, Alfons Mucha. He achieved the subtle coloring by painting rather than staining the glass.

If you walk halfway up the right-hand aisle you will find the exquisitely ornate **Svatováclavská kaple** (Chapel of St. Wenceslas). With a 14th-century tomb holding the saint's remains, this square chapel is the ancient heart of the cathedral. Wenceslas (the "good king" of Christmas-carol fame) was a determined Christian in an era of widespread paganism. In 925, as prince of Bohemia, he founded a rotunda church dedicated to St. Vitus on this site. But the prince's brother, Boleslav, was impatient to take power and ambushed Wenceslas four years later near a church at Stará Boleslav, northeast of Prague. Wenceslas was originally buried in that church, but his grave produced so many miracles that he rapidly became a symbol of piety for the common people, something that greatly irritated the new Prince Boleslav. In 931 Boleslav was finally forced to honor his brother by reburying the body in the St. Vitus rotunda. Shortly afterward, Wenceslas was canonized.

The rotunda was replaced by a Romanesque basilica in the late 11th century. Work was begun on the existing building in 1344, on the initiative of the man who was later to become Charles IV. For the first few years the chief architect was the Frenchman Mathias d'Arras, but after his death in 1352, the work was continued by the 22-year-old German architect Peter Parler, who went on to build the Charles Bridge and many other Prague treasures.

The small door in the back of the chapel leads to the **Korunní komora** (Crown Chamber), the repository of the Bohemian crown jewels. It remains locked with seven keys held by seven different people and is definitely not open to the public.

A little beyond the Wenceslas Chapel on the same side, stairs lead down to the underground **royal crypt,** interesting primarily for the information it provides about the cathedral's history. As you descend the stairs, on the right you'll see parts of the old Romanesque basilica. A little farther, in a niche to the left, are portions of the foundations of the rotunda. Moving around into the second room, you'll find a rather eclectic group of royal remains ensconced in new sarcophagi dating from the 1930s. In the center is Charles IV, who died in 1378. Rudolf II, patron of Renaissance Prague, is entombed at the rear in the original tin coffin. To his right is Maria Amalia, the only child of Maria Theresa to reside in Prague. Ascending the wooden steps back into the cathedral, you'll come to the white-marble **Kralovské mausoleum** (Royal Mausoleum), atop which lie stone statues of the first two Hapsburg kings to rule in Bohemia, Ferdinand I and Maximilian II.

The cathedral's **Kralovské oratorium** (Royal Oratory) was used by the kings and their families when attending mass. Built in 1493, the work is a perfect example of late Gothic, laced on the outside with a stone network of gnarled branches very similar in pattern to the ceiling vaulting in the Královský palác (☞ *below*). The oratory is connected to the palace by an elevated covered walkway, which you can see from outside.

A few steps farther toward the east end, you can't fail to catch sight of the ornate silver **sarcophagus of St. John of Nepomuk,** designed by the famous Viennese architect Fischer von Erlach. According to legend, when Nepomuk's body was exhumed in 1721 to be reinterred, the tongue was found to be still intact and pumping with blood. These strange tales sadly served a highly political purpose. The Catholic Church and the Hapsburgs were seeking a new folk hero to replace the Protestant forerunner Jan Hus, whom they despised. The late Father Nepomuk was sainted and reburied a few years later with great ceremony in the 3,700-pound silver tomb, replete with angels and cherubim; the tongue was enshrined in its own reliquary.

The eight chapels around the back of the cathedral are the work of the original architect, Mathias d'Arras. A number of old tombstones, including some badly worn grave markers of medieval royalty, can be seen within, amid furnishings from later periods. Opposite the wooden relief, depicting the looting of the cathedral by Protestants in 1619, is the **Valdštejnská kaple** (Wallenstein Chapel). Since the last century, it has housed the Gothic tombstones of its two architects, Mathias d'Arras and Peter Parler, who died in 1352 and 1399, respectively. If you look up to the balcony, you can just make out the busts of these two men, designed by Parler's workshop. The other busts around the triforium depict various Czech kings.

The Hussite wars in the 15th century put an end to the first phase of the cathedral's construction. During the short era of illusory peace before the Thirty Years' War, lack of money laid to rest any idea of finishing the building, and the cathedral was closed by a wall built across from the Wenceslas Chapel. Not until the 20th century was the western side of the cathedral, with its two towers, completed according to Parler's original plans.

A key element of the cathedral's teeming, rich exterior decoration is the **Last Judgment mosaic** above the ceremonial entrance, called the Golden Portal, on the south side. The use of mosaic is quite rare in countries north of the Alps; this work, dating from the 1370s, is made of 1 million glass and stone chunks. It's currently undergoing an extensive, desperately needed restoration led by the Getty Conservation Institute. Just visible are the faded central image of Christ in glory, adored by Charles IV, his wife, and several saints; the risen dead and attendant angels to the left; and on the right-hand side, Satan surrounded by the flames of Hell. ⊠ *St. Vitus Cathedral.* ▣ *Western section free; chapels, crypt, and tower accessible with castle-wide ticket* (see *Informační středisko,* below). ☾ *Apr.–Oct., daily 9–5; Nov.–Mar., daily 9–4.*

❸ **Druhé nádvoří** (Second Courtyard). Empress Maria Theresa's court architect, Nicolò Pacassi, received the imperial approval to remake the castle in the 1760s, as the castle was badly damaged by Prussian shelling during the War of the Austrian Succession in 1757. The Second Courtyard was the main victim of Pacassi's attempts at imparting classical grandeur to what had been a picturesque collection of Gothic and Renaissance styles. This courtyard also houses the reliquary of Charles IV inside the **Kaple svatého Kříže** (Chapel of the Holy Cross). Displays include Gothic silver busts of the major Bohemian patron saints as well as bones and vestments that supposedly belonged to various saints. However, except for the view of the spires of St. Vitus Cathedral towering above the palace, there's little for the eye to feast upon here.

Built in the late-16th and early 17th centuries, the Second Courtyard was originally part of a reconstruction program commissioned by Rudolf II, under whom Prague enjoyed a period of unparalleled cultural development. Once the Prague court was established, the emperor gathered around him some of the world's best craftsmen, artists, and scientists, including the brilliant astronomers Johannes Kepler and Tycho Brahe.

Rudolf also amassed a large and famed collection of fine and decorative art, scientific instruments, philosophic and alchemical books, natural wonders, coins, and everything else under the sun. The bulk of the collection was looted by the Swedes during the Thirty Years' War, removed to Vienna when the imperial capital returned there after

Rudolf's death, or auctioned off during the 18th century, but a small part of the painting hoard was rediscovered in unused castle rooms in the 1960s. Renaissance and Baroque paintings, for the most part acquired after Rudolf's time, are displayed in the **Obrazárna** (Picture Gallery), on the left side of the courtyard as you face St. Vitus. It reopened at long last in summer 1998, elegantly redecorated by the official castle architect, Bořek Šípek. The passageway by the gallery entrance forms the northern entrance to the castle and leads out over a luxurious ravine known as the **Jelení příkop** (Stag Moat). ⊠ *North side of Second Courtyard.* 🖼 *100 Kč.* ☉ *Daily 10–6.*

⑤⑤ Informační středisko (Castle Information Office). This is the place to come for entrance tickets, guided tours, headphones for listening to recorded tours in English, tickets to cultural events held at the castle, and money changing. Tickets are valid for three consecutive days and allow admission to the older parts of St. Vitus Cathedral, the Královský palác, St. George's Basilica (but not the adjacent National Gallery exhibition), and a medieval bastion called Mihulka with an exhibition on alchemy. These sights may be visited only on the three-day ticket (the 20th-century section of the cathedral is free). Buy tickets to other castle sights at the door. If you just want to walk through the castle grounds, note that the gates close at midnight from April through October, at 11 PM the rest of the year, while the gardens are open from April through October only. ⊠ *Třetí nádvoří, across from the entrance to Chrám svatého Víta.* ☎ *02/ 2437–3368.* 🖼 *3-day tickets 100 Kč (English-language guided tours 50 Kč per person, minimum 5 people), grounds and gardens free.* ☉ *Apr.– Oct., daily 9–5; Nov.–Mar., daily 9–4.*

⑥⓪ Klášter svatého Jiří (St. George's Convent). The first convent in Bohemia, founded in 973 next to the even older St. George's Basilica (☞ *above*), now houses the Old Bohemian Collection of the **Národní galerie** (Czech National Gallery). The works run through the history of Czech art from the Middle Ages to the rather more secular themes of the Mannerist school and the voluptuous work of the court painters of Rudolf II. Treasures of the Gothic include the wonderful paintings of Master Theodoric, statues, icons, and triptychs. This is the best place in Prague to gain an overview of Czech art during the medieval and Hapsburg periods. ⊠ *Nám. U sv. Jiří,* ☎ *02/5732–0536.* 🖼 *70 Kč.* ☉ *Tues.–Sun. 10–6.*

⑤④ Královská zahrada (Royal Garden). This peaceful swath of greenery affords an unusually lovely view of St. Vitus Cathedral and the castle's walls and bastions. Originally laid out in the 16th century, it endured devastation in war, neglect in times of peace, and many redesigns, reaching its present parklike form early this century. Luckily, its Renaissance treasures survive. The garden front of the **Míčovna** (Ball Game Hall), built by Bonifaz Wohlmut in 1568, is completely covered by a dense tangle of allegorical sgraffiti; it was restored in the 1970s after fading to near invisibility.

The **Královský letohrádek** (Royal Summer Palace, also known as the Belvedere), at the garden's eastern end, deserves its usual description as one of the most beautiful Renaissance structures north of the Alps. Italian architects began it; Wohlmut finished it off in the 1560s with a copper roof like an upturned boat's keel riding above the graceful arcades of the ground floor. In the 18th and 19th centuries, military engineers tested artillery in the interior, which had already lost its rich furnishings to Swedish soldiers during their siege of the city in 1648. The Renaissance-style *giardinetto* (little garden) adjoining the summer palace centers on another masterwork, the Italian-designed, Czech-cast *Singing Fountain,* which resonates to the sound of falling water. ⊠ *Gar-*

den entrances from U Prašného mostu ul. and Mariánské hradby ul. near Chotkovy Sady Park. 🖅 *Free.* 🕒 *Apr.–Oct., daily 10–5:45.*

⑤⑧ Královský palác (Royal Palace). The palace is a congeries of styles and add-ons accumulated over many centuries. The best way to grasp its size is from within the **Vladislavský sál** (Vladislav Hall), the largest secular Gothic interior space in Central Europe. The enormous hall was completed in 1493 by Benedict Ried, who was to late-Bohemian Gothic what Peter Parler was to the earlier version. The room imparts a sense of space and light, softened by the sensuous lines of the vaulted ceilings and brought to a dignified close by the simple oblong form of the early Renaissance windows, a style that was just beginning to make inroads in Central Europe. In its heyday, the hall was the site of jousting tournaments, festive markets, banquets, and coronations. In more recent times, it has been used to inaugurate presidents, from the Communist Klement Gottwald in 1948 to Václav Havel in 1989, 1993, and 1998.

From the front of the hall, turn right into the rooms of the **Česká kancelář** (Bohemian Chancellery). This wing was built by the same Benedict Ried only 10 years after the hall was completed, but it shows a much stronger Renaissance influence. Pass through the Renaissance portal into the last chamber of the chancellery. This room was the site of the second defenestration of Prague, in 1618, an event that marked the beginning of the Bohemian rebellion and, ultimately, of the Thirty Years' War. This peculiarly Bohemian method of expressing protest (throwing someone out a window) had first been used in 1419 in the New Town Hall, an event that formed part of the lead-up to the Hussite wars. Two hundred years later the same conflict was reexpressed in terms of Hapsburg-backed Catholics versus Bohemian Protestants. Rudolf II had reached an uneasy agreement with the Bohemian nobles, allowing them religious freedom in exchange for financial support. But his next-but-one successor, Ferdinand II, was a rabid opponent of Protestantism and disregarded Rudolf's tolerant "Letter of Majesty." Enraged, the Protestant nobles stormed the castle and chancellery and threw two Catholic officials and their secretary, for good measure, out the window. Legend has it they landed on a mound of horse dung and escaped unharmed, an event the Jesuits interpreted as a miracle. The square window in question is on the left as you enter the room.

At the back of the Vladislav Hall, a staircase leads up to a gallery of the **Kaple všech svatých** (All Saints' Chapel). Little remains of Peter Parler's original work, but the church contains some fine works of art. The large room to the left of the staircase is the **Stará sněmovna** (council chamber), where the Bohemian nobles met with the king in a kind of prototype parliament. Portraits of the Hapsburg rulers line the walls. The descent from Vladislav Hall toward what remains of the **Romanský palác** (Romanesque palace) is by way of a wide, shallow set of steps; you can still see the high barrel-vaulting. This **Jezdecké schody** (Riders' Staircase) was the entranceway for knights who came for the jousting tournaments. ✉ *Royal Palace, Třetí nádvoří.* 🖅 *For admission information,* see *Castle Information Office,* above. 🕒 *Apr.–Oct., daily 9–5; Nov.–Mar., daily 9–4.*

⑥② Lobkovický palác (Lobkowicz Palace). From the beginning of the 17th century until the 1940s, this building was the residence of the powerful Catholic Lobkowicz family. It was supposedly to this house that the two defenestrated officials escaped after landing on the dung hill in 1618. During the 1970s the building was restored to its early Baroque appearance and now houses the National Museum's permanent exhibition on Czech history. If you want to get a chronological understanding of Czech history from the beginnings of the Great

Moravian Empire in the 9th century to the Czech national uprising in 1848, this is the place. Copies of the crown jewels are on display here; but it is the rich collection of illuminated Bibles, old musical instruments, coins, weapons, royal decrees, paintings, and statues that makes the museum well worth visiting. Detailed information on the exhibits is available in English. ✉ *Jiřská ul.* ✒ *40 Kč.* ☉ *Tues.–Sun. 9–5.*

㊿ Matyášova brána (Matthias Gate). Built in 1614, the stone gate once stood alone in front of the moats and bridges that surrounded the castle. Under the Hapsburgs, the gate survived by being grafted as a relief onto the palace building. As you go through it, notice the ceremonial white-marble entrance halls on either side, which lead up to President Václav Havel's reception rooms (only rarely open to the public).

㊾ První nádvoří (First Courtyard). The main entrance to Prague Castle from Hradčanské náměstí is a little disappointing. Going through the wrought-iron gate, guarded at ground level by Czech soldiers and from above by the ferocious *Battling Titans* (a copy of Ignaz Platzer's original 18th-century statues), you'll enter this courtyard, built on the site of old moats and gates that once separated the castle from the surrounding buildings and thus protected the vulnerable western flank. The courtyard is one of the more recent additions to the castle, designed by Maria Theresa's court architect, Nicolò Pacassi, in the 1760s. Today it forms part of the presidential office complex. Pacassi's reconstruction was intended to unify the eclectic collection of buildings that made up the castle, but the effect of his work is somewhat flat. From a distance, the effect is monumental. As you move farther into the castle, large parts appear to be relatively new, while in reality they cover splendid Gothic and Romanesque interiors.

㊿③ Staré zámecké schody (Old Castle Steps). Unending lines of tourists pass by dozens of trinket sellers as they troop up and down this long, walled staircase. It starts from the Black Tower, a square, Romanesque structure at the far eastern end of the castle, and comes out just above the Malostranská metro station. There you can catch the subway or take a tram toward Malostranské náměstí.

㊾⑥ Třetí nádvoří (Third Courtyard). The contrast between the cool, dark interior of St. Vitus Cathedral (☞ *above*) and the brightly colored Pacassi facades of the Third Courtyard just outside is startling. The courtyard's clean lines are the work of Slovenian architect Jože Plečnik in the 1930s, but the modern look is a deception. Plečnik's paving was intended to cover an underground world of house foundations, streets, and walls dating from the 9th through the 12th centuries—rediscovered when the cathedral was completed. (You can see a few archways through a grating in a wall of the cathedral.) Plečnik added a few eclectic features to catch the eye: a granite obelisk to commemorate the fallen of the First World War, a black-marble pedestal for the Gothic statue of St. George (the original is in the museum at St. George's Convent), the inconspicuous entrance to his Bull Staircase leading down to the south garden, and the peculiar golden ball topping the eagle fountain near the eastern end of the courtyard.

㊿① Zlatá ulička (Golden Lane). An enchanting collection of tiny, ancient, brightly colored houses crouches under the fortification wall, looking remarkably like a set for *Snow White and the Seven Dwarfs*. Legend has it that these were the lodgings of the international group of alchemists whom Rudolf II brought to the court to produce gold. The truth is a little less romantic: The houses were built during the 16th century for the castle guards, who supplemented their income by practicing various crafts outside the jurisdiction of the powerful guilds. By the early

20th century, Golden Lane had become the home of poor artists and writers. Franz Kafka, who lived at No. 22 in 1916 and 1917, described the house on first sight as "so small, so dirty, impossible to live in and lacking everything necessary." But he soon came to love the place. As he wrote to his fiancée: "Life here is something special . . . to close out the world not just by shutting the door to a room or apartment but to the whole house, to step out into the snow of the silent lane." The lane now houses tiny stores selling books, music, and crafts.

🄫 Above Golden Lane runs a timber-roofed corridor within the walls, lined with replica suits of armor and weapons (some of it for sale), mock torture chambers, and the like (entrance between house No. 23 and No. 24). 🖃 *Free.* 🕐 *Tues.–Sun. 10–6, Mon. 1–6.*

🄫 The other end of the lane, furthest from the cathedral, overlooks a court-yard and house where a high royal official called the Supreme Burgrave once lived; today a private **Muzeum hraček** (Toy Museum) is there. It covers everything from ancient Greek toys to Barbie. ⊠ *Jiřská ul.* 🖃 *40 Kč.* 🕐 *Daily 9:30–5:30.*

Nové město (New Town) and Vyšehrad

To this day, Charles IV's building projects are tightly woven into the daily lives of Praguers. His most extensive scheme, Nové město (the New Town), is still such a lively, vibrant area you may hardly realize that its streets, Gothic churches, and squares were planned as far back as 1348. With Prague fast outstripping its Old Town parameters, Charles IV extended the city's fortifications; a high wall surrounded the newly developed 2½-square-km (1½-square-mi) area south and east of the Old Town, tripling the walled territory on the Vltava's right bank. The wall extended south to link with the fortifications of the citadel called Vyšehrad. In the mid-19th century, new building in the New Town boomed in a welter of Romantic and neo-Renaissance styles, particularly on Wenceslas Square and avenues such as Vodičkova, Na Poříčí, and Spálená. One of the most important structures was the Národní divadlo (National Theater), meant to symbolize in stone the revival of Czechs' history, language, and sense of national pride. Both preceding and following Czechoslovak independence in 1918, mod-ernist architecture entered the mix, particularly on the outer fringes of the Old Town and in the New Town. One of modernism's most un-expected products was Cubist architecture, a form unique to Prague, which produced four notable examples at the foot of ancient Vyšehrad.

A Good Walk
Start at the **Národní divadlo** ㊸ and follow the embankment, Masarykovo nábřeží, south toward Vyšehrad. Below the Národní divadlo on Masarykovo nábřeží, note the Art Nouveau architecture of No. 32, the amazingly eclectic design by Kamil Hilbert at No. 26, and the tile-decorated Hlahol building at No. 16. Opposite, on a narrow island, is a 19th century, yellow-and-white ballroom-restaurant, Žofín. Strad-dling an arm of the river at Myslíkova ulice are the modern Galerie Mánes (1928–1930) and its attendant 15th-century water tower, where, from a lookout on the sixth floor, communist-era secret police used to observe Václav Havel's apartment at Rašínovo nábřeží 78. This building, still part-owned by the president, and the adjoining **Tančicí dům** ("Dancing House") by Frank Gehry and Vlado Milunić, are on the far side of Jiráskovo náměstí, a square named after the historical novelist Alois Jirásek. From the square, Resslova street leads uphill four blocks to **Karlovo náměstí** ㊹.

A convenient place to rejoin the riverfront is Palackého náměstí via Na Moráni street at the southern end of Karlovo náměstí. This square, with its (melo)dramatic monument to the 19th-century historian František Palacký, "awakener of the nation," lies 1 km (½ mi) south of the Národní divadlo. The view of the Benedictine Klášter Emauzy from here is lovely. The houses grow less attractive south of here, so you may wish to hop a tram (tram no. 3, 16, or 17 at the stop on Rašínovo nábřeží) and ride one stop to Výtoň, at the base of the **Vyšehrad** ㊹ citadel. Walk under the railroad bridge on Rašínovo nábřeží to find the closest of four nearby **Cubist buildings.** Another lies a few dozen yards farther along the embankment; two more are a couple of minutes' walk "inland" along Vnislavova to Neklanova. Alternatively, just before reaching Neklanova, veer right onto Vratislavova, an ancient road that runs tortuously up into the heart of Vyšehrad.

It's about 2¼ km (1½ mi) between Národní divadlo and the Vyšehrad. Note that tram no. 17 travels the length of the embankment, if you'd like to make a quicker trip between the two points.

TIMING

A leisurely stroll from the Národní divadlo to Vyšehrad may easily absorb two hours, as may an exploration of Karlovo náměstí and the Klášter Emauzy. Vyšehrad is open every day, year-round, and the views are stunning on a clear day or evening, but keep in mind that there is little shade along the river walk on hot afternoons.

Sights to See

Cubist buildings. Born of zealous modernism, Prague's Cubist architecture followed a great Czech tradition in that it fully embraced new ideas while adapting them to existing artistic and social contexts. Between 1912 and 1914, Josef Chochol (1880–1956) designed several of the city's dozen or so Cubist projects. His apartment house **Neklanova 30**, on the corner of Neklanova and Přemyslova streets, is magnificent. The pyramidal, kaleidoscopic window mouldings and roof cornices are completely novel while making an expressive link to Baroque forms; the faceted corner balcony column elegantly alludes to Gothic forerunners. On the same street, at **Neklanova 2**, is another apartment house attributed to Chochol; like the building at Neklanova 30, it uses pyramidal shapes and the suggestion of Gothic columns. ✉ *Neklanova 30 and Neklanova 2, Prague 2.*

Chochol's **villa**, on the embankment at Libušina 3, has an undulating effect created by smoothly articulated forms. The wall and gate around the back of the house are superb as well, using triangular moldings and metal grating to create an effect of controlled energy. The **three-family house**, about 100 yards away from the villa at Rašínovo nábřeží 6–10, was completed slightly earlier, when Chochol's Cubist style was still developing. Here, the design is touched with Baroque and neoclassical influence, with a mansard roof and end gables. The somewhat incongruous relief above the central door shows motifs from the legends of Vyšehrad.

㊺ **Karlovo náměstí** (Charles Square). This square began life as a cattle market, a function chosen by Emperor Charles IV when he established the New Town in 1348. The Horse Market (now Wenceslas Square) quickly overtook it as a livestock-trading center, and an untidy collection of shacks accumulated here until the mid-1800s, when it became a green park named for its patron. ✉ *Vodičkova ul., Spálená ul., Resslova ul., and Na Moráni ul. lead into square.*

Novoměstská radnice (New Town Hall), at the northern edge of the square, has a late-Gothic tower similar to that of the Old Town Hall and three superb, tall Renaissance gables. The "First Defenestration

of Prague" occurred here on July 30, 1419; a mob of townspeople, followers of the martyred religious reformer Jan Hus, hurled Catholic town
councillors out the windows. Historical exhibitions and contemporary
arts shows are held regularly, and you may climb the tower for a view
of the New Town. (Admission to the exhibits varies.) ⊠ *Karlovo
náměstí at Vodi kova, Prague 2. ☎ Tower: 20 Kč. ۞ Tower June 1–
Sept. 30, Tues.–Sun. 10–6.*

On the east side of the square, south of Ječná street, the glowing white-
and-gold Jesuit church of St. Ignatius and adjoining plain lines of a hospital building that was once a Jesuit college form a continuous long
facade. The south end of Karlovo náměstí is dominated by the Faustův
dům (Faust House), said to have been a residence of the legendary Doctor Faustus, who sold his soul to the devil. More certain residents included the Elizabethan alchemist Edward Kelley. (The house is usually
closed to the public.) Next door is the almost always locked gate to
Kilian Dientzenhofer's dynamic Kostel sv. Jana Nepomuckého (Church
of St. John of Nepomuk), called *na skalce* (on the rock), for a self-evi-
dent reason—perched on a rock above ground level, it has two exterior staircases leading down to the street.

Just south of the square and across from St. John of Nepomuk lies another of Charles IV's gifts to the city: the Benedictine **Klášter Emauzy**
(Emmaus Monastery). It is often called Na Slovanech, literally "At the
Slavs'," in reference to its purpose when established in 1347: the emperor invited Croatian monks here to celebrate mass in Old Slavonic
and thus cultivate religion among the Slavs in a city largely controlled
by Germans. A faded but substantially complete cycle of biblical scenes
by Charles's court artists lines the four cloister walls. The frescoes, and
especially the abbey church, suffered heavy damage from a February
14, 1945, raid by Allied bombers that may have mistaken Prague for
75-mi-distant Dresden. The church lost its spires and the interior remains a blackened shell. Some years after the war two arcing concrete
"spires" were set atop the church. ⊠ *Vyšehradská 49 (cloister entrance
is on the left at the rear of the church), Prague 2. ☎ 10 Kč. ۞ Weekdays 10–6.*

㊸ **Národní divadlo** (National Theater). The idea for a Czech national theater began during the revolutionary decade of the 1840s and soon became a popular cause. In a telling display of national pride, donations
to fund the plan poured in from all over the country, from people of
every socioeconomic stratum. The cornerstone was laid in 1868; the
"National Theater generation" who designed the neo-Renaissance
structure became the architectural and artistic establishment for decades
to come. Its designer, Josef Zítek (1832–1909), was the leading neo-
Renaissance architect in Bohemia. The nearly finished interior was gutted by a fire in 1881, and Zítek's onetime student Josef Schulz
(1840–1917) saw the reconstruction through to completion two years
later. Statues representing Drama and Opera rise above the riverfront
side entrances; two gigantic chariots flank figures of Apollo and the
nine Muses above the main facade. The rich decorations in the foyer
include a sequence of legendary scenes and a series of busts, while the
performance space itself is filled with gilding, voluptuous plaster figures, and plush upholstery. Next door is the modern (1970s–80s)
Nová scéna (New Stage), where the popular Magic Lantern black-light
shows are staged. The Národní divadlo is one of the best places to see
a performance; ticket prices here start as low as 30 Kč. ⊠ *Národní
třída 2,* ☎ *02/2491–3437.*

Tančící dům (Dancing House). This whimsical building was partnered
into life in 1996 by architect Frank Gehry (he of the Guggenheim-Mu-

seum-in-Bilbao fame) and his Croatian-Czech collaborator Vlado Milunić. A wasp-waisted glass-and-steel tower sways into the main structure as though they were a couple on the dance floor—a "Fred and Ginger" effect that gave the wacky, yet somehow appropriate, building its nickname. A French restaurant occupies the top floors (☞ La Perle de Prague *in* Dining, *below*), and there is a café at street level. ⊠ *Rašínovo nábřeží 80, Prague 2.*

🆖 **Vyšehrad.** Bedřich Smetana's symphonic poem *Vyšehrad* opens with four stirring harp chords; these bardic notes seem to echo the legendary associations with Vyšehrad's ancient fortifications. Today, the flat-topped bluff standing over the right bank of the Vltava is a green, tree-dotted expanse showing few signs that splendid medieval monuments once made it a landmark to rival Prague Castle. The Kapitulní kostel sv. Petra a Pavla dominates the plateau as it has since the 11th century; next to the church lies the burial ground of the nation's revered cultural figures. Most of the buildings still standing are from the 19th century; scattered among them are a few older structures and some foundation stones of the medieval palaces. Surrounding the ruins are gargantuan, excellently preserved brick fortifications built in the 17th to the mid-19th centuries; their broad tops allow strollers to take in sweeping vistas up- and downriver.

The historical father of Vyšehrad, the "High Castle," is Vratislav II (1061–1092), a Přemyslide duke who became the first king of Bohemia. He made the fortified hilltop his capital, but, under subsequent rulers, it fell into disuse until the 14th century, when Charles IV transformed the site into an ensemble of palaces, the Gothicized Kapitulní kostel sv. Petra a Pavla, battlements, and a massive gatehouse called *Špička,* whose scant remains are on V Pevnosti street. By the 17th century royalty had long since departed, most of the structures they built were crumbling, and Vyšehrad became a fortress occupying a key point in the city's defensive system.

Vyšehrad's place in the modern Czech imagination is largely thanks to the National Revivalists of the 19th century, particularly writer Alois Jirásek (1851–1930), who mined medieval chronicles for legends and facts to glorify the early Czechs. In his rendition, Vyšehrad was the court of the prophetess-ruler Libuše, who had a vision of her husband-to-be, the ploughman Přemysl—father of the Přemyslide line—and of "a city whose glory shall reach the heavens" called Praha. (In truth, the Czechs first came to Vyšehrad around the beginning of the 900s, slightly later than the building of Prague Castle.)

A concrete result of the National Revival was the establishment of the **Hřbitov** (cemetery) in the 1860s; it peopled the legend-haunted fortress with the remains of luminaries from the arts and sciences. The grave of Smetana faces the **Slavín**, a mausoleum for more than 50 honored men and women including Alfons Mucha, sculptor Jan Štursa, inventor František Křižík, and the opera diva Ema Destinnová—all guarded by a winged genius who hovers above the inscription AČ ZEMŘELI, JEŠTĚ MLUVÍ ("Although they have died, they yet speak"). Antonín Dvořák (1841–1904) rests in the arcade along the north wall. Among the many writers buried here are Jan Neruda, Božena Němcová, Karel Čapek, and the Romantic poet Karel Hynek Mácha, whose grave was visited by students on their momentous November 17, 1989, protest march.

Traces of the citadel's distant past do remain. A heavily restored **Ro-manesque rotunda,** built by Vratislav II, stands on the east side of the compound. Foundations and a few embossed floor tiles from the late-10th-century **Basilika sv. Vavřince** (St. Lawrence Basilica) are in a structure on Soběslavova street (if it is locked, you can ask for the key at the refreshment stand just to the left of the basilica entrance; admission is 5 Kč). Part of the medieval fortifications stand next to the surprisingly confined foundation mounds of a medieval palace overlooking a ruined watchtower called Libuše's Bath. A statue of Libuše and her consort Přemysl is nearby in a plot of grass next to the Kapitulní kostel sv. Petra a Pavla (☞ *below*), one of four large sculpted images of couples from Czech legend by J. V. Myslbek (1848–1922), the sculptor of the St. Wenceslas monument.

The stone spires of the **Kapitulní kostel sv. Petra a Pavla** (Chapter Church of Sts. Peter and Paul) are visible from all over Prague. Founded by Vratislav II and rebuilt several times, the church owes its present appearance to the re-Gothicizing carried out at the turn of the 20th century. The other standing buildings are also mainly neo-Gothic; some are used by the Catholic chapter established by Vratislav in 1070.

The military history of the fortress and the city is covered in a small exposition inside the **Cihelná brána** (Brick Gate). Here also is the entrance to the casemates—a long, dark passageway within the walls that ends at a dank hall used to store several original pollution-scarred Charles Bridge sculptures. A guided tour into the casemates and the statue storage room starts at the military history exhibit (10 Kč admission to expostion; tour 20 Kč). ✉ *Entrances on Vratislavova and V Pevnosti Sts., Prague 2.* ☉ *Grounds: daily. Military history exhibit, casemates, St. Lawrence Basilica Apr.–Oct., daily 9:30–5:30; Nov.–Mar., daily 9:30–4:30. Cemetery Apr.–Oct., daily 8–6; Nov.–Mar., daily 9–5.*

Vinohrady

From Riegrovy sady and its sweeping view of the city from above the National Museum, the elegant residential neighborhood called Vinohrady extends its streets of eclectic apartment houses and villas eastward and southward. The pastel-tinted ranks of turn-of-the-century apartment houses—many crumbling after years of neglect—are slowly but unstoppably being transformed into upscale flats, slick offices, eternally packed new restaurants, and a range of shops unthinkable only a half decade ago. Much of the development lies on or near Vinohradská, the main street, which extends from the top of Wenceslas Square to a belt of enormous cemeteries about 3 km (2 mi) eastward. Yet the flavor of daily life persists: Smoky old pubs still ply their trade on the quiet side streets; the stately theater, Divadlo na Vinohradech, keeps putting on excellent shows as it has for decades; and on the squares and in the parks nearly everyone still practices Prague's favorite form of outdoor exercise—walking the dog.

㊻ Kostel Nejsvětějšiho Srdce Páně (Church of the Most Sacred Heart). If you've had your fill of Romanesque, Gothic, and Baroque, take the metro to the Jiřího z Poděbrad station (Line A) for a look at a startling Art Deco edifice. Designed in 1927 by Slovenian architect Josip Plečnik (the same architect commissioned to update Prague Castle), the church resembles a luxury ocean liner more than a place of worship. The effect was conscious; during the 1920s and '30s, the avant-garde imitated mammoth objects of modern technology. Plečnik used many modern elements on the inside: Notice the hanging speakers, seemingly designed to bring the word of God directly to the ears of each worshiper. You may be able to find someone at the back entrance of the church who will let you walk up the long ramp into the fascinating glass clock tower. ✉ *Nám. Jiřího z Poděbrad, Prague 3.* ☉ *Daily 10–5.*

Nový Židovský hřbitov (New Jewish Cemetery). Tens of thousands of Czechs find eternal rest in Vinohrady's cemeteries. In this, the newest of the city's half-dozen Jewish cemeteries, you'll find the modest **tombstone of Franz Kafka,** which seems grossly inadequate to Kafka's stature but oddly in proportion to his own modest ambitions. The cemetery is usually open, although men may be required to wear a yarmulke (you can buy one there), and guards sometimes inexplicably seal off the grounds. Turn right at the main cemetery gate and follow the wall for about 100 yards. Kafka's thin, white tombstone, usually covered with flowers and remembrances, lies at the front of Section 21. ⊠ *Vinohradská at Jana Želivského, Prague 3 (metro station Želivského).* ▣ *Free.* ☉ *June–Aug., Sun.–Thurs. 8–5; Sept.–May, Mon.–Thurs. 9–4, Sun. 9–3.*

NEED A BREAK? The cool and quiet basement café of one of the city's best English-language bookstores, **U knihomola,** serves delicious and wholesome light meals as well as fabulous carrot cake and a variety of coffees—perfect for a lazy Sunday with the newspapers. Often there's live acoustic music as well. ⊠ *Mánesova 79, Prague 2,* ☎ *02/627-7770.*

㊆ Pavilon (Vinohrady Pavilion market hall). This gorgeous, turn-of-the-century, neo-Renaissance, three-story market hall is one of the most attractive sites in Vinohrady. It used to be a major old-style market, a vast space filled with stalls selling all manner of foodstuffs, plus the requisite grimy pub. After being spiffed up several years ago, its settled into life as an upscale shopping mall. As a shopping center far from the tourist track, though, the Pavilon is still waiting to hit its stride; most locals cannot afford the gleaming designer pens and Italian shoes that are sold there nowadays. ⊠ *Vinohradská 50, Prague 2,* ☎ *02/2209-7111.*

NEED A BREAK? A symbol of this bucolic neighborhood's intellectual leanings, the literary café **Literární kavárna** serves coffees and light desserts in a well-lit and welcoming shop brimming with books, newspapers, and magazines (most in Czech). Several nights a week, the café hosts readings as well as intimate concerts of folk, jazz, or Romany (Gypsy) music. ⊠ *Čerchovská 4, Prague 2,* ☎ *02/627-3332.*

㊽ Židovský hřbitov (Jewish Burial Ground). In an odd visual juxtaposition, this small cemetery huddles at the foot of the soaring rocket ship–like television tower that broke ground in the last years of communism and used to be mockingly called "Big Brother's Finger." The cemetery once spread where the tower now stands, but Jewish community leaders agreed (under pressure) to let it be dug up and the most historic tombstones crammed into one corner of the large square. The stones date back as far as the 17th century; a little neoclassical mausoleum stands forlornly just outside the fence. The cemetery gate is almost always locked, but the bars are widely spaced enough for small people to squeeze through (the cemetery is unsupervised). ⊠ *Fibichova at Kubelíkova, Prague 3.*

Letná and Holešovice

From above the Vltava's left bank, the large, grassy plateau called Letná affords one of the classic views of the Old Town and the many bridges crossing the river. (To get to Letná from the Old Town above Parizska street, cross the Čechův Bridge and climb the stairs.) Beer gardens, tennis, and Frisbee attract people of all ages, while amateur soccer players emulate the professionals of Prague's top team, Sparta, which plays in the stadium just across the road. Ten minutes' walk from Letná, down into the residential neighborhood of Holešovice, brings you to a massive, gray-blue building that might have been designed by a young postmodernist architect. In fact it dates to the 1920s, and the cool exterior gives no hint of the cavernous halls within or of the treasures of Czech and French modern art that line its corridors. Just north along Dukelských hrdinů Street, Stromovka—a royal hunting preserve turned gracious park—offers quiet strolls under huge old oaks and chestnuts.

49 Letenské sady (Letna Gardens). Come to this large, shady park for an unforgettable view of Prague's bridges. From the enormous cement pedestal at the center of the park, the largest statue of Stalin in Eastern Europe once beckoned to citizens on the Old Town Square far below. The statue was ripped down in the 1960s, when Stalinism was finally discredited. The walks and lawns that stretch out behind the pedestal are perfect for relaxing on a warm afternoon. On sunny Sundays expatriates often meet up here to play ultimate Frisbee. ⊠ *Bordered by Milady Horákové, Nad Štolou, and Badeniho streets, Prague 7.*

50 Veletržní palác sbírka moderního a soucasného umění (Veletržní palác Museum of Modern Art). The National Gallery's newest museum, housed in a trade-fair hall in the Holešovice neighborhood, set off a furor when it opened in 1995. The lighting, the exhibit design, the unused empty spaces in the building's two enormous halls, even the selection of paintings and sculpture—all came under critics' scrutiny. The discouraging voices couldn't deny, though, that the palace—itself a key work of constructivist architecture—serves a vital purpose in permanently displaying hundreds of pieces of 20th-century Czech art. Most of the collections languished in storage for decades, either because some cultural commissar forbade their public display or because there was no exhibition space. The collection of 19th- and 20th-century French art, including an important group of early Cubist paintings by Picasso and Braque, is also here, moved from the Sternberg Palace (☞ The Castle District, *above*). ⊠ *Veletržní at Dukelských hrdinů, Prague 7,* ☎ *02/2430–1111.* ⊠ *120 Kč.* ☉ *Tues.–Wed. and Fri.–Sun. 10–6, Thurs. 10–9.*

OFF THE BEATEN PATH   **ZOOLOGICKÁ ZAHRADA–** Prague's small but delightful zoo is north of the city in Troja, under the shadow of the Troja Castle. Take the metro Line C to Nádraží Holešovice and change to Bus 112. ⊠ U trojského zámku 3, Prague 7, ☎ 02/688-0480. ⊠ 40 Kč. ☉ May–Sept., daily 9–6; Oct.–Apr., daily 9–4.

DINING

For a cheaper and quicker alternative to the sit-down establishments listed below, try a light meal at one of the city's growing number of street stands and fast-food places. Look for stands offering *párky* (hot dogs) or *smažený syr* (fried cheese). McDonald's, with several locations in the city, heads the list of Western imports. For more exotic fare, try a gyro (made from pork) at the stand on Old Town Square or the very good vegetarian fare at **Country Life** (⊠ Melantrichova ul. 15, ☎ 02/2421–3366), open Sunday–Friday. The German coffeemaker **Tchibo** has teamed up with a local bakery and now offers tasty sandwiches and excellent coffee at convenient locations on Old Town Square and at the top of Wenceslas Square.

For price range information, *see* Dining *in* Pleasures and Pastimes, *above.*

Old Town (Staré Město)

$$$$ ✗ **Bellevue.** The first choice for visiting dignitaries and businesspeople blessed with expense accounts, Bellevue has creative, freshly prepared cuisine, more nouvelle than Bohemian—and the elegant setting not far from Charles Bridge doesn't hurt. Look for the lamb carpaccio with fresh rosemary, garlic, and extra-virgin olive oil, or the wild berries marinated in port and cognac, served with vanilla and walnut ice cream. Window seats afford stunning views of Prague Castle. There is a small, mostly Czech, vintage wine list. ⊠ *Smetanovo nábřeží 18,* ☎ *02/2422–7614. AE, DC, MC, V.*

$$$$ ✗ **Jewel of India.** Although generally Asian cooking of any stripe is not Prague's forte, here is a sumptuous spot well worth seeking out for Northern Indian tandooris and other moderately spiced specialties, including some delicious vegetarian dishes. ⊠ *Pařížská 20 (near metro Staroměstská), Prague 1,* ☎ *02/2481–1010. AE, MC, V.*

$$$$ ✗ **V Zátiši.** White walls and casual grace accentuate the subtle flavors
★ of smoked salmon, plaice, beef Wellington, and other non-Czech specialties. Order the house *Rulandské červené,* a fruity Moravian red wine that meets the exacting standards of the food. In behavior unusual for the city, the benign waiters fairly fall over each other to serve diners. ⊠ *Liliová 1, Betlémské nám.,* ☎ *02/2422–8977. AE, DC, MC, V.*

$$ ✗ **Chez Marcel.** At this authentic French bistro on a quiet, picturesque street, you can get a little taste of that *other* riverside capital. French owned and operated, Chez Marcel has an extensive menu suitable for lingering over a three-course meal—try deciding among salads, pâtés, cheeses, rabbit, and some of the best steaks in Prague. Or polish off a quick espresso and one of their divine desserts, such as the exquisite crème brûlée. ⊠ *Haštalská 12,* ☎ *02/231–5676. No credit cards.*

$$ ✗ **La colline oubliée.** In "The Forgotten Hill," remember to try *brik* (spicy ratatouille or ground meat in pastry) or the all-you-can-eat couscous. Indecisive diners may be whisked into the kitchen by one of the charming North African team for a convincing sample. The decor in this intimate restaurant is bright and cheerful, as is the music; the Old Town location is ideal, just off Pařížská street. ⊠ *Elišky Krásnohorské 11,* ☎ *02/232–9522. AE, V.*

$ ✗ **Lotos.** Banana ragout with polenta and broccoli strudel are two favorites at what is undoubtedly the best of the city's scant selection of all-vegetarian restaurants. Blond-wood tables and billowing tie-dyed fabric festooning the ceiling set an informal yet elegant atmosphere. The salads and soups are wonderful. ⊠ *Platnéřská 13,* ☎ *02/232–2390. AE, MC, V.*

$ ✗ **Pizzeria Azzurra.** This bright and spacious pizzeria with a nautical motif is just a couple of blocks from Old Town Square, yet it remains relatively undiscovered by all but hungry locals. Whet your appetite by watching the pizza bake in the kiln; toppings may include grilled eggplant or prosciutto. An extensive array of pastas is also available; the lasagna is especially good. Moravian wine by the glass is reasonably priced, as are the Italian wines, including the old standby, Chianti. ⊠ *Dlouhá 35,* ☎ *02/2481–5613. No credit cards.*

$ ✗ **Profit.** The unfortunate name masks a clean, spacious pub that serves such excellent Czech standbys as goulash and pork with dumplings and sauerkraut at astonishingly reasonable prices. The central location could hardly be better. ⊠ *Betlémské nám. 8,* ☎ *02/2421–8557. No credit cards.*

$ ✗ **Slávia kavárna.** This legendary hangout for the best and brightest
★ in Czech arts—from composer Bedřich Smetana and poet Jaroslav Seifert to then-dissident Václav Havel—is back in business after being held hostage in absurd real-estate wrangles for most of the '90s. Its Art

Prague Dining and Lodging

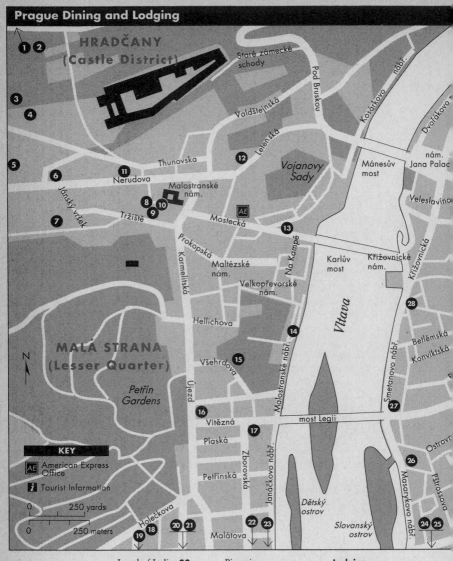

KEY

AE American Express Office

i Tourist Information

0 — 250 yards

0 — 250 meters

N

Dining
Adonis, **58**
Bella Napoli, **61**
Bellevue, **28**
Bohemia Bagel, **16**
Café Savoy, **17**
Chez Marcel, **35**
Circle Line Brasserie, **8**
Dolly Bell, **24**
Fakhreldine, **43**
Fromin, **56**
Govinda Vegetarian Club, **42**

Jewel of India, **33**
La Cambusa, **20**
La colline oubliée, **34**
La Crêperie, **41**
La Perle de Prague, **25**
Lobkovická, **7**
Lotos, **32**
Mailsi, **52**
Myslivna, **64**
Novoměstský pivovar, **60**
Pasha, **12**
Penguin's, **22**
Pizzeria Azzurra, **36**

Pizzeria Coloseum, **57**
Profit, **31**
Radost FX, **63**
Rusalka, **26**
Rybářský klub, **14**
Slávia kavárna, **27**
U bakaláře, **50**
U Mecenáše, **9**
U Počtů, **40**
U ševce Matouše, **6**
U Tří Zlatých Hvězd, **10**
U Zlaté Hrušky, **4**
V Krakovské, **62**
V Zátiši, **29**

Lodging
Apollo, **38**
Astra, **65**
Axa, **46**
Balkan, **23**
Central, **48**
City Hotel Moráň, **59**
Diplomat, **1**
Dům U Červeného Lva, **11**
Grand Hotel Bohemia, **49**
Harmony, **45**
Hotel Bern, **53**
Hotel Olšanka, **54**
Kampa, **15**

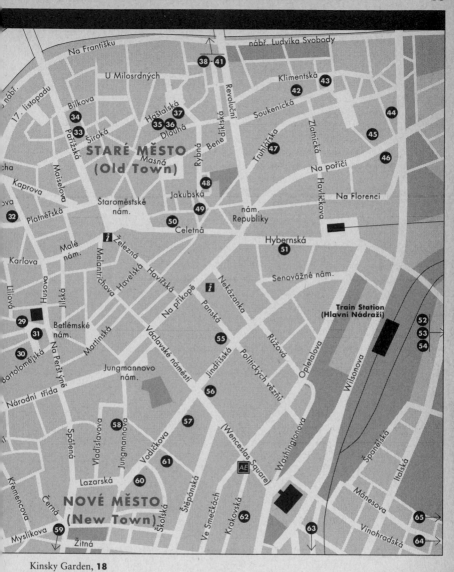

Deco decor is a perfect backdrop for people-watching, and the vistas (the river and Prague Castle on one side, the National Theater on the other) are a compelling reason to linger for hours over an espresso. Although the Slavia is principally a café, you can also get a light meal, such as a small salad with Balkan cheese or an open-face sandwich. And despite what the old-guard coat-check lady will tell you on your way in, it is not obligatory to check your coat with her. ⊠ *Smetanovo nábřeží 1012/2,* ☎ *02/2422–0957. No credit cards.*

$ ✕ **U bakaláře.** "At the Graduate's" is a clean, friendly, cafeteria-style eatery connected to a library of Charles University, just off Old Town Square. The selection of hot and cold dishes is mostly vegetarian and almost invariably on the salty side, yet the prices make it a good bet for a quick snack, lunch, or early dinner. (In the early evening, for an hour or two before the place closes at 7 PM, the management may set out lit candles on the tables, creating a romantic atmosphere under the vaulted ceilings.) ⊠ *Celetná 13,* ☎ *02/2481–1870. No credit cards.*

New Town (Nové Město)

$$$$ ✕ **La Perle de Prague.** Delicious Parisian cooking awaits at the top of Frank Gehry and Vlado Milunić's curvaceous "Fred and Ginger" building. The restaurant's interior is washed with soft tones of lilac and sea green . . . and a quiet sense of humor (parading elephants are the motif for one table setting). The semiprivate dining room at the very top affords a view so riveting diners might almost forget they were enjoying red snapper Provençal, freshwater pike-perch (*candát*), tournedos of beef Béarnaise, and other classic French dishes. Make reservations as early as you can; this is also a good reason to unpack your tie. ⊠ *Rašínovo nábřeží 80,* ☎ *02/2198–4160. AE, DC, MC, V. Closed Sun. No lunch Mon.*

$$$ ✕ **Fakhreldine.** This elegant Lebanese restaurant, crowded with diplomats who know where to find the real thing, has an excellent range of Middle Eastern dishes, such as *kibbey bisayniyeh* (lamb and ground pine-nut patty), *warakinab* (stuffed grape leaves), and three kinds of baklava. For a moderately priced meal, try several appetizers—hummus and garlic yogurt, perhaps—instead of a main course. ⊠ *Klimentská 48,* ☎ *02/232–7970. AE, DC, MC, V.*

$$ ✕ **Bella Napoli.** The decor may be a little much, but the food is gen-
★   uine and the price-to-quality ratio is hard to beat. Close your eyes to the alabaster Venus de Milos astride shopping-mall fountains and head straight for the antipasto bar, which will distract you with fresh olives, eggplant, squid, and mozzarella. For your main course, go with any of a dozen superb pasta dishes or splurge with shrimp or chicken parmigiana. The Italian-American chef hails from Brooklyn and knows his stuff. ⊠ *V jámě 8,* ☎ *02/2422–7315. No credit cards.*

$$ ✕ **Fromin.** Come dressed to the teeth—flourishing your mobile phone, preferably—for dinner at this so-chic loft high above Wenceslas Square. The food is better than average, with entrées unusual for hereabouts, such as turkey *piccata,* lamb chops, and fresh tuna steaks. The upstairs café is quiet in the mornings; then at 10 PM it becomes a disco whose doorman will turn away unstylishly dressed guests. ⊠ *Václavské nám. 21,* ☎ *02/2423–2319. AE, MC, V.*

$ ✕ **Adonis.** Ideal for a late lunch or early supper when the heaviness of Czech cooking doesn't appeal, this small, bustling cafeteria serves Middle Eastern standards: falafel, gyros, tabbouleh, hummus. Expect to eat standing up at lunchtime. ⊠ *Jungmannova 21,* ☎ *no phone. No credit cards. Closed Sun. No dinner Sat.*

$ ✕ **Govinda Vegetarian Club.** Owned and operated by the Hare Krishnas, Govinda offers cheap, wholesome food with nary a whisper of proselytizing. (Although it calls itself a "club," there is no membership requirement.) The selection of chutney, rice, curried vegetables, and bread is mild and perhaps overly sweet by Indian standards, and it does not vary much from day to day, but lunch here is surely the least expensive in the downtown area. No chance for dinner, as it closes at 5 PM. ✉ *Soukenická 27 (off Revoluční),* ☎ *02/2481–6016. No credit cards. Closed Sun.*

$ ✗ **Novoměstský pivovar.** It's easy to lose your way in this crowded microbrewery-restaurant; there's a maze of rooms, some painted in mock-medieval style, others covered with murals of Prague street scenes. *Vepřové koleno* (pork knuckle) is a favorite dish. The beer is the cloudy, fruity "fermented" style. ✉ *Vodičkova 20, Prague 1,* ☎ *02/ 2423–3533. AE, MC, V.*

$ ✗ **Pizzeria Coloseum.** Of the swarms of pizzerias that have cropped up in the past few years, most spots have proved to be mediocre, but this one has kept its popularity, due largely to its position right off Wenceslas Square. Location doesn't have everything to do with it, though; the pizzas have a wonderfully thin, crisp crust, and the pasta with Gorgonzola sauce will have you blessing Italian cows. Long picnic tables make this an ideal spot for an informal lunch or dinner. There's a salad bar, too. ✉ *Vodičkova 32,* ☎ *02/2421–4914. AE, MC, V.*

$ ✗ **Radost FX.** Colorful and campy in design, this lively café is a street-level adjunct to the popular dance club Radost and CD shop next door. It's a vegetarian heaven for both Czechs and expatriates: The rotating tofu special is bound to be good, and there are usually creative specials of a Mexican or Italian persuasion. If you suddenly find yourself craving a brownie, this is the place to get a fudge-fix. Another plus: It's open until 4 AM. ✉ *Bělehradská 120,* ☎ *02/2425–4776. No credit cards.*

$ ✗ **Rusalka.** This quiet, cozy nook is the perfect pre- or post-theater dining spot; not only is it right behind the National Theater, but it's named after Dvořák's beloved opera. Fish and pasta are the draws, such as the halibut with *Hermelín* (a Brie-like Czech cheese), calamari, and fettuccini with asparagus and smoked meat. ✉ *Na struze 1/277,* ☎ *02/2491–5876. AE, MC, V.*

$ ✗ **V Krakovské.** At this clean, proper pub close to the major tourist sights, the food is traditional and hearty; this is the place to try *svíčková na smetaně* (thinly sliced sirloin beef in cream sauce) paired with an effervescent Krušovice beer. ✉ *Krakovská 20,* ☎ *02/2221–0204. No credit cards.*

Lesser Quarter (Malá Strana)

$$$$ ✗ **Circle Line Brasserie.** Bypass the cozy-looking sister restaurant, Avalon, on the ground-floor level as you enter the building (the food and service are nothing special for the price) and head straight downstairs for the fresh, delicious seafood of Circle Line. The decor here is sophisticated without being stuffy, and the service can't be faulted. There are creative seasonal specials such as the warm foie gras with cherries, but be sure to save room for the *cokoládový talíř* (chocolate plate) for dessert. ✉ *Malostranské nám. 12,* ☎ *02/530308. AE, DC, MC, V.*

$$$$ ✗ **Pasha.** This inviting Middle Eastern spot at the foot of Prague Castle hits just the right notes of luxury and easiness. The à la carte menu includes luscious *adana kebab* (skewer of minced lamb), pilaf, and shish kebab. Baklava served with fresh mint tea makes a splendid dessert. ✉ *Letenská 1,* ☎ *02/549773. AE, DC, MC, V. Closed Mon.*

$$$ ✗ **Lobkovická.** This dignified *vinárna* (wine hall) set inside a 17th-century town palace serves innovative, imaginative dishes by Prague standards. Chicken breast with crabmeat and curry sauce is an excellent main dish and typical of the kitchen's approach to sauces and spices.

Deep-red carpeting sets the perfect mood for enjoying bottles of Moravian wine brought from the musty depths of the restaurant's wine cellar. ⊠ *Vlašská 17,* ☎ *02/530185. AE, MC, V.*

$$$ ✕ **U Mecenáše.** An enticing Renaissance inn from the 17th century, with dark, high-backed benches in the front room and cozy, elegant sofas and chairs in back, this is the place to splurge. From the aperitifs to the specialty steaks or beef Wellington and the cognac (swirled lovingly in oversize glasses), the presentation is seamless. ⊠ *Malostranské nám. 10,* ☎ *02/533881. AE, MC, V.*

$$ ✕ **U Tří Zlatých Hvězd.** The "Three Golden Stars" is a perfect spot for a romantic evening; the cuisine is hearty, classic Czech with thoughtful European touches, such as roast duck Bohemian style with apples, bacon, dumplings, and red cabbage. Fondue is served in the downstairs wine bar. ⊠ *Malostranské nám. 8,* ☎ *02/539–660. AE, MC, V.*

$ ✕ **Bohemia Bagel.** It's not New York, but the friendly, American-owned Bohemia Bagel still serves up a plentiful assortment of fresh bagels from raisin walnut to "supreme," with all kinds of spreads and toppings. Their thick soups are among the best in Prague for the price, and the bottomless cups of coffee are a further draw. It's a popular choice for weekend brunches. ⊠ *Újezd 16,* ☎ *02/531002. No credit cards.*

$ ✕ **Café Savoy.** Opened in 1887 as a grand café, the Savoy lasted only a few years before the long, airy room was divided up to be made into shops. In 1992 the café was reborn, and best of all, the painted and stuccoed ceiling that had long been covered over was restored. It's best as a spot for coffee, a drink, or a fine apple strudel; typical meat dishes such as pork steak with horseradish are also available. ⊠ *Vítězná 5,* ☎ *02/535–000. AE, DC, MC, V.*

$ ✕ **Rybářský klub.** The "Fishing Club" restaurant shares its building with
★   a real fishing club's headquarters; it's a great place to try a wide variety of freshwater fish. Perch, eel, barbel, and the esteemed pike-perch (*candát*) are served at picnic-style tables or by the water in summer. ⊠ *U Sovových mlýnů 1, Kampa Island,* ☎ *02/530–223. No credit cards.*

Hradčany

$$$$ ✕ **U Zlaté Hrušky.** At this bustling bistro perched on one of Prague's prettiest cobblestone streets, slide into one of the cozy dark-wood booths and let the cheerful staff advise on wines and specials. Among the regular offerings are a superb leg of venison with pears and millet gnocchi and an excellent appetizer of duck liver in wine sauce. After dinner, stroll to the castle for an unforgettable panorama. ⊠ *Nový Svět 3,* ☎ *02/2051–4778. Jacket and tie. AE, DC, MC, V.*

$$ ✕ **U ševce Matouše.** Steaks are the raison d'être at this former shoemaker's shop; the gold shoe still hangs from the ceiling of the arcade outside to guide patrons into the vaulted dining room. Appetizers are hit-and-miss; stick with the dozen or so tenderloins and filet mignons. ⊠ *Loretánské nám. 4,* ☎ *02/2051–4536. MC, V.*

Vinohrady

$$ ✕ **Myslivna.** The name means "hunting lodge," and the cooks at this neighborhood eatery certainly know their way around venison, quail, and boar. Attentive staff can advise on wines: Try Vavřinecké, a hearty red that holds its own with any beast. The stuffed quail and the leg of venison with walnuts both get high marks. A cab from the city center to Myslivna should cost under 200 Kč. ⊠ *Jagellonská 21, Prague 3,* ☎ *02/627–0209. No credit cards.*

Letná and Holešovice

$ ✕ **La Crêperie.** Run by a Czech-French couple, this creperie near the Globe Bookstore (☞ Shopping, *below*) and Veletržní palá Museum of Modern Art serves all manner of crepes (thin pancakes), both sweet and savory. (It may take at least three or four to satisfy a hearty appetite.) Make sure to leave room for the dessert crepe with cinnamon-apple purée layered with lemon cream. ✉ *Janovského 4, Holešovice,* ☎ *02/878040. No credit cards.*

$ ✕ **U Počtů.** This is a charmingly old-fashioned neighborhood eatery with comparatively skilled service. Garlic soup and chicken livers in wine sauce are flawlessly rendered, and the grilled trout is delicious. ✉ *Milády Horakové 47, Letná,* ☎ *02/3337–1419. AE, MC, V.*

Smíchov

$$$ ✕ **La Cambusa.** Despite a less-than-ideal location, this is an accomplished seafood restaurant. The small, changing menu has a northern Italian bent; it could offer simply prepared octopus, lobster, or monkfish. It's situated on a grimy street near a large construction site; to reach it from the nearby metro station Anděl (Line B), walk one block east on Plzeňská to Stroupežnického, turn left, and walk to the corner of Klicperova. ✉ *Klicperova 2 (entrance on Stroupežnického),* ☎ *02/ 541–533. AE, DC, MC, V. Closed Sun. No lunch.*

$$ ✕ **Penguin's.** The emphasis at this popular eatery is on classic Czech and pasta dishes with a Czech bent (a liberal use of local flavors like ham and mild peppers). Try any of the steaks or the chicken breast with potatoes. The penguin in the name refers to the Pittsburgh variety, of hockey fame—the owner's favorite team. ✉ *Zborovská 5,* ☎ *02/ 5731–1019. AE, MC, V.*

Žižkov

$ ✕ **Mailsi.** Funky paintings of Arabian Nights–type scenes in a low-ceil-
★ ing cellar make for a casual, cheerful setting at this Pakistani restaurant—normal in some other cities but practically unique in Prague. The menu offers beef, chicken, lamb, and vegetable curries, delicious chapati and nan bread, and a tasty *murgh tikka* appetizer of thin-sliced marinated chicken. Take tram 5, 9, or 26 to the Lipanská stop, and then walk one block uphill. ✉ *Lipanská 1,* ☎ *02/0603/466–626. No credit cards.*

Vyšehrad

$$ ✕ **Dolly Bell.** This restaurant's whimsical design, with upside-down ta-
★ bles hanging from the ceiling, provides a clever counterpoint to the extensive selection of well-prepared Yugoslav dishes. There's an emphasis on meat and seafood—especially worth sampling are the corn bread (polenta) with Balkan cheese, *čevapčiči* (pork sausage), and *tufahija* (baked apple with a smooth nut filling). ✉ *Neklanova 20,* ☎ *02/ 298–815. AE, DC, MC, V.*

LODGING

Helpful room-finding agencies include **Hello Ltd.** (✉ Senovážné nám. 3, Nové Město, ☎ ℻ 02/2421–2647 or 02/2421–4212), open daily 9 AM–9 PM; it's a 10-minute walk from the main train station. The bluntly named **Accommodation Service** (✉ Haštalská 7, Staré Město, ☎ 02/ 231–0202, ℻ 02/231–6640), open daily between April and October from 10–noon and 1–7 and from November to March 9–1 and 2–6, specializes in Old Town rooms and apartments from 1,800 Kč for double occupancy. If all else fails, just take a walk through the Old Town: The number of places advertising ACCOMMODATION (often written in German as UNTERKUNFT) is astounding.

For price range information, *see* Lodging *in* Pleasures and Pastimes, *above*.

Old Town (Staré Město)

$$$$ ⊞ **Grand Hotel Bohemia.** This beautifully refurbished Art Nouveau town palace, probably the most expensive hotel in Prague, is just a stone's throw from Old Town Square. The Austrian owners opted for a muted, modern decor in the rooms but left the sumptuous public areas just as they were. Sweeping, long drapes frame spectacular views of the Old Town; each room's amenities include a fax, trouser press, and answering machine. ⊠ *Králodvorská 4, 110 00 Prague 1,* ☎ *02/2480–4111,* ⅨX *02/232–9545. 73 rooms, 5 suites. Restaurant, bar, café, minibars, in-room safes. AE, DC, MC, V.*

$$$ ⊞ **Maximilian.** Oversize beds, French cherry-wood Art Nouveau furniture, and thick drapes make for a relaxing stay in this luxurious hotel. A relatively new property (opened in 1995), it's located on a peaceful square, well away from traffic, noise, and crowds, yet within easy walking distance to Old Town Square and Pařížská Street. There are fax machines and satellite TVs in every room. ⊠ *Haštalská 14, 113 03 Prague 1,* ☎ *02/2180–6111,* ⅨX *02/2180–6110. 72 rooms. Minibars, in-room safes. AE, DC, MC, V.*

$$ ⊞ **Central.** Quite conveniently, this hotel lives up to its name, with a site on a relatively quiet sidestreet near Celetná Street and Republic Square. Rooms are sparely furnished, but all have baths, and the English-speaking concierge is very helpful and accommodating. The Baroque glories of the Old Town are steps away. ⊠ *Rybná 8, 110 00 Prague 1,* ☎ *02/2481–2041,* ⅨX *02/232–8404. 62 rooms, 4 suites. Restaurant, bar. AE, DC, MC, V.*

$ ⊞ **Pension Unitas.** Now operated by the Christian charity Unitas, the spartan rooms of this former convent used to serve as interrogation cells for the Communist secret police. (Václav Havel was once a "guest.") Conditions are much more comfortable nowadays, if far from luxurious. There's a common (but clean) bathroom on each floor. You'll need to reserve well in advance, even in off-season. Note that there is an adjacent three-star hotel, Cloister Inn, using the same location and phone number; when calling, just specify the pension. ⊠ *Bartolomějská 9, 110 00 Prague 1,* ☎ *02/232–7700,* ⅨX *02/232–7709. 40 rooms, none with bath. Restaurant. AE, MC, V.*

New Town (Nové Město)

$$$$ ⊞ **Palace.** For the well-heeled, this is Prague's most coveted address—
★ a beautiful Art Nouveau–style building perched on a busy corner only a block from Wenceslas Square. The hotel's spacious, well-appointed rooms, each with a white-marble bathroom (with its own phone), are fitted in velvety pinks and greens cribbed straight from an Alfons Mucha print. All have satellite TV. The hotel's restaurant is pure Continental, from the classic garnishes to the creamy sauces. Two rooms are set aside for travelers with disabilities; children 12 and under stay for free. ⊠ *Panská 12, 111 21 Prague 1,* ☎ *02/2409–3120,* ⅨX *02/ 2422–1240. 114 rooms, 10 suites. 2 restaurants, piano bar, 2 no-smoking floors, room service, sauna, meeting rooms. AE, DC, MC, V.*

$$$ ⊞ **Axa.** Funky and functional, this 1932 high-rise was a mainstay of the budget-hotel crowd until a makeover forced substantial price hikes

several years ago. The rooms, now with color television sets and modern plumbing, are certainly improved; however, the lobby and public areas are still decidedly tacky, with plastic flowers, lots of mirrors, and glaring lights. However, the scores of free weights in Axa's gym make it one of the best in Prague. ⊠ *Na Poříčí 40, 113 03 Prague 1,* ☎ *02/2481–2580,* FAX *02/232–2172. 109 rooms. Restaurant, bar, pool, exercise room, nightclub. AE, DC, MC, V.*

$$$ ▦ **City Hotel Moráň.** This renovated 19th-century town house has a bright, inviting lobby, made over in an updated Jugendstil style. The modern, if slightly bland, rooms are a cut above the Prague standard for convenience and cleanliness; some on the top floors afford a good view of Prague Castle. ⊠ *Na Moráni 15 (corner of Václavská), 120 00 Prague 2,* ☎ *02/2491–5208,* FAX *02/297–533. 57 rooms. Restaurant. AE, DC, MC, V.*

$$$ ▦ **Harmony.** This is one of the renovated, formerly state-owned standbys. A stern 1930s facade clashes with the bright, nouveau riche–type 1990s interior, but cheerful receptionists, comfortably casual rooms, and an easy 10-minute walk to the Old Town compensate for the aesthetic flaws. Ask for a room away from the bustle of one of Prague's busiest streets, which during the day is a major route for trams. ⊠ *Na Poříčí 31, 110 00 Prague 1,* ☎ *02/232–0016,* FAX *02/231–0009. 60 rooms. Restaurant, snack bar. AE, DC, MC, V.*

$$$ ▦ **Meteor Plaza.** This popular hotel, operated by the Best Western chain, combines modern conveniences with historical ambience (Empress Maria Theresa's son, Emperor Joseph II, stayed here when he was passing through in the 18th century). The setting is ideal: a Baroque building that is only five minutes on foot from downtown. For a better sense of the hotel's age, visit the original 14th-century wine cellar. ⊠ *Hybernská 6, 110 00 Prague 1,* ☎ *02/2419–2111,* FAX *02/2421–3005. 90 rooms, 6 suites. Restaurant, exercise room. AE, DC, MC, V.*

$$$ ▦ **Opera.** Once the lodging of choice for divas performing at the nearby State Theater, the Opera greatly declined under the Communists. The mid-'90s saw the grand fin-de-siècle facade rejuvenated with a perky pink-and-white exterior paint job; this exuberance is still strictly on the outside, though, as the rooms have an easy-on-the-eyes, modern decor. In the off-season a double room can be had for around 2,800 Kč. ⊠ *Těšnov 13, 110 00 Prague 1,* ☎ *02/231–5609,* FAX *02/231–1477. 66 rooms. Restaurant, bar. AE, DC, MC, V.*

$$ ▦ **Salvator.** An efficiently run establishment just outside the Old Town, this pension offers more comforts than most in its class, including satellite TV and minibars in most rooms, and a breakfast room–cum–bar with a billiard table. Rooms are pristine if plain, with the standard narrow beds; those without private bath also lack TVs but are good value nonetheless. Parking (for a 200 Kč-a-day fee) is available in the courtyard. ⊠ *Truhlářská 10 (near metro Náměstí Republiky), 110 00 Prague 1,* ☎ *02/231–2234,* FAX *02/231–6355. 13 rooms, 9 with bath, 7 suites. AE (in high season only).*

Malá Strana

$$$$ ▦ **Dům U Červeného Lva.** On Mala Strana's main, historic thorough-
★ fare, a five-minute walk from Prague Castle's front gates, the Baroque House at the Red Lion is an intimate, immaculately kept hotel. The spare but comfortable guest rooms have parquet floors, 17th-century painted-beam ceilings, superb antiques, and all-white bathrooms with brass fixtures. The two top-floor rooms can double as a suite. Note: There is no elevator, and stairs are steep. ⊠ *Nerudova 41, 118 00 Prague 1,* ☎ *02/537–239 or 02/538–192,* ⊠ *02/538–193. 11 rooms. 2 restaurants, bar. AE, MC, V.*

$$$ ⊞ **Kampa.** This early Baroque armory turned hotel is tucked away on
★   a leafy corner at the southern end of Malá Strana. The rooms are clean,
      if sparse; the bucolic setting and comparatively low rates make up for
      any discomforts. Note the late-Gothic vaulting in the massive dining
      room. ⊠ *Všehrdova 16, 118 00 Prague 1,* ☎ *02/5732–0508,* FAX *02/*
      5732–0262. 85 rooms. Restaurant. AE, MC, V.

$$$ ⊞ **U Tří Pštrosů.** The location could not be better—a romantic corner
      just a stone's throw from the river and within arms' reach of the
      Charles Bridge. The airy rooms of the centuries-old building still have
      their original oak-beamed ceilings and antique furniture; many also have
      views over the river. Massive walls keep out the noise of the crowds
      on the bridge. An excellent in-house restaurant serves traditional Czech
      dishes to guests and nonguests alike. (It does not accept credit cards.)
      Rates drop slightly in July and August—probably because there's no
      air-conditioning, though the building's thick walls help keep it cool.
      ⊠ *Dražického nám. 12, 118 00 Prague 1,* ☎ *02/5732–0565,* FAX *02/*
      5732–0611. 14 rooms, 4 suites. Restaurant. AE MC, V.

Hradčany

$$$$ ⊞ **Savoy.** A restrained yellow Jugendstil facade conceals one of the city's
★   most luxurious small hotels, whose extra touches include in-room
      breakfast and complimentary afternoon tea in the small library. The
      erstwhile budget hotel was gutted and lavishly refurbished in the mid-
      1990s; rooms have spacious bathrooms, harmonious maroon and
      brown color schemes, and fax machines. Some are purely modern, while
      others have a faux-rococo flourish. The only drawback: Although
      Prague Castle is just up the road, none of the rooms have a view of it.
      ⊠ *Keplerova 6, 118 00 Prague 6,* ☎ *02/2430–2430,* FAX *02/2430–2128.*
      55 rooms, 6 suites. Restaurant, café, exercise room, sauna, meeting
      rooms. AE, DC, MC, V.

$$$ ⊞ **Pension U Raka.** This private guest house, since 1997 a member of
★   the Romantik Hotels & Restaurants organization, offers the coziness
      of an Alpine lodge, plus a quiet location on the ancient, winding streets
      of Nový Svět, just behind the Loreto Church and a 10-minute walk
      from Prague Castle. One side of the 18th-century building presents a
      rare example of half-timbering; the rooms carry on the country feel
      with heavy furniture reminiscent of a Czech farmhouse. There are
      only six rooms, but if you can get a reservation (try at least a month
      in advance), you will nab a wonderful base for exploring the city. ⊠
      Černínská 10/93, 118 00 Prague 1, ☎ *02/2051–1100,* FAX *02/2051–*
      0511. 5 rooms, 1 suite. Breakfast room. AE, MC, V.

Smíchov

$$$ ⊞ **Kinsky Garden.** You could walk the mile or so from this hotel to
      Prague Castle entirely on the tree-lined paths of Petřín, the hilly park
      that starts across the street. Opened in 1997, the hotel takes its name
      from a garden established by Count Rudolf Kinsky in 1825 on the south-
      ern side of Petřín. The public spaces and some rooms are not spacious,
      but everything is tasteful and comfortable; try to get a room on one
      of the upper floors for a view of the park. The management and restau-
      rant are Italian. ⊠ *Holečkova 7, 150 00 Prague 5,* ☎ *02/5731–1173,*
      FAX *02/5731–1184. 60 rooms. Restaurant, bar, meeting room. AE,*
      DC, MC, V.

$$ ⊞ **Mepro.** Standard rooms and service and a reasonably central loca-
      tion make this small hotel worth considering. The Smíchov neighbor-
      hood offers a good range of restaurants (for one, the U Mikuláše
      Dačického wine tavern, across the street from the hotel) and nice
      strolls along the river or up the Petřín hill. ⊠ *Viktora Huga 3, 150 00*

Prague 5, ☎ *02/5721–5263,* FAX *02/527–343. 26 rooms. Snack bar. AE, MC, V.*

$$ 🏨 **Petr.** Set in a quiet part of Smíchov, just a few minutes' stroll from Malá Strana, this is an excellent value. As a "garni" hotel, it does not have a full-service restaurant, but it does serve breakfast (included in the price). The rooms are simply but adequately furnished. It's a 10-minute walk from metro Anděl, Line B. ✉ *Drtinova 17, 150 00 Prague 5,* ☎ *02/5731–4068,* FAX *02/5731–4072. 37 rooms, 2 suites. AE, MC, V.*

$ 🏨 **Balkan.** One of the few central hotels that can compete in cost with private rooms, the spartan Balkan is on a busy street, not far from Malá Strana and the National Theater. Room prices do not include breakfast. ✉ *Svornosti 28, 150 00 Prague 5,* ☎ FAX *02/540777, 02/540196, or 02/540670. 24 rooms. Restaurant. AE.*

Žižkov

$$ 🏨 **Hotel Bern.** The cream-colored Bern is a comfortable alternative to staying in the city center. Although geographically the hotel is rather far out, it is situated on a series of city bus routes that run frequently even on evenings and weekends; there are two direct bus routes to the Old Town and the ride takes about 10 minutes. Rooms are decorated in faux–Art Nouveau black and white. ✉ *Koněvova 28, 130 00 Prague 3,* ☎ *02/697–5807,* FAX *02/697–4420. 26 rooms with shower. Restaurant, bar. AE, DC, MC, V.*

$$ 🏨 **Hotel Olšanka.** The main calling card of this boxy modern hotel is its outstanding 50-m swimming pool and modern sports center, which includes a pair of tennis courts and aerobics classes. Rooms are clean and, though basic, have the most important hotel amenities. There's also a relaxing sauna with certain nights reserved for men, women, or both. (Please note that the sports facilities may be closed for August.) The neighborhood is nondescript, but the Old Town is only 10 minutes away by direct tram. ✉ *Táboritská 23, 130 87 Prague 3,* ☎ *02/ 6709–2202,* FAX *02/273–386 or 02/278–434. 225 rooms. Restaurant, bar, pool, health club. AE, DC, MC, V.*

Eastern Suburbs

$$ 🏨 **Apollo.** This is a standard, no-frills, square-box hotel where clean rooms come at a fair price. Its primary flaw is its location: roughly 20 minutes away by metro or bus from the city center. ✉ *Kubišova 23, 182 00 Prague 8,* ☎ *02/688–0628,* FAX *02/688–4570. 35 rooms. AE, MC, V. Metro: Holešovice, Line C, then Tram 5, 17, or 25 to the Hercovka stop.*

$$ 🏨 **Astra.** The location best serves drivers coming into town from the east, although the nearby metro station makes this modern hotel easy to reach from the center. The neighborhood is quiet, if ordinary, and the rooms are more comfortable than most in this price range. ✉ *Mukařovská 1740/18, 100 00 Prague 10,* ☎ *02/781–3595,* FAX *02/781– 0765. 43 rooms, 10 suites. Restaurant, nightclub. AE, DC, MC, V. Metro: Skalka, Line A, then walk south on Na padesátém about 5 mins to Mukařovská.*

$ 🏨 **Pension Louda.** The friendly owners of this family-run guest house,
★ set in a suburb roughly 20 minutes by tram from the city center, go out of their way to make you feel welcome. The large, spotless rooms are an unbelievable bargain, and the hilltop location offers a stunning view of greater Prague from the south-facing rooms. ✉ *Kubišova 10, 182 00 Prague 8,* ☎ *02/688–1491,* FAX *02/688–1488. 9 rooms. Sauna, exercise room. No credit cards. Metro: Holešovice, Line C, then Tram 5, 17, or 25 to the Hercovka stop.*

Western Suburbs

$$$$ ⊞ **Diplomat.** This sprawling complex opened in 1990 and remains pop-
★   ular with business travelers thanks to its location between the airport
and downtown. The city center is easily reached by metro (the closest
stop is Metro Dejvická on Line A). The modern rooms may not exude
much character, but they are tastefully furnished and quite comfortable. Many of the hotel staff members speak English. You can drive a
miniature racing car at the indoor track next door. ⊠ *Evropská 15,
160 00 Prague 6,* ☎ *02/2439–4111,* FAX *02/2439–4215. 369 rooms,
13 suites. 2 restaurants, bar, café, no-smoking floor, exercise room, sauna,
nightclub, meeting room. AE, DC, MC, V.*

$ ⊞ **Penzion Sprint.** Straightforward, no-surprises rooms, most of which
have their own bathroom (however tiny), make the Sprint a fine choice.
This pension is on a quiet residential street in the outskirts of Prague
about 20 minutes from the airport. Tram 18 rumbles directly to the
Old Town, and the closest stop (Batérie) is just two blocks away. ⊠
Cukrovárnická 62, 160 00 Prague 6, ☎ *02/312–3338,* FAX *02/312–
1797. 12 rooms, 9 with bath. AE, MC, V.*

NIGHTLIFE AND THE ARTS

The fraternal twins of the performing arts and nightlife are having an
exhilarating growth spurt. Except for Czech-language theater—which
is suffering from severe state budget cuts—the number of concerts, art
exhibitions, and the like is on the rise. Some venues in the city center
pitch themselves to tourists, but there are dozens of places where you
can join the local crowds for music, dancing, or the rituals of beer and
conversation. For details of cultural and nightlife events, look for the
English-language newspaper the *Prague Post* or the monthly *Prague
Guide* (also in English), available at hotels, tourist offices, and newsstands.

Nightlife

Cabaret
For adult stage entertainment (with some nudity) try the **Varieté Praga**
(⊠ Vodičkova ul. 30, ☎ 02/2421–5945).

Discos
Dance clubs come and go with predictable regularity. The longtime fa-
vorite is **Radost FX** (⊠ Bělehradská 120, ☎ 02/251210), with imported
DJs playing the latest dance music and techno from London. **Lávka**
(⊠ Novotného lávká 1, ☎ 02/2421–4797), near the Charles Bridge,
has open-air dancing by the bridge on summer nights; there's also the
Corona Club and Latin Café (⊠ Novotného lávká, ☎ 02/2108–2357),
which highlights Latin, Gypsy, and other dance-friendly live music. Dis-
cos catering to a very young crowd blast sound onto lower Wenceslas
Square.

Jazz Clubs
Jazz gained notoriety under the Communists as a subtle form of protest,
and the city still has some great jazz clubs, featuring everything from
swing to blues and modern. The following clubs have a cover charge.
Reduta (⊠ Národní 20, ☎ 02/2491–2246) features a full program of
local and international musicians. **AghaRTA** (⊠ Krakovská 5, ☎ 02/
2221–1275) offers a variety of jazz acts in an intimate café-nightclub
atmosphere. Music starts around 9 PM, but come earlier to get a seat.
Jazz Club Železná (⊠ Železná 16, ☎ 02/2421–2541) mixes its jazz
acts with world music. **Jazz Club U staré paní** (⊠ Michalská 9, ☎ 02/

264–920) has a rotating list of tried-and-true Czech bands; **Jazz & Blues Café** (✉ Na Příkopě 23, ☏ 02/2422–8788) is in the same vein.

Pubs, Bars, and Lounges

Bars or lounges are not traditional Prague fixtures, but bars catering to a young, often foreign, crowd have elbowed their way in over the past few years. Still, most social life of the drinking variety takes place in pubs (*pivnice* or *hospody*), which are liberally sprinkled throughout the city's neighborhoods. Tourists are welcome to join in the evening ritual of sitting around large tables and talking, smoking, and drinking beer. Before venturing in, however, it's best to familiarize yourself with a few points of pub etiquette. Always ask if a chair is free before sitting down (*Je tu volno?*). To order a beer (*pivo*), do not wave the waiter down or shout across the room; he will usually assume you want beer—most pubs serve one brand—and bring it over to you without asking. He will also bring subsequent rounds to the table without asking. To refuse, just shake your head or say no thanks (*ne, děkuju*). At the end of the evening, usually around 10:30 or 11, the waiter will come to tally the bill. There are plenty of popular pubs in the city center, such as **U Medvídků** (✉ Na Perštýně 7, ☏ 02/2422–0930), which was a brewery at least as long ago as the 15th century. Beer is no longer made on the premises; rather, draft Budvar is shipped from České Budějovice, the South Bohemian town known as Budweis to Germans, who call the beer Budweiser—but this is not the stuff made in St. Louis. **U Sv. Tomáše** (✉ Letenská 12, ☏ 02/5732–0101) brewed beer for Augustinian monks starting in 1358. Now they serve commercially produced dark beer in a tourist-friendly mock-medieval hall in Malá Strana. **U Zlatého Tygra** (✉ Husova ul. 17, ☏ 02/2422–9020) is famed as one of the three best Prague pubs for Pilsner Urquell, the original and perhaps the greatest of the pilsners. It was also a hangout for such raffish types as the writer Bohumil Hrabal, who died in 1997. All can get impossibly crowded.

One of the oddest phenomena of Prague's post-1989 renaissance is the sight of travelers and tour groups from the United States, Britain, Australia, and even Japan descending on this city to experience the life of— American expatriates. There are a handful of bars guaranteed to ooze Yanks and other native English speakers. **Jo's Bar** (✉ Malostranské nám. 7, ☏ no phone) is a haven for younger expats, serving bottled beer, mixed drinks, and good Mexican food. The **James Joyce Pub** (✉ Liliová 10, 02/2424–8793) is authentically Irish (it has Irish owners), with Guinness on tap and excellent food of the fish-and-chips persuasion. **U Malého Glena** (✉ Karmelitská 23, ☏ 02/535–8115) puts on live jazz, folk, and rock; lots of expat groups perform here. The major hotels also run their own bars and nightclubs. The **Piano Bar** in the Palace hotel (☞ Lodging, *above*) is the most pleasant of the lot; jacket and tie are suggested.

Rock Clubs

Prague's rock scene is thriving. Hard-rock enthusiasts should check out the **Rock Café** (✉ Národní 20, ☏ 02/2491–4416); you can also slouch into the **Lucerna Music Bar** (✉ Vodičkova 3, ☏ 02/2421–7108). For dance tracks, hip locals congregate at **Roxy** (✉ Dlouhá 33, ☏ 02/2481–0951). **Malostranská Beseda** (✉ Malostranské nám. 21, ☏ 02/539–024) is a dependable bet for sometimes bizarre but always good musical acts from around the country. The cavernous **Palác Akropolis** (✉ Kubelíkova 27, ☏ 02/9000–2310) has top Czech acts and major international world-music performers; as the name suggests, the space has an Acropolis theme.

The Arts

Prague's cultural flair is legendary, and performances are sometimes booked far in advance by all sorts of Praguers. The concierge at your hotel may be able to reserve tickets for you. Otherwise, for the cheapest tickets go directly to the theater box office a few days in advance or immediately before a performance. The biggest ticket agency, **Ticketpro,** has outlets all over town and accepts all major credit cards (main branch: ✉ Salvátorská 10, ☎ 02/2481–4020). **Bohemia Ticket International** (✉ Na Příkopě 16, ☎ 02/2421–5031; ✉ Václavské nám. 25, ☎ 02/2422–7253) sells tickets for major cultural events, though at semi-inflated prices. Tickets can also be purchased at **American Express** (☞ Travel Agencies *in* Prague A to Z, *below*).

Film

If a film was made in the United States or Britain, the chances are good that it will be shown with Czech subtitles rather than dubbed. (Film titles, however, are usually translated into Czech, so your only clue to the movie's country of origin may be the poster used in advertisements.) Movies in the original language are normally indicated with the note "*českými titulky*" (with Czech subtitles). Popular cinemas are **Blaník** (✉ Václavské nám. 56, ☎ 02/2421–6698), **Lucerna** (✉ Vodičkova 36, ☎ 02/2421–6972), **Praha** (✉ Václavské nám. 17, ☎ 02/262–035), and **Světozor** (✉ Vodičkova 39, ☎ 02/263616). Prague's English-language publications carry film reviews and full timetables.

Music

Classical concerts are held all over the city throughout the year. One of the best orchestral venues is the resplendent Art Nouveau **Obecní dům** (✉ Smetana Hall, Nám Republiky 5, ☎ 02/2200–2336), home of the Prague Symphony Orchestra. **Dvořák Hall** (✉ In the Rudolfinum, nám. Jana Palacha, ☎ 02/2489–3111) is home to one of Central Europe's best orchestras, the Czech Philharmonic, which has been racked in recent years by bitter disputes among players, conductors, and management but still plays sublimely.

Performances also are held regularly at many of the city's palaces and churches, including the **Garden on the Ramparts** below Prague Castle (where the music comes with a view); the two **churches of St. Nicholas** (☞ Staré Město [the Old Town] *in* Exploring Prague, *above*); the **Church of Sts. Simon and Jude** (✉ Dušní ul., Old Town); the **Church of St. James** (✉ Malá Štupartská, near Old Town Square); the **Zrcadlová kaple** (✉ Mirror Chapel, Klementinum, Mariánské náměstí, Old Town); and the **Lobkowicz Palace** at Prague Castle. Classical ensembles are the most common finds, and the standard of performance ranges from adequate to superb, though the programs tend to take few risks. Serious fans of Baroque music may have the opportunity to hear works of little-known Bohemian composers at these concerts. Some of the best chamber ensembles are the **Talich Chamber Orchestra,** the **Guarneri Trio,** the **Wihan Quartet,** the **Czech Piano Trio,** and the **Agon** contemporary music group.

Concerts at the **Villa Bertramka** (☞ Karlův Most [Charles Bridge] and Malá Strana [Lesser Quarter] *in* Exploring Prague, *above*) emphasize the music of Mozart and his contemporaries.

If you're an organ-music buff, you'll most likely have your pick of recitals held in Prague's historic halls and churches. Popular programs are offered at **St. Vitus Cathedral** in Hradčany, **U Křížovníků** (✉ Křížovnické nám., ☎ no phone) near the Charles Bridge, the **Church of St. Nicholas** in Malá Strana, and the **Church of St. James** (☞ *above*), where the organ plays amid a complement of Baroque statuary.

BONUS MILES MAKE GREAT SOUVENIRS.

Earn Miles With Your MCI Card.

Take the MCI Card along on this trip and start earning miles for the next one. You'll earn frequent flyer miles on all your calls and save with the low rates you've come to expect from MCI. Before you know it, you'll be on your way to some other international destination.

Sign up for MCI by calling 1-800-FLY-FREE

Earn Frequent Flyer Miles.

Is this a great time, or what? :-)

Easy To Call Home.

1. To use your MCI Card, just dial the WorldPhone access number of the country you're calling from.
2. Dial or give the operator your MCI Card number.
3. Dial or give the number you're calling.

# Austria (CC) ♦	022-903-012
# Belarus (CC)	
From Brest, Vitebsk, Grodno, Minsk	8-800-103
From Gomel and Mogilev regions	8-10-800-103
# Belgium (CC) ♦	0800-10012
# Bulgaria	00800-0001
# Croatia (CC) ★	0800-22-0112
# Czech Republic (CC) ♦	00-42-000112
# Denmark (CC) ♦	8001-0022
# Finland (CC) ♦	08001-102-80
# France (CC) ♦	0-800-99-0019
# Germany (CC)	0800-888-8000
# Greece (CC) ♦	00-800-1211
# Hungary (CC) ♦	00▼800-01411
# Iceland (CC) ♦	800-9002
# Ireland (CC)	1-800-55-1001
# Italy (CC) ♦	172-1022
# Kazakhstan (CC)	8-800-131-4321
# Liechtenstein (CC) ♦	0800-89-0222
# Luxembourg	0800-0112
# Monaco (CC) ♦	800-90-019
# Netherlands (CC) ♦	0800-022-9122
# Norway (CC) ♦	800-19912
# Poland (CC) ÷	00-800-111-21-22
# Portugal (CC) ÷	05-017-1234
Romania (CC) ÷	01-800-1800
# Russia (CC) ÷ ♦	
To call using ROSTELCOM ■	747-3322
For a Russian-speaking operator	747-3320
To call using SOVINTEL ■	960-2222
# San Marino (CC) ♦	172-1022
# Slovak Republic (CC)	00-421-00112
# Slovenia	080-8808
# Spain (CC)	900-99-0014
# Sweden (CC) ♦	020-795-922
# Switzerland (CC) ♦	0800-89-0222
# Turkey (CC) ♦	00-8001-1177
# Ukraine (CC) ÷	8▼10-013
# United Kingdom (CC)	
To call using BT ■	0800-89-0222
To call using C&W ■	0500-89-0222
# Vatican City (CC)	172-1022

Or pounds for London. Or Deutschmarks for Düsseldorf. Or any of 75 foreign currencies. Call **Chase Currency To Go**[SM] at **935-9935** in area codes 212, 718, 914, 516 and Rochester, N.Y.; all other area codes call 1-800-935-9935. We'll deliver directly to your door.* Overnight. And there are no exchange fees. Let Chase make your trip an easier one.

CHASE. The right relationship is everything.[SM]

3

Opera and Ballet

The Czech Republic has a strong operatic tradition, and performances at the **Národní divadlo** (National Theater; ⊠ Národní třída 2, ☎ 02/2421–5001) and the **Statní Opera Praha** (State Opera House; ⊠ Wilsonova 4, ☎ 02/265–353), near the top of Wenceslas Square, can be excellent. It's always worthwhile to buy a cheap ticket (for as little as 30 Kč) just to take a look at these stunning 19th-century halls. Now, unlike during the Communist period, operas are almost always sung in their original tongue, and the repertoire offers plenty of Italian favorites and the Czech national composers Janáček, Dvořák, and Smetana. These two theaters also often stage ballets. The historic **Stavovské divadlo** (Estates' Theater; ⊠ Ovocný trh. 1, ☎ 02/2421–5001), where *Don Giovanni* premiered in the 18th century, plays host to a mix of operas and dramatic works. Simultaneous translation into English via a microwave transmitter and headsets is sometimes offered at drama performances. Appropriate attire is recommended for all venues; the National and Estates' theaters instituted a "no jeans" rule in 1998.

Puppet Shows

This traditional form of Czech popular entertainment has been given ○ new life thanks to the productions mounted at the **Národní divadlo marionet** (National Marionette Theater; ⊠ Žatecká 1, ☎ 02/232–2536) and **Divadlo v Celetné** (⊠ Celetná 17, ☎ 02/232–6843). Children and adults alike can enjoy the hilarity and pathos of these performances; one long-running show was a version of *Don Giovanni*.

Theater

A dozen or so professional theater companies play in Prague to ever-packed houses; the language barrier can't obscure the players' artistry. Tourist-friendly, nonverbal theater abounds as well, notably "Black Light Theater," a melding of live acting, mime, video, and stage trickery, which continues to draw crowds despite signs of fatigue. The famous **Laterna Magika** (Magic Lantern) puts on a similar extravaganza (⊠ Národní třída 4, ☎ 02/2491–4129). Performances usually begin at 7 or 7:30 PM. The popular **Archa Theater** (⊠ Na Poříčí 26, ☎ 02/232–8800) offers avant-garde and experimental theater, music, and dance and has hosted world-class visiting ensembles such as the Royal Shakespeare Company. Several English-language theater groups operate sporadically; pick up a copy of the *Prague Post* for complete listings.

OUTDOOR ACTIVITIES AND SPORTS

Fitness Clubs

The best fitness clubs in the city are at the **Forum Hotel** (⊠ Kongresova ul. 1, ☎ 02/6119–1111; Vyšehrad metro station), which has a well-equipped weight room and a pool; the more centrally located **Hilton Hotel** (⊠ Pobřežní 1, ☎ 02/2484–1111; Florenc metro station) with its lap pool and weight machines; and the much less costly **Axa** hotel (⊠ Na Poříčí 40). All three are open to nonguests, but call first to inquire about rates.

Golf

You can golf year-round, weather permitting, at Prague's only course, located in the western suburbs at the **Hotel Golf** (⊠ Plzeňská ul. 215, ☎ 02/523251). Take a taxi to the hotel or Tram 4, 7, or 9 from metro station Anděl to the Hotel Golf stop.

Jogging

The best place for jogging is the **Letenské sady,** the large park east of the Royal Garden at Prague Castle, across Chotkova street. Cross the Svatopluka Čecha Bridge, climb the stairs, and turn to the right for a

good, long run far away from the car fumes. For safety's sake, unac-
companied women should avoid the more obscure corners of this
park. The **Riegrový sady,** a park in Vinohrady behind the main train
station, is also nice, but it is small and a bit out of the way.

Spectator Sports

Prague plays host to a wide variety of spectator sports, including
world-class ice hockey, soccer, and tennis. The best place to find out
what's going on (and where) is the weekly sports page of the *Prague
Post,* or you can inquire at your hotel.

Soccer
National and international matches are played regularly at the Sparta
Stadium in Letná, behind the Letenské sady (☞ Jogging, *above*). To
reach the stadium, take Tram 1, 25, or 26 to the Sparta stop. Prague's
other first-division clubs are Slavia, whose Slavia Stadium is in the
Vršovice neighborhood (Prague 10), and Victoria Žižkov, who play in
a tiny park in the working-class Žižkov quarter.

Swimming
The best public swimming pool in Prague is at the **Podolí Swimming
Stadium** in Podolí, easily reached in 15 minutes or less from the city
center via Tram 3 or 17 to the Kublov stop. The indoor pool is 50 m
long, and the complex also includes two open-air pools, a sauna, a steam
bath, and a wild-ride water slide. (A word of warning: Podolí, for all
its attractions, is notorious as a local hot spot of petty thievery; don't
entrust any valuables to the lockers—it's best either to check them in
the safe with the *vrátnice* [superintendent], or better yet, don't bring
them at all.) The pool at the **Hilton Hotel** (☞ Fitness Clubs, *above*) is
smaller, but the location is more convenient. Another pool to try is in
the **Hotel Olšanka** (✉ Táboritská 23, ☎ 6709–2202).

Tennis
There are public courts at the **Strahov Stadium** in Břevnov. Take Bus
176 from Karlovo náměstí in the New Town, or Bus 143 from the Dejvická metro station (Line A) to the Stadion Strahov stop. The **Hilton
Hotel** (☞ Fitness Clubs, *above*) has two indoor courts available for public use.

SHOPPING

Despite the relative shortage of quality clothes—Prague has a long way
to go before it can match shopping meccas Paris and Rome—the capital is a great place to pick up gifts and souvenirs. Bohemian crystal
and porcelain deservedly enjoy a worldwide reputation for quality, and
plenty of shops offer excellent bargains. The local market for antiques
and artworks is still relatively undeveloped, while dozens of antiquarian bookstores can yield some excellent finds, particularly German and Czech books and graphics.

Shopping Districts

The major shopping areas are **Národní třída,** running past Můstek to
Na Příkopě, and the area around **Old Town Square. Pařižská ulice,
Karlova ulice** (on the way to the Charles Bridge), and the area just south
of the **Jewish Quarter** are also good places to find boutiques and antiques shops. In the Malá Strana, try **Nerudova ulice,** the street that
runs up to the Castle Hill district.

Department Stores

These are not always well stocked and often have everything except the one item you're looking for, but a stroll through one may yield some interesting finds and bargains. **Bilá Labuť** (✉ Na poříčí 23, ☎ 02/2481–1364) has a decent selection, but the overall shabbiness harkens back to socialist times. **Kotva** (✉ Nám. Republiky 8, ☎ 02/2480–1111) is comparatively upscale; it's got a nice stationery shop and a basement supermarket with good wine and cheese sections. **Krone**'s (✉ Václavské nám. 21, ☎ 02/2423–0477) main virtues are its basement supermarket and its location near the Mustek metro. Otherwise it is cramped and poorly stocked, with a bewildering layout to boot. **Tesco** (✉ Národní třída 26, ☎ 02/2200–3111) is generally the best place for one-stop shopping—especially if you're caving in to homesickness. It's got same-day film developing, a news agent stocking English-language newspapers and magazines, American-brand toiletries, a supermarket with Western groceries (if you're dying for corn chips, you'll find them here), and a multilingual staff.

Street Markets

For fruits and vegetables, the best street market in central Prague is on **Havelská ulice** in the Old Town. You'll need to arrive early in the day if you want something a bit more exotic than tomatoes and cucumbers. The best market for nonfood items is the flea market in **Holešovice**, north of the city center, although there isn't really much of interest here outside of cheap tobacco and electronics products. Take the metro Line C to the Vltavská station and then ride any tram heading east (running to the left as you exit the metro station). Exit at the first stop and follow the crowds.

Specialty Stores

Antiques

For antiques connoisseurs, Prague can be a bit of a letdown. Even in comparison with other former Communist capitals like Budapest, the choice of antiques in Prague might seem depressingly slim, as the city lacks large stores with a diverse selection of goods. The typical Prague *Starožitnosti* (antiques shop) tends to be a small, one-room jumble shop selling old glass and bric-a-brac. The good ones distinguish themselves by focusing on one particular specialty. On the pricey end of the scale is the Prague affiliate of the Austrian **Dorotheum** auction house (✉ Havelsk 19, ☎ 02/2489–2921) in the Old Town. It is an elegant pawnshop that specializes in small things: jewelry, porcelain knickknacks, and standing clocks as well as the odd military sword. The small **JHB Starožitnosti** (✉ Panská 1, ☎ 02/261–425) in the New Town is the place for old clocks: everything from rococo to Empire standing clocks and Bavarian cuckoo clocks. The shop also has a wide array of antique pocket watches. **Nostalgie Antique** (✉ Jánský Vršek 8, ☎ 02/532–628) specializes in old textiles and jewelry. Most of the textiles are pre–World War II and include clothing, table linens, curtains, hats, and laces. **Papillio** (✉ Ungelt 1, ☎ 02/2489–5454), in the courtyard behind Tyn church, is probably one of the best antiques shops in Prague, offering furniture, paintings, and especially museum-quality antique glass. Here you can find colorful Biedermeier goblets by Moser and wonderful Art Nouveau Loetz vases, as well as French glass by Émile Gallé. **Zlatnictvi** (✉ Vomáčka Ná prstkova 9, ☎ 02/295–2525) is a jumble shop that redeems itself with its selection of old jewelry in a broad price range, including rare Art Nouveau rings and antique garnet brooches. In the shop's affiliate next door, jewelry is repaired, cleaned, and made to order.

Art Galleries

The best galleries in Prague are quirky and eclectic affairs, places to sift through artworks rather than browse at arms' length. Many galleries are also slightly off the beaten track and away from the main tourist thoroughfares. Prague's as-yet-untouristed Novy Svět neighborhood is something of a miniature artist's quarter and home to two of Prague's more interesting galleries. One is **Galerie Gambra** (✉ Černinska 5, ☎ 02/2051–4527), owned by the surrealist animator Jan Švankmayer. The space was originally Švankmayer's kitchen, where dissident surrealists used to gather and trade ideas; now the gallery displays Švankmayer's bizarre collages as well as his wife's anthropomorphic ceramics. Books and magazines focusing on Czech surrealist art are also for sale. There's also **Galerie Novy Svět** (✉ Novy Svě 5, ☎ 02/2051–4611), a small gallery displaying interesting paintings and drawings by somewhat obscure Czech artists, as well as ceramics, glass, and art books.

At the higher end is **Galerie Lichtenfels** (✉ Michalská 12, ☎ 02/2422–7680) in the Old Town, which specializes in modern Czech art. Paintings, prints, and drawings crowd the walls and are propped against glass cases and window sills. Rifle through works by Czech Cubists, currently fetching high prices at international auctions. **Galerie Litera** (✉ Karlinske námešsti 13, ☎ 02/231–7195) is in Karlín, a neighborhood rarely set foot in by tourists—it's not rough but pretty seedy. (It's northeast of the city center; get off at Florenc metro station and walk five minutes up Sokolovská.) Most of the gallery space is given over to temporary shows of unique, high-quality graphics. There are also some lovely ceramics as well as a refined selection of antiquarian art books.

Books and Prints

By the same token as antiques shops, Prague's rare book shops, or *antikvariáts,* were once part of a massive state-owned consortium that since privatization has split up and diversified. Now, while appealing to varied interests, most shops tend to cultivate their own specialties. Some places do have a small English-language section displaying a motley blend of potboilers, academic texts, classics, and tattered paperbacks; books in German, on the other hand, can be found in abundance.

Antikvariát Karel Křenek (✉ Celetná 31, ☎ 02/231–4734), near the Powder Tower in the Old Town, specializes in books with a humanist slant. It also has a good selection of modern graphics and prides itself on its avant-garde periodicals and journals from the 1920s and '30s. It also has a small collection of English books. **Antikvariát Makovský and Gregor** (✉ Kaprova 9, 02/232–8835) is a great all-around bookstore as attested by the constant traffic of philosophy students from the nearby Charles University. The art section is particularly good hunting ground, where you could turn up the memoirs of Casanova with illustrations by Aubrey Beardsley or a book on Leni Reifenstahl's mountaineering movies. If you'd just like a good read, be sure to check out the **Globe Bookstore and Coffeehouse** (✉ Janovského 14, ☎ 02/6671–2610), which is a magnet for the local English-speaking community.

U Karlova Mostu (✉ Karlova ul. 2, Staré Město, ☎ 02/2422–9205) is the preeminent Prague bookstore. In a suitably bookish location opposite the National Library, it's the place to go if you are looking for that elusive 15th-century manuscript. In addition to housing ancient books too precious to be leafed through, the store has a good selection of books on local subjects, a small foreign-language section, and a host of prints, maps, drawings, and paintings. **U Knihomola Book-**

store and Café (✉ Mánesova 79, ☎ 02/627–7770) is a close contender to the Globe for the best place to find the latest in English literature; it also stocks the best selection of new English-language art books and guidebooks. It's near the metro stop Jiřího z Poděbrad.

Glass

Glass has traditionally been Bohemia's biggest export, and it was one of the few products manufactured during communist times that managed to retain an artistically innovative spirit. Today Prague has plenty of shops selling Bohemian glass, much of it tourist kitsch. A good spot for traditional glass is the stylish **Galerie A** (✉ Na Perštýné, ☎ 02/261–334), which stocks Art Nouveau, Biedermeier, and medieval replica glass in Art Deco vitrines from the 1920s. For purely artistic glass check out **Galerie Mozart** (✉ Platyz 1, ☎ 02/2421–1127), off Národní Třidda, which offers glass sculptures as well as some colorful vases and bowls. Much more contemporary and decidedly less practical is **Galerie 'Z'** (✉ U luzickeho semináře 7, 02/2161–1555), which sells limited-edition mold-melted and blown glass. **Moser** (✉ Na Příkopě 12, ☎ 02/2421–1293), the flagship store for the world-famous Karlovy Vary glassmaker, offers the widest selection of traditional glass. Even if you're not in the market to buy, stop by the store simply to look at the elegant wood-paneled salesrooms on the second floor. The staff will gladly pack goods for traveling.

Home Design

Czech design is wonderfully rich both in quality and imagination, emphasizing old-fashioned craftsmanship while often taking an off-beat, even humorous approach. Strained relations between Czech designers and producers has reined in the potential selection, but there are nevertheless a handful of places showcasing Czech work. **Fast** (✉ Sázavská 32, Vinohrady, ☎ 02/242–50538) is a little bit off the beaten track but worth the trek. Besides ultramodern furniture, there are ingenious (and more portable) pens, binders, and other office accoutrements. **Genia Loci** (✉ Ujezd 11, ☎ 02/539–468) is one of Prague's hippest design shops; you can find irreverent things like a Kafka-themed coffee service. The shop also has a good selection of Czech architecture and design magazines. **Tekton Gallery** (✉ Truhlářska 20, ☎ 02/231–7743) is a father-and-son operation focusing exclusively on Czech-made furniture. Look for Jaroslav Dubsky's intaglio jewelry cases with inset gemstones.

Jewelry

Alfons Mucha is perhaps most famous for his whiplash Art Nouveau posters, but he also designed furniture, lamps, clothing, and jewelry. **Art Décoratif** (✉ U Obecního domu, ☎ 02/2200–2350), right next door to the Art Nouveau Obecní Dum, sells Mucha-inspired designs—the jewelry is especially remarkable. The Old Town's **Granát** (✉ Dlouhá 30, ☎ 02/231–5612) has a comprehensive selection of garnet jewelry, plus contemporary and traditional pieces set in gold and silver. **Hlada** (✉ Karlova 25, ☎ 02/24238928) offers sleek, Czech-designed silver jewelry; an affiliate shop at Na Příkopé 16 specializes in gold, diamonds, and pearls.

Marionettes

Marionettes have a long tradition in Bohemia, going back to the times when traveling troupes used to entertain children with morality plays on town squares. Now, while this art form survives, it's become yet another tourist lure; you'll continually stumble across stalls selling hand-carved marionettes. However, the marionettes at **Manhartský Dùm** (✉ Celetná 7, ☎ 02/2480–9156) are the real thing. These puppets—knights, princesses, and cloven-hoofed devils—are made by the same

artists who work for the Theater Institute. Prices may be higher than
for the usual stuff on the street, but the craftsmanship is well worth it.

Museum Shops

In general, Prague's museum shops are nothing to write home about.
At the **Museum of Decorative Arts** (☞ Staré Město [the Old Town] *in*
Exploring Prague, *above*) you can find replicas of classic glass and porcelain, as well as a limited but thoughtful selection of books and postcards. Perhaps the best place for art souvenirs is **Museum Shop** (⊠ U
Havličkových Sadů 11, ☎ 02/2425–3777), which has a fine selection
of Czech-related art books, sgraffito mugs, ties and scarves patterned
with facsimiles of Prague Castle grillwork and Czech Art Deco motifs,
Prague jigsaw puzzles, and other fun knickknacks.

Musical Instruments

Melodia (⊠ Jungmannova nám. 17, ☎ 02/2422–2500) carries a complete range of quality musical instruments at reasonable prices. **Capric-
cio** (⊠ Újezd 15, ☎ 02/532507) is a great place to find sheet music of
all kinds.

Food

Specialty food stores have been slow to catch on in Prague. **Fruits de
France** (⊠ Jindřišská 9, Nové Město, ☎ 02/2422–0304) stocks Prague's
freshest fruits and vegetables imported directly from France at Western prices. The bakeries at the **Krone** and **Kotva** department stores sell
surprisingly delicious breads and pastries. Both stores also have large,
well-stocked basement grocery stores.

Fun Things for Children

Nearly every stationery store has beautiful watercolor and colored-chalk
sets available at rock-bottom prices. The Czechs are also master illus-
trators, and the books they've made for young "pre-readers" are some
of the world's loveliest. For delightful wooden toys, look in at **Obchod
Vším Možným** (⊠ Nerudova 45, ☎ 02/536941). **Object** (⊠ U lužického semináře 19, ☎ 02/900–5544) also stocks wooden toys as well
as handsome art and school supplies. For older children and teens, it's
worth considering a Czech or Eastern European watch, telescope, or
set of binoculars. The quality/price ratio is unbeatable.

Sports Equipment

Sport Centrum (⊠ Revoluční 1, ☎ 02/2180–3311) is a sprawling
shop selling everything from ski-equipment to climbing gear.

SIDE TRIP TO THE
BOHEMIAN SPA TOWNS

Until World War II, western Bohemia was the playground of Central
Europe's rich and famous. Its three well-known spas, Karlovy Vary,
Mariánské Lázně, and Františkový Lázně (better known by their German names: Karlsbad, Marienbad, and Franzensbad, respectively),
were the annual haunts of everybody who was anybody—Johann
Wolfgang von Goethe, Ludwig van Beethoven, Karl Marx, and England's
King Edward VII, to name but a few. Although strictly "proletarian-
ized" in the Communist era, the spas still exude a nostalgic aura of a
more elegant past and, unlike most of Bohemia, offer a basic tourist
infrastructure that makes dining and lodging a pleasure.

For price range information, *see* Dining *and* Lodging *in* Pleasures and
Pastimes, *above*.

*Numbers in the margin correspond to numbers on the Western Bohemia
map.*

Western Bohemia

Karlovy Vary

★ ⑥⑤ *132 km (79 mi) due west on Route 6 (E48) from Prague. By car the trip takes about two hours.*

Karlovy Vary, better known outside the Czech Republic by its German name, Karlsbad, is the most famous Bohemian spa. It is named for Emperor Charles (Karl) IV, who allegedly happened upon the springs in 1358 while on a hunting expedition. As the story goes, the emperor's hound—chasing a harried stag—fell into a boiling spring and was scalded. Charles had the water tested and, familiar with spas in Italy, ordered baths to be established in the village of Vary. The spa reached its heyday in the 19th century, when royalty came here from all over Europe for treatment. The long list of those who "took the cure" includes Goethe (no fewer than 13 times, according to a plaque on one house in the Old Town), Schiller, Beethoven, and Chopin. Even Karl Marx, when he wasn't decrying wealth and privilege, spent time at the resort and wrote some of *Das Kapital* here between 1874 and 1876.

The shabby streets of modern Karlovy Vary, though, are vivid reminders that those glory days are long over. Aside from a few superficial changes, the Communists made little new investment in the town for 40 years; many of the buildings are crumbling behind their beautiful facades. Today officials face the daunting tasks of financing the town's reconstruction and carving out a new role for Karlovy Vary, in an era when few people can afford to set aside weeks or months at a time for a leisurely cure. To raise some quick cash, many sanatoriums have turned to offering short-term accommodations to foreign visitors (at rather expensive rates). It's even possible at some spas to receive "treatment," including carbon-dioxide baths and massage. For most visitors, though, it's enough simply to stroll the streets and parks and allow the eyes to feast awhile on the splendors of the past.

Whether you're arriving by bus, train, or car, your first view of the town on the approach from Prague will be of the ugly new section on the banks of the Ohře River. Don't despair: Continue along the main road—following the signs to the Grandhotel Pupp—until you reach the lovely main street of the older spa area, situated gently astride the banks of the little Teplá River. The walk from the New Town to the spa area is about 20 minutes; take a taxi if you're carrying a heavy load. The **Historická čtvrt** (Historic District) is still largely intact. Tall 19th-century houses, boasting decorative and often eccentric facades, line the spa's proud, if dilapidated, streets. Throughout you'll see colonnades full of the healthy and the not so healthy sipping the spa's hot sulfuric water from odd pipe-shaped drinking cups. At night the streets fill with steam escaping from cracks in the earth, giving the town a slightly macabre feel.

Karlovy Vary's jarringly modern **Vřídlo** (Vřídlo Colonnade), home of the spring of the same name, is the town's hottest and most dramatic spring. The Vřídlo is indeed unique, shooting its scalding water to a height of some 40 ft. Walk inside the arcade to watch the hundreds of patients here take the famed Karlsbad drinking cure. You'll recognize them promenading somnambulistically up and down, eyes glazed, clutching a drinking glass filled periodically at one of the five "sources." The waters are said to be especially effective against diseases of the digestive and urinary tracts. They're also good for the gout-ridden (which probably explains the spa's former popularity with royals!). If you want to join the crowds and take a sip, you can buy your own spouted cup from vendors within the colonnade.

Walk in the direction of the New Town, past the wooden **Tržni kolonáda** (Market Colonnade). Continue down the winding street until you reach the **Mlýnská kolonáda** (Mill Colonnade). This neo-Renaissance pillared hall, built in 1871–81, offers four springs bearing the romantic names of Rusalka, Libussa, Prince Wenceslas, and Millpond. If you continue down the valley, you'll soon arrive at the very elegant **Sádová kolonáda** (Park Colonnade), a white wrought-iron construction built in 1882 by the Viennese architectural duo of Fellner and Helmer, who sprinkled the Austro-Hungarian Empire with many such edifices during the late 19th century and who also designed the town's theater (1886), the Market Colonnade (1883), and one of the old bathhouses (1895), now a casino.

The 20th century emerges at its most disturbing a little farther along the valley across the river, in the form of the huge, bunkerlike **Thermal Hotel,** built in the late 1960s. Although the building is a monstrosity, the view of Karlovy Vary from the rooftop pool is nothing short of spectacular. (The pool is open from 8 AM to 8 PM.) Even if you don't feel like a swim, it's worth taking the winding road up to the baths for the view. ⊠ *I.P. Pavlova.*

The **Imperial** (Imperial Sanatorium) is a perfect example of turn-of-the-century architecture, with its white facade and red-roofed tower. The Imperial was once the haunt of Europe's wealthiest financiers. Under the Communists, though, the sanatorium was used to house visiting Soviet dignitaries—a gesture of "friendship" from the Czech government. The Imperial has recently reopened as a private hotel, but it will be many years before it can again assume its former role. ⊠ *Libušina 18.*

Across the little Gogol Bridge, you'll find the steep road **Zámecký vrch,** which will lead you to a handful of other sights. Walk uphill until you come to the redbrick **Kostel sv. Lukáše** (Victorian Church) at the intersection of Zámecký vrch and Petra Velikeho; it was once used by the local English community. A few blocks farther along Petra Velikeho street, you'll come to a splendid **Kostel sv. Petra a Pavla** (Russian Orthodox church), once visited by Czar Peter the Great. Return to the English church and take a sharp right uphill on the redbrick road. Then turn left onto a footpath through the woods, following the signs to **Jeleni Skok** (Stag's Leap). After a while you'll see steps leading up to a bronze statue of a deer towering over the cliffs, the symbol of Karlovy Vary. From here a winding path leads up to **Altán Jeleni Skok**, a little red gazebo opening onto a fabulous panorama of the town.

NEED A BREAK?	Reward yourself for making the climb to Stag's Leap with a light meal at the nearby restaurant **Jeleni Skok.** You may have to pay an entrance fee if there is a live band (but you'll also get the opportunity to polka). If you don't want to walk up, you can drive up a signposted road from the Victorian church.

The **Grandhotel Pupp** (☞ Dining and Lodging, *below*), perched on the edge of the spa district, is the former favorite of the Central European nobility. The Pupp's reputation was tarnished somewhat during the years of Communist rule (the hotel was renamed the Moskva-Pupp), but the hotel's former grandeur is still in evidence. Even if you're not staying here, be sure to stroll around the impressive facilities and have a drink in the elegant cocktail bar.

Diagonally across from the Grandhotel Pupp (☞ *above*), behind a little park, is the pompous Fellner and Helmer **Imperial Spa,** now known as **Lázně I** and housing the local casino. If you walk back toward the town center along the river on Stará louka, you'll pass a variety of interesting stores, including the Moser glass store and the Elefant, one of the last of a dying breed of sophisticated coffeehouses in the Czech Republic.

To the right of the Vřídlo Colonnade (☞ *above*) are steps up to the white **Kostel svatej Maři Magdaleny** (Church of Mary Magdalene). Designed by Kilian Dientzenhofer (architect of the two St. Nicholas churches in Prague), this church is the best of the few Baroque buildings still standing in Karlovy Vary. ⊠ *Moravská ul.,* ☎ *no phone.* ☉ *Weekends 10–5.*

Dining and Lodging

$$$ ✕ **Embassy.** This cozy, sophisticated wine restaurant, conveniently located near the Grandhotel Pupp, serves an innovative menu: Tagliatelle with smoked salmon in cream sauce makes an excellent main course, as does roast duck with cabbage and dumplings. Highlights of the varied dessert menu include plum dumplings with *fromage blanc* (a soft, fresh cream cheese). On the wine list, look for Czech wines like Rulandské bílé and Ryzlink Rýnský. ⊠ *Nová Louka 21,* ☎ *017/322–3049,* FAX *017/322–3146. AE, DC, MC, V.*

$$ ✕ **Karel IV.** Its location atop an old castle not far from the Market colon-★ nade affords diners the best view in town. Good renditions of traditional Czech standbys—*bramborák* (potato pancake) and chicken breast with peaches—are served in small, secluded dining areas that are particularly intimate after sunset. ⊠ *Zámecký vrch 2,* ☎ *017/322–7255. AE, MC.*

$$$$ 🏨 **Dvořák.** Consider a splurge here if you're longing for Western stan-★ dards of service and convenience. Opened in late 1990, this Austrian-owned hotel occupies three renovated town houses that are just a five-minute walk from the main spas. The staff is helpful, and the rooms are spotlessly clean. If possible, request a room with a bay-window view of the town. Breakfast is included. ⊠ *Nová Louka 11, 360 21,* ☎ *017/*

322–4145, ℻ *017/322–2814. 87 rooms. Restaurant, café, pool, beauty salon, massage, sauna, exercise room. AE, DC, MC, V.*

$$$–$$$$ 🏨 **Grandhotel Pupp.** This enormous 300-year-old hotel is one of
★   Karlovy Vary's landmarks—it's also one of Central Europe's most fa-
mous resorts. Standards and service slipped under the Communists (when
the hotel was known as the Moskva-Pupp), but the highly professional
management has more than made up for the decades of neglect. Ask
for a room furnished in 19th-century period style. The food in the ground-
floor restaurant is decent, but it's the elegant setting that makes the
hotel worth a splurge. Every July, the Pupp becomes a temporary
home base for international movie stars who come to the Karlovy Vary
International Film Festival. (The adjacent Parkhotel Pupp, under the
same management, is an affordable alternative to the Grandhotel.) Break-
fast is included. ✉ *Mírové nám. 2, 360 91,* ☎ *017/310–9111,* ℻ *017/
310–9620 or 017/322–4032. 214 rooms, 10 suites. 4 restaurants,
lounge, sauna, exercise room, 2 nightclubs. AE, DC, MC, V.*

$$$ 🏨 **Elwa.** Renovations have successfully integrated modern comforts into
this older, elegant spa resort located midway between the Old and New
Towns. Modern features include clean, comfortable rooms (most with
television) with contemporary furnishings like overstuffed chairs.
There's also an on-site fitness center. Breakfast is included. ✉ *Zahradní
29, 360 21,* ☎ *017/322–8472,* ℻ *017/322–8473. 30 rooms. Restaurant, bar, beauty salon, health club. AE, DC, MC, V.*

Nightlife and the Arts

In Karlovy Vary, the action centers on the two nightclubs of the **Grandhotel Pupp** (☞ Dining and Lodging, *above*). The "little dance hall" is
open daily 8 PM–1 AM. The second club is open Wednesday through
Sunday 7 PM–3 AM; it spins pop music. **Club Propaganda** (✉ Jaltska
7, ☎ no phone) is Karlovy Vary's best venue for live rock and new music.

Shopping

In western Bohemia, Karlovy Vary is best known to glass enthusiasts
as home of **Moser** (✉ Tržiště 7, ☎ 017/323–5303), one of the world's
leading producers of crystal and decorative glassware. A number of
outlets for lesser-known, although also high-quality, makers of glass
and porcelain can also be found along Stará Louka.

For excellent buys in porcelain, try **Karlovarský porcelán** (✉ Tržiště
27, ☎ 017/322–5660).

A cheaper but nonetheless unique gift from Karlovy Vary would be a
bottle of the ubiquitous bittersweet (and potent) **Becherovka,** a liqueur
produced by the town's own Jan Becher distillery. Another neat gift
would be one of the pipe-shaped ceramic drinking cups used to take
the drinking cure at spas; you can find them at the colonnades in
Karlovy Vary and Mariánské Lázně. You can also buy boxes of tasty
Oplatky wafers, sometimes covered with chocolate, at shops in all of
the spa towns.

Františkovy Lázně

🔤 *6 km (4 mi) from Cheb, 40 km (25 mi) west of Karlovy Vary.*

Františkovy Lázně, or Franzensbad, the smallest of the three main Bohemian spas, isn't really in the same league as the other two (Karlovy
Vary and Mariánské Lázně). Built on a more modest scale at the start
of the 19th century, the town's ubiquitous kaiser-yellow buildings
have been prettified after their neglect under the previous regime and
now present cheerful facades, almost too bright for the few strollers.
The poorly kept parks and the formal yet human-scale neoclassical ar-

chitecture retain much of their former charm. Overall, a pleasing tor-
por reigns in Františkovy Lázně. There is no town to speak of, just
Národní ulice, the main street, which leads down into the spa park.
The waters, whose healing properties were already known in the 16th
century, are used primarily for curing infertility—hence the large number of young women wandering the grounds.

The most interesting sight in town may be the small **Lázeňský muzeum**
(Spa Museum), just off Národní ulice. There is a wonderful collection
of spa-related antiques, including copper bathtubs and a turn-of-the-
century exercise bike called a Velotrab. The guest books (*Kurbuch*) provide an insight into the cosmopolitan world of pre–World War I
Central Europe. The book for 1812 contains the entry "Ludwig van
Beethoven, composer from Vienna." ⊠ *Ul. Doktora Pohoreckého 8,*
☎ *0166/542–344.* ⌨ *30 Kč.* ☉ *Oct.–May, weekdays 9–noon and 2–*
5; June–Sept., weekdays 9–noon and 2–5, weekends 9–4.

The main spring, **Františkuv prameň,** is under a little gazebo filled with
brass pipes. The colonnade to the left was decorated with a bust of
Lenin that was replaced in 1990 by a memorial to the American liberation of the town in April 1945. Walk along the path to the left until
you come to the *Lázeňská poliklinika* (spa clinic), where you can arrange for a day's spa treatment for around 350 Kč. ⊠ *Národní ul.*

NEED A BREAK?	Only insipid pop music (the scourge of eating and drinking places everywhere in the country) interrupts the cheerful atmosphere of the little café of the **Hotel Slovan** on Národní. The tiny gallery and lively frescoes make it a great spot for cake, coffee, or drinks.

Dining and Lodging

$$$ ✕⌨ **Slovan.** This gracious place is the perfect complement to this re-
★ laxed little town. The eccentricity of the original turn-of-the-century
design survived a thorough renovation during the 1970s; the airy
rooms are clean and comfortable, and some have a balcony over-
looking the main street. The main-floor restaurant serves above-aver-
age Czech dishes such as tasty *svíčková* (beef sirloin in a citrusy cream
sauce); consider a meal here even if you're staying elsewhere. ⊠
Národní 5, 35101, ☎ *0166/542–841,* ⌷ *0166/542–843. 25 rooms,*
19 with bath. Restaurant, bar, café. DC, V.

$$$ ⌨ **Centrum.** Renovations have left the rooms clean and well appointed
if a bit sterile. Still, it is among the best-run hotels in town and only a
short walk from the main park and central spas. ⊠ *Anglická 41, 351*
01, ☎ *0166/543–156 or 543–157,* ⌷ *0166/542–843. 30 rooms.*
Restaurant, bar. MC, V.

$$$ ⌨ **Tři Lilie.** Reopened in 1995 after an expensive refitting, this place once
accommodated the likes of Goethe, Metternich, and Hapsburg emperor
Ferdinand V ("the Benign"). Though too new to have developed a style
of its own, the "Three Lilies" has certainly become the best-equipped
hotel in town. Spa treatments are conducted off-premises. For reserva-
tions, you need to go through the town's spa management. ⊠ *Národní*
3, ☎ *0166/542–415. 31 rooms. Restaurant, brasserie, café. No credit*
cards. Reservations: Obchodní oddělení, Lázně Františkovy Lázně a.s.,
Jiráskova 17, 351 01, ☎ *0166/542–063,* ⌷ *0166/542–970.*

$$ ⌨ **Bajkal.** This is an offbeat, older hotel with acceptably clean rooms
and a friendly staff. It is on the far side of the park from the main spas,
roughly a 10-minute walk from the city center. The travel agency in
the building also books private accommodations. ⊠ *Americká ul. 84/*
4, 351 01, ☎ *0166/542–501,* ⌷ *0166/542–503. 25 rooms, 17 with*
bath. Restaurant. V.

Mariánské Lázně

★ ⑥⑥ *47 km (29 mi) south of Karlovy Vary.*

Your expectations of what a spa resort should be may come nearest to full reality here. It's far larger and better maintained than Františkovy Lázně and is greener and quieter than Karlovy Vary (☞ *above*). This was the spa favored by Britain's Edward VII; Goethe and Chopin, among other luminaries, also repaired here frequently. Mark Twain, on a visit to the spa in 1892, labeled the town a "health factory" and couldn't get over how new everything looked. Indeed, at that time everything was new. The sanatoriums, all built in the middle of the 19th century in a confident, outrageous mixture of "neo" styles, fan out impressively around a finely groomed oblong park. Cure takers and curiosity seekers alike parade through the two stately colonnades, both placed near the top of the park. Buy a spouted drinking cup (available at the colonnades) and join the rest of the sippers taking the drinking cure. Be forewarned, though: The waters from the Rudolph, Ambrose, and Caroline springs, though harmless, all have a noticeable diuretic effect. For this reason they're used extensively in treating disorders of the kidney and bladder. Several spa hotels offer more extensive treatment, including baths and massage. Prices are usually reckoned in U.S. dollars or German marks. For more information, inquire at the main spa offices (⊠ Masarykova 22, ☎ 0165/623–061). A stay in Mariánské Lázně, however, can be healthful even without special treatment. Special walking trails of all difficulty levels surround the resort in all directions. The best advice is simply to put on comfortable shoes, buy a hiking map, and head out. One of the country's few golf courses lies 3 or 4 km (2 or 3 mi) from town to the east. Hotels can also help to arrange special activities, such as tennis and horseback riding. For the less intrepid, a simple stroll around the gardens, with a few deep breaths of the town's famous air, is enough to restore a healthy sense of perspective.

Dining and Lodging

$$ ✕ **Filip.** This bustling wine bar is where locals come to find relief from the sometimes large horde of tourists. A tasty selection of traditional Czech dishes—mainly pork, grilled meats, and steaks—is served by a friendly and efficient staff. ⊠ *Poštovní 96,* ☎ *0165/626–161. No credit cards.*

$$ ✕ **Koliba.** This combination hunting lodge and wine tavern, set in the
★ woods roughly 20 minutes on foot from the spas, is an excellent alternative to the hotel restaurants in town. Grilled meats and shish kebabs, plus tankards of Moravian wine (try the cherry-red Rulandské Červené), are served with traditional gusto. ⊠ *Dusíkova, Route 24 in direction of Karlovy Vary,* ☎ *0165/90144. AE, DC, MC, V.*

The best place to look for private lodgings is along Paleckého ulice and Hlavní třída, south of the main spa area. Private accommodations can also be found in the neighboring villages of Zádub and Závišín and along roads in the woods to the east of Mariánské Lázně.

$$$$ 🏨 **Excelsior.** This lovely older hotel is on the main street and is convenient to the spas and colonnade. Rooms have traditional cherrywood furniture and marble bathrooms, and the views over the town are enchanting. The staff is friendly and multi-lingual. While the food in the adjoining restaurant is only average, the romantic setting provides adequate compensation. ⊠ *Hlavní tř. 121, 353 01,* ☎ *0165/622–705,* FAX *0165/625–346. 64 rooms. Restaurant, café. AE, DC, MC, V.*

$$$$ 🏨 **Hotel Golf.** Book in advance to secure a room at this stately villa situated 3½ km (2 mi) out of town on the road to Karlovy Vary. A major renovation in the 1980s left the large, open rooms with a cheery, modern look. The restaurant on the main floor is excellent, but the big draw

is the 18-hole golf course on the premises, one of the few in the Czech Republic. ⊠ *Zádub 55, 353 01,* ☎ *0165/622–651 or 0165/622–652,* FAX *0165/622655. 25 rooms. Restaurant, pool, 18-hole golf course, tennis court. AE, DC, MC, V.*

$$$ 🏨 **Bohemia.** At this spa resort, beautiful crystal chandeliers in the
★   main hall set the stage for a comfortable and elegant stay. The crisp beige-and-white rooms let you spread out and *really* unpack; they're spacious and high-ceilinged. (If you want to be really decadent, request one of the enormous suites overlooking the park). The helpful staff can arrange spa treatments and horseback riding. ⊠ *Hlavní třída 100, 353 01,* ☎ *0165/623–251,* FAX *0165/622–943. 73 rooms, 4 suites. 2 restaurants, café. AE, DC, MC, V.*

Nightlife and the Arts

Mariánske Lázně sponsors a **music festival** each June, with numerous concerts featuring Czech and international composers and orchestras. The town's annual Chopin festival each autumn brings in fans of the Polish composer's work from around the world.

Mariánské Lázně's **Casino Marienbad** (⊠ Anglická 336, ☎ 0165/ 623–292) is open daily 6 AM–2 AM. For late-night drinks, try the **Hotel Golf** (☞ Dining and Lodging, *above*), which has a good nightclub with dancing in season.

The Bohemian Spa Towns A to Z

Arriving and Departing

Prague is the main gateway to western Bohemia and the spa towns (☞ Arriving and Departing *in* Prague A to Z, *below*). Major trains from Munich and Nürnberg stop at some of the spa towns. It is also an easy drive across the border from Bavaria on the E48 to Cheb and from there to any of the spas.

Getting Around

Good, if slow, train service links all the major towns west of Prague. The best stretches are from Františkovy Lázně to Prague via Plzeň. The Prague–Karlovy Vary run takes far longer than it should but has a romantic charm all its own. Frequent bus service between Prague and Karlovy Vary, by contrast, makes the journey only about two hours each way. Note that most trains heading west to Germany (in the direction of Nürnberg) stop at Mariánské Lázně. Most trains leave from Prague's Hlavní nádraží (main station), but be sure to check on which station if in doubt. If you're driving, take the E48 directly from Prague to Karlovy Vary. Roads in the area tend to be in good condition, though they can sometimes be quite narrow.

Contacts and Resources

EMERGENCIES
Police (☎ 158). **Ambulance** (☎ 155).

GUIDED TOURS
Čedok (☎ 02/2419–7111) offers several specialized tours covering western Bohemia's major sights. Tour "G-O" combines a trip to Lidice in northern Bohemia with a visit to Karlovy Vary. The trip takes a full day and departs three times weekly. Prague departure points are at the Čedok offices at Na Příkopě 18 and Bílkova ulice 6, and the Panorama, Forum, and Hilton hotels.

VISITOR INFORMATION
Karlovy Vary (⊠ Ul. Dr. Bechera 21–23, ☎ 017/22281). **Mariánské Lázně** (⊠ Třebízského 2/101, ☎ 0165/2254; Infocentrum, ⊠ Hlavní 47, ☎ 0165/5330, 0165/5892, 0165/3757).

PRAGUE A TO Z

Arriving and Departing

By Bus

The Czech complex of regional bus lines known collectively as **ČSAD** operates its dense network from the sprawling main bus station on Křižíkova (metro stop: Florenc, Lines B or C). For information about routes and schedules call ☎ 02/1034, consult the confusingly displayed timetables posted at the station, or visit the information window, situated at the bus unloading area, open weekdays 6 AM–7:45 PM, Saturday 6–4, and Sunday 8–6.

By Car

Prague is well served by major roads and highways from anywhere in the country. On arriving in the city, simply follow the signs to CENTRUM (city center). During the day, traffic can be stop-and-go on all approaches to the center. Pay particular attention to the trams, which have the right-of-way in every situation. Note that parts of the historic center of Prague, including Wenceslas Square and Old Town Square, are closed to private vehicles.

Parking is permitted in the center of town on a growing number of streets with parking meters or in the few small lots within walking distance of the historic center. An underground lot is at Náměstí Jana Palacha, near Old Town Square.

By Plane

Ruzyně Airport, 20 km (12 mi) northwest of the downtown area, is small but easily negotiated. Allow yourself plenty of time when departing Prague because the airport is still too small to handle the large numbers of travelers who move through it, and you may encounter long lines at customs and check-in.

ČSA (the Czech national carrier) offers direct flights all over the world from Ruzyně. Major airlines with offices in Prague are **Air France** (☎ 02/2422–7164); **Alitalia** (☎ 02/2481–0079 or 02/232–5966); **Austrian Airlines** (☎ 02/231–1872); **British Airways** (☎ 02/2211–4444); **British Midland** (☎ 02/2423–9280); **ČSA** (☎ 02/2010–4310); **Delta** (☎ 02/2423–3638); **KLM** (☎ 02/2422–8678); **Lufthansa** (☎ 02/2481–1007); **SAS** (☎ 02/2421–4749); and **Swissair** (☎ 02/2481–2111).

BETWEEN THE AIRPORT AND DOWNTOWN

The **Cedaz** minibus shuttle links the airport with Republic Square (just off the Old Town). It runs hourly, more often at peak periods, between 6 AM and 9:30 PM daily and makes an intermediate stop at the Dejvická metro station. The one-way fare is 90 Kč. Regular municipal bus service (Bus 119) also connects the airport and the Dejvická metro stop; the fare is 12 Kč. From Dejvická you can take a subway to the city center. To reach Wenceslas Square, get off at the Můstek station.

Taxis offer the easiest and most convenient way of getting downtown. The trip is a straight shot down Evropská Boulevard and takes approximately 20 minutes. The road is not usually busy, but anticipate an additional 20 minutes during rush hour (7 AM–9 AM and 3 PM–6 PM). The ride costs about 500 Kč.

By Train

International trains arrive at and depart from either the main station, **Hlavní nádraží** (✉ Wilsonova ulice, about 500 yards east of Wenceslas Square); or the suburban **Nádraží Holešovice** (✉ About 2 km/1½ mi north of the city center). This is an unending source of confusion—

always make certain you know which station your train is using. For train times, consult timetables in stations or get in line at the **information offices** (☎ 02/2422–4200, 02/2461–4030, or 02/2461–4031) upstairs at the main station or downstairs near the exits under the ČD Centrum sign. Both offices are open daily 6 AM–10 PM. The **Čedok** office at Na Příkopě 18 (☞ Visitor Information, *below*) also provides train information and issues tickets.

Wenceslas Square is a convenient five-minute walk from the main station, or you can take the subway (Line C) one stop in the Haje direction to Muzeum. A taxi ride from the main station to the center will cost about 100 Kč. To reach the city center from Nádraží Holešovice, take the subway (Line C) four stops to Muzeum. A taxi ride should cost roughly 200 Kč–250 Kč.

Getting Around

To see Prague properly, there is no alternative to walking, especially since much of the city center is off-limits to cars. And the walking couldn't be more pleasant—most of it along the beautiful bridges and cobblestone streets of the city's historic core. Before venturing out, however, be sure you have a good map. The city is divided into 10 administrative districts; Prague 1 and part of Prague 2 lie entirely within the historic center.

By Bus and Tram

Prague's extensive bus and streetcar network allows for fast, efficient travel throughout the city. Tickets are the same as those used for the metro, although you validate them at machines inside the bus or streetcar. Tickets (*jízdenky*) can be bought at hotels, newsstands, and from dispensing machines in the metro stations. The price of a ticket increased in 1998 from 10 Kč to 12 Kč; the tickets permit one hour's travel throughout the metro, tram, and bus network between 5 AM and 8 PM on weekdays, or 90 minutes' travel between 8 PM and midnight and on weekends. You can also buy a one-day pass allowing unlimited use of the system for 70 Kč, a three-day pass for 180 Kč, a seven-day pass for 250 Kč, and a 15-day pass for 280 Kč. The passes can be purchased at the main metro stations and at some newsstands in the center. A pass is not valid until stamped in the orange machines in metro stations or aboard trams *and* the required information is entered on the back (instructions are provided in English). A refurbished old tram, No. 91, plies a route in the Old Town and Lesser Quarter on summer weekends. Trams 50–59 and Buses 500 and above run all night, after the metro shuts down at midnight. All night-tram routes intersect at the corner of Lazarská and Spálená streets in the New Town near the Národní Třída metro station.

By Car

Traveling by car is the easiest and most flexible way of seeing the Czech Republic—other than Prague. If you intend to visit only the capital, you can do without a car. The city center is congested and difficult to navigate, and you'll save yourself a lot of hassle by sticking to public transportation.

A permit is required to drive on expressways and other four-lane highways. They cost 800 Kč and are sold at border crossings, some service stations, and all post offices.

For accidents, call the **emergency number** (☎ 154). In case of breakdown, get in touch with the 24-hour **Yellow Angel** road service (☎ 123 [in some areas, 0123]). Autoturist offices throughout the Czech Republic (main office: ✉ Na Rybníčku 16, ☎ 02/2491–1830) can provide motoring information of all kinds.

PARKING

Parking spaces are scarce in Prague, but parking meters have been installed in the city center, significantly easing the competition. The meters with green stripes let you park up to six hours; an orange stripe means two hours is allowed. (Use change in the meters). Signs with a blue circle outlined in red with a diagonal red slash indicate a no-parking zone. Avoid the blue-marked spaces, which are reserved for local residents. Violaters may find a "boot" immobilizing their vehicle.

ROAD CONDITIONS

The city center is mostly a snarl of traffic, off-limits areas, and tram lines. If you plan to drive outside the capital, there are few four-lane highways, but most of the roads are in reasonably good shape, and traffic is usually light. Roads can be poorly marked, however, so before you start out, buy one of the multilingual, inexpensive auto atlases available at any bookstore.

RULES OF THE ROAD

The Czech Republic follows the usual Continental rules of the road. A right turn on red is permitted only when indicated by a green arrow. Signposts with yellow diamonds indicate a main road where drivers have the right of way. The speed limit is 110 kph (68 mph) on four-lane highways, 90 kph (56 mph) on open roads, and 50 kph (30 mph) in built-up areas. The fine for speeding is 300 Kč, payable on the spot. Seat belts are compulsory, and drinking before driving is absolutely prohibited. Passengers under 12 years of age, or less than 150 cm (5 ft) in height, must ride in the back seat.

By Subway

Prague's subway system, the metro, is clean and reliable; the stations are marked with red "M" signs. Trains run daily from 5 AM to midnight. Validate the tickets at the orange machines before descending the escalators; tickets are valid on trams and buses as well (☞ *above*). Trains are patrolled often; the fine for riding without a valid ticket is 200 Kč. Beware of pickpockets, who often operate in large groups on crowded trams and metro cars.

By Taxi

Dishonest taxi drivers are the shame of the nation. Luckily you probably won't need to rely on taxis for trips within the city center (it's usually easier to walk or take the subway). Typical scams include drivers doctoring the meter or simply failing to turn the meter on and then demanding an exorbitant sum at the end of the ride. In an honest cab, the meter starts at 25 Kč and increases by 17 Kč per km (½ mi) or 2 Kč per minute at rest. (Taxis operating from, but not to, the airport have a monopoly and charge slightly higher rates.) Most rides within town should cost no more than 80 Kč–100 Kč. To minimize the chances of getting ripped off, avoid taxi stands in Wenceslas Square, Old Town Square, and other heavily touristed areas. The best alternative is to phone for a taxi in advance. Some reputable firms are **AAA Taxi** (☎ 02/1080) and **Profitaxi** (☎ 02/1035). Many firms have English-speaking operators.

Contacts and Resources

Car Rentals

The following rental agencies are based in Prague:

Alamo Rent a Car (✉ Revoluční 25, ☎ 231–0122 or 231–6947); **Avis** (✉ Klimentská 46, ☎ 02/2185–1225); **A Rent-A-Car** (✉ Washingtonova 9, ☎ 02/2421–1587 or 02/2422–9848); **Budget** (✉ Hotel

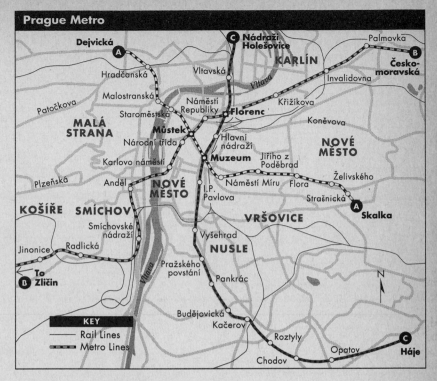

Prague Metro

KEY
—— Rail Lines
▬▬▬ Metro Lines

Inter-Continental, nám. Curieových 5, ☎ 02/2418–0777 or 02/2061–
0095); **Hertz** (✉ Karlovo nám. 28, ☎ 02/291851 or 02/290122).

Embassies

United States (✉ Tržiště 15, Malá Strana, ☎ 02/5732–0663). **United
Kingdom** (✉ Thunovská 14, Malá Strana, ☎ 02/5732–0355). **Canada**
(✉ Mickiewiczova 6, Hradčany, ☎ 02/2431–1108). There are no
Australian or New Zealand embassies.

Emergencies

Police (☎ 158). **Ambulance** (☎ 155). **Medical emergencies: Foreigners' Department of Na Homolce Hospital** (✉ Roentgenova 2, ☎ 02/
5292–2146 weekdays, ☎ 02/5721–1111 or 02/5292–2191 evenings
and weekends); **First Medical Clinic of Prague** (✉ Vyšehradská 35, ☎
02/292–286, 2421–6200, or ☎ 02/0601–225050 24-hr emergency
mobile phone); **American Medical Center** (✉ Janovského 48, ☎ 02/
807–756 weekdays). Be prepared to pay in cash for medical treatment,
whether you are insured or not. **Dentists** (✉ Palackého 5, ☎ 02/2421–
6032 for 24-hr emergency service).

Lost credit cards: American Express (☎ 02/2421–9978 or 02/2421–
9992); **Diners Club, Visa** (☎ 02/2412–5353); **MasterCard** (☎ 02/
2442–3135).

English-Language Bookstores

In the central city these are too numerous to list. *See* Shopping, *above,*
for a few recommended bookstores a bit off the tourist routes. Street
vendors on Wenceslas Square and Na Příkopě carry leading foreign newspapers and periodicals. For hiking maps and auto atlases, try the
downstairs level of the **Jan Kanzelsberger** bookstore on Wenceslas Square
(✉ Václavské nám. 42, ☎ 02/2421–7335).

Guided Tours

Čedok's (☞ Visitor Information, *below*; ☎ 02/231–8255 for tour information) three-hour "Historical Prague" tour, offered year-round, is a combination bus-walking venture that covers all the major sights with commentary in English. It departs daily at 10 AM and 2 PM from the Čedok office at Pařížská 6 (near the Inter-Continental Hotel), and the price is 590 Kč. Between May and October, "Panoramic Prague," an abbreviated version of the above tour, departs Wednesday, Friday, and Saturday at 11 AM from the Čedok office at Na Příkopě 18. The price is 300 Kč. On Friday Čedok also offers "Prague on Foot," a slower-paced, three-hour walking tour that departs at 10 AM from Na Příkopě 18. The price is 300 Kč. More tours are offered, especially in summer, and the above schedule may well vary according to demand. Prices may also go up in high season.

Many private firms now offer combination **bus-walking tours** of the city that typically last two or three hours and cost 300 Kč–400 Kč or more. For more information, check with any of the dozen operators with booths on Wenceslas Square, Old Town Square (near the Jan Hus monument), or Republic Square (near the Obecní Dům).

PERSONAL GUIDES

You can contact the Čedok office at Na Příkopě 18 (☞ Visitor Information, *below*) to arrange a personalized walking tour. Times and itineraries are negotiable; prices start at around 500 Kč per hour.

Late-Night Pharmacies

There are two 24-hour pharmacies close to the city's center, both called **Lékárna** (✉ Štefánikova 6, ☎ 02/537039 or 02/5732–0918; ✉ Belgická 37, ☎ 02/2423–7207 or 02/258189).

Mail

POSTAL RATES

Postcards to the United States and Canada cost 7 Kč; letters up to 20 grams in weight, 11 Kč. Postcards to Great Britain cost 6 Kč; a letter, 10 Kč. You can buy stamps at post offices, hotels, and shops that sell postcards.

RECEIVING MAIL

If you don't know where you'll be staying, **American Express** mail service is a great convenience, available at no charge to anyone holding an American Express credit card or carrying American Express traveler's checks. The American Express office is at Václavské náměstí 56 (Wenceslas Square) in central Prague. You can also have mail held *poste restante* (general delivery) at Prague's main post office (✉ Jindřišská ul. 14), but the letters should be marked *Pošta 1*, to designate the city's main post office. You will be asked for identification when you collect your mail.

Money and Expenses

COSTS

Despite rising inflation, the Czech Republic is still generally a bargain by Western standards. Prague remains the exception, however. Hotel prices in particular are often higher than the standard of facilities would warrant. Nevertheless, you can still find bargain private accommodations. The prices at tourist resorts outside the capital are lower and, in the outlying areas and off the beaten track, very low. Tourists can now legally pay for hotel rooms in crowns, although some hotels still insist on payment in "hard" (i.e., Western) currency. It is an unfortunate fact that many venues such as galleries, museums, castles, and certain clubs charge a higher entrance fee for foreigners than they charge for Czechs. The entrance fees are usually posted, with the Czech citizens' rate written in words rather than figures. Ticket vendors can be quite militant about defending this policy, which is legally acceptable in the Czech Republic, and protesting such discrimination when it happens will usually get you nowhere.

CURRENCY
The unit of currency in the Czech Republic is the koruna, or crown (Kč), which is divided into 100 haléř, or hellers. There are (little-used) coins of 10, 20, and 50 hellers; coins of 1, 2, 5, 10, 20, and 50 Kč; and notes of 20, 50, 100, 200, 500, 1,000, 2,000, and 5,000 Kč. Notes of 1,000 Kč and up may not always be accepted for small purchases.

Try to avoid exchanging money at hotels or private exchange booths, including the ubiquitous Čekobanka and Exact Change booths. They routinely take commissions of 8%–10%. The best places to exchange are at bank counters, where the commissions average 1%–3%, or at ATMs. The koruna became fully convertible late in 1995 and can now be purchased outside the country and exchanged into other currencies. Ask about current regulations when you change money, however, and keep your receipts. At press time the exchange rate was around 30 Kč to the U.S. dollar, 20 Kč to the Canadian dollar, and 50 Kč to the pound sterling.

SAMPLE PRICES
A cup of coffee will cost about 30 Kč; museum or castle entrance, 20 Kč–300 Kč; a good theater seat, up to 500 Kč; a cinema seat, 60 Kč–100 Kč; ½ liter (pint) of beer, 15 Kč–25 Kč; a 2-km (1-mi) taxi ride, 60 Kč–100 Kč; a bottle of Moravian wine in a good restaurant, 140 Kč–320 Kč; a glass (2 deciliters or 7 ounces) of wine, 35 Kč–45 Kč.

Passports and Visas

United States, Canadian, and British citizens require only a valid passport to visit the Czech Republic as tourists. U.S. citizens may stay for 30 days without a visa; British and Canadian citizens, six months. Canadians may be required to register with the police if staying with friends or family. It's advisable to contact the Czech Embassy (✉ Embassy of the Czech Republic, 541 Sussex Dr., Ottawa, Ontario K1N 6Z6, ☎ 613/562–3875, ℻ 613/562–3878) about changes to the rules regarding Canadian citizens. U.S. citizens can receive additional information from the Czech Embassy (✉ 3900 Spring of Freedom St. NW, Washington, DC 20008, ☎ 202/274–9100, ℻ 202/966–8540).

Student and Youth Travel

CKM (Youth Travel Service; ✉ Jindřišská 28, Prague 1, ☎ 02/2423–0218) provides information on travel bargains within the Czech Republic and abroad to students, travelers under 26, and teachers. **KMC** (Young Travelers' Club; ✉ Karoliny Světlé 30, Prague 1, ☎ 02/2423–0633) issues IYH cards (50 Kč for those under 26, 200 Kč for others) and books hostel beds throughout the country. For general information about student identity cards, work-abroad programs, and youth hostels, *see* Student Travel *in* the Gold Guide.

Telephones

COUNTRY CODE
The country code for the Czech Republic is 420. When dialing a number in the Czech Republic from abroad, drop the initial zero from the regional area code.

INTERNATIONAL CALLS
To reach an English-speaking operator in the United States, call **AT&T** (☎ 00–420–00101), **MCI** (☎ 00–420–00112), or **Sprint** (☎ 00–420–87187). For **CanadaDirect,** dial 00–420–00151; for **B.T.Direct** to the

United Kingdom, call 00–420–04401. The operator will connect
your collect or credit-card call at the carrier's standard rates. In
Prague, many phone booths allow direct international dialing; if you
can't find one, the telephone office of the **main post office** (Hlavní pošta,
⊠ Politických vĕznu 4), open 24 hours, is the best place to try. Once
inside, follow signs for "Telegraf/Telefax." The international dialing
code is 00. Rates to the U.S. are roughly 42 Kč per minute; a call to
the U.K. costs about 25 Kč per minute. For international inquiries,
dial 0132 for the United States, Canada, or the United Kingdom. Otherwise, ask the receptionist at any hotel to put a call through for you,
though beware: The more expensive the hotel, the more expensive the
call will be.

LOCAL CALLS
The few remaining coin-operated telephones take 2- and 5-Kč coins.
Most newer public phones operate only with a special telephone card,
available from newsstands and tobacconists in denominations of 150
Kč, 240 Kč, and 300 Kč. A call within Prague costs 2 Kč from a coin-
operated phone or the equivalent of 3 Kč (1 unit) from a card-operated phone. The dial tone is a series of short and long buzzes.

Tipping
Service is usually not included in restaurant bills. Round the bill up to
the nearest multiple of 10 (if the bill comes to 83 Kč, for example, give
the waiter 90 Kč); 10% is considered appropriate in all but the most
expensive places. Tip porters who bring bags to your rooms 40 Kč total.
For room service, a 20-Kč tip is enough. In taxis, round the bill up by
10%. Give tour guides and helpful concierges between 50 Kč and 100
Kč for services rendered.

Travel Agencies
American Express (⊠ Václavské nám. 56, ☏ 02/2421–9992, FAX 02/
2211–1131); **Thomas Cook** (⊠ Národní třída 28, ☏ 02/2110–5276).

For bus tickets to just about anywhere in Europe, try **Bohemia Tour**
(⊠ Zlatnická 7, ☏ 02/232–877) or Čedok's main office (☞ Visitor
Information, *below*).

Visitor Information
There are three central offices for the municipal **Prague Information
Service** (PIS; ⊠ Staroměstské nám. 22, ☏ 02/2448–2018; ⊠ Na
Příkopě 20, ☏ 02/264–020; ⊠ Hlavní nádraží, lower hall, ☏ 02/2423–
9258). The Staroměstské náměstí (Old Town Square) branch is open
weekdays 9–6 and weekends 9–5, while the Na Příkopě office, just a
few doors down from Čedok's main office, is open weekdays 9–6 and
Saturday 9–3. From April to October, the Hlavní ńdraží branch is open
on weekdays 9–7, weekends 9–4; from November to March, it's open
weekdays 9–6 and Saturday 9–3. PIS locates lodging, offers city maps
and general tourist information, sells tickets to cultural events, and arranges group and individual tours.

Čedok, the ubiquitous travel agency, also provides general tourist information and city maps. Čedok will also exchange money, book accommodations, arrange guided tours, and book passage on airlines,
buses, and trains. You can pay for Čedok services, including booking
rail tickets, with any major credit card. Note limited weekend hours.
⊠ *Main office: Na Příkopě 18,* ☏ *02/2419–7111,* FAX *02/2422–5339.*
⊙ *Weekdays 8:30–6, Sat. 9–1. Other downtown offices:* ⊠ *Rytířská
16,* ☏ *02/262–714,* ⊙ *Weekdays 9–6;* ⊠ *Pařížská 6,* ☏ *02/231–4302,*
⊙ *Weekdays 9–6, Sat. 9–noon.*

The **Czech Tourist Authority** (⊠ Národní třída 37, ☎ FAX 02/2421–1458) can provide information on tourism outside Prague but does not sell tickets or book accommodations.

To find out what's on for the month and to get the latest tips for shopping, dining, and entertainment, consult Prague's weekly English-language newspaper, the *Prague Post.* It prints comprehensive entertainment listings and can be bought at most downtown newsstands as well as in major North American and European cities. The monthly *Prague Guide,* available at newsstands and tourist offices for about 25 Kč, provides a good overview of major cultural events and has listings of restaurants, hotels, and organizations offering traveler assistance.

3 Budapest

After decades under Soviet rule, newly democratic Hungary is in the midst of full-swing revitalization. Budapest pairs breathtaking Old World grandeur with a thriving cultural life—its hearty meals spiced with rich red paprika are matched by the generosity and warmth of the Magyar soul.

HUNGARY SITS AT THE CROSSROADS of Central Europe, having retained its own identity by absorbing countless invasions and foreign occupa-
By Alan Levy and Julie Tomasz
tions. Its industrious, resilient people have a history of brave but unfortunate uprisings: against the Turks in the 17th century, the Hapsburgs in 1848, and the Soviet Union in 1956. Each has resulted in a period of readjustment, a return to politics as the art of the possible.

The 1960s and '70s saw matters improve politically and materially for the majority of Hungarians. Communist Party leader János Kádár remained relatively popular at home and abroad, allowing Hungary to expand and improve trade and relations with the West. The bubble began to burst during the 1980s, however, when the economy stagnated and inflation escalated. The peaceful transition to democracy began when young reformers in the party shunted aside the aging Kádár in 1988 and began speaking openly about multiparty democracy, a market economy, and a break from Moscow—daring ideas at the time.

Events quickly gathered pace, and by spring 1990, as the Iron Curtain fell, Hungarians went to the polls in the first free elections in 40 years. A center-right government led by Prime Minister József Antal took office, sweeping away the Communists and their renamed successor party, the Socialists, who finished fourth. Ironically, four years later, in the nation's next elections, Hungarians voted out the ailing center-right party in favor of none other than the Hungarian Socialist Party, which ruled in coalition with the Free Democrats until it was ousted again in the 1998 elections. Voting the center-right FIDESZ party, led by 35-year-old Viktor Orbán, into power, the nation has chosen an entirely new generation to take it into the new millennium.

Because Hungary is a small, agriculturally oriented country, visitors are often surprised by its grandeur and Old World charm, especially in the capital, Budapest, which bustles with life as never before. Situated on both banks of the Danube, Budapest unites the colorful hills of Buda and the wide, businesslike boulevards of Pest. Though it was the site of a Roman outpost during the 1st century, the city was not officially created until 1873, when the towns of Óbuda, Pest, and Buda were joined. Since then, Budapest has been the cultural, political, intellectual, and commercial heart of Hungary; for the 20% of the nation's population who live in the capital, anywhere else is simply *vidék* ("the country").

Budapest has suffered many ravages in the course of its long history. It was totally destroyed by the Mongols in 1241, captured by the Turks in 1541, and nearly destroyed again by Soviet troops in 1945. But this bustling industrial and cultural center survived as the capital of the People's Republic of Hungary after the war—and then, as the 1980s drew to a close, it became one of the Eastern Bloc's few thriving bastions of capitalism. Today, judging by the city's flourishing cafés and restaurants, markets and bars, the stagnation enforced by the Communists seems a thing of the very distant past.

Much of the charm of a visit to Budapest lies in unexpected glimpses into shadowy courtyards and in long vistas down sunlit cobbled streets. Although some 30,000 buildings were destroyed during World War II and in 1956, the past lingers on in the often crumbling architectural details of the antique structures that remain.

Hungarians are known for their hospitality and love talking to foreigners, although their unusual language can be a problem. Today, however, everyone seems to be learning English, especially young people. But

Hungary (Magyarország)

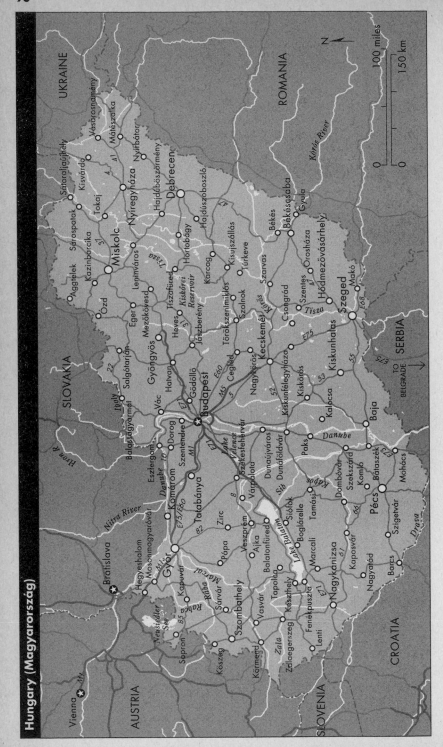

what all Hungarians share is a deep love of music, and the calendar is studded with it, from Budapest's famous opera to its annual spring music festival. And everywhere Gypsy violinists are likely to serenade you during your evening meal.

Pleasures and Pastimes

Dining

Through the lean postwar years the Hungarian kitchen lost none of its spice and sparkle. Meats, rich sauces, and creamy desserts predominate, but the more health-conscious will also find salads, even out of season. (Strict vegetarians should note, however, that even meatless dishes are usually cooked with lard [*zsír*].) In addition to the ubiquitous dishes with which most foreigners are familiar, such as chunky beef *gulyás* (goulash) and *paprikás csirke* (chicken paprika) served with *galuska* (little pinched dumplings), traditional Hungarian classics include fiery *halászlé* (fish soup), scarlet with hot paprika; *fogas* (pike perch) from Lake Balaton; and goose liver, duck, and veal specialties. Lake Balaton is the major source of fish in Hungary, particularly for *süllő*, a kind of perch. Hungarians are also very fond of carp (*ponty*), catfish (*harcsa*), and eel (*angolna*), which are usually stewed in a garlic-and-tomato sauce.

Portions are large, so don't plan to eat more than one main Hungarian meal a day. Desserts are lavish, and every inn seems to have its house *torta* (cake), though *rétes* (strudels), *Somlói galuska* (a steamed sponge cake soaked in chocolate sauce and whipped cream), and *palacsinta* (stuffed crepes) are ubiquitous. Traditional rétes fillings are *mák* (sugary poppy seeds), *meggy* (sour cherry), and *túró* (sweetened cottage cheese); palacsintas always come rolled with *dió* (sweet ground walnut), *túró*, or *lekvár* (jam)—usually *barack* (apricot).

In major cities, there is a good selection of restaurants, from the grander establishments that echo the imperial past of the Hapsburg era to the less expensive, rustic spots favored by locals. In addition to trying out the standard *vendéglő* or *étterem* (restaurants), visitors can eat at an *önkiszolgáló étterem* (self-service restaurant), a *bistró étel bár* (sit-down snack bar), a *büfé* (snack counter), an *eszpresszó* (café), or a *söröző* (pub). And no matter how strict your diet, don't pass up a visit to at least one *cukrászda* (pastry shop). Our dining choices focus primarily on Hungarian and Continental cuisine; however, Budapest has plenty of restaurants whose menus roam further afield.

Although prices are steadily increasing, there are plenty of good, affordable restaurants offering a variety of Hungarian dishes. Even in Budapest, eating out can provide you with some of the best value for the money of any European capital. In almost all restaurants, an inexpensive prix-fixe lunch called a *menü* is available, usually for as little as 350 Ft. It includes soup or salad, an entrée, and a dessert. One caveat: Some of the more touristy restaurants sometimes follow the international practice of embellishing tourists' bills; it doesn't hurt to check the prices discreetly before ordering and the total before paying. Budapest made international news last year for a flagrant overcharging incident; authorities have since cracked down on the guilty establishments. Also note that many restaurants have a fine-print policy of charging for each slice of bread consumed from the bread basket.

Hungarians eat early—you risk offhand service and cold food after 9 PM. Lunch, the main meal for many, is served from noon to 2. At most moderately priced and inexpensive restaurants, casual but neat dress is acceptable.

CATEGORY	COST*
$$$$	over 3,200 Ft.
$$$	2,300 Ft.–3,200 Ft.
$$	1,400 Ft.–2,300 Ft.
$	under 1,400 Ft.

per person for a three-course meal, excluding wine and tip

Folk Art and Porcelain

Hungary's centuries-old traditions of handmade, often regionally specific folk art are still beautifully alive. Intricately carved wooden boxes,
vibrantly colorful embroidered tablecloths and shirts, matte-black pottery pitchers, delicately woven lace collars, ceramic plates splashed with
painted flowers and birds, and decorative heavy leather whips are
among the favorite handcrafted pieces a visitor can purchase. You'll
find them in folk-art stores but can purchase them directly from the
artisans at crafts fairs and from peddlers on the streets. Dolls dressed
in national costume are also popular souvenirs.

Among the most sought-after items are the exquisite hand-painted
Herend and Zsolnay porcelain, created in Herend and Pécs, respectively.
Unfortunately, the prices on all makes of porcelain have risen considerably in the last few years. For guaranteed authenticity without heading to the factories, make your purchases in Budapest's specific Herend
and Zsolnay stores.

Lodging

Budapest is well equipped with hotels and hostels, but the increase in
tourism since 1989 has put a strain on the city's often crowded lodgings. Advance reservations are strongly advised, especially at the lower-
price hotels. Many of the major luxury and business-class hotel chains
are represented in Budapest; however, all of them are Hungarian-run
franchise operations with native touches that you won't find in any
other Hilton or Marriott.

In winter it's not difficult to find a hotel room, even at the last minute,
and prices are usually reduced by 20%–30%. Guest houses, also
called *panziók* (pensions), provide simple accommodations—well
suited to people on a budget. Like B&Bs, most are run by couples or
families and offer simple breakfast facilities and usually have private
bathrooms; they're generally outside the city or town center. Arrangements can be made directly with the panzió or through local tourist
offices and travel agents abroad. By far the cheapest and most accessible beds in the city are rooms ($20–$25 for a double room) in private homes. The supply is limited, so if you plan to arrange something
on your own, try to arrive in Budapest early in the morning. Look for
signs reading SZOBA KIADÓ (or the German ZIMMER FREI). Reservations
and referrals can also be made by any tourist office, and if you go that
route, you have someone to complain to if things don't work out.

Apartments in Budapest and cottages at Lake Balaton are available for
short- and long-term rental and can make the most economic lodging
for families—particularly for those who prefer to cook their own
meals. Rates and reservations can be obtained from tourist offices in
Hungary and abroad. Also consult the free annual accommodations
directory published by **Tourinform** (☞ Visitor Information *in* Budapest A to Z, *below*); published in five languages, it lists basic information about hotels, pensions, bungalows, and tourist hostels throughout
the country. A separate brochure lists the country's campgrounds.

For single rooms with bath, count on paying about 80% of the dou-
ble-room rate. During the off-season (in Budapest, September through
March; at Lake Balaton, May and September), rates can drop consid-

erably. Prices at Lake Balaton tend to be significantly higher than those in the rest of the countryside. Note that most large hotels require payment in hard currency (either U.S. dollars or Deutschemarks).

CATEGORY	BUDAPEST*	OTHER AREAS*
$$$$	over $200	over $70
$$$	$140–$200	$50–$70
$$	$80–$140	$30–$50
$	under $80	under $30

All prices are for a standard double room with bath and breakfast during peak season (June through August).

Spas and Thermal Baths

Several thousand years ago, the first settlers of the area that is now Budapest chose their home because of its abundance of hot springs. Centuries later, the Romans and the Turks built baths and developed cultures based on medicinal bathing. Now there are more than 1,000 medicinal hot springs bubbling up around the country. Budapest alone has some 14 historic working baths, which attract ailing patients with medical prescriptions for specific water cures as well as "recreational" bathers—locals and tourists alike—wanting to soak in the relaxing waters, try some of the many massages and treatments, and experience the architectural beauty of the bathhouses themselves.

For most, a visit to a bath involves soaking in several thermal pools of varying temperatures and curative contents—perhaps throwing in a game of aquatic chess—relaxing in a steam room or sauna, and getting a brisk, if not brutal, massage (average cost: 200 Ft. for a half hour). Many bath facilities are single-sex or have certain days set aside for men or women only, and most people walk around nude or with miniature loincloths, provided at the door. Men should be aware that some baths have a strong gay clientele.

In addition to the ancient beauties there are newer, modern baths open to the public at many spa hotels. They lack the charm and aesthetic appeal of their older peers but provide the latest treatments in sparkling facilities. For more information, page through the "Hungary: Land of Spas" brochure published by the Hungarian Tourist Board, available free from most tourist offices.

Wine, Beer, and Spirits

Hungary tempts wine connoisseurs with its important wine regions, especially Villány, near Pécs, in the south; Eger and Tokaj in the north; and the northern shore of Lake Balaton. Kéknyelű, Szürkebarát, and especially Olaszrizling are all common white table wines; Tokay, one of the great wines of the world, can be heavy, dark, and sweet, and is generally drunk as an aperitif or a dessert wine. It's expensive, especially by Hungarian standards, so it's usually reserved for special occasions.

The gourmet red table wine of Hungary, Egri Bikavér (Bull's Blood of Eger, usually with *el toro* himself on the label), is the best buy and the safest bet with all foods. Other good reds and the best rosés come from Villanyi; the most adventurous reds—with sometimes successful links to both Austrian and Californian wine making and viticulture—are from the Sopron area.

Before- and after-dinner drinks tend toward schnapps, most notably *Barack-pálinka,* an apricot brandy. A plum brandy called *Kosher szilva-pálinka,* bottled under rabbinical supervision, is very chic. Unicum, Hungary's national liqueur, is a dark, thick, vaguely minty, and quite potent drink that could be likened to Germany's Jägermeister. Its chubby green bottle makes it a good souvenir to take home.

Major Hungarian beers are Köbányai, Dreher, Aranyhordó, Balaton Világos, and Aszok.

EXPLORING BUDAPEST

Numbers in the text correspond to numbers in the margin and on the Exploring Budapest and Castle Hill (Várhegy) maps.

The principal sights of the city fall roughly into three areas, each of which can be comfortably covered on foot. The Budapest hills are best explored by public transportation. Note that street names have been changed in the past several years to purge all reminders of the Communist regime. Underneath the new names, the old ones remain, canceled out by a big red slash. Also note that a Roman-numeral prefix listed before an address refers to one of Budapest's 22 districts.

Great Itineraries

IF YOU HAVE 1-2 DAYS

A whistle-stop visit should start at the Várhegy (Castle Hill), where you can walk along cobblestone streets lined with Baroque, Gothic, and Renaissance houses and visit the Királyi Palota (Royal Palace). Zip down the hill for a soak or massage at one of the beautiful baths, such as those at the Gellért Hotel, and then cross to the Pest side of the river for a walk along the *korzó* (promenade) up toward the lovely Széchenyi lánchíd (Chain Bridge). If you're determined to shop, Váci utca is your best bet—the pedestrian-only street is unabashedly touristy, but there's a wealth of shops selling everything from paprika to crystal. Vörösmarty tér (Vörösmarty Square) is a good place to find a café and take a break. With extra time, you could visit Szent István Bazilika (St. Stephen's Basilica) and then walk up the grand avenue Andrássy út to Hősök tere (Heroes' Square). If at all possible, catch a performance at the neo-Renaissance Operaház (Opera House).

IF YOU HAVE 3-5 DAYS

Take time to thoroughly explore the museums, squares, and religious buildings on Castle Hill, including the Mátyás templom (Matthias Church), the Budapesti Történeti Múzeum (Budapest History Museum), and the quiet, tree-lined Tóth Árpád sétány promenade. (This could easily take a full day and a half.) Spend a couple of afternoons in Budapest's other wonderful museums, such as the Magyar Nemzeti Múzeum (Hungarian National Museum), where you can see the Crown of St. Stephen, the Szépművészeti Múzeum (Museum of Fine Arts), which has Hungary's finest collection of European art, or the Néprajzi Múzeum (Museum of Ethnography) and its detailed exhibit on Hungarian folk cuture. You could also visit Europe's largest synagogue, the Nagy Zsinagóga (Great Synagogue). If it's a sunny afternoon and you can't bear to be indoors, head to Margit-sziget (Margaret Island). If you enjoy classical music, try to nip in to a performance at the Liszt Ferenc Zeneakadémia (Franz Liszt Academy of Music).

IF YOU HAVE 5-7 DAYS

After spending a few days exploring the city as described above, take a trip to the north shore of Lake Balaton (☞ Side Trip to Lake Balaton, *below*). Here you can swim, hike up the vineyard-covered slopes of Mount Badacsony, do some wine tasting, and have incredible fresh fish for dinner. Tihany is a good place to overnight; in the morning you can wander its twisting streets and visit its hilltop abbey. Alternatively, you could spend the night in the busy spa town of Balatonfüred.

Várhegy (Castle Hill)

Most of the major sights of Buda are on Várhegy (Castle Hill), a long, narrow plateau laced with cobblestone streets, clustered with beautifully preserved Baroque, Gothic, and Renaissance houses, and crowned by the magnificent Royal Palace. The area is theoretically banned to private cars (except for those of neighborhood residents and Hilton Hotel guests), but the streets manage to be lined bumper to bumper with Trabants and Mercedes all the same—sometimes the only visual element to verify you're not in a fairy tale. As in all of Budapest, thriving urban new has taken up residence in historic old; international corporate offices, diplomatic residences, restaurants, and boutiques occupy many of its landmark buildings. But these are still the exceptions, as most flats and homes are lived in by private families. The most striking example, perhaps, is the Hilton Hotel on Hess András tér, which has ingeniously incorporated remains of Castle Hill's oldest church (a tower and one wall), built by Dominican friars in the 13th century.

A Good Walk

Castle Hill's cobblestone streets and numerous museums are made to be explored on foot: Plan to spend about a day here. Most of the transportation options for getting to Castle Hill deposit you on Szent György tér or Dísz tér. It's impossible not to find Castle Hill, but it is possible to be confused about how to get on top of it. If you're already on the Buda side of the river, you can take the Castle bus—*Várbusz*—from the Moszkva tér metro station, northwest of Castle Hill. If you're starting out from Pest, you can take a taxi or Bus 16 from Erzsébet tér or, the most scenic alternative, cross the Széchenyi Lánchíd (Chain Bridge) on foot to Clark Ádám tér and ride the *Sikló* (funicular rail) up Castle Hill (☞ Clark Ádám tér *in* Downtown Pest and the Kis körút [Little Ring Road], *below*).

Begin your exploration by walking slightly farther south to visit the **Királyi Palota** at the southern end of the hill. Of the palace's several major museums, the **Magyar Nemzeti Galéria** ② and the **Budapesti Történeti Múzeum** ③ are particularly interesting. From here, you can cover the rest of the area by walking north along its handful of charming streets. From Dísz tér, start with Tárnok utca, whose houses and usually open courtyards offer glimpses of how Hungarians have integrated contemporary life into Gothic, Renaissance, and Baroque settings; of particular interest are the houses at No. 16, now the Arany Hordo restaurant, and at No. 18, the 15th-century Arany Sas Patika (Golden Eagle Pharmacy Museum), with a naïf Madonna and child in an overhead niche. This tiny museum displays instruments, prescriptions, books, and other artifacts from 16th- and 17th-century pharmacies. Modern commerce is also integrated into Tárnok utca's historic homes; you'll encounter numerous folk souvenir shops and tiny boutiques lining the street. Tárnok utca funnels into Szentháromság tér, home of **Mátyás templom** ⑦ and, just behind it, the **Halászbástya** ⑧.

After exploring them, double back to Dísz tér and set out northward again on Úri utca, which runs parallel to Tárnok utca; less commercialized by boutiques and other shops, it is also the longest and oldest street in the castle district, lined with many stately houses, all worth special attention for their delicately carved details. Both gateways of the Baroque palace at Nos. 48–50 are articulated by Gothic niches. The funny little Telefónia Museum, at No. 49, is worth a stop, as is the **Budavári Labirintus** ⑥, at No. 9. At the end of Úri utca you'll reach **Kapisztrán tér** ⑬. From here, you can walk south again on a parallel

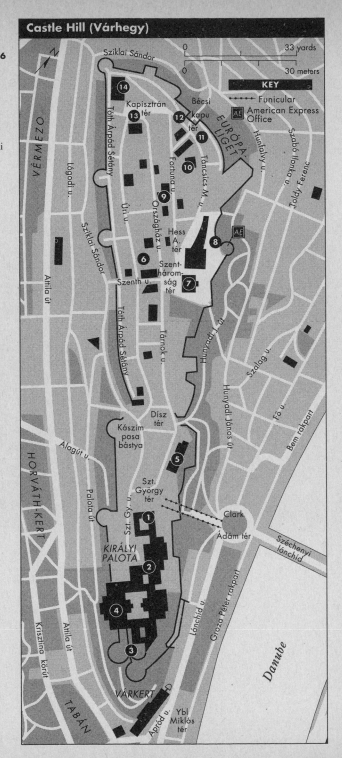

street, Országház utca (Parliament Street), the main thoroughfare of 18th-century Buda; it takes its name from the building at No. 28, which was the seat of Parliament from 1790 to 1807. Before it was appropriated for secular use, this building was the church and convent of the Order of St. Clare. You'll end up back at Szentháromság tér, with just two streets remaining to explore.

You can stroll down charming little Fortuna utca, named for the 18th-century Fortuna Inn, which now houses the **Magyar Kereskedelmi és Vendéglátóipari Múzeum** ⑨. At the end of Fortuna utca you'll reach **Bécsi kapu tér** ⑫, opening to Moszkva tér just below. Go back south on the last of the district's streets, Táncsics Mihály utca, stopping at the **Középkori Zsidó Imaház** ⑪ and the **Zenetörténeti Múzeum** ⑩. Next door, at No. 9, is the Baroque house (formerly the Royal Mint) where rebel writer Tancsics Mihály was imprisoned in the dungeons and freed by the people on the Day of Revolution, March 15, 1848. You'll find yourself in front of the Hilton Hotel, back at Hess András tér, bordering Szentháromság tér. Those whose cobblestone-jostled feet haven't yet protested can finish off their tour of Castle Hill by doubling back to the northern end and strolling south back to Dísz tér on **Tóth Árpád sétány,** the romantic, tree-lined promenade along the Buda side of the hill.

TIMING
Castle Hill is small enough to cover in one day, but perusing its major museums and several tiny exhibits will require more time.

Sights to See

⑫ **Bécsi kapu tér** (Vienna Gate Square). Marking the northern entrance to Castle Hill, the stone gateway (rebuilt in 1936) called Vienna Gate opens toward Vienna—or, closer at hand, Moszkva tér just below. The square named after it has some fine Baroque and rococo houses but is dominated by the enormous neo-Romanesque (1913–17) headquarters of the **Országos Levéltár** (Hungarian National Archives), which resembles a cathedral-like shrine to paperwork.

❸ **Budapesti Történeti Múzeum** (Budapest History Museum). The palace's Baroque southern wing (E) contains the Budapest History Museum, displaying a fascinating permanent exhibit of modern Budapest history from Buda's liberation from the Turks in 1686 through the 1970s. Viewing the vintage 19th- and 20th-century photos and videos of the castle, the Széchenyi Lánchíd, and other Budapest monuments—and seeing them as the backdrop to the horrors of World War II and the 1956 Revolution—helps to put your later sightseeing in context; while you're browsing, peek out one of the windows overlooking the Danube and Pest and let it start seeping in.

Through historical documents, objects, and art, other permanent exhibits depict the medieval history of the Buda fortress and the capital as a whole. This is the best place to view remains of the medieval Royal Palace and other archaeological excavations. Some of the artifacts unearthed during excavations are in the vestibule in the basement; others are still among the remains of medieval structures. Down in the cellars are the original medieval vaults of the palace; portraits of King Matthias and his second wife, Beatrice of Aragon; and many late-14th-century statues that probably adorned the Renaissance palace. ⊠ *Royal Palace (Wing E), Szt. György tér 2,* ☎ *1/375–7533.* ▩ *270 Ft.* ☉ *Mar.–mid-May and mid-Sept.–Oct., Wed.–Mon. 10–6; mid-May–mid-Sept., daily 10–6; Nov.–Feb., Wed.–Mon. 10–4.*

❻ **Budavári Labirintus** (Labyrinth of Buda Castle). Used as a wine cellar and a source of water during the 16th and 17th centuries and then as an air-raid shelter during World War II, the labyrinth—entered at Úri utca 9 below an early 18th-century house—can be explored with a tour or, if you dare, on your own. There are some English-language brochures available. ⊠ *Úri utca 9,* ☎ *1/375–6858.* 🖾 *750 Ft.* ⊘ *Daily 9:30–7:30.*

For a light snack, pastry, and coffee, **Café Miro** (⊠ Úri u. 30, ☎ 1/375–5458) is a fresh, hip alternative to the Old World Budapest cafés.

⑭ **Hadtörténeti Múzeum** (Museum of Military History). Fittingly, this museum is lodged in a former barracks, on the northwestern corner of Kapisztrán tér. The exhibits, which include collections of uniforms and military regalia, trace the military history of Hungary from the original Magyar conquest in the 9th century through the period of Ottoman rule to the middle of this century. You can arrange an English-language tour in advance for roughly 1,000 Ft. ⊠ *I, Tóth Árpád sétány 40,* ☎ *1/356–9522.* 🖾 *270 Ft.* ⊘ *Apr.–Sept., Tues.–Sun. 10–6; Oct.–Mar., Tues.–Sun. 10–4.*

★ ⑧ **Halászbástya** (Fishermen's Bastion). The wondrous porch overlooking the Danube and Pest is the neo-Romanesque Fishermen's Bastion, a merry cluster of white stone towers and arches and columns above a modern bronze statue of St. Stephen, Hungary's first king. Medieval fishwives once peddled their wares here, but the site is now home to souvenirs, crafts, and music. On a sunny summer morning you might hear a brass band in full uniform as well as a Hungarian zitherist sporting a white handlebar mustache and full folkloric garb, both competing for your ear as you marvel at the exquisite Danube view.

⑬ **Kapisztrán tér** (Capistrano Square). Castle Hill's northernmost square was named after St. John of Capistrano, an Italian friar who in 1456 recruited a crusading army to fight the Turks who were threatening Hungary. There's a statue of this honored Franciscan on the northwest corner; also here are the **Museum of Military History** (☞ *above*) and the remains of the 12th-century Gothic **Mária Magdolna templom** (Church of St. Mary Magdalene). Its *torony* (tower), completed in 1496, is the only part left standing; the rest of the church was destroyed by air raids during World War II.

★ **Királyi Palota** (Royal Palace, commonly called Buda Castle). During a seven-week siege at the end of 1944, the entire Castle Hill district of palaces, mansions, and churches was turned into one vast ruin. The final German stand was in the Royal Palace, which was utterly gutted by fire; by the end of the siege its walls were reduced to rubble, and just a few scarred pillars and blackened statues protruded from the wreckage. The destruction was incalculable, yet it gave archaeologists and art historians an opportunity to discover the medieval buildings that once stood on the site of this Baroque and neo-Baroque palace. Fortunately, details of the edifices of the kings of the Árpád and Anjou dynasties, of the Holy Roman Emperor Sigismund, and of the great 15th-century king Mátthiás Corvinus had been preserved in some 80 medieval reports, travelogues, books, and itineraries that were subsequently used to reconstruct the complex.

The postwar rebuilding was slow and painstaking. In some places debris more than 20 ft deep had to be removed; the remains found on the medieval levels were restored to their original planes. Freed from mounds of rubble, the foundation walls and medieval castle walls were completed, and the ramparts surrounding the medieval royal residence were re-created as close to their original shape and size as possible. Out of this herculean labor emerged the Royal Palace of today, a vast cultural center and museum complex (☞ Budapest His-

In case you want to be welcomed there.

We're here to see that you're always welcomed at establishments everywhere. That's why millions of people carry the American Express® Card – for peace of mind, confidence, and security, around the world or just around the corner.

do more

Cards

In case you're running low.

We're here to help with more than 118,000 Express Cash locations around the world. In order to enroll, just call American Express before you start your vacation.

do more

Express Cash

And just in case.

We're here with American Express® Travelers Cheques and Cheques *for Two®.* They're the safest way to carry money on your vacation and the surest way to get a refund, practically anywhere, anytime.

Another way we help you...

do more®

Travelers Cheques

tory Museum, *above, and* Ludwig Múzeum, Magyar Nemzeti Galéria, *and* Országos Széchenyi Könyvtár, *below).*

⑪ Középkori Zsidó Imaház (Medieval Synagogue). The excavated one-room Medieval Synagogue is now used as a museum. On display are objects relating to the Jewish community, including religious inscriptions, frescoes, and tombstones dating to the 15th century. There are a number of Hebrew gravestones in the entranceway. ⊠ *Táncsics Mihály u. 26,* ☎ *1/355–8849.* ▦ *120 Ft.* ⊙ *May–Oct., Tues.–Fri. 10–2, weekends 10–6.*

❶ Ludwig Múzeum. This collection of more than 200 pieces of Hungarian and contemporary international art, including works by Picasso and Lichtenstein, occupies the castle's northern wing. ⊠ *Royal Palace (Wing A), Dísz tér 17,* ☎ *1/375–7533.* ▦ *120 Ft., free Tues.* ⊙ *Tues.–Sun. 10–6.*

❾ Magyar Kereskedelmi és Vendéglátóipari Múzeum (Hungarian Museum of Commerce and Catering). The 18th-century Fortuna Inn now serves visitors in a different way—as the Catering Museum. Displays in a permanent exhibit show the city as a tourist destination from 1870 to the 1930s; you can see, for example, what a room at the Gellért Hotel, still operating today, would have looked like in 1918. The Commerce Museum, just across the courtyard, chronicles the history of Hungarian commerce from the late 19th century to 1947, when the new Communist regime "liberated" the economy into socialism. The four-room exhibit includes everything from an antique chocolate-and-caramel vending machine to early shoe-polish advertisements. You can rent an English-language recorded tour for 200 Ft. ⊠ *Fortuna utca 4,* ☎ *1/375–6249.* ▦ *120 Ft., free Fri.* ⊙ *Wed.–Fri. 10–5, weekends 10–6.*

❷ Magyar Nemzeti Galéria (Hungarian National Gallery). The immense center block of the Royal Palace (made up of Wings B, C, and D) contains this fine gallery, which exhibits a wide range of Hungarian fine art, from medieval ecclesiastical paintings and statues, through Gothic, Renaissance, and Baroque art, to a rich collection of 19th- and 20th-century works. Especially notable are the works of the romantic painter Mihály Munkácsy, the impressionist Pál Szinyei Merse, and the surrealist Kosztka Csontváry, whom Picasso much admired. There is also a large collection of modern Hungarian sculpture. There are labels and commentary in English for both permanent and temporary exhibits. If you contact the museum in advance, you can book a tour for up to five people with an English-speaking guide. ⊠ *Royal Palace (entrance in Wing C), Dísz tér 17,* ☎ *1/375–7533.* ▦ *Gallery 220 Ft., tour 1,000 Ft.* ⊙ *Mid-Mar.–Oct., Tues.–Sun. 10–6; Nov.–mid-Mar., Tues.–Sun. 10–4. (Note: Mid-Jan.–mid-Mar. hrs. may be reduced to Fri.–Sun. only, 10–4).*

★ ❼ Mátyás templom (Matthias Church). The Gothic Matthias Church is officially the Buda Church of Our Lady but better known by the name of the 15th century's "just king" of Hungary, who was married here twice. It is sometimes called the Coronation Church, because the last two kings of Hungary were crowned here: the Hapsburg emperor Franz Joseph in 1867 and his grandnephew Karl IV in 1916. Originally built for the city's German population in the mid-13th century, the church has endured many alterations and assaults. For almost 150 years it was the main mosque of the Turkish overlords—and the predominant impact of its festive pillars is decidedly Byzantine. Badly damaged during the recapture of Buda in 1686, it was completely rebuilt between 1873 and 1896 by Frigyes Schulek, who gave it an asymmetrical western front, with one high and one low spire, and a fine rose window; the south porch is from the 14th century.

The Szentháromság Kápolna (Trinity Chapel) holds an *encolpion*, an enameled casket containing a miniature copy of the Gospel to be worn on the chest; it belonged to the 12th-century king Béla III and his wife, Anne of Chatillon. Their burial crowns and a cross, scepter, and rings found in their excavated graves are also displayed here. The church's **treasury** contains Renaissance and Baroque chalices, monstrances, and vestments. High Mass is celebrated every Sunday at 10 AM with full orchestra and choir—and often with major soloists; get here early if you want a seat. During the summer there are usually organ recitals on Friday at 8 PM. Tourists are asked to remain at the back of the church during weddings and services (it's least intrusive to come after 9:30 AM weekdays and between 1 and 5 PM Sundays and holidays). ✉ *I, Szentháromság tér 2,* ☎ *1/355–5657.* ☉ *Daily 7 AM–8 PM.* 💰 *Church free, except during concerts; treasury 100 Ft.* ☉ *Treasury daily 9:30–5:30.*

④ Országos Széchenyi Könyvtár (Széchenyi National Library). The western wing (F) of the Royal Palace is home to the National Library, which houses more than 2 million volumes. Its archives include well-preserved medieval codices, manuscripts, and the correspondence of historic eminences. This is not a lending library, but the reading rooms are open to the public (though you must show a passport), and even the most valuable materials can be viewed on microfilm. Small, temporary exhibits on rare books and documents are usually on display; the hours and admission fees for these are quite variable. Note that the entire libary closes for one month every summer, usually in July or August; call ahead to confirm it's open. ✉ *Buda Castle (Wing F). To arrange a tour with an English-speaking guide,* ☎ *1/375–7533.* 💰 *300 Ft.* ☉ *Reading rooms Mon. 1–9, Tues.–Sat. 9–9; exhibits Mon. 1–6, Tues.–Sat. 10–6.*

Statue of Prince Eugene of Savoy. In front of the Royal Palace, facing the Danube by the entrance to Wing C, stands an equestrian statue of Prince Eugene of Savoy, a commander of the army that liberated Hungary from the Turks at the end of the 17th century. From the terrace on which the statue stands there is a superb view across the river to Pest.

Szentháromság tér (Holy Trinity Square). This square is named for its Baroque **Trinity Column**, erected in 1712–13 as a gesture of thanksgiving by survivors of a plague. The column stands in front of the famous Gothic Matthias Church (☞ *above*), its large pedestal a perfect seat from which to watch the wedding spectacles that take over the church on spring and summer weekends: From morning till night, in a continuous cycle accompanied by organ music, frilly engaged pairs flow in one after the other and, after a brief transformation inside, back out onto the square just as the next couple in line begins.

★ **Tóth Árpád sétány.** This romantic, tree-lined promenade along the Buda side of the hill is often mistakenly overlooked by sightseers. Beginning at the Museum of Military History (☞ *above*) the promenade takes you "behind the scenes" along the back sides of the matte-pastel Baroque houses you saw on Úri utca, with their regal arched windows and wrought-iron gates. On a late spring afternoon, the fragrance of the cherry trees may be enough to revive even the most wearied feet and spirits.

Úri utca. Running parallel to Tárnok utca, Úri utca has been less commercialized by boutiques and other shops; the longest and oldest street in the castle district, it is lined with many stately houses, all worth special attention for their delicately carved details. Both gateways of the Baroque palace at Nos. **48–50** are articulated by Gothic niches. The Telefónia Múzeum (Telephone Museum), at No. 49, is an endearing little museum entered through a peaceful, shady central courtyard shared with the local district police station. Although vintage telephone systems are still in use all over the country, both the oldest and most recent products of telecommunication—from the 1882 wooden box with hose attachment to the latest, slickest fax machines—can be observed and tested here. *Telefónia Múzeum:* ✉ *Úri utca 49,* ☎ *1/201–8188.* 🎫 *60 Ft.* ☉ *Nov.–Apr., Tues.–Sun. 10–4; May–Oct., Tues.–Sun. 10–6.*

⑤ Várszínház (Castle Theater). Once a Franciscan church, this was transformed into a more secular royal venue in 1787 under the supervision of courtier Farkas Kempelen. The first theatrical performance in Hungarian was held here in 1790. Heavily damaged during World War II, the theater was rebuilt and reopened in 1978. While the building retains its original late-Baroque-style facade, the interior was renovated with marble and concrete. It is now used as the studio theater of the National Theater and occasionally for classical recitals, and there is usually a historical exhibition in its foyer—usually theater-related, such as a display of costumes. ✉ *Színház utca 1–3,* ☎ *1/375–8011.*

⑩ Zenetörténeti Múzeum (Museum of Music History). This handsome gray-and-pearl-stone 18th-century palace is where Beethoven allegedly stayed in 1800 when he came to Buda to conduct his works. Now a museum, it displays rare manuscripts and old instruments downstairs in its permanent collection and temporary exhibits upstairs in a small, sunlit hall. The museum also often hosts intimate classical recitals. ✉ *Táncsics Mihály u. 7,* ☎ *1/214–6770.* 🎫 *170 Ft.* ☉ *Mid-Nov.–late-Dec. and first two wks of Mar., Tues.–Sun. 10–5; mid-Mar.–mid-Nov., Tues.–Sun. 10–6.*

Tabán and Gellért-hegy (Tabán and Gellért Hill)

Spreading below Castle Hill is the old quarter called the Tabán (from the Turkish word for "armory"). A onetime suburb of Buda, it was known at the end of the 17th century as Little Serbia (*Rác*) because so many Serbian refugees settled here after fleeing from the Turks. It later became a quaint and romantic district of vineyards and small taverns. Though most of the small houses characteristic of this district have been demolished—mainly in the interest of easing traffic—a few picturesque buildings remain.

Gellért-hegy (Gellért Hill), 761 ft high, is the most beautiful natural formation on the Buda bank. It takes its name from St. Gellért (Gerard) of Csanad, a Venetian bishop who came to Hungary in the 11th century and was supposedly flung to his death from the top of the hill by pagans. The walk up can be tough, but take solace from the cluster of hot springs at the foot of the hill, which soothe and cure bathers at the Rác, Rudas, and Gellért baths.

Numbers in the text correspond to numbers in the margin and on the Exploring Budapest map.

A Good Walk

From the **Semmelweis Orvostörténeti Múzeum** ⑮, walk around the corner to Szarvas tér and a few yards toward the river to the **Tabán plébánia-templom** ⑯. Walking south on Attila út and crossing to the other side of Hegyalja út, you'll be at the foot of Gellért Hill. From here, take a deep breath and climb the paths and stairs to the **Citadella** ⑳ (fortress) at the top of the hill (about 30 minutes). After taking in the views and exploring the area, you can descend and treat yourself to a soak or a swim at the **Gellért Szálloda és Thermál Fürdő** ⑲ at the southeastern foot of the hill. On foot, take the paths down the southeastern side of the hill. You can also take Bus 27 down the back of the hill to Móricz Zsigmond körtér and walk back toward the Gellért on

102

Exploring Budapest

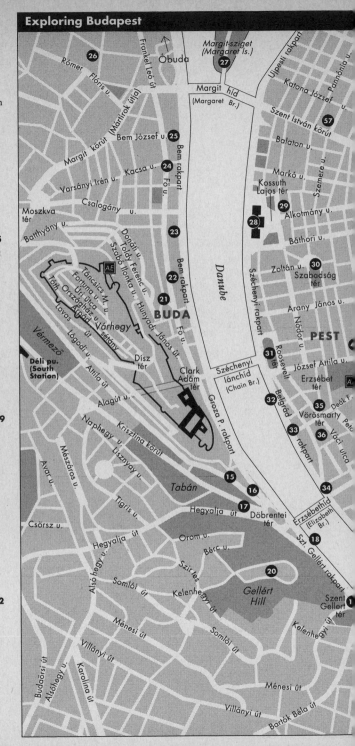

busy Bartók Béla út, or take Tram 47, 49, 18, or 19 a couple of stops
to Szent Gellért tér.

TIMING

The Citadella and Szabadság Szobor are lit in golden lights every night,
but the entire Gellért-hegy is at its scenic best every year on August
20, when it forms the backdrop to the spectacular St. Stephen's Day
fireworks display.

Sights to See

★ ⑳ **Citadella.** The fortress atop the hill was a much-hated sight for Hungarians. They called it the Gellért Bastille, for it was erected, on the site
of an earlier wooden observatory, by the Austrian army as a lookout
after the 1848–49 War of Independence. But no matter what its history may be, the views from this ring of walls are breathtaking. Its transformation into a tourist site during the 1960s improved its image, with
the addition of cafés, a beer garden, wine cellars, and a hostel. In its
inner wall is a small graphic exhibition (with some relics) of Budapest's
2,000-year history. ☎ *No phone.* ⊠ *Free.* ☉ *Accessible at all times.*

Erzsébethíd (Elizabeth Bridge). This bridge was named for Empress Elizabeth (1837–1898), otherwise known as Sissi, of whom the Hungarians were particularly fond. The beautiful but unhappy wife of Franz
Joseph, she was stabbed to death in 1898 by an anarchist while boarding a boat on Lake Geneva. The original bridge was built between 1897
and 1903; at the time, it was the longest single-span suspension bridge
in Europe. It was destroyed by the Germans in 1945, and its modern
replacement dates from 1964.

★ ⑲ **Gellért Szálloda és Thermál Fürdő** (Gellért Hotel and Thermal Baths).
At the foot of the Gellért Hill, by the base of the green wrought-iron
Szabadsághíd (Liberty Bridge), are these beautiful art-nouveau establishments. The Danubius Hotel Gellért (☞ Lodging, *below*) is the oldest spa hotel in Hungary, with hot springs that have supplied curative
baths for nearly 2,000 years. It is the most popular among tourists, as
you don't need reservations, it's quite easy to communicate, and there's
a wealth of treatments—including chamomile steam baths, salt-vapor
inhalations, and hot mud packs. Many of these treatments require a
doctor's prescription; they will accept prescriptions from foreign doctors. Men and women have separate steam and sauna rooms; both the
indoor pool and the outdoor wave pool (☞ Outdoor Activities and
Sports, *below*) are coed. ⊠ *XI, Gellért tér 1,* ☎ *1/385–3555 (baths).*
⊠ *Indoor baths and steam rooms 500 Ft. per 1½ hrs; indoors and pool
1,300 Ft. per day.* ☉ *Baths weekdays 6 AM–6 PM, weekends 6:30 AM–
1 (May–Sept. until 4 PM). May–Sept. weekend massage only until 1
PM. Wave pool May–Sept., daily 6 AM–6 PM.*

⑰ **Rác Fürdő** (Rác Baths). The bright-yellow building tucked away at the
foot of Gellért Hill near the Elizabeth Bridge houses these baths, built
during the reign of King Zsigmond in the early 15th century and rebuilt by Miklós Ybl in the mid-19th century. Its waters contain alka-
line salts and other minerals; you can also get a massage. Women can
bathe on Monday, Wednesday, and Friday; men on Tuesday, Thursday, and Saturday (☞ Outdoor Activities and Sports, *below*). These
baths are particularly popular with the gay community. ⊠ *I, Hadnagy
utca 8–10,* ☎ *1/356–1322.* ⊠ *450 Ft.* ☉ *Mon.–Sat. 6:30 AM–6 PM.*

⑱ **Rudas Fürdő** (Rudas Baths). This bath is on the riverbank, the original Turkish pool making its interior possibly the most dramatically beautiful of Budapest's baths. A high, domed roof admits pinpricks of
bluish-green light into the dark, circular stone hall with its austere
columns and arches. Fed by eight springs with a year-round tempera-

ture of 44°C (111°F), the Rudas's highly fluoridated waters have been known for 1,000 years. The facility is open to men only (though it does not have a large gay following); a less interesting outer swimming pool is open to both sexes (☞ Outdoor Activities and Sports, *below*). Massages are available. ⊠ *I, Döbrentei tér 9,* ☎ *1/356–1322.* ▣ *400 Ft.* ◷ *Weekdays 6 AM–6 PM, weekends 6 AM–noon.*

⑮ **Semmelweis Orvostörténeti Múzeum** (Semmelweis Museum of Medical History). This splendid Baroque house was the birthplace of Ignác Semmelweis (1818–65), the great Hungarian physician who proved the contagiousness of puerperal (childbed) fever. It's now a museum that traces the history of healing. Semmelweis's grave is in the garden. ⊠ *Apród utca 1–3,* ☎ *1/375–3533.* ▣ *100 Ft.* ◷ *Tues.–Sun. 10:30–5:30.*

Szabadság Szobor (Liberation Memorial). Visible from many parts of the city, this 130-ft-high 1947 memorial, which starts just below the southern edge of the Citadella and towers above it, honors the 1944–45 siege of Budapest and the Russian soldiers who fell in the battle. It is the work of noted Hungarian sculptor Zsigmond Kisfaludi-Stróbl, and from a distance it looks light, airy, and even liberating. A sturdy young girl, her hair and robe swirling in the wind, holds a palm branch high above her head. Until recently, she was further embellished with sculptures of giants slaying dragons, Red Army soldiers, and peasants rejoicing at the freedom that Soviet liberation promised (but failed) to bring to Hungary. Since 1992, her mood has lightened: In the Budapest city government's systematic purging of Communist symbols, the Red Combat infantrymen who had flanked the Liberation statue for decades were hacked off and carted away. The soldier who had stood the highest and the one who was shaking hands with a grateful Hungarian worker are now on display among the other evicted statues in the Szobor Park in the city's 22nd district (☞ Off the Beaten Path, *below*). ⊠ *Gellért-hegy.*

OFF THE **SZOBOR PARK** (Statue Park) – For a look at Budapest's too-recent Iron
BEATEN PATH Curtain past, make the 30-minute trip out to this open-air exhibit, cleverly nicknamed "Tons of Socialism," where 42 of the Communist statues and memorials that once dominated the city's streets and squares have been put out to pasture since the political changes in 1989. Here you can wander among mammoth Lenin and Marx statues and buy socialist-nostalgia souvenirs while songs from the Hungarian and Russian workers' movement play bombastically in the background. ⊠ *XXII, Balatoni út, corner of Szabadkai út,* ☎ FAX *1/227-7446.* ▣ *250 Ft.* ◷ *Mid-Apr.–Oct., daily 8–8; Nov.–mid-Apr., weekends 10–dusk.*

Szarvas-ház (Stag House). This Louis XVI–style building is named for the former Szarvas Café or, more accurately, for its extant trade sign, with an emblem of a stag not quite at bay, which can be seen above the triangular arched entryway. For years, the structure housed the Arany Szarvas restaurant, which preserved some of the mood of the old Tabán, but at press time it was closed for renovations and seemed likely to change hands and reopen as something else. ⊠ *Szarvas tér 1.*

⑯ **Tabán plébánia-templom** (Tabán Parish Church). In 1736, this church was built on the site of a Turkish mosque and subsequently renovated and reconstructed several times. Its present form—mustard-colored stone with a rotund, green clock tower—could be described as restrained Baroque. ⊠ *I, Attila u. 1.*

North Buda

Most of these sights are along Fő utca (Main Street), a long, straight thoroughfare that starts at the Chain Bridge and runs parallel to the

Danube. It is lined on both sides with multistory late-18th-century houses—many darkened by soot and showing their age more than those you've seen in sparklingly restored areas like Castle Hill. This north-bound exploration can be done with the help of Bus 86, which covers the waterfront, or on foot, although distances are fairly great.

Numbers in the text correspond to numbers in the margin and on the Exploring Budapest map.

A Good Walk

Beginning at **Batthyány tér** ㉓, with its head-on view of Parliament across the Danube, continue north on Fő utca, passing (or stopping to bathe at) the famous Turkish **Király-fürdő** ㉔. From **Bem József tér** ㉕, one block north, turn left (away from the river) up Fekete Sas utca, cross-ing busy Margit körút and turning right, one block past, up Mecset utca. This will take you up the hill to **Gül Baba türbéje** ㉖.

TIMING

The tour can fit easily into a few hours, including a good hour-and-a-half soak at the baths; expect the walk from Bem József tér up the hill to Gül Baba türbéje to take about 25 minutes. Fő utca and Bem József tér can get congested during rush hours (around 8 and 9 AM and 5 and 6 PM). Remember that museums are closed Mondays and that the Király Baths are open to men and women on different days of the week.

Sights to See

㉓ **Batthyány tér.** This lovely square, open on its river side, affords a grand view of Parliament, directly across the Danube. The M2 subway, the HÉV electric railway from Szentendre, and various suburban and local buses converge on the square, as do peddlers hawking everything from freshly picked flowers to tattered, mismatched pairs of shoes. At No. 7 Batthyány tér is the beautiful, Baroque twin-towered **Szent Anna-templom** (Church of St. Anne), dating from 1740–62, its interior in-spired by Italian art and its oval cupola adorned with frescoes and stat-uary.

NEED A BREAK?
The **Angelika** café (✉ Batthyány tér 7, ☎ 1/212–3784), housed in the Church of St. Anne building, serves swirled meringues, chestnut-filled layer cakes, and a plethora of other heavenly pastries, all baked on the premises from family recipes. You can sit inside on small velvet chairs at marble-topped tables or at one of the umbrella-shaded tables outdoors. It's open daily 10 AM–10 PM.

㉕ **Bem József tér.** This square near the river is not particularly picturesque and can get heavy with traffic, but it houses the statue of its important namesake, Polish general József Bem, who offered his services to the 1848 revolutionaries in Vienna and then Hungary. Reorganizing the rebel forces in Transylvania, he inflicted numerous defeats on the Hapsburgs and was the war's most successful general. It was at this statue on Oc-tober 23, 1956, that a great student demonstration in sympathy with the Poles' striving for liberal reforms exploded into the brave and tragic Hungarian uprising suppressed by the Red Army.

OFF THE BEATEN PATH
JÁNOSHEGY (Janos Hill) – A *libegő* (chairlift) will take you to Janos Hill—at 1,729 ft, the highest point in Budapest—where you can climb a lookout tower for the best view of the city. ✉ *Take Bus 158 from Moszkva tér to the last stop, Zugligeti út,* ☎ *1/395–6494 or 1/376–3764.* ✇ *One-way 200 Ft., round-trip 300 Ft.* ⊙ *Mid-May–mid-Sept., daily 9–5; mid-Sept.–mid-May (depending on weather), daily 9:30–4; closed every other Mon.*

㉑ **Corvin tér.** This charming, small, shady square on Fő utca is the site of the turn-of-the-century Folk Art Institute administration building and the concert hall Budai Vigadó (☞ Nightlife and the Arts, *below*) at No. 8.

㉖ **Gül Baba türbéje** (Tomb of Gül Baba). Gül Baba, a 16th-century dervish and poet whose name means "father of roses" in Turkish, was buried in a tomb built of carved stone blocks with four oval windows. He fought in several wars waged by the Turks and fell during the siege of Buda in 1541. The tomb remains a place of pilgrimage; it is considered Europe's northernmost Muslim shrine and marks the spot where he was slain. Set at an elevation on Rózsadomb (Rose Hill), the tomb is near a good lookout for views of Buda and across the river to Pest. ⊠ *Mecset utca 14,* ☎ *1/355–8764.* 🎫 *100 Ft.* ☉ *May–Oct., Tues.–Sun. 10–4.*

� **Gyermek vasút** (Children's Railway). The 12-km (7-mi) Children's Railway runs from Széchenyihegy to Hűvösvölgy. The sweeping views make the trip well worthwhile for children and adults alike. Departures are from Széchenyi-hegy, which you can reach by taking a cogwheel railway. ⊠ *Cogwheel railway station: intersection of Szilágyi Erzsébet fasor and Pasaréti út.* 🎫 *140 Ft. each way.* ☉ *Trains run mid-Jan.–late Mar. and mid-Sept.–Dec., Wed.–Sun. 8–4; mid-Jan. and Apr.–mid-Sept., Tues.–Sun. 8–5.*

Kapucinus templom (Capuchin Church). This church was converted from a Turkish mosque at the end of the 17th century. Damaged during the revolution in 1849, it acquired its current romantic-style exterior when it was rebuilt a few years later. ⊠ *Fő utca.*

㉔ **Király-fürdő** (King Baths). The royal gem of Turkish baths in Budapest was built in the 16th century by the Turkish pasha of Buda. Its stone cupola, crowned by a golden moon and crescent, arches over the steamy, dark pools indoors. It is open to men on Monday, Wednesday, and Friday; to women on Tuesday, Thursday, and Saturday (☞ Outdoor Activities and Sports, *below*). These baths are very popular with the gay community. ⊠ *II, Fő utca 84,* ☎ *1/202–3688.* 🎫 *400 Ft.* ☉ *Weekdays 6:30 AM–6 PM, Sat. 6:30 AM–noon.*

㉒ **Szilágyi Dezső tér.** This is another of the charming little squares punctuating Fő utca; here you'll find the composer Béla Bartók's house, at No. 4.

Margit-sziget (Margaret Island)

More than 2½ km (1½ mi) long and covering nearly 200 acres, **Margit-sziget** ㉗ is ideal for strolling, jogging, sunbathing, or just loafing. In good weather, the island draws a multitudinous cross section of the city's population out to its gardens and sporting facilities. The outdoor pool complex of the Palatinus Baths (toward the Buda side), built in 1921, can attract tens of thousands of people on a summer day. Nearby are a tennis stadium, a youth athletic center, boathouses, sports grounds, and, most impressive of all, the Nemzeti Sportuszoda (National Sports Swimming Pool), designed by the architect Alfred Hajós (while still in his teens, Hajós won two gold medals in swimming at the first modern Olympic Games, held in Athens in 1896). In addition, walkers, joggers, bicyclists, and rollerbladers do laps around the island's perimeter and up and down the main road, closed to traffic except for Bus 26 (and a few official vehicles), which travels up and down the island and across the Margaret Bridge to and from Pest.

The island's natural curative hot springs have given rise to the Danubius Grand and Thermal hotels on the northern end of the island (☞

Lodging, *below*) and are piped in to two spa hotels on the mainland, the Aquincum on the Buda bank and the Hélia on the Pest side.

A Good Walk

Entering the island from its southern end at the **Margit-híd,** stroll (or rent a bicycle and pedal) north along any of the several tree-shaded paths, including the **Művész sétány,** pausing for a picnic on an open lawn, and eventually ending up at the rock garden at the northern end. From here, you can wander back to the southern end or take Bus 26 on the island's only road. A walk around the circumference of the island on the popular jogging path is also pleasant.

TIMING

A leisurely walk simply from one end to the other would take about 40 minutes, but it's nice to spend extra time wandering. To experience Margaret Island's role in Budapest life fully, go on a Saturday or Sunday afternoon to join and/or watch people picnicking, strolling, kicking a soccer ball, and otherwise whiling away the day. Sunday is a particularly good choice for strategic sightseers, who can utilize the rest of the week to cover those city sights and areas that are closed on Sundays. On weekdays, you'll share the island only with joggers and kids playing hooky from school.

Sights to See

Margit-híd (Margaret Bridge). At the southern end of the island, the Margaret Bridge is the closer of the two entrances for those coming from downtown Buda or Pest. Just north of the Chain Bridge, the bridge walkway provides gorgeous midriver views of Castle Hill and Parliament. Toward the end of 1944, the bridge was blown up by the retreating Nazis while it was crowded with rush-hour traffic. It was rebuilt in the same unusual shape—forming an obtuse angle in midstream, with a short leg leading down to the island. The original bridge was built during the 1840s by French engineer Ernest Gouin in collaboration with Gustave Eiffel.

㉗ Margit-sziget (Margaret Island). The island was first mentioned almost 2,000 years ago as the summer residence of the commander of the Roman garrison at nearby Aquincum. Later known as Rabbit Island (Insula Leporum), it was a royal hunting ground during the Árpád dynasty. King Imre, who reigned from 1196 to 1204, held court here, and several convents and monasteries were built here during the Middle Ages. (During a walk round the island, you'll see the ruins of a few of these buildings.) It takes its current name from St. Margaret, the pious daughter of King Béla IV, who at the ripe old age of 10 retired to a Dominican nunnery here.

Margit-sziget Vadaspark (Margaret Island Game Park). Just east of the rose garden is a small would-be petting zoo, if the animals were allowed to be petted. A fenced-in compound houses a menagerie of goats, rabbits, donkeys, assorted fowl and ducks, and gargantuan peacocks that sit heavily on straining tree branches and make loud crying noises that can be heard around the island. ⌨ *Free.*

Marosvásárhelyi zenélő kút (Marosvásárhely Musical Fountain). At the northern end of the island is a copy of the water-powered Marosvásárhely Musical Fountain, which plays songs and chimes. The original was designed more than 150 years ago by a Transylvanian named Péter Bodor. It stands near a picturesque, artificial **rock garden** with Japanese dwarf trees and lily ponds. The stream coursing through it never freezes, for it comes from a natural hot spring causing it instead to give off thick steam in winter that enshrouds the garden in a mystical cloud.

Művész sétány (Artists' Promenade). Through the center of the island runs the Artists' Promenade, lined with busts of Hungarian artists, writers, and musicians. Shaded by giant plane trees, it's a perfect place to stroll on a hot summer afternoon. The promenade passes close to the **rose garden** (in the center of the island), a large grassy lawn surrounded by blooming flower beds planted with hundreds of kinds of flowers. It's a great spot to picnic or to watch a game of soccer or Ultimate Frisbee, both of which are regularly played here on weekend afternoons.

Downtown Pest and the Kis körút (Little Ring Road)

Budapest's urban heart is full of bona fide sights plus innumerable tiny streets and grand avenues where you can wander for hours admiring the city's stately old buildings—some freshly sparkling after their first painting in decades, others silently but still elegantly crumbling.

Dominated by the Parliament building, the district surrounding Kossuth tér is the legislative, diplomatic, and administrative nexus of Budapest; most of the ministries are here, as are the National Bank and Courts of Justice. Downriver, the romantic Danube promenade, the Duna Korzó, extends along the stretch of riverfront across from Castle Hill. With Vörösmarty tér and pedestrian shopping street Váci utca just inland, this area forms Pest's tourist core. Going south, the Korzó ends at Március 15 tér. One block in from the river, Ferenciek tere marks the beginning of the university area, spreading south of Kossuth Lajos utca. Here, the streets are narrower and the echoes of your footsteps louder as they resound off of the elegantly aging stone buildings.

Pest is laid out in broad circular *körúts* ("ring roads" or boulevards). Vámház körút is the first sector of the 2½-km (1½-mi) Kis körút (Little Ring Road), which traces the route of the Old Town wall from Szabadsághíd (Liberty Bridge) to Deák tér. Construction of the inner körút began in 1872 and was completed in 1880. Changing names as it curves, after Kálvin tér it becomes Múzeum körút (passing by the National Museum), and then Károly körút for its final stretch ending at Deák tér. Deák tér, the only place where all three subway lines converge, could be called the dead-center of downtown. East of the körút are the weathered streets of Budapest's former ghetto, where the Great Synagogue presides proudly.

A Good Walk

Starting at Kossuth tér to see the **Országház** ㉘ and the **Néprajzi Múzeum** ㉙, it's worth walking a few blocks southeast to take in stately **Szabadság tér** ㉚ before heading back to the Danube and south to the foot of the **Széchenyi Lánchíd** at **Roosevelt tér** ㉛. As this tour involves quite a bit of walking, you may want to take Tram 2 from Kossuth tér a few stops downriver to Roosevelt tér to save your energy. While time and/or energy may not allow it just now, at some point during your visit, a walk across the Chain Bridge is a must. From Roosevelt tér go south, across the street, and join the **korzó** ㉜ along the river, strolling past the **Vigadó** ㉝ at Vigadó tér, all the way to the **Belvárosi plébánia templom** ㉞ at Március 15 tér, just under the Elizabeth Bridge. Double back up the korzó to Vigadó tér and walk in from the river on Vigadó utca to **Vörösmarty tér** ㉟.

Follow the crowds down pedestrian-only **Váci utca** ㊱, crossing busy Kossuth Lajos utca near Ferenciek tere and continuing along Váci utca's southern stretch to the **Vásárcsarnok** ㊲. Doubling back a few blocks on Váci utca, turn right onto Szerb utca and stroll past the **Szerb Ortodox templom** to the street's end at **Egyetem tér** ㊳. Here, you are going through the darker, narrower streets of this student-filled, increasingly trendy area. A detour into any of the other side streets will give you a good flavor of the area. Walking south on Kecskeméti utca, you will reach **Kálvin tér** ⑩. To save time and energy, you can also take Tram 47 or 49 from Fővám tér, in front of the Vásárcsarnok, one stop away from the Danube to Kálvin tér. Just north of Kálvin tér on Múzeum körút is the **Magyar Nemzeti Múzeum** ㊶. The **Nagy Zsinagóga** ㊷ is about ¾ km (⅓ mi) farther north along the Kis körút (Small Ring Road)—a longish walk or a short tram ride. From here, more walking along the körút, or a tram ride to the last stop, brings you to Pest's main hub, Deák tér. The **Szent István Bazilika** ㊺ is an extra but rewarding 500-yard walk north on Bajcsy-Zsilinszky út.

TIMING

This is a particularly rich part of the city; the suggested walk will take the better part of a day, including time to visit the museums, stroll on the korzó, and browse on Vaci utca—not to mention time for lunch.

Sights to See

③④ **Belvárosi plébánia templom** (Inner City Parish Church). Dating to the 12th century, this is the oldest ecclesiastical building in Pest. It's actually built on something even older—the remains of the Contra Aquincum, a 3rd-century Roman fortress and tower, parts of which are visible next to the church. There is hardly any architectural style that cannot be found in some part or another, starting with a single Romanesque arch in its south tower. The single nave still has its original Gothic chancel and some 15th-century Gothic frescoes. Two side chapels contain beautifully carved Renaissance altarpieces and tabernacles of red marble from the early 16th century. During Budapest's years of Turkish occupation, the church served as a mosque—and this is remembered by a *mihrab*, a Muslim prayer niche. During the 18th century, the church was given two Baroque towers and its present facade. In 1808 it was enriched with a rococo pulpit, and still later a superb winged triptych was added to the main altar. From 1867 to 1875, Franz Liszt lived only a few steps away from the church, in a town house where he held regular "musical Sundays" at which Richard and Cosima Wagner were frequent guests and participants. Liszt's own musical Sunday mornings often began in this church. An admirer of its acoustics and organ, he conducted many masses here, including the first Budapest performance of his *Missa Choralis*, in 1872. ✉ *V, Március 15 tér 2*, ☎ *1/317–3322*.

③⑧ **Egyetem tér** (University Square). Budapest's University of Law sits on University Square in the heart of the city's university neighborhood. On one corner is the cool gray-and-green marble **Egyetemi Templom** (University Church), one of Hungary's most beautiful Baroque buildings. Built between 1725 and 1742, it has an especially splendid pulpit.

④④ **Evangélikus Templom and Evangélikus Múzeum** (Lutheran Church and Lutheran Museum). The neoclassical Lutheran Church sits in the center of it all on busy Deák tér. Classical concerts are regularly held here. The church's interior designer, János Krausz, flouted then-traditional church architecture by placing a single large interior beneath the huge vaulted roof structure. The adjoining school, which the revolutionary poet Petőfi attended in 1833–34, is now the Lutheran Museum, which traces the role of Protestantism in Hungarian history and contains Martin Luther's original will. ✉ *Deák Ferenc tér 4*, ☎ *1/317–4173*. ☜ *Museum 200 Ft.; church free (except during concerts)*. ⊙ *Museum Tues.–Sun. 10–6.*

③⑦ **Ferenciek Templom** (Franciscan church). This pale-yellow church was built in 1743. On the wall facing Kossuth Lajos utca is a bronze relief showing a scene from the devastating flood of 1838, which swept away many houses and people; the detail is so vivid that it almost makes you seasick. A faded arrow below the relief indicates the high-water mark of almost 4 ft. Next to it is the **Nereids Fountain,** a popular meeting place for students from the nearby Eötvös Loránd University, which elaborates on the square's nautical motif. ✉ *V, Ferenciek tere.*

Görög Ortodox templom (Greek Orthodox Church). Built at the end of the 18th century in late-Baroque style, the Greek Orthodox Church was remodeled a century later by Miklós Ybl, who designed the Opera House and many other important Budapest landmarks. The church retains some fine wood carvings and a dazzling array of icons by late-18th-century Serbian master Miklós Jankovich. ✉ *V, Petőfi tér 2/b.*

40 **Kálvin tér** (Calvin Square). Calvin Square takes its name from the neoclassical Protestant church that tries to dominate this busy traffic hub; more glaringly noticeable, however, is the billboard of a giant Pepsi adverstisement. The Kecskeméti Kapu, a main gate of Pest, once stood here, as well as a cattle market that was a notorious den of thieves. At the beginning of the 19th century, this was where Pest ended and the prairie began.

NEED A BREAK? The Hotel Korona's popular café, **Korona Passage** (✉ Kecskeméti utca 14, ☎ 1/317–4111), has a *palacsinta* (crepe) bar where you can watch the cooks prepare giant Hungarian crepes brimming with such fillings as apple, chocolate, and *túró* (sweetened cottage cheese). The café also serves soups and sandwiches and has a salad bar.

★ 32 **Korzó.** The neighborhood to the south of Roosevelt tér has regained much of its past elegance—if not its architectural grandeur—with the erection of the Atrium Hyatt, Inter-Continental, and Budapest Marriott luxury hotels. Traversing all three and continuing well beyond them is the riverside Korzó, a pedestrian promenade lined with park benches and appealing outdoor cafés from which one can enjoy postcard-perfect views of Gellért Hill and Castle Hill directly across the Danube. Try to take a stroll in the evening, when the views are lit up in shimmering gold. In summer and during holidays and festivals, you'll often find stalls selling colorful folk crafts and souvenirs, usually next to the Marriott Hotel.

NEED A BREAK? The **Bécsi Kávéház** (Viennese Café; ✉ V, Apáczai Csere János u. 12–14, ☎ 1/327–6333), in the Hotel Inter-Continental, serves mouthwatering *isler* (giant chocolate-covered cookies filled with apricot or raspberry jam) and cream pastries.

Közgazdagsági Egyetem (University of Economics). Just below the Liberty Bridge on the waterfront, the monumental neo-Renaissance building was once the Customs House. Built in 1871–74 by Miklós Ybl, it is now also known as *közgáz,* after a stint during the Communist era as Karl Marx University. ✉ *Fővám tér.*

41 **Magyar Nemzeti Múzeum** (Hungarian National Museum). Built between 1837 and 1847, the museum is a fine example of 19th-century classicism—simple, well proportioned, and surrounded by a large garden. In front of this building on March 15, 1848, Sándor Petőfi recited his revolutionary poem, the "National Song" ("Nemzeti dal"), and the "12 Points," a list of political demands by young Hungarians calling on the people to rise up against the Hapsburgs. Celebrations of the national holiday commemorating the failed revolution are held on these steps every year on March 15.

The museum's most sacred treasure, the **Szent Korona** (Holy Crown), reposes with other royal relics in a domed Hall of Honor off the main lobby. The crown sits like a golden soufflé above a Byzantine band of holy scenes in enamel and pearls and other gems. It seems to date from the 12th century, so it could not be the crown that Pope Sylvester II presented to St. Stephen in the year 1000, when he was crowned the first king of Hungary. Nevertheless, it is known as the Crown of St. Stephen and has been regarded—even by Communist governments—as the legal symbol of Hungarian sovereignty and unbroken statehood for nearly a millennium. In 1945 the fleeing Hungarian army handed over the crown and its accompanying regalia to the Americans rather than have them fall into Soviet hands. They were restored to Hungary in 1978.

Other rarities include a completely furnished Turkish tent; masterworks of cabinet making and wood carving, including pews from churches in Nyírbátor and Transylvania; a piano that belonged to both Beethoven and Liszt; and, in the treasury, masterpieces of goldsmithing, among them the 11th-century Constantions Monomachos crown from Byzantium and the richly pictorial 16th-century chalice of Miklós Pálffy. Looking at it is like reading the "Prince Valiant" comic strip in gold. The epic Hungarian history exhibit has exhibits chronicling the end of communism and the much-celebrated exodus of the Russian troops. ⊠ *IX, Múzeum körút 14–16,* ☎ *1/338–2122.* ⌨ *270 Ft.* ☽ *Mid-Mar.– mid-Oct., Wed.–Sun. 10–6; mid-Oct.–mid-Mar., Wed.–Sun. 10–5. Museum may open Tues. also, depending on demand; call ahead to check.*

★ ㊷ **Nagy Zsinagóga** (Great Synagogue). Seating 3,000, Europe's largest synagogue was designed by Ludwig Förs and built between 1844 and 1859 in a Byzantine-Moorish style described as "consciously archaic Romantic-Eastern." Desecrated by German and Hungarian Nazis, it was painstakingly reconstructed with donations from all over the world; its doors reopened in fall 1996. While it is used for regular services during much of the year, it is generally not used in midwinter as the space is too large to heat; between December and February, visiting hours are erratic. In the courtyard behind the synagogue, a weeping willow made of metal honors the victims of the Holocaust. Liszt and Saint-Saëns are among the great musicians who have played its grand organ. ⊠ *Dohány u. 2–8,* ☎ *1/342–1335.* ⌨ *Free.* ☽ *Weekdays 10–3, Sun. 10–1. Closed Jewish holidays and Dec.*

★ ㉙ **Néprajzi Múzeum** (Museum of Ethnography). The 1890s neoclassical temple opposite Parliament formerly housed the Supreme Court. Now a vast, impressive permanent exhibition, "The Folk Culture of the Hungarian People," explains all aspects of peasant life from the end of the 18th century until World War I; explanatory texts are provided in both English and Hungarian. Besides embroideries and carvings—the authentic pieces you can't see at touristy folk shops—there are farming tools, furniture, and traditional costumes. The central room of the building alone is worth the entrance fee: a majestic, cavernous hall with ornate marble staircases and pillars, and towering stained-glass windows. ⊠ *V, Kossuth tér 12,* ☎ *1/332–6340.* ⌨ *250 Ft., Tues. free.* ☽ *Mid-Mar.–mid-Oct., Tues.–Sun. 10–6; mid-Oct.–mid-Mar., Tues.–Sun. 10–4.*

★ ㉘ **Országház** (Parliament). The most visible, though not highly accessible, symbol of Budapest's left bank is the huge neo-Gothic Parliament. Mirrored in the Danube much the way Britain's Parliament is reflected by the Thames, it lies midway between the Margaret and Chain bridges and can be reached by the M2 subway (Kossuth tér station) and waterfront Tram 2. A fine example of historicizing, eclectic fin-de-siècle architecture, it was designed by the Hungarian architect Ímre Steindl and built by a thousand workers between 1885 and 1902. The grace and dignity of its long facade and 24 slender towers, with spacious arcades and high

windows balancing its vast central dome, lend this living landmark a re-
freshingly baroque spatial effect. The exterior is lined with 90 statues of
great figures in Hungarian history; the corbels are ornamented by 242
allegorical statues. Inside are 691 rooms, 10 courtyards, and 29 staircases; some 88 pounds of gold were used for the staircases and halls.
These halls are also a gallery of late-19th-century Hungarian art, with
frescoes and canvases depicting Hungarian history, starting with Mihály
Munkácsy's large painting of the Magyar Conquest of 896. Unfortunately,
because Parliament is a workplace for legislators, the building is not open
to individual visitors and must be toured in groups at certain hours on
specific city tours organized by IBUSZ Travel (☞ Visitor Information *in*
Budapest A to Z, *below*). ✉ V, *Kossuth tér*.

㉛ **Roosevelt tér** (Roosevelt Square). This square opening onto the Danube
is less closely connected with the U.S. president than with the progressive
Hungarian statesman Count István Széchenyi, dubbed "the greatest Hungarian" even by his adversary, Kossuth. The neo-Renaissance palace
of the **Magyar Tudományos Akadémia** (Academy of Sciences) on the
north side was built between 1862 and 1864, after Széchenyi's suicide.
It is a fitting memorial, for in 1825, the statesman donated a year's income from all his estates to establish the academy. Another Széchenyi
project, the Széchenyi Lánchíd (☞ *below*), leads into the square; there
stands a statue of Széchenyi near one of another statesman, Ferenc Deák,
whose negotiations led to the establishment of the dual monarchy
after Kossuth's 1848–49 revolution failed. Both men lived on this square.

★ **㉚** **Szabadság tér** (Liberty Square). This is the site of the **Magyar Tele-
vizió** (Hungarian Television Headquarters), a former stock exchange
with what look like four temples and two castles on its roof, and a
solemn-looking neoclassical shrine, the **Nemzeti Bank** (National Bank).
The bank's Postal Savings Bank branch, adjacent to the main building but visible from behind Szabadság tér on Hold utca, is another exuberant Art Nouveau masterpiece of architect Ödön Lechner, built in
1901 with colorful majolica mosaics, characteristically curvaceous
windows, and pointed decorative towers ending in swirling gold flourishes. In the square's center remains one of the few monuments to the
Russian "liberation" that were spared the recent cleansing of symbols
of the past regime. The decision to retain this obelisk—because it represents liberation from the Nazis during World War II—caused out-
rage among many groups, prompting some to vow to haul it away
themselves (though for the moment it remains). With the Stars and Stripes
flying out in front, the **American Embassy** is at Szabadság tér 12.
Movie fans may notice that scenes from the film *Evita*, starring
Madonna and Antonio Banderas, were filmed on the square.

Széchenyi Lánchíd (Chain Bridge). This is the oldest and most beautiful of the Danube's eight bridges. Before the lánchíd was built, the river
could be crossed only by ferry or by a pontoon bridge that had to be
removed when ice blocks began floating downstream in winter. It was
constructed at the initiative of the great Hungarian reformer and phi-
lanthropist Count István Széchenyi, using an 1839 design by the French
civil engineer William Tierney Clark, who had also designed London's
Hammersmith Bridge. This classical, almost poetically graceful and sym-
metrical suspension bridge was finished by his Scottish namesake,
Adam Clark, who also built the 383-yard tunnel under Castle Hill, thus
connecting the Danube quay with the rest of Buda. After it was destroyed by the Nazis, the bridge was rebuilt in its original form (though
slightly widened for traffic) and was reopened in 1949, on the centenary of its inauguration. At the Buda end of the bridge is **Clark Ádám
tér** (Adam Clark Square), where you can zip up to Castle Hill on the

sometimes crowded Sikló funicular rail. ☎ *250 Ft.* ⊙ *Funicular daily 7:30 AM–10 PM; closed every other Mon.*

★ ㊺ **Szent István Bazilika** (St. Stephen's Basilica). Dark and massive, this is one of the chief landmarks of Pest and the city's largest church—it can hold 8,500 people. Its very Holy Roman front porch greets you with a tympanum bustling with statuary. The basilica's dome and the dome of Parliament are by far the most visible in the Pest skyline, and this is no accident: With the Magyar Millennium of 1896 in mind, both domes were planned to be 315 ft high.

The millennium was not yet in sight when architect József Hild began building the basilica in neoclassical style in 1851, two years after the revolution was suppressed. After Hild's death, the project was taken over in 1867 by Miklós Ybl, the architect who did the most to transform modern Pest into a monumental metropolis—in contrast to medieval Buda across the river. Wherever he could, Ybl shifted Hild's motifs toward the neo-Renaissance mode that Ybl favored. When the dome collapsed, partly damaging the walls, he made even more drastic changes. Ybl died in 1891, five years before the 1,000-year celebration, and the basilica was completed in neo-Renaissance style by József Kauser—but not until 1905.

Below the cupola, the interior is surprisingly cool and restful, a rich collection of late-19th-century Hungarian art: mosaics, altarpieces, and statuary (what heady days the millennium must have meant for local talents!). There are 150 kinds of marble, all from Hungary except for the Carrara in the sanctuary's centerpiece: a white statue of King (St.) Stephen I, Hungary's first king and patron saint. Stephen's mummified right hand is preserved as a relic in the **Szent Jobb Kápolna** (Holy Right Chapel); the guard will illuminate it for you for two minutes for a minimal charge. Visitors can also climb the 364 stairs (or take the elevator) to the top of the cupola for a spectacular view of the city. Extensive restorations have been under way at the aging basilica for years, with a target completion date of 2010, and some part of the structure is likely to be under scaffolding when you visit. ⊠ *V, Szt. István tér,* ☎ *1/317–2859.* 🖃 *Church free, Szt. Jobb chapel 100 Ft., cupola 350 Ft.* ⊙ *Church Mon.–Sat. 7–7, Sun. 1–7; Szt. Jobb Chapel Apr.–Sept., Mon.–Sat. 9–5, Sun. 1–5; Oct.–Mar., Mon.–Sat. 10–4, Sun. 1–4; Cupola Apr. and Sept.–Oct., daily 10–5; May–Aug., daily 9–6.*

Szerb Ortodox templom (Serbian Orthodox Church). Built in 1688, this lovely burnt-orange church, one of Budapest's oldest buildings, sits in a shaded garden surrounded by thick stone walls of the same color detailed with large-tile mosaics and wrought-iron gates. ⊠ *V, Szerb utca.*

㊱ **Váci utca.** Immediately north of Elizabeth Bridge is Budapest's best-known shopping street and most unabashed tourist zone, Váci utca, a pedestrian precinct with electrified 19th-century lampposts, smart shops with credit-card emblems on ornate doorways. No bargain basement, Váci utca gets its special flavor from the mix of native furriers, tailors, designers, shoemakers, and folk artists, as well as an increasing number of internationally known boutiques. There are also bookstores—first- and secondhand in addition to foreign-language—and china and crystal shops, as well as gourmet food stores redolent of paprika. Váci utca's second half, south of Kossuth Lajos utca, was transformed into another pedestrian-only zone a few years ago and has a different character from its northern side. Still changing, as new leases are bought and old ones hang on, the street is lined with a clash of past and future: A tiny button shop and a knife and scissor sharpening store struggle alongside tacky souvenir vendors and flashy boutiques. Watch your purses and wallets—against inflated prices *and* active pickpockets.

43 **Városház.** The monumental former city council building, which used to be a hospital for wounded soldiers and then a resort for the elderly ("home" would be too cozy for so vast a hulk), is now Budapest's city hall. It's enormous enough to loom over the row of shops and businesses lining Károly körút in front of it but can only be entered through courtyards or side streets (Gerlóczy utca is the most accessible). Its 57-window facade, interrupted by five projections, fronts on Városház utca, which parallels the körút. The Tuscan columns at the main entrance and the allegorical statuary of *Atlas, War,* and *Peace* are especially splendid. There was once a chapel in the center of the main facade, but now only its spire remains. ✉ *V, Városház u. 9–12,* ☎ *1/318–6066.*

39 **Vásárcsarnok** (Central Market Hall). The magnificent hall, a 19th-century iron-frame construction, was reopened in late 1994 after years of renovation (and disputes over who would foot the bill). Even during the leanest years of Communist shortages, the abundance of food came as a revelation to shoppers from East and West. Today, the cavernous, three-story hall once again teems with people browsing among stalls packed with salamis and red-paprika chains, crusty bread, fresh fish, and other tastes of Hungary. Upstairs you can buy folk embroideries and souvenirs. ✉ *IX, Vámhaz körút 1–3.* ☉ *Mon. 6 AM–5 PM, Tues.–Fri. 6 AM–6 PM, Sat. 6 AM–2 PM.*

33 **Vigadó** (Concert Hall). Designed in a striking romantic style by Frigyes Feszl and inaugurated in 1865 with Franz Liszt conducting his own *St. Elizabeth Oratorio,* the concert hall is a curious mixture of Byzantine, Moorish, Romanesque, and Hungarian motifs, punctuated by dancing statues and sturdy pillars. Brahms, Debussy, and Casals are among the other phenomenal musicians who have graced its stage. Mahler's *Symphony No. 1* and many works by Bartók were first performed here. Severely damaged in World War II, the hall was rebuilt and reopened in 1980. While you can go into the lobby on your own, the hall is open only for concerts. ✉ *V, Vigadó tér 2.*

★ **35** **Vörösmarty tér** (Vörösmarty Square). This large, handsome square at the northern end of Váci utca is the heart of Pest's tourist life. Street musicians and sidewalk cafés make it one of the liveliest places in Budapest and a good spot to sit and relax—if you can manage to ward off the aggressive caricature sketchers. Grouped around a white-marble statue of the 19th-century poet and dramatist Mihály Vörösmarty are luxury shops, airline offices, and an elegant former pissoir. Now a lovely kiosk, it displays gold-painted historic scenes of the square's golden days.

NEED A
BREAK?

The best-known, tastiest, and most tasteful address on Vörösmarty Square belongs to the **Gerbeaud** pastry shop (✉ Vörösmarty tér 7, ☎ 1/318–1311), founded in 1858 by a French confectioner, Henri Kugler, and later taken over by the Swiss family Gerbeaud. Filling most of a square block, it offers dozens of sweets (as well as sandwiches, coffee, and other not so sugary snacks), served in a salon with green-marble tables and Regency-style marble fireplaces or at tables outside in summer. A mildly hostile staff is an integral part of the Gerbeaud tradition.

Zsidó Múzeum (Jewish Museum). The four-room museum, around the corner from the Great Synagogue (☞ *above*) has displays explaining the effect of the Holocaust on Hungarian and Transylvanian Jews, as well as exhibits on Jewish rituals and traditions. (There are labels in English.) In late 1993, burglars ransacked the museum and got away with approximately 80% of its priceless collection; several months later, the stolen objects were found in Romania and returned to their home. ✉ *Dohány utca 2,* ☎ *1/342–8949.* 🎟 *150 Ft. suggested donation.* ⏲ *Mon.–Thurs. 10–6, Fri. 10–3, Sun. 10–2.*

Andrássy út

Behind St. Stephen's Basilica, at the crossroad along Bajcsy-Zsilinszky út, begins Budapest's grandest avenue, **Andrássy út.** For too many years, this broad boulevard of music and mansions bore the tongue-twisting, mind-bending name of Népköztársaság (Avenue of the People's Republic) and, for a while before that, Stalin Avenue. In 1990, however, it reverted to its old name honoring Count Gyula Andrássy, a statesman who in 1867 became the first constitutional premier of Hungary. The boulevard that would eventually bear his name was begun in 1872, as Buda and Pest (and Óbuda) were about to be unified. Most of the mansions that line it were completed by 1884. It took another dozen years before the first **underground railway** on the Continent was completed for—you guessed it—the Magyar Millennium in 1896. Though preceded by London's Underground (1863), Budapest's was the world's first electrified subway. Only slightly modernized but refurbished for the 1996 millecentenary, this "Little Metro" is still running a 4-km (2½-mi) stretch from Vörösmarty tér to the far end of City Park. Using tiny yellow trains with tanklike treads, and stopping at antique stations marked FÖLDALATTI (Underground) on their wrought-iron entranceways, Line 1 is a tourist attraction in itself. Six of its 10 stations are along Andrássy út.

A Good Walk

A walking tour of Andrássy út's sights is straightforward: Begin at its downtown end, near Deák tér, and stroll its length (about 2 km [1¼ mi]) all the way to **Hősök tere** ⑤①. The first third of the avenue, from Bajcsy-Zsilinszky út to the eight-sided intersection called Oktogon, boasts a row of eclectic city palaces with balconies held up by stone giants. Pause at the **Operaház** ④⑦ and other points along the way. One block past the Operaház, Andrássy út intersects Budapest's Broadway: Nagymező utca contains several theaters, cabarets, and nightclubs. Andrássy út alters when it crosses the Nagy körút (Outer Ring Road), at the Oktogon crossing. Four rows of trees and scores of flower beds make the thoroughfare look more like a garden promenade, but its cultural character lingers. Farther up, past **Kodály körönd,** the rest of Andrássy út is dominated by widely spaced mansions surrounded by private gardens. At Hősök tere, browse through the **Műcsarnok** ⑤② and/or the **Szépművészeti Múzeum** ⑤③, and finish off with a stroll into the Vajdahunyad Vár (Vajdahunyad Castle) and Városliget (City Park; ☞ Városliget [City Park], *below*). You can return to Deák tér on the subway, the Millenniumi Földalatti (Millennial Underground).

TIMING

As most museums are closed Mondays, it's best to explore Andrássy Út on other days, preferably weekdays or early Saturday, when stores are also open for browsing. During opera season, you can time your exploration to land you at the Operaház stairs just before 7 PM to watch the spectacle of opera goers flowing in for the evening's performance.

Sights to See

Budapest Bábszínház (Budapest Puppet Theater). In this templelike, eclectic building, you'll find colorful shows that both children and adults deem enjoyable even if they don't understand Hungarian. Watch for showings of *Cinderella* (*Hamupipőke*) and *Snow White and the Seven*

Dwarfs (*Hófehérke*), part of the theater's regular repertoire. ✉ *VI, Andrássy út 69,* ☎ *1/322–5200.*

Drechsler Kastély (Drechsler Palace). Across the street from the Operaház is the French Renaissance–style Drechsler Palace. An early work by Ödön Lechner, Hungary's master of Art Nouveau, it is now the home of the National Ballet School. ✉ *VI, Andrássy út 25.*

Hopp Ferenc Kelet-Ázsiai Művészeti Múzeum (Ferenc Hopp Museum of Eastern Asiatic Arts). Stop in here to see the rich collection of exotica from the Indian subcontinent, such as sculpture and devotional pieces, and Far Eastern ceramics. ✉ *Andrássy út 103,* ☎ *1/322–8476.* 🎫 *80 Ft.* ⏲ *Oct.–mid-Apr., Tues.–Sun. 10–4; mid-Apr.–Sept., Tues.–Sun. 10–6.*

★ (51) **Hősök tere** (Heroes' Square). Andrássy út ends in grandeur at Heroes' Square, with Budapest's answer to Berlin's Brandenburg Gate. Cleaned and refurbished in 1996 for the millecentenary, the **Millenniumi Emlékmű** (Millennial Monument) is a semicircular twin colonnade with statues of Hungary's kings and leaders between its pillars. Set back in its open center, a 118-ft stone column is crowned by a dynamic statue of the archangel Gabriel, his outstretched arms bearing the ancient emblems of Hungary. At its base ride seven bronze horsemen: the Magyar chieftains, led by Árpád, whose tribes conquered the land in 896. Before the column lies a simple marble slab, the **National War Memorial**, the nation's altar, at which every visiting foreign dignitary lays a ceremonial wreath. England's Queen Elizabeth upheld the tradition during her royal visit in May of 1992. In 1991 Pope John Paul II conducted a mass here. Just a few months earlier, half a million Hungarians had convened to recall the memory of Imre Nagy, the reform-minded Communist prime minister who partially inspired the 1956 revolution. Heroes' Square is flanked by the **Műcsarnok** and the **Szépművészeti Múzeum** (☞ *below*).

Kodály körönd. A handsome traffic circle with imposing statues of three Hungarian warriors—leavened by a fourth one of a poet—the Kodály Körönd is surrounded by plane and chestnut trees. Look carefully at the towered mansions on the north side of the circle—behind the soot you'll see the fading colors of ornate frescoes peeking through. The circle takes its name from the composer Zoltán Kodály, who lived just beyond it at Andrássy út 89.

㊿ **Liszt Ferenc Emlékmúzeum** (Franz Liszt Memorial Museum). Andrássy út No. 67 was the original location of the old Academy of Music and Franz Liszt's last home; entered around the corner, it now houses a museum. Several rooms display the original furniture and instruments from Liszt's time there; another room shows temporary exhibits. The museum hosts excellent, free classical concerts year round, except in August. ✉ *Vörösmarty u. 35,* ☎ *1/342–7320.* 🎫 *100 Ft.* ⏲ *Weekdays 10–6, Sat. 9–5. Classical concerts (free with admission) Sept.–July, Sat. 11* AM. *Closed Aug. 1–20.*

㊾ **Liszt Ferenc Zeneakadémia** (Franz Liszt Academy of Music). Along with the **Vigadó** (☞ Downtown Pest and the Kis körút [Little Ring Road], *above*), this is one of the city's main concert halls. The academy in fact has two auditoriums: a green-and-gold 1,200-seat main hall and a smaller hall for chamber music and solo recitals. Outside this exuberant Art Nouveau building, a statue of Liszt oversees the square. The academy has been operating as a highly revered teaching institute since 1907; Liszt was its first chairman and Erkel its first director. The pianist Ernő (formerly Ernst) Dohnányi and composers Béla Bartók and Zoltán Kodály were teachers here. ✉ *Liszt Ferenc tér 8,* ☎ *1/342–0179.*

NEED A
BREAK?

Lukács (⊠ VI, Andrássy út 70, ☎ 1/332–7942) shares its entrance with a glossy international bank, but its upstairs salon is steeped in classic café elegance—it was built in 1912, during Budapest's café-culture glory days. The room is anchored at one end by an ornate fireplace; marble-topped tables cluster under a sparkling chandelier. Stop in for a jolt of espresso and something sweet from the pastry display. Despite the glamour, there is an unsettling element; in the repressive 1950s the café was taken over by the secret police to serve as a meeting spot, and to many locals, it still evokes those dark times.

48 Mai Manó Fotógaléria (Mai Manó Photo Gallery). This weathered yet ornate turn-of-the-century building was built as a photography studio, where the wealthy bourgeoisie would come to be photographed by imperial and royal court photographer Manó Mai. Inside, ironwork and frescoes ornament the curving staircase leading up to the tiny gallery, the only one in Budapest that is exclusively devoted to photography. Established in late 1995, the gallery displays changing exhibits and sells books and publications. Restorations are under way to rejuvenate the tired old building and to expand the facilities. ⊠ V, Nagymező u. 20, ☎ 1/302–4398. 🎫 Free. ◐ Weekdays 2–6.

52 Műcsarnok (Palace of Exhibitions). The city's largest hall for special exhibitions is a striking 1895 temple of culture with a colorful tympanum. After four years of exhaustive renovations, the Palace of Exhibitions reopened its doors during the 1995 Budapest Spring Festival. Its program of events includes exhibitions of contemporary Hungarian and international art and a rich series of films, plays, and concerts. ⊠ XIV, Dózsa György út 37, ☎ 1/343–7401. 🎫 250 Ft., Tues. free. ◐ Tues.–Sun. 10–6.

★ **47 Operaház** (Opera House). Miklós Ybl's crowning achievement is the neo-Renaissance Opera House, built between 1875 and 1884. There are those who prefer its architecture to that of the Vienna State Opera or the Paris Opera. Badly damaged during the siege of 1944–45, Budapest's Opera House was restored for its 1984 centenary. Two buxom marble sphinxes guard the driveway; the main entrance is flanked by Alajos Strobl's "romantic-realist" limestone statues of Liszt and of another 19th-century Hungarian composer, Ferenc Erkel, the father of Hungarian opera (his patriotic opera Bánk bán is still performed for national celebrations).

Inside, the spectacle begins even before the performance does. You glide up grand staircases and through wood-paneled corridors and gilt lime-green salons into a glittering jewel box of an auditorium. Its four tiers of boxes are held up by helmeted sphinxes beneath a frescoed ceiling by Károly Lotz. Lower down there are frescoes everywhere, with intertwined motifs of Apollo and Dionysus. In its early years, the Budapest Opera was conducted by Gustav Mahler (from 1888 to 1891) and, after World War II, by Otto Klemperer.

The best way to experience the Opera House's interior is to see a ballet or opera; and while performance quality varies, tickets are relatively cheap and easy to come by, at least by tourist standards. And descending from La Bohème into the Földalatti station beneath the Opera House was described by travel writer Stephen Brook in The Double Eagle as stepping "out of one period piece and into another." There are no performances in summer, except for the weeklong BudaFest international opera and ballet festival in mid-August. Fifty-minute tours (in English) are usually conducted daily at 3 PM and 4 PM; meet by the sphinx at the Dálszínház utca entrance. (Call ahead to confirm that one is being given). The cost is about 900 Ft. ⊠ *VI, Andrássy út 22,* ☎ *1/331–2550 (ext. 156 for tours).*

㊻ **Postamúzeum** (Postal Museum). The best of Andrássy út's many marvelous stone mansions is luckily visitable, for the Postal Museum occupies an apartment with frescoes by Károly Lotz (whose work adorns St. Stephen's Basilica and the Opera House). Among the displays is an exhibition on the history of Hungarian mail, radio, and telecommunications. There are English-language pamphlets available. Even if the exhibits don't thrill you, the venue is worth the visit. ⊠ *Andrássy út 3,* ☎ *1/269–6838.* 🖃 *70 Ft.* ☉ *Tues.–Sun. 10–6.*

★ **㊾** **Szépművészeti Múzeum** (Museum of Fine Arts). Across Heroes' Square from the Palace of Exhibitions and built by the same team of Albert Schickedanz and Fülöp Herzog, the Museum of Fine Arts houses Hungary's finest collection, rich in Flemish and Dutch old masters. With seven fine El Grecos and five beautiful Goyas as well as paintings by Velázquez and Murillo, the collection of Spanish old masters is one of the best outside Spain. The Italian school is represented by Giorgione, Bellini, Correggio, Tintoretto, and Titian masterpieces and, above all, two superb Raphael paintings: *Eszterházy Madonna* and his immortal *Portrait of a Youth,* rescued after a world-famous art heist. Nineteenth-century French art includes works by Delacroix, Pissarro, Cézanne, Toulouse-Lautrec, Gauguin, Renoir, and Monet. There are also more than 100,000 drawings (including five by Rembrandt and three studies by Leonardo), Egyptian and Greco-Roman exhibitions, late-Gothic winged altars from northern Hungary and Transylvania, and works by all the leading figures of Hungarian art up to the present. A 20th-century collection was added to the museum's permanent exhibits in 1994, comprising an interesting series of statues, paintings, and drawings by Chagall, Le Corbusier, and others. Labels are in both Hungarian and English; there's also an English-language booklet on the permanent collection for sale. ⊠ *XIV, Dózsa György út 41,* ☎ *1/343–9759.* 🖃 *250 Ft.* ☉ *Tues.–Sun. 10–5:30.*

Városliget (City Park)

A Good Walk

Heroes' Square is the gateway to the **Városliget** (City Park): a square km (almost half a square mi) of recreation, entertainment, beauty, and culture. A bridge behind the Millennial Monument leads across a boating basin that becomes an artificial ice-skating rink in winter; to the south of this lake stands a statue of George Washington, erected in 1906 with donations by Hungarian emigrants to the United States. Next to the lake stands **Vajdahunyad Vár**, built in myriad architectural styles. Visitors can soak or swim at the turn-of-the-century Széchenyi Fürdő, jog along the park paths, or careen on Vidám Park's roller coaster. There's also the Petőfi Csarnok, a leisure-time youth center and major concert hall on the site of an old industrial exhibition.

TIMING

Fair-weather weekends, when the children's attractions are teeming with kids and parents and the Széchenyi Fürdő brimming with bathers, are the best time for people-watchers to visit City Park; if you go on a weekday, the main sights are rarely crowded.

Sights to See

☻ **Budapesti Állatkert** (Budapest Zoo). This fairly depressing urban zoo is brightened—for humans, anyway—by an elephant pavilion decorated with Zsolnay majolica and glazed ceramic animals. The zoo cares for a variety of exotic animals, including hippos, a favorite of local young-

sters. ⊠ *XIV, Állatkerti körút 6–12,* ☎ *1/343–6073.* ☲ *400 Ft.* ◷
Mar. and Oct., daily 9–5; Apr. and Sept., daily 9–6; May, daily 9–
6:30; June–Aug., daily 9–7; Nov.–Feb., daily 9–4 (last tickets sold 1
hr before closing).

◐ **Fővárosi Nagycirkusz** (Municipal Grand Circus). This circus puts on
colorful performances by local acrobats, clowns, and animal trainers,
as well as by international guests, in its small ring. The performance
schedule varies from November to June; you'll need to call ahead. ⊠
XIV, Állatkerti körút 7, ☎ *1/343–8300.* ☲ *Weekdays 350–650 Ft.,*
weekends 400–750 Ft. ◷ *July–Aug., Wed.–Sat. 3 PM and 7 PM, Sun.*
10 AM and 3 PM; closed Sept.–Oct.

Széchenyi Fürdő (Széchenyi Baths). Dating from 1876, these vast baths
are in a beautiful neo-Baroque building in the middle of City Park; they
comprise one of the biggest spas in Europe. There are several thermal
pools indoors as well as two outdoors, which remain open even in winter, when dense steam hangs thick over the hot water's surface—you
can just barely make out the figures of elderly men, submerged shoul-
der deep, crowded around waterproof chess boards (☞ Outdoor Activities and Sports, *below*). ⊠ *XIV, Állatkerti körút 11,* ☎ *1/321–0310.*
☲ *450 Ft.* ◷ *May–Sept., daily 6–6; Oct.–Apr., daily 6–5.*

★ **Vajdahunyad Vár** (Vajdahunyad Castle). Beside the City Park's lake
stands this castle, an art historian's Disneyland, named for the Transylvanian home (today in Hunedoara, Romania) of János Hunyadi, a
15th-century Hungarian hero in the struggle against the Turks. This
fantastic medley borrows from all of Hungary's historic and architectural past, starting with the Romanesque gateway of the cloister of Jak
in western Hungary. A Gothic castle, Transylvanian turrets, Renaissance loggia, Baroque portico, and Byzantine decoration are all guarded
by a spooky modern (1903) bronze statue of the anonymous medieval
chronicler who was the first recorder of Hungarian history. Designed
for the millennial celebration in 1896 but not completed until 1908,
this hodgepodge houses the surprisingly interesting **Mezőgazdasági**
Múzeum (Agricultural Museum), with intriguingly arranged sections
on animal husbandry, forestry, horticulture, hunting, and fishing. ⊠
XIV, Városliget, Széchenyi Island, ☎ *1/343–3198.* ☲ *Museum 170*
Ft. ◷ *Mid-Feb.–Nov., Tues.–Sat. 10–5, Sun. 10–6; Dec.–mid-Feb.,*
Tues.–Fri. 10–4, weekends 10–5.

◐ **Vidám Park.** Budapest's somewhat weary amusement park is next to the
zoo and is crawling with happy children with their parents or grandparents
in tow. Rides cost around $1 (some are for preschoolers). There are also
game rooms and a scenic railway. Next to the main park is a separate,
smaller section for toddlers. In winter, only a few rides operate. ⊠
Városliget, Állatkerti krt. 14–16, ☎ *1/343–0996.* ☲ *100 Ft.* ◷ *Mid-*
Mar.–Aug., daily 10–7; Sept.–mid-Mar., daily 10–late afternoon.

Eastern Pest and the Nagy körút (Great Ring Road)

This section covers primarily Kossuth Lajos–Rákóczi út and the Nagy
körút (Great Ring Road)—busy, less touristy urban thoroughfares full
of people, cars, shops, and Budapest's unique urban flavor.

Beginning a few blocks from the Elizabeth Bridge, Kossuth Lajos utca
is Budapest's busiest shopping street. Try to look above and beyond
the store windows to the architecture and activity along Kossuth Lajos
utca and its continuation, Rákóczi út, which begins when it crosses the
Kis körút (Small Ring Road) at the busy intersection called Astoria.
Most of Rákóczi út is lined with hotels, shops, and department stores,
and it ends at the grandiose Keleti (Eastern) Railway Station.

Pest's Great Ring Road, the Nagy körút, was laid out at the end of the 19th century in a wide semicircle anchored to the Danube at both ends; an arm of the river was covered over to create this 114-ft-wide thoroughfare. The large apartment buildings on both sides also date from this era. Along with theaters, stores, and cafés, they form a boulevard unique in Europe for its "unified eclecticism," which blends a variety of historic styles into a harmonious whole. Its entire length of almost 4½ km (2¾ mi) from Margaret Bridge to Petőfi Bridge is traversed by Trams 4 and 6, but strolling it in stretches is also a good way to experience the hustle and bustle of downtown Budapest.

Like its smaller counterpart, the Kis körút (Small Ring Road), the Great Ring Road comprises sectors of various names. Beginning with Ferenc körút at the Petőfi Bridge, it changes to József körút at the intersection marked by the Museum of Applied Arts, then to Erzsébet körút at Blaha Lujza Square. Teréz körút begins at the busy Oktogon crossing with Andrássy út—boasting the biggest Burger King in the world—and ends at the Nyugati (West) Railway Station, where Szent István takes over for the final stretch to the Margaret Bridge.

A Good Walk

Beginning with a visit to the **Iparművészeti Múzeum** ⑤④, near the southern end of the boulevard, walk or take Tram 4 or 6 north (away from the Petőfi Bridge) to the New York Kávéház on Erzsébet körút, just past Blaha Lujza tér—all in all about 1¾ km (1 mi) from the museum. The neo-Rennaissance **Keleti pályaudvar** is a one-metro-stop detour away from Blaha Lujza tér. Continuing in the same direction on the körút, go several stops on the tram to **Nyugati pályaudvar** and walk the remaining sector, Szent István körút, past the **Vígszínház** ⑤⑦ to Margaret Bridge. From the bridge, views of Margaret Island to the north, and Parliament, Castle Hill, the Chain Bridge, and Gellért Hill to the south, are gorgeous.

TIMING

As this area is packed with stores, it's best to explore during store hours—weekdays until around 5 PM and Saturdays until 1 PM; Saturdays will be most crowded. Keep in mind that the Iparművészeti Múzeum is closed Mondays.

Sights to See

★ ⑤④ **Iparművészeti Múzeum** (Museum of Applied and Decorative Arts). The templelike structure housing this museum is indeed a shrine to Hungarian Art Nouveau, and in front of it, drawing pen in hand, sits a statue of its creator, Hungarian architect Ödön Lechner. Opened in the millennial year of 1896, it was only the third museum of its kind in Europe. Its dome of tiles is crowned by a majolica lantern from the same source: the Zsolnay ceramic works in Pécs. Inside its central hall are playfully swirling whitewashed, double-decker, Moorish-style galleries and arcades. The museum, which collects and studies objects of interior decoration and use, has five departments: furniture, textiles, goldsmithing, ceramics, and everyday objects. ⊠ *Üllői út 33–37,* ☎ *1/ 217–5222.* 🎟 *170 Ft.* ☉ *Tues.–Sun. 10–6.*

⑤⑤ **Kapel Szent Roch** (St. Roch Chapel). The impact of this charming, yellow, 18th-century chapel is rendered even more colorful by peasant women peddling lace and embroidery on its small square. The chapel is the oldest remnant of Pest's former outer district. It was built beside a hospice where doomed victims of the great plague of 1711 were sent to die as far away as possible from residential areas. ⊠ *Corner of Rákóczi út and Gyulai Pál utca.*

Once the haunt of famous writers and intellectuals, whose caricatures decorate the walls, the **New York Kávéház** (⊠ VII, Erzsébet krt. 9–11, ☎ 1/322-1648) is an eclectic, neo-Baroque café and restaurant in the ornate 1894 New York Palace building.

Keleti pályaudvar (Eastern Railway Station). The grandiose, imperial-looking Eastern Railway Station was built in 1884 and considered Europe's most modern until well into this century. Its neo-Renaissance facade, which resembles a gateway, is flanked by statues of two British inventors and railway pioneers, James Watt and George Stephenson. ⊠ *VII, Rákóczi út.*

Klotild and Matild buildings. Braced on either side of heavily trafficked Kossuth Lajos utca, the imposing Klotild and Matild buildings, with their distinctive twin towers, were built in an interesting combination of Art Nouveau and eclectic styles. They house the headquarters of the IBUSZ travel agency, among other tenants.

❺❻ Köztársaság tér (Square of the Republic). Surrounded by faceless concrete buildings, this square is not particularly alluring aesthetically but is significant because it was where the Communist Party of Budapest had its headquarters, and it was also the scene of heavy fighting in 1956. Here also is the city's second opera house, and Budapest's largest, the **Erkel Ferenc színház** (Ferenc Erkel Theatre).

Nyugati pályaudvar (Western Railway Station). The iron-laced glass hall of the Western Railway Station is in complete contrast to—and much more modern than—the newer Eastern Railway Station. Built in the 1870s, it was designed by a team of architects from Gustav Eiffel's office in Paris. ⊠ *VI, Teréz krt.*

Párizsi Udvar (Paris Court). This glass-roofed arcade was built in 1914 in richly ornamental neo-Gothic and eclectic styles—it's one of the most attractive sights of Pest. Nowadays it's filled with touristy boutiques. ⊠ *Corner of Petőfi Sándor utca and Kossuth Lajos utca.*

★ ❺❼ Vígszínház (Comedy Theater). Designed in neo-Baroque style by the Viennese imperial architectural team of Fellner and Helmer and built in 1895–86, the gemlike theater twinkles with just a tiny, playful anticipation of Art Nouveau and sparkles inside and out since its 1994 refurbishment. The theater hosts primarily musicals, such as Hungarian adaptations of *Cats* and *West Side Story,* as well as dance performances and classical concerts. ⊠ *XIII, Pannónia u. 1,* ☎ *1/329-2340.*

Óbuda

Until its unification with Buda and Pest in 1872 to form the city of Budapest, Óbuda (the name means Old Buda) was a separate town that used to be the main settlement; now it is usually thought of as a suburb. Although the vast new apartment blocks of Budapest's biggest housing project and busy roadways are what first strike the eye, the historic core of Óbuda has been preserved in its entirety as an ancient monument.

A Good Walk
Óbuda is easily reached by car, bus, or streetcar via the Árpád Bridge from Pest or by the HÉV suburban railway from Batthyány tér to the Árpád Bridge. Once you're there, covering all the sights on foot involves large but manageable distances along major exhaust-permeated roadways. One way to tackle it is to take Tram 17 from its southern terminus at the Buda side of the Margaret Bridge to Kiscelli utca and walk uphill to the **Kiscelli Múzeum.** Then walk back down the same street all the way past **Flórián tér,** continuing toward the Danube and mak-

ing a left onto Hídfő utca or Szentlélek tér to enter **Fő tér.** After exploring the square and taking in the museums in the **Zichy Kúria,** walk a block or two southeast to the HÉV suburban railway stop and take the train just north to the museum complex at **Aquincum.**

TIMING

It's best to begin touring Óbuda during the cooler, early hours of the day, as the heat on the area's busy roads can get overbearing. Avoid Mondays, when museums are closed.

Sights to See

Aquincum. This complex comprises the reconstructed remains of a Roman settlement dating from the 1st century AD and the capital of the Roman province of Pannonia. Careful excavations at Aquincum have unearthed a varied selection of artifacts and mosaics, giving a tantalizing inkling of what life was like in the provinces of the Roman Empire. A gymnasium and a central heating system have been unearthed, along with the ruins of two baths and a shrine to Mithras, the Persian god of light, truth, and the sun. The **Aquincum múzeum** (Aquincum Museum) displays the dig's most notable finds: ceramics signed by the city's best-known potter, Ressatus of Aquincum; a red-marble sarcophagus showing a triton and flying Eros on one side and on the other, Telesphorus, the angel of death, depicted as a hooded dwarf; and jewelry from a Roman lady's tomb. ⊠ *III, Szentendrei út 139,* ☎ *1/250–1650.* 🎫 *350 Ft.* ☉ *Mid-Apr.–end of Apr. and Oct., Tues.–Sun. 10–5; May–Sept., Tues.–Sun. 10–6. Grounds open at 9.*

Flórián tér. The center of today's Óbuda is Flórián tér, where Roman ruins were first discovered when the foundations of a house were dug in 1778. Two centuries later, careful excavations were carried out during the reconstruction of the square, and today the restored ancient ruins lie in the center of the square in boggling contrast to the racing traffic and cement-block housing projects.

Fő tér. Óbuda's charming old main square is its most picturesque part. The square has been spruced up in recent years, and there are now several good restaurants and interesting museums in and around the Baroque **Zichy Kúria** (☞ *below*), which has become a neighborhood cultural center. Among the most popular offerings are the summer concerts in the courtyard and the evening jazz concerts.

Hercules Villa. A fine 3rd-century Roman dwelling, it takes its name from the myth depicted on its beautiful mosaic floor. The ruin was unearthed between 1958 and 1967 and is now only open by request (inquire at Aquincum). ⊠ *III, Meggyfa u. 19–21.*

Kiscelli Múzeum (Kiscelli Museum). A strenuous climb up the steep, dilapidated sidewalks of Remethegy (Hermit's Hill) will deposit you at this elegant, mustard-yellow Baroque mansion. Built between 1744 and 1760 as a Trinitarian monastery, today it holds an eclectic mix of paintings, sculptures, engravings, and sundry items related to the history of Budapest. Included here is the printing press on which poet and revolutionary Sándor Petőfi printed his famous "Nemzeti Dal" ("National Song"), in 1848, inciting the Hungarian people to rise up against the Hapsburgs. ⊠ *III, Kiscelli u. 108,* ☎ *1/250–0304.* 🎫 *170 Ft.* ☉ *Nov.–Mar., Tues.–Sun. 10–4; Apr.–Oct., Tues.–Sun. 10–6.*

Római amfiteátrum (Roman Amphitheater). Probably dating back to the 2nd century, Óbuda's Roman military amphitheater once held some 16,000 people and, at 144 yards in diameter, was one of Europe's largest. A block of dwellings called the Round House was later built by the Romans above the amphitheater; massive stone walls found in the Round House's cellar were actually parts of the amphitheater. Below the amphitheater are the cells where prisoners and lions were held while awaiting confrontation. It's open to the public, more by nonchalance than design—people sometimes use it as a dog run. ⊠ *Pacsirtamező u. at the junction where it meets Bécsi út.*

Zichy Kúria (Zichy Mansion). One wing of the Zichy Mansion is taken up by the **Óbudai Múzeum** (Óbuda Museum); permanent exhibitions here include traditional rooms from typical homes in the district of Békásmegyer and a popular exhibit covering the history of toys from 1860 to 1960. Another wing houses the **Kassák Múzeum,** which honors the literary and artistic works of a pioneer of the Hungarian avant-garde, Lajos Kassák. ⊠ *Zichy Mansion, Fő tér 1. Óbuda Museum:* ☎ *1/250–1020.* ☜ *100 Ft.* ⊙ *Mid-Mar.–mid-Oct., Tues.–Fri. 2–6, weekends 10–6; mid-Oct.–mid-Mar. Tues.–Fri. 2–5, weekends 10–5. Kassák Museum:* ☎ *1/368–7021.* ☜ *50 Ft.* ⊙ *Oct.–Feb., Tues.–Sun. 10–4; Mar.–Sept., Tues.–Sun. 10–6.*

DINING

In Budapest, numerous new ethnic restaurants—from Chinese to Mexican to Hare Krishna Indian—are springing up all the time. The pulse of the city's increasingly vibrant restaurant scene is in downtown Pest; restaurants on Castle Hill tend to be more touristy and expensive. Our choice of restaurants is primarily Hungarian and Continental, but if you get a craving for sushi or tortellini, consult the restaurant listings in the *Budapest Sun* (☞ Contacts and Resources *in* Budapest A to Z, *below*) for the latest information on what's cooking where. Remember that some restaurants, particularly the tourist-oriented ones, occasionally fall into the international practice of embellishing tourists' bills. Authorities in Budapest, however, have been cracking down on establishments reported for overcharging. Don't order from menus without prices, and don't accept dining or drinking invitations from women hired to lure people into shady situations.

Addresses below are preceded by the district number (in Roman numerals) and include the Hungarian postal code. Districts V, VI, and VII are in downtown Pest; I includes Castle Hill, the main tourist district of Buda. For price range information, *see* Dining *in* Pleasures and Pastimes, *above*.

Castle Hill

$$$$ ✕ **Alabárdos.** As medieval as its name, the Halberdier (the wielder of that ancient weapon, the halberd), this vaulted wooden room in a 400-year-old Gothic house sits across from the Matthias Church. It has only a handful of tables, set with exquisite Herend and Zsolnay porcelain, though in summer a courtyard garden doubles its capacity. The impeccable service, flowery decor, quiet music, and overriding discretion make this an excellent place for a serious business meal. For extra flair, order the popular flambéed mixed grill: waiters turn the room's lights off before delivering it to your table. Late lunchers and early diners should note that Alabárdos is closed between 4 and 7 PM. ⊠ *I, Országház u. 2,* ☎ *1/356–0851. Reservations essential. Jacket and tie. AE, DC, MC, V. Closed Sun. No lunch mid-Oct.–mid-Apr.*

Downtown Pest and the Small Ring Road

$$$–$$$$ ✕ **Múzeum.** The gustatory anticipation sparked by this elegant, candlelit salon with mirrors, mosaics, and swift-moving waiters is matched by wholly satisfying, wonderful food. The salads are generous, the Hungarian wines excellent, and the chef dares to be creative. ⊠ *VIII, Múzeum körút 12,* ☎ *1/267–0375. Jacket and tie. AE. Closed Sun.*

$$$ ✕ **Lou Lou.** This glowing bistro tucked onto a sidestreet near the Danube has been the hottest restaurant in Budapest for years. Blending local and Continental cuisines, the menu includes an excellent rack of lamb and succulent fresh salmon with lemongrass; the venison fillet with wild berry sauce is another mouthwatering choice. At press time, Lou Lou was planning to relocate to a larger space in fall 1998; check with Tourinform (☞ Visitor Information *in* Budapest A to Z, *below*) for the latest information. The restaurant closes between 3 PM and 7 PM. ⊠ *V, Vigyázó Ferenc u. 4,* ☎ *1/312–4505. Reservations essential. AE. Closed Sun. No lunch Sat.*

$$$ ✕ **Művészinas.** Walls hung with framed vintage prints and photos, antique vitrines filled with old books, and tall slender candles on the tables create a romantic haze in this bustling restaurant in the heart of Pest. Dozens of Hungarian specialties fill the long menu; beef, veal, and poultry are each prepared a half-dozen ways, from sirloin "Budapest style" (smothered in a goose-liver, mushrooms, and sweet-pepper ragout) to spinach-stuffed turkey breast in garlic sauce. Poppy-seed palacsinta with plum sauce are a sublime dessert. ⊠ *VI, Bajcsy-Zsilinszky út 9,* ☎ *1/268–1439. Reservations essential. AE, MC, V.*

$$ ✕ **Amstel River Café.** Just steps from the tourist-filled Váci utca, you'll find this welcoming Dutch pub; simple dark wood tables and chairs and low-key service make it a haven of sincere, cozy informality. The menu has something for everyone—from rabbit to Caesar salad to grilled chicken. Besides the Amstel beers (of course), there's a weekly changing wine list. The breakfast menu—a rarity in Budapest—has everything from corn flakes to omelets to cold goose liver. ⊠ *V, Párizsi u. 6,* ☎ *1/266–4334. No credit cards.*

$$ ✕ **Cyrano.** This smooth young bistro just off Vörösmarty tér has an arty, contemporary bent, with wrought-iron chairs, green-marble floors, and long-stemmed azure glasses. The creative kitchen sends out elegantly presented Hungarian and Continental dishes, from standards such as goulash and chicken *paprikás* to more eclectic tastes like tender fried Camembert cheese with blueberry jam and peaches stuffed with Roquefort cream and dressed with a lightly herbed sauce. ⊠ *V, Kristóf tér 7–8,* ☎ *1/266–3096. Reservations essential. AE, DC, MC.*

$$ ✕ **Duna-Corso.** Having stood on this riverfront square for nearly two decades, this restaurant continues to offer good, solid food at reasonable prices right in the center of Pest's luxury-hotel belt. The bean-and-cabbage soup (laced with smoked pork), roast duck with sauerkraut, and goose cracklings with potatoes are as simple and hearty as ever, and the service is still pokey and friendly. For views of the castle and Chain Bridge, a table on the vast outdoor terrace is the best seat in town. ⊠ *V, Vigadó tér 3,* ☎ *1/318–6362. No credit cards.*

$ ✕ **Fészek.** Hidden away inside the nearly 100-year-old Fészek Artists' Club is this large, neoclassical dining room. Inside it has high ceilings and mustard-color walls trimmed with ornate moldings, but if you come on a warm day, you can eat in a beautiful Venetian-style courtyard, originally monks' cloisters, with pillared archways, colorful majolica decorations, and blooming chestnut trees. The extensive, almost daunting menu features all the heavy Hungarian classics, with such specialties as turkey stuffed with goose liver and a variety of game dishes. You'll have to pay a 150-Ft. Artists' Club cover charge upon entering the building; if you've reserved a table in advance, it will be charged to your bill instead. ⊠ *VII, Kertész u. 36 (corner of Dob u.),* ☎ *1/322–6043. AE, DC, MC, V.*

$ ✕ **Kispipa.** Under the same management as Fészek (☞ *above*), this tiny, well-known restaurant with arched yellow-glass windows and piano

126

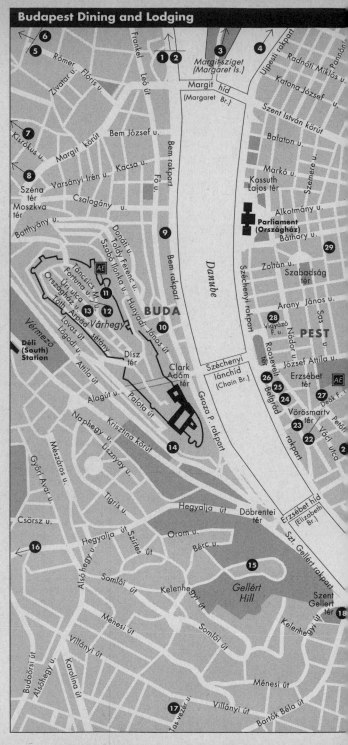

Budapest Dining and Lodging

Visegrádi u.

Váci út

Ferdinánd híd

Rippl-Rónai u.

Dózsa György út

38 37 36

Hősök
tere

Városliget

Olof Palme sétány

Szinyei Merse u.

Bajza u.

35

Benczúr u.

Ajtósi Dürer sor

**Nyugati
(West)
Station**

Podmaniczky utca

Szondi u.

Rózsa u.

Felső erdősor

Városligeti fasor

Nyugati
tér

Teréz körút

34

Eötvös u.

Aradi u.

Damjanich u.

Dózsa György út

Bajcsy-Zsilinszky út

Jókai u.

Oktogon
(Square)

Vörösmarty u.

Dob u.

Rottenbiller utca

Dembinszky u.

István u.

Nagymező u.

Mozsár u.

Andrássy út

Liszt
Ferenc
tér

Erzsébet körút

Hársfa u.

Thököly út

Verseny u.

Hajós u.

Lázár u.

Paulay Ede u.

Király u.

33 Kertész u.

**Keleti (East)
Station**

32

Akácfa u.

Rákóczi út.

Baross
tér

Kerepesi út

30

Deák
tér

Károly krt.

Dob utca

Nagy Diófa u.

Wesselényi utca

Klauzál u.

Dohány utca

Rákóczi út.

31

Köztársaság
tér

Fiumei út

Kerepesi
temető
(Cemetery)

Szenkirályi u.

József körút

Somogyi Béla u.

Népszinház u.

Bérkocsis u.

Déri Miksa u.

Teleki
László
tér

Luiza u.

i

1

Sándor u.

Kossuth L. u.

20

Múzeum krt.

Magyar u.

Puskin u.

19

Bródy Sándor u.

Múzeum u.

József u.

Mátyás
tér

Dankó u.

N

Ferenciek
tere

Kecskeméti u.

Krúdy u.

Baross utca

Veres Pálné u.

Váci utca

Kálvin
tér

Baross utca

Molnár u.

Fővám
tér.

Vámház krt.

Üllői út

Nap u.

Práter u.

Szigony u.

Diószeghy Sámuel u.

Szabadság híd
[Liberty Br.]

Lónyay u.

Ráday u.

Tömő u.

Üllői út

Korányi S. u.

Danube

Műegyetem rakpart

Közraktár u.

Kinizsi u.

Knézits u.

Ferenc körút

Mester u.

Boráros
tér

Thaly Kálmán u.

Márton u.

0   550 yards

0   500 meters

Petőfi híd
[Petőfi Br.]

bar features a similar expansive menu of first-rate Hungarian food. The kitchen has a loyal following of both locals and foreigners (drawn in part by unexpectedly low prices); the venison ragout soup with tarragon is excellent. A singer at the piano entertains from 7 PM. ⊠ *VII, Akácfa u. 38,* ☎ *1/342–2587. Reservations essential. AE, MC. Closed Sun. and July–Aug.*

$ ✕ **Tüköry Söröző.** Solid, hearty, decidedly non-vegetarian Hungarian fare comes in big portions at this popular state-owned spot close to Parliament. Best bets include pork cutlets stuffed with savory liver or apples and cheese, paired with a big mug of inexpensive beer. Courageous carnivores can sample the beefsteak tartare, topped with a raw egg; many say it's the best in town. ⊠ *V, Hold u. 15,* ☎ *1/269–5027. MC, V. Closed weekends.*

North Buda

$$$$ ✕ **Vadrózsa.** The "Wild Rose" always has fresh ones on the table; the restaurant is in a romantic old villa perched on a hilltop in the exclusive Rózsadomb district of Buda. It's elegant to the last detail, with white-glove service, and the garden is delightful in summer. Try the venison or grilled fish; the house specialty, grilled goose liver, is succulent perfection. ⊠ *II, Pentelei Molnár u. 15,* ☎ *1/326–5817. Reservations essential. AE, DC, MC, V.*

$$$–$$$$ ✕ **Udvarház.** The views from this Buda hilltop restaurant are unsurpassed. As you dine indoors at tables set with white linens and candles or outdoors on the open terrace, your meals are accompanied by vistas of the Danube bridges and Parliament far below. Excellent fresh fish is prepared tableside; you could also try veal and goose liver in paprika sauce, served with salty cottage cheese dumplings. Catering to the predominantly tourist crowd, folklore shows and live Gypsy music frequently enliven the scene. The buses up here are infrequent; it's easier to take a car or taxi. ⊠ *III, Hármashatárhegyi út 2,* ☎ *1/ 388–6921. AE, DC, MC, V. Closed Mon. Nov.–Mar. No lunch weekdays Nov.–Mar.*

$$ ✕ **Náncsi Néni.** Aunt Nancy's restaurant is a perennial favorite, de-
★ spite its out-of-the-way location. Irresistibly cozy, the dining room feels like Grandma's country kitchen: Chains of paprika and garlic dangle from the low wooden ceiling above tables set with red-and-white gingham tablecloths, candles, and fresh bread tucked into tiny baskets. Shelves along the walls are crammed with jars of home-pickled beets, peppers, and the like, which you can purchase to take home. On the home-style Hungarian menu (large portions!) turkey dishes feature a creative flair, such as breast fillets stuffed with apples, peaches, mushrooms, cheese, and sour cream. Special touches include a popular outdoor garden in summer and free champagne for all couples in love. ⊠ *II, Ördögárok út 80,* ☎ *1/397–2742. Reservations essential July–Aug. AE, MC, V.*

$ ✕ **Marxim.** Two years after the death of socialism in Hungary, this simple pizza-and-pasta restaurant opened up to mock the old regime— and milk it for all it's worth. From the flashing red star above the door outside to the clever puns on the menu, the theme is "communist nostalgia." Classic black-and-white photos of decorated hard-liners and papier-mâché doves stuck in gnarled barbed-wire fences line the walls. Crowds of teenagers and blaring rock music make Marxim best suited for a lunch or snack. ⊠ *II, Kisrókus u. 23,* ☎ *1/212–4183. AE, DC, MC, V. No lunch Sun.*

Óbuda

$$$ ✕ **Kehli.** This pricey but laid-back neighborhood tavern is on a hard-to-find street near the Óbuda end of the Árpád Bridge. The inn is small, paneled, and sepia-toned, with an old wooden wagon out front and a garden (which in summer more than doubles the restaurant's capacity). The food is hearty and heavy, just the way legendary Hungarian writer and voracious eater Gyula Krúdy (to whom the restaurant is dedicated) liked it when he lived in the neighborhood. Select from appetizers, such as hot bone marrow with garlic toast, before moving on to fried goose livers with mashed potatoes or turkey breast stuffed with cheese and goose liver. ⊠ *III, Mókus utca 22*, ☎ *1/250–4241 or 1/ 368–0613. AE, MC, V. No lunch weekdays*

$$$ ✕ **Kisbuda Gyöngye.** Considered one of the city's finest restaurants, this
★ intimate Óbuda restaurant is filled with antique furniture, and its walls are creatively decorated with an eclectic but elegant patchwork of carved wooden cupboard doors and panels. A violin-piano duo sets a romantic mood, and in warm weather you can dine outdoors in the cozy back garden. Try the venison with Transylvanian mushrooms or the popular *liba lakodalmas* (goose wedding feast), a roast goose leg, goose liver, and goose cracklings. ⊠ *III, Kenyeres u. 34*, ☎ *1/368–6402 or 1/368– 9246. Reservations essential. AE, DC, MC, V. Closed Sun.*

Tabán and Gellért Hill

$$ ✕ **Tabáni Kakas.** This popular restaurant just below Castle Hill has a distinctly friendly atmosphere and specializes in large helpings of poultry dishes, particularly goose. Try the catfish *paprikás* or the roast duck with steamed cabbage. ⊠ *I, Attila út 27*, ☎ *1/375–7165. AE, MC, V.*

City Park

$$$$ ✕ **Gundel.** George Lang, Hungary's best-known restaurateur, showcases
★ his native country's cuisine at this lauded turn-of-the-century palazzo. Dark-wood paneling, a dozen oil paintings by exemplary Hungarian artists, and tables set with Zsolnay porcelain make this the city's plushest, most handsome dining room. Violinist György Lakatos, of the legendary Lakatos Gypsy musician dynasty, strolls from table to table playing folk music, as waiters in black tie serve traditional favorites such as tender veal in a paprika-and-sour-cream sauce and carp *Dorozsma* (panfried with mushrooms). ⊠ *XIV, Állatkerti út 2*, ☎ *1/321–3550. Reservations essential. Jacket and tie. AE, DC, MC, V.*

$$$$ ✕ **Robinson Restaurant.** At this intimate dining room on the park's small lake, service is doting and the menu creative, with dishes such as crisp roast suckling pig flavored with champagne or fresh *fogas* (pike-perch) stuffed with spinach. Finish it off with a flaming cup of coffee *Diablo*, fueled with Grand Marnier. Padded pastel decor and low lighting wash the room in pleasant, if not Hungarian, elegance. ⊠ *XIV, Városliget*, ☎ *1/343–0955. Reservations essential. Jacket and tie. AE, DC, MC, V. Closed daily 4–6 PM.*

$$ ✕ **Bagolyvár.** George Lang opened this restaurant next door to his gas-
★ tronomic palace, Gundel (☞ *above*), in 1993. The immaculate dining room with a soaring wooden-beam ceiling has an informal yet elegantly professional atmosphere, and the kitchen produces first-rate daily menus of home-style Hungarian specialties. Soups, served in shiny silver tureens, are particularly good. Musicians entertain with cimbalom music nightly from 7 PM. In warm weather there is outdoor dining in a lovely back garden. ⊠ *XIV, Állatkerti út 2*, ☎ *1/343–0217. AE, DC, MC, V.*

LODGING

Addresses below are preceded by the district number (in Roman numerals) and include the Hungarian postal code. Districts V, VI, and VII are in downtown Pest; I includes Castle Hill, the main tourist district of Buda. For price range information, *see* Lodging *in* Pleasures and Pastimes, *above.*

$$$$ 🖬 **Atrium Hyatt.** The spectacular 10-story interior—a mix of glass capsule elevators, cascading tropical greenery, an open bar, and café—is surpassed only by the views across the Danube to the castle (rooms with a river view cost substantially more). After major renovations, rooms have been tastefully redesigned with classy, unobtrusive decor in muted blues and light woods, and sparkling bathrooms. ⊠ *V, Roosevelt tér 2, H-1051,* ☎ *1/266–1234,* 𝖥𝖠𝖷 *1/266–9101. 328 rooms, 27 suites. 3 restaurants, 2 bars, air-conditioning, in-room modem lines, no-smoking rooms, indoor pool, beauty salon, sauna, exercise room, casino, business services, meeting rooms, travel services, parking (fee). AE, DC, MC, V.*

$$$$ 🖬 **Budapest Hilton.** Built in 1977 around a 13th-century monastery
★   adjacent to the Matthias Church, this perfectly integrated architectural wonder overlooks the Danube from the choicest site on Castle Hill. Every contemporary room has a remarkable view; Danube vistas cost more. Complete renovations during 1999 promise a welcome update in room decor. Children, regardless of age, get free accommodations when sharing a room with their parents. Note: Breakfast is not included in room rates. ⊠ *I, Hess András tér 1–3, H-1014,* ☎ *1/214–3000,* ☎ *800/445–8667 in the U.S. and Canada,* 𝖥𝖠𝖷 *1/356–0285. 295 rooms, 27 suites. 3 restaurants, 2 bars, café, air-conditioning, in-room modem lines, beauty salon, sauna, exercise room, casino, laundry services and dry cleaning, business services, meeting rooms, travel services, parking (free and fee). AE, DC, MC, V.*

$$$$ 🖬 **Budapest Marriott.** In this sophisticated yet friendly hotel on the Danube
★   in downtown Pest, attention to detail is evident, from the impeccable buffet of colorfully glazed pastries to the feather-light ring of the front-desk bell. Public spaces have hard-to-argue-with decor—marble floors, forest-green leather couches, and fresh flower arrangements in the lobby. Guest rooms have lushly patterned carpets, floral bedspreads, and etched glass. The layout takes full advantage of the hotel's prime Danube location, offering breathtaking views of Gellért Hill, the Chain and Elizabeth bridges, and Castle Hill from the lobby, ballroom, every guest room, and even the impressive health club—which is unquestionably the best hotel fitness center in the city. ⊠ *V, Apáczai Csere János u. 4, H-1364,* ☎ *1/266–7000,* ☎ *800/831–4004 in the U.S. and Canada,* 𝖥𝖠𝖷 *1/266–5000. 362 rooms, 20 suites. 3 restaurants, bar, air-conditioning, in-room modem lines, no-smoking rooms, health club, squash, shops, baby-sitting, laundry service and dry cleaning, business services, meeting rooms, travel services, parking (fee). AE, DC, MC, V.*

$$$$ 🖬 **Danubius Hotel Gellért.** The double-deck rotunda of this grand
★   Hungarian spa hotel leads you to expect a string orchestra, concealed behind massive marble pillars, playing "The Emperor Waltz." Built in 1918, the Jugendstil Gellért was favored by Otto von Habsburg, son of the last emperor. Rooms come in all shapes and sizes—from palatial suites to awkward, tiny spaces. Now part of the Danubius hotel chain, the Gellért began an ambitious three- to four-year overhaul in 1998—including the addition of air-conditioning and refurnishing of all rooms in the mood of the original Jugendstil style. The best views—across the Danube or up Gellért Hill—are more expensive; avoid those that face the building's inner core. Though the hotel's service can be

a bit inconsistent, its famous pièce de résistance will make up for it: the monumental, ornate thermal baths, including an outdoor pool with a wave machine. Admission to the spa is free to hotel guests (medical treatments cost extra); corridors and an elevator lead directly to the baths from the second, third, and fourth floors. ⊠ *XI, Gellért tér 1, H-1111,* ☎ *1/385–2200,* FAX *1/466–6631. 199 rooms, 13 suites. Restaurant, bar, brasserie, café, no-smoking rooms, indoor pool, beauty salon, spa, baby-sitting, business services, meeting rooms, parking (fee). AE, DC, MC, V.*

$$$$ ★ 🏨 **Hotel Inter-Continental Budapest.** Formerly the Fórum Hotel, this boxy, modern, riverside hotel consistently wins applause for its gracious appointments, excellent service, and gorgeous views across the Danube to Castle Hill. Sixty percent of the rooms have river views (these are more expensive); rooms on higher floors ensure the least noise. The hotel café, Bécsi Kávéház, is locally known for its pastries. The central location and efficient business services make the Inter-Continental popular with businesspeople. Note: Breakfast is not included in the room rates. ⊠ *V, Apáczai Csere János u. 12–14, Box 231, H-1368,* ☎ *1/ 327–6333,* FAX *1/327–6357. 392 rooms, 16 suites. 2 restaurants, bar, café, air-conditioning, in-room modem lines, no-smoking floors, pool, health club, business center, meeting rooms, car rental, parking (fee). AE, DC, MC, V.*

$$$$ ★ 🏨 **Kempinski Hotel Corvinus Budapest.** Opened in August 1992, this sleek luxury hotel is the favored lodging of visiting VIPs—from rock superstars to business moguls and foreign dignitaries—offering a central-city location and superior facilities. From overnight shoe-shine service to afternoon chamber music in the lobby, the Kempinski exudes solicitousness. Unlike those of other nearby hotels, rooms are spacious, with blond and black Swedish geometric inlaid woods and an emphasis on functional touches, such as three phones in every room. Large, sparkling bathrooms, most with tubs and separate shower stalls and stocked with every toiletry, are the best in Budapest. The hotel's business services also stand out as the city's best. An automatic current in the smallish pool allows you to swim long distances without getting anywhere. Breakfast is not included in the room rates. ⊠ *V, Erzsébet tér 7–8, H-1051,* ☎ *1/266–1000, 800/426–3135 in the U.S. and Canada,* FAX *1/266–2000. 337 rooms, 28 suites. 2 restaurants, bar, lobby lounge, pub, air-conditioning, in-room modem lines, no-smoking rooms, indoor pool, barbershop, beauty salon, massage, health club, shops, laundry service and dry cleaning, business services, meeting rooms, travel services, parking (fee). AE, DC, MC, V.*

$$$ 🏨 **Danubius Grand Hotel Margitsziget.** Built in 1873 and long in disrepair, this venerable hotel reopened in 1987 as a Ramada Inn and was recently taken over by the Danubius hotel chain. Room rates may have increased since the 1870s, but the high ceilings haven't been lowered. Nor have the old-fashioned room trimmings—down comforters, ornate chandeliers—been lost in the streamlining. Graham Greene always took the same suite that he had before World War II, and the U.S. Embassy likes to send visitors here. Choose between views across the Danube onto a less attractive, industrial section of Pest or out onto the verdant lawns and trees of a tranquil park. Because it's connected to a bubbling thermal spa next door and is located on car-free Margaret Island in the Danube right between Buda and Pest, the Danubius Grand feels removed from the city but is still only a short taxi or bus ride away. ⊠ *XIII, Margit-sziget, H-1138,* ☎ *1/329–2300 or 1/349–2769 (reservations),* FAX *1/353–3029. 164 rooms, 10 suites. 2 restaurants, no-smoking rooms, indoor pool, beauty salon, massage, spa, sauna, exercise room, bicycles, meeting rooms, travel services, free parking. AE, DC, MC, V.*

$$$ 🏨 **Danubius Thermal Hotel Helia.** A sleek Scandinavian design and less hectic location upriver from downtown make this spa hotel on the Danube a change of pace from its Pest peers. Its neighborhood is nondescript, but guests can be in town in minutes or take advantage of the thermal baths and special health packages—including everything from Turkish baths to electrotherapy and fitness tests. The staff is friendly and helpful, and most of the comfortable rooms have Danube views. ⊠ *XIII, Kárpát u. 62–64, H-1133,* ☎ *1/270–3277,* FAX *1/270–2262. 254 rooms, 8 suites. Restaurant, bar, café, indoor pool, beauty salon, hot tub, massage, sauna, spa, steam room, tennis courts, exercise room, business services, meeting rooms, free parking. AE, DC, MC, V.*

$$$ 🏨 **Flamenco.** Classy though sometimes overlooked, this hotel in the Buda foothills is a welcome addition to this side of the river. A wall of windows in the low-ceilinged lobby opens out onto views of a park. Service is professional, and the well-kept contemporary rooms are priced at the lowest end of this category. ⊠ *XI, Tas Vezér utca 7, H–1113,* ☎ *1/372–2068 or* ☎ *1/372–2000,* FAX *1/372–2100. 352 rooms, 8 suites. 2 restaurants, indoor pool, beauty salon, sauna, business services, meeting rooms, travel services, parking (fee). AE, DC, MC, V.*

$$$ 🏨 **Radisson SAS Béke.** The well-situated Béke (on a main boulevard near the Nyugati [West] Railroad Station) is a budget family inn turned luxury hotel—it now has a glittering turn-of-the-century facade, liveried doormen, a lobby lined with mosaics and statuary, and bellmen bowing before the grand marble staircase. Popular with Italians and Americans, this hotel has all the business amenities plus the efficient services of a helpful staff. Guest rooms resemble solidly modern living rooms, with two-tone wood furnishings and pastel decor. ⊠ *VI, Teréz krt. 43, H-1067,* ☎ *1/301–1600,* FAX *1/301–1615. 238 rooms, 8 suites. 2 restaurants, 2 bars, café, air-conditioning, in-room modem lines, no-smoking rooms, pool, sauna, beauty salon, casino, business center, meeting rooms, travel services, parking (fee). AE, DC, MC, V.*

$$ 🏨 **Alba Hotel.** Tucked behind an alleyway at the foot of Castle Hill, this spotless, modern hotel is a short walk via the Chain Bridge from lively business and shopping districts. Rooms are snug and quiet, with clean white-and-pale-gray contemporary decor and charmingly typical Budapest views over a kaleidoscope of rooftops and chimneys. Half have bathtubs. Service is efficient. ⊠ *I, Apor Péter u. 3, H-1011,* ☎ *1/375–9244,* FAX *1/375–9899. 95 rooms. Bar, breakfast room, air-conditioning, no-smoking rooms, meeting room, parking (fee). AE, DC, MC, V.*

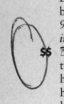

$$ 🏨 **Astoria.** At a busy intersection in downtown Pest stands a revitalized turn-of-the-century hotel that remains an oasis of quiet and serenity in hectic surroundings. Staff members are always—but unobtrusively—on hand. Rooms are genteel, spacious, and comfortable, and renovations have remained faithful to the original furnishings and decor: rather like Grandma's sitting room, in Empire style with an occasional antique. The Astoria's opulent café is a popular meeting place. ⊠ *V, Kossuth Lajos u. 19–21, H-1053,* ☎ *1/317–3411,* FAX *1/318–6798. 125 rooms, 5 suites. Restaurant, bar, café, no-smoking rooms, nightclub, business services, meeting rooms, free parking. AE, DC, MC, V.*

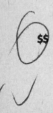

$$ 🏨 **Hotel Centrál.** Relive history—stay in this hotel, well situated in a leafy diplomatic quarter just one block from Heroes' Square, as visiting Communist dignitaries once did. The architecture and furnishings are straight out of the 1950s, but rooms are comfortable and most have unusually large bathrooms. Suites, however, as well as six of the standard rooms, are classically elegant, with turn-of-the-century Hungarian furnishings; ask for the suite that was Rudolf Nureyev's favorite. ⊠ *VI, Munkácsy Mihály u. 5–7, H-1063,* ☎ *1/321–2000,* FAX *1/322–9445. 36 rooms, 6 suites. Restaurant, free parking. AE, MC, V.*

$$ ⌧ **Nemzeti.** With a lovely, baby-blue Baroque facade, the Nemzeti reflects the grand mood of the turn of the century. The high-ceiling lobby and public areas—with pillars, arches, and wrought-iron railings—are elaborately elegant. A timely renovation begun in late 1997 is transforming the once small, dark, unexceptional guest rooms with pretty, new furnishings and air-conditioning; be sure to ask for one of these rooms (20 DM extra) for optimal comfort. The hotel is located at bustling Blaha Lujza tér in the center of Pest, which tends toward the seedy after dark; although windows are double-paned, to ensure a quiet night, ask for a room facing the inner courtyard. ⊠ *VIII, József körút 4, H-1088,* ☎ *1/303–9310,* ℻ *1/314–0019,* ☎℻ *1/303– 9162. 75 rooms, 1 suite. Restaurant, air-conditioning, piano bar, meeting room, travel services. AE, DC, MC, V.*

$$ ⌧ ★ **Victoria.** The dark, stately Parliament building and city lights twinkling over the river can be seen from the picture windows of every room at this young establishment right on the Danube. The tiny hotel mixes the charm of a small inn with the modern comforts and efficiency of a business hotel. The absence of conventioneers and tours is a plus, and the location—an easy walk from Castle Hill sights and downtown Pest—couldn't be better. ⊠ *I, Bem rakpart 11, H-1011,* ☎ *1/457–8080,* ℻ *1/457–8088. 27 rooms, 1 suite. Bar, air-conditioning, sauna, meeting room, travel services, parking (fee). AE, DC, MC, V.*

$ ⌧ **Citadella.** Comparatively basic, the Citadella is nevertheless very popular for its price and for its stunning location—right inside the fortress. Half of the rooms compose a youth hostel, giving the hotel a lively communal atmosphere. None of the rooms have bathrooms, but half have showers. Breakfast is not included in the rates. ⊠ *XI, Citadella sétány, Gellérthegy, H-1118,* ☎ *1/366–5794,* ℻ *1/386–0505. 20 rooms, none with bath. Breakfast room. No credit cards.*

$ ⌧ ★ **Kulturinov.** One wing of a magnificent 1902 neo-Baroque castle now houses basic budget accommodations. Rooms come with two or three beds and are clean and delightfully peaceful; they have showers but no tubs. The neighborhood—one of Budapest's most famous squares in the luxurious castle district—is magical. ⊠ *I, Szentháromság tér 6, H-1014,* ☎ *1/355–0122 or 1/375–1651,* ℻ *1/375–1886. 16 rooms. Snack bar, library, meeting rooms. AE, DC, MC, V.*

$ ⌧ **Molnár Panzió.** Fresh air and peace and quiet could lure you to this immaculate guest house nestled high above Buda on Széchenyi Hill. Rooms in the octagonal main house are polyhedric, clean, and bright, with pleasant wood paneling and pastel-color modern furnishings; most have distant views of Castle Hill and Gellért Hill, and some have balconies. Service is at once friendly and professional, and the restaurant is first-rate. Eight rooms in a new (1997) addition next door are more private and have superior bathrooms. Breakfast here is more appealing than usual—with scrambled eggs in addition to the standard breads and jams. ⊠ *XII, Fodor u. 143, H-1124,* ☎ *1/395–1873,* ☎ ℻ *1/395–1872. 23 rooms. Restaurant, bar, sauna, exercise room, playground, travel services, free parking. AE, DC, MC, V.*

NIGHTLIFE AND THE ARTS

Nightlife

Budapest's nightlife is vibrant and diverse. For basic beer and wine drinking, *sörözős* (beer bars) and *borozős* (wine bars) abound, although the latter tend to serve the early-morning-spritzer-before-work types rather than nighttime revelers. For quiet conversation there are *drink-bárs* in most hotels and all over town, but beware of the inflated prices and steep cover charges. Cafés are preferable for unescorted women.

Most nightspots and clubs have bars, pool tables, and dance floors. Although some places do accept credit cards, it's best to expect to pay cash for your night on the town. As is the case in most other cities, the life of a club or disco in Budapest can be somewhat ephemeral. In one year, several different clubs may open and close at the same address. Those listed below are quite popular and seem to be here to stay. But for the very latest on the more transient "in" spots, consult the nightlife sections of the *Budapest Sun* and *Budapest Week*.

Budapest also has its share of seedy go-go clubs and so-called "cabarets," some of which are known for scandalously excessive billing and physical intimidation. Be wary if you are "invited" in by women lingering nearby, and don't order anything without first seeing the price.

A word of warning to the smoke-sensitive: Budapest is a city of smokers. No matter where you spend your night out, chances are you'll come home smelling of cigarette smoke.

Bars and Clubs

Angel Bar and Disco (⊠ VII, Szövetség u. 33, ☎ 1/351–6490) is one of Budapest's enduring and most popular gay bars (though all persuasions are welcome), with a rollicking dance floor. It's closed Monday–Wednesday.

Bahnhof (⊠ VI, Váci út 1, at Nyugati pu.) is, appropriately, in the Nyugati (Western) train station and attracts swarms of young people to its large, crowded dance floor to live bands and DJ'd music. It's closed Sunday–Tuesday.

The most popular of Budapest's Irish pubs and a favorite expat watering hole is **Becketts** (⊠ V, Bajcsy-Zsilinszky út 72, ☎ 1/311–1035), where Guinness flows freely and excellent Irish fare is served amid the gleams of polished wood and brass.

One of the city's hottest spots is **Café Capella** (⊠ V, Belgrád rakpart 23, ☎ 1/318–6231), where a welcoming, gay-friendly crowd flocks to the glittery drag shows (held a few times a week) and revels to DJ'd club music until dawn.

A hip, mellow crowd mingles at the stylish **Cafe Incognito** (⊠ VI, Liszt Ferenc tér 3, ☎ 1/351–9428), with low lighting and funky music kept at a conversation-friendly volume. Couches and armchairs in the back are comfy and private. It closes relatively early—at midnight.

Café Pierrot (⊠ I, Fortuna u. 14, ☎ 1/375–6971), an elegant café and piano bar on a small street on Castle Hill, is well suited to a secret rendezvous.

The look is sophisticated and stylish but the mood low-key and unpretentious at the **Fél 10 Jazz Club** (⊠ VIII, Baross u. 30, cellular ☎ 06–60/318-467), near Kálvin tér. Three open levels with balconylike sitting areas, a dance floor, and two bars are impeccably decorated with wrought-iron tables and maroon-cushioned chairs.

Established Hungarian jazz headliners and young up-and-comers play nightly at the **Long Jazz Club** (⊠ VII, Dohány u. 22–24, ☎ 1/322–0066). It's closed Sunday.

Housed in an old stone mansion near Heroes' Square, the conceptually schizophrenic **Made Inn** (⊠ VI, Andrássy út 112, ☎ 1/311–3437) has an elaborate decor modeled on an underground mine shaft, a kitchen specializing in Mediterranean foods, a large outdoor bar, and a disco dance floor packed with local and international Beautiful People with cell phones and fake-bake tans. Live bands play most nights.

Cool (and trendily dark) **Underground** (✉ VI, Teréz krt. 30, ☎ 1/311–1481) is below the artsy Művész movie theater. Exposed metal beams and girders and wackily shaped scrap-metal chairs and tables give this bar the requisite industrial look; the DJ spins progressive popular music. Weekends are packed with younger, sometimes rowdy, hipsters.

Casinos

Most casinos are open daily from 2 PM until 4 or 5 AM and offer gambling in hard currency—usually dollars—only.

The **Gresham Casino** (✉ V, Roosevelt tér 5, ☎ 1/317–2407) is in the famous Gresham Palace at the Pest end of the Chain Bridge. Sylvester Stallone is alleged to be an owner of the popular **Las Vegas Casino** (✉ V, Roosevelt tér 2, ☎ 1/317–6022), in the Atrium Hyatt Hotel. In an 1879 building designed by prolific architect Miklós Ybl, who also designed the State Opera House, the **Várkert Casino** (✉ I, Miklós Ybl tér 9, ☎ 1/202–4244) is the most attractive of the city's casinos.

The Arts

For the latest on arts events, consult the entertainment listings of the English-language newspapers (☞ Contacts and Resources *in* Budapest A to Z, *below*). Their weekly entertainment calendars map out all that's happening in Budapest's arts and culture world—from thrash bands in wild clubs to performances at the Opera House and traditional Hungarian folk-dancing lessons at local cultural houses. Another option is to stop in at the **National Philharmonic ticket office** (✉ Vörösmarty tér 1, ☎ 1/318–0281) and browse through the scores of free programs and fliers and scan the walls coated with upcoming concert posters. Hotels and tourist offices will also provide you with a copy of the monthly publication *Programme,* which contains details of all cultural events.

Tickets can be bought at the venues themselves, but many ticket offices sell them without extra charge. Prices are still very low, so markups of even 30% shouldn't dent your wallet if you book through your hotel. Inquire at Tourinform (☞ Visitor Information *in* Budapest A to Z, *below*) if you're not sure where to go. Ticket availability depends on the performance and season—it's usually possible to get tickets a few days before a show, but performances by major international artists sell out early. Tickets to Budapest Festival Orchestra concerts and other festival events also go particularly quickly.

Theater and opera tickets are sold at the **Central Theater Booking Office** (Pest: ✉ VI, Andrassy út 18, ☎ 1/312–0000). For classical concert, ballet, and opera tickets, as well as tickets for major pop and rock shows, go to the **National Philharmonic ticket office** (☞ *above*). **Music Mix Ticket Service** (✉ V, Váci utca 33, ☎ 1/338–2237 or 1/317–7736) specializes in popular music but handles other genres as well.

Classical Music and Opera

The tiny recital room of the **Bartók Béla Emlékház** (Béla Bartók Memorial House; ✉ II, Csalán út 29, ☎ 1/376–2100) hosts intimate Friday evening chamber music recitals by well-known ensembles from mid-March to June and September to mid-December.

The **Budapest Kongresszusi Központ** (Budapest Convention Center; ✉ XII, Jagelló út 1–3, ☎ 1/209–1990) is the city's largest-capacity (but least atmospheric) classical concert venue and usually hosts the largest-selling events of the Spring Festival.

The homely little sister of the Opera House, the **Erkel Színház** (Erkel Theater; ✉ VII, Köztársaság tér 30, ☎ 1/333–0540) is Budapest's other main opera and ballet venue. There are no regular performances in the summer.

Liszt Ferenc Zeneakadémia (Franz Liszt Academy of Music; ⊠ VI, Liszt Ferenc tér 8, ☎ 1/342–0179), usually referred to as the Music Academy, is Budapest's premier classical concert venue, hosting orchestra and chamber music concerts in its splendid main hall. It's sometimes possible to grab a standing-room ticket just before a performance here.

The glittering **Magyar Állami Operaház** (Hungarian State Opera House; ⊠ VI, Andrassy út 22, ☎ 1/331–2550), Budapest's main venue for operas and classical ballet, presents an international repertoire of classical and modern works as well as such Hungarian favorites as Kodály's *Háry János*. Except during the one-week BudaFest international opera and ballet festival in mid-August, the Opera House is closed during the summer.

Colorful operettas like those by Lehár and Kalman are staged at their main Budapest venue, the **Operetta Theater** (⊠ VI, Nagymező u. 19, ☎ 1/332–0535); also look for modern dance productions and Hungarian renditions of popular Broadway classics.

Classical concerts are held regularly at the **Pesti Vigadó** (Pest Concert Hall; ⊠ V, Vigadó tér 2, ☎ 1/318–9167).

English-Language Movies
Many of the English-language movies that come to Budapest are subtitled in Hungarian rather than dubbed. There are more than 30 cinemas that regularly show films in English, and tickets are very inexpensive by Western standards (about 800 Ft.). Consult the movie matrix in the *Budapest Sun* or *Budapest Week* for a weekly list of what's showing.

Folk Dancing
Many of Budapest's district cultural centers regularly hold traditional regional folk-dancing evenings, or dance houses (*táncház*), often with general instruction at the beginning. These sessions provide a less touristy way to taste Hungarian culture. Ask your hotel clerk to find out the latest programs at these more popular cultural centers.

Almássy Recreation Center (⊠ VII, Almássy tér 6, ☎ 1/352–1572) holds numerous folk-dancing evenings, representing Hungarian as well as Greek and other ethnic cultures. Traditionally the wildest táncház is held Saturday nights at the **Inner City Youth and Cultural Center** (⊠ V, Molnár u. 9, ☎ 1/317–5928), where the stomping and whirling go on way into the night. Hungary's best-known folk ensemble, Muzsikás, hosts a weekly dance house at the **Marczibányi téri Művelődési ház** (Marczibányi tér Cultural Center; ⊠ II, Marczibányi tér 5/a, ☎ 1/212–5789), usually on Thursday nights. Muzsikás lead singer Márta Sebestyén appears less and less frequently with the group since her singing was featured in the movie *The English Patient,* launching her into international recognition; call ahead to find out when she'll perform next.

Folklore Performances
The Hungarian State Folk Ensemble performs regularly at the **Budai Vigadó** (⊠ I, Corvin tér 8, ☎ 1/201–5846); shows incorporate music, dancing, and singing.

The **Folklór Centrum** (⊠ XI, Fehérvári út 47, ☎ 1/203–3868) has been a major venue for folklore performances for more than 30 years. It hosts regular traditional folk concerts and dance performances from spring through fall.

Theaters
The **Madách Theater** (⊠ VII, Erzsébet körút 31–33, ☎ 1/322–2015) produces colorful musicals in Hungarian, including a popular adap-

tation of *Cats*. English-language dramas are not common in Budapest, but when there are any, they are usually staged at the **Merlin Theater** (✉ V, Gerlóczy utca 4, ☎ 1/317–9338). In summer, the Merlin usually hosts an English-language theater series. Another musical theater is the **Thália Theater** (✉ VI, Nagymező u. 22–24, ☎ 1/331–0500). The sparkling **Vígszínház** (Comedy Theater; ✉ XIII, Pannónia út 1, ☎ 1/269–5340) hosts classical concerts and dance performances but is primarily a venue for musicals, such as the Hungarian adaptation of *West Side Story*.

OUTDOOR ACTIVITIES AND SPORTS

Bicycling

Because of constant thefts, bicycle rentals are difficult to find in Hungary. **Bringóhintó,** a rental outfit on Margaret Island (✉ Hajós Alfréd sétány 1, across from Thermal Hotel, ☎ 1/329–2072), offers popular four-wheel pedaled contraptions called *Bringóhintók,* as well as traditional two-wheelers; standard bikes cost about 450 Ft. per hour, 600 to 1,000 Ft. for 24 hours. For more information about renting in Budapest, contact **Tourinform** (✉ V, Sütő u. 2, ☎ 1/317–9800). For brochures and general information on bicycling conditions and suggested routes, try Tourinform or contact the **Magyar Kerékpáros Túrázók Szövetsége** (Bicycle Touring Association of Hungary; ✉ V, Bajcsy-Zsilinszky út 31, 2nd floor, Apt. 3, ☎ 1/332–7177).

Golf

Golf is still a new sport in Hungary, one that many Hungarians can't afford. The closest place to putt is 35 km (22 mi) north of the city at the **Budapest Golfpark** (☎ 1/317–6025, 1/317–2749, or 06–26/392–463) in Kisoroszi. The park has an 18-hole, 72-par course and a driving range. Greens fees range from 5,000 Ft. to 6,000 Ft. Carts and equipment can be rented. The club also has two tennis courts. The park is closed November–February.

Health and Fitness Clubs

Andi Stúdió (✉ V, Hold u. 29, ☎ 1/311–0740) is a trendy fitness club with adequate but sometimes overcrowded facilities. For about 550 Ft. you can work out on the weight machines (no real cardiovascular equipment to speak of) and sit in the sauna, or take an aerobics class, held every hour. **Gold's Gym** (✉ VIII, Szentkirályi u. 26, ☎ 1/267–4334) stands out as having the least cramped facilities, with good weight-training and cardiovascular equipment and hourly aerobics classes in larger-than-usual spaces. A one-visit pass costs around 750 Ft.

Horseback Riding

Experienced riders can ride at the **Nemzeti Lovarda** (National Horse Academy; ✉ VIII, Kerepesi út 7, ☎ 1/313–5210) for about 800 Ft. per hour. Call ahead to assure yourself a horse. In the verdant outskirts of Buda, the **Petneházy Club** (✉ 1029 Feketefej út 2, Adyliget, ☎ 1/376–5992) is a fully equipped resort with horseback-riding lessons and trail rides for around 1,500 Ft. per hour.

Jogging

The path around the perimeter of **Margaret Island,** as well as the numerous pathways in the center, is level and inviting for a good run. **Városliget** (City Park) in flat Pest has paths and roads good for jogging.

Spas and Thermal Baths

In addition to those listed below, newer, modern baths are open to the public at hotels, such as the **Danubius Grand Hotel Margitsziget** (⊠ XIII, Margitsziget, ☎ 1/329–2300) and the **Thermal Hotel Helia** (⊠ XIII, Kárpát u. 62, ☎ 1/270–3277). They lack the charm and aesthetic appeal of their older peers but provide the latest treatments in sparkling facilities.

Gellért Thermal Baths (☞ Tabán and Gellért Hill *in* Exploring Budapest, *above*); **Király Baths** (☞ North Buda *in* Exploring Budapest, *above*); **Rác Baths** (☞ Tabán and Gellért Hill *in* Exploring Budapest, *above*); **Rudas Baths** (☞ Tabán and Gellért Hill *in* Exploring Budapest, *above*); **Széchenyi Baths** (☞ Városliget [City Park] *in* Exploring Budapest, *above*).

The **Lukács Baths** (⊠ II, Frankel Leó u. 25–29, ☎ 1/326–1695) were built in the 19th century but modeled on the Turkish originals and fed with waters from a source dating from the Bronze Age and Roman times. It's open Monday–Saturday 6:30–6, Sunday 6:30–4; the facilities are coed. Admission to the baths costs 450 Ft.

For more information on the spa and thermal bath experience, *see* Pleasures and Pastimes, *above*.

Tennis and Squash

On Margaret Island, **Euro-Gym Fitness Club** (⊠ XIII, Europa House, Margitsziget, ☎ 1/339–8672) charges 500 Ft.–700 Ft. per hour to play on one of its eight clay courts; it's open from mid-April to mid-October, and you'll need to reserve a day or two in advance. **On-line Squash Club** (⊠ Budaörs, Forrás u. 8, ☎ 23/416–945), on the near outskirts of town (about 10 minutes by car from the centrum), is a trendy full-facility fitness club with five squash courts. Hourly rates are around 1,900 Ft.–2,700 Ft., depending on when you play. The club rents equipment and stays open until 11 PM. **Városmajor Tennis Academy** (⊠ XII, Városmajor u. 63–69, ☎ 1/202–5337) has five outdoor courts (clay and hexapet) available daily 7 AM–9 PM. They are lit for night play and covered by a tent in winter. Court fees are around 1,200 Ft. per hour in summer, 1,800 Ft.–2,800 Ft. in winter. Racket rentals and lessons are also offered. The Marriott Hotel's **World Class Fitness Center** (⊠ V, Apáczai Csere János u. 4, ☎ 1/266–4290) has one excellent squash court available for 3,000 Ft. an hour; be sure to reserve it a day or two in advance.

SHOPPING

Shopping Districts

You'll find plenty of expensive boutiques, folk-art and souvenir shops, foreign-language bookstores, and classical-record shops on or around touristy **Váci utca,** Budapest's famous, upscale, pedestrian-only promenade. While a stroll along Váci utca is integral to a Budapest visit, browsing among some of the smaller, less touristy, more typically Hungarian shops in Pest—on the **Kis körút** (Small Ring Road) and **Nagy körút** (Great Ring Road)—may prove more interesting and less pricey. Lots of arty boutiques are springing up in the section of District V **south of Ferenciek tere and toward the Danube,** and around **Kálvin tér.** Charming **Falk Miksa utca,** also in the fifth district, running south from Szent István körút, is one of the city's best antiques districts, lined on both sides with atmospheric little shops and galleries.

Department Stores

Skála Metro (✉ VI, Nyugati tér 1–2, ☎ 1/353–2222), opposite the Nyugati (Western) Railroad Station, is one of the largest and best-known department stores, selling a little bit of not entirely everything. Váci utca's sleekest department store, **Fontana,** has several floors of cosmetics, clothing, and other goods, all with price tags reflecting the store's expensive address.

Markets

For true bargains and possibly an adventure, make an early morning trip to the vast **Ecseri Piac** (✉ IX, Nagykőrösi út; take Bus 54 from Boráros tér), on the outskirts of the city. A colorful, chaotic market that shoppers have flocked to for decades, it is an arsenal of second-hand goods, where you can find everything from frayed Russian army fatigues to Herend and Zsolnay porcelain vases to 150-year-old hand-made silver chalices. Goods are sold at permanent tables set up in rows, from trunks of cars parked on the perimeter, and by lone, shady characters clutching just one or two items. As a foreigner, you may be over-charged, so prepare to haggle—it's part of the flea-market experience. Also, watch out for pickpockets. Ecseri is open weekdays 8–4, Saturday 8–3, but the best selection is on Saturday mornings.

A colorful outdoor flea market is held weekend mornings from 7 to 2 at **Petőfi Csarnok** (✉ XIV, Városliget, Zichy Mihály út 14, ☎ 1/251–7266), in City Park. The quantity and selection are smaller than at Ecseri Piac, but it offers a fun flea-market experience closer to the city center. Many visitors buy red-star medals, Russian military watches, and other memorabilia from Communist days here. One other option is **Vásárcsarnok** (☞ Downtown Pest and the Kis körút [Little Ring Road] *in* Exploring Budapest, *above*).

Specialty Stores

Antiques

Falk Miksa utca (☞ Shopping Districts, *above*), lined with antiques stores, is a delightful street for multiple-shop browsing.

The shelves and tables at tiny **Anna Antikvitás** (✉ V, Falk Miksa u. 18–20, ☎ 1/302–5461) are stacked with exquisite antique textiles—from heavily embroidered wall hangings to dainty lace gloves. Wonderful cloth and lace parasols line the ceiling, but these, unfortunately, are not for sale; similar ones are, however, sometimes available. The store also carries assorted antique objets d'art. **BÁV Műtárgy** (✉ V, Ferenciek tere 12, ☎ 1/318–3381; ✉ V, Kossuth Lajos u. 3, ☎ 1/318–4403; ✉ V, Szent István krt. 3, ☎ 1/331–4534), the State Commission Trading House, has antiques of all shapes, sizes, kinds, and prices at its several branches around the city. While they all have a variety of objects, porcelain is the specialty at the branch on Kossuth Lajos utca, and paintings at the Szent István körút store. **Polgár Galéria és Aukciósház** (✉ V, Kossuth Lajos u. 3, ☎ 1/318–6954) sells everything from jewelry to furniture and also holds several auctions a year. **Qualitás** (✉ V, Falk Miksa u. 32; ✉ V, Kígyó u. 5; ✉ VII, Dohány u. 1) sells paintings, furniture, and decorative objects at its branches around town.

Art Galleries

Budapest has dozens of art galleries showing and selling old works as well as the very latest. **Dovin Gallery** (✉ V, Galamb u. 6, ☎ 1/318–3673) specializes in Hungarian contemporary paintings. New York celebrity Yoko Ono opened **Gallery 56** (✉ V, Falk Miksa u. 7, ☎ 1/269–2529) to show art by internationally famed artists, such as Keith

Haring, as well as works by up-and-coming Hungarian artists. You can also visit **Mai Manó Fotógaléria** (☞ Andrássy út *in* Exploring Budapest, *above*).

Books

You'll encounter bookselling stands throughout the streets and metro stations of the city, many of which sell English-language souvenir picturebooks at discount prices. **Váci utca** is lined with bookstores that sell glossy coffee-table books about Budapest and Hungary.

Atlantisz (⊠ V, Váci u. 31–33) has a selection of English classics, as well as academic texts. **Bestsellers** (⊠ V, Október 6 u. 11, ☎ 1/312–1295) sells exclusively English-language books and publications, including best-selling paperbacks and a variety of travel guides about Hungary and beyond. The **Central European University Bookshop** (⊠ V, Nádor u. 9, ☎ 1/327–3096), in the Central European University, is a more academically focused branch of Bestsellers bookstore. If you're interested in reading up on this part of the world, this is the store for you. You'll also find a good selection of books in English at **Idegennyelvű Könyvesbolt** (⊠ V, Petőfi Sándor u. 2 [in Párisi udvar]), which specializes in foreign-language books. **Írók boltja** (Writers' Bookshop; ⊠ VI, Andrássy út 45, ☎ 1/322–1645), one of Budapest's main literary bookstores, has a small but choice selection of Hungarian fiction and poetry translated into English. The hushed, literary atmosphere is tangible, and small tables are set out for reading and enjoying a cup of self-serve tea or instant coffee.

China, Crystal, and Porcelain

Hungary is famous for its age-old Herend porcelain, which is hand-painted in the village of Herend near Lake Balaton. For the Herend name and quality without the Herend price tag, visit **Herend Village Pottery** (⊠ II, Bem rakpart 37, ☎ 1/356–7899), where you can choose from Herend's less costly, practical-use-oriented line of durable ceramic cups, dishes, and table settings. The brand's Budapest store, **Herendi Porcelán Márkabolt** (⊠ V, József Nádor tér 11, ☎ 1/317–2622), sells a variety of the delicate (and pricey) pieces, from figurines to dinner sets. Hungary's exquisite Zsolnay porcelain, created and hand-painted in Pécs, is sold at the **Zsolnay Márkabolt** (⊠ V, Kígyó u. 4, ☎ 1/318–3712).

Hungarian and Czech crystal is considerably less expensive here than in the United States. **Goda Kristály** (⊠ V, Váci u. 9, ☎ 1/318–4630) has beautiful colored and clear pieces. **Haas & Czjzek** (⊠ VI, Bajcsy-Zsilinszky út 23, ☎ 1/311–4094) has been in the business for more than 100 years, selling a variety of porcelain, glass, and ceramic pieces in traditional and contemporary styles. Crystal and porcelain dealers also sell their wares at the Ecseri Piac flea market (☞ Markets, *above*), often at discount prices, but those looking for authentic Herend and Zsolnay should beware of imitations.

Clothing

Fidji Boutique (⊠ V, Váci u. 30, ☎ 1/266–7113) has racks of snazzy men's clothes by international designers like Christian Dior. The **Hugo Boss Shop** (⊠ V, Erzsébet tér 7–8, ☎ 1/266–7867), in the Kempinski Hotel, has a good selection of men's suits. High-fashion women's outfits by top Hungarian designers are for sale at **Monarchia** (⊠ V, Szabadsajtó út 6, ☎ 1/318–3146), a tiny boutique with rich burgundy velvet draperies and ceilings higher than its floor space. **Manier** (⊠ V, Váci u. 48 [entrance at Nyári Pál u. 4], ☎ 1/318–1812) is a popular haute couture salon run by talented Hungarian designer Anikó Németh offering women's pieces ranging from quirky to totally outrageous. The store's second branch is across the street at Váci utca 53.

Folk Art

Handmade articles, such as embroidered tablecloths and painted plates, are sold all over the city by Transylvanian women wearing traditional scarves and colorful skirts. You can usually find them standing at **Moszkva tér, Jászai Mari tér,** outside the **Kossuth tér** metro, around **Váci utca,** and in the larger metro stations.

Éva Dolls (⊠ V, Kecskeméti u. 10, ☎ 1/266–5373), a small store near Kálvin tér, has pricey but beautiful crafts. All types of folk art—pottery, blouses, jewelry boxes, wood carvings, embroidery—can be purchased at one of the many branches of Népművészet Háziipar, also called **Folkart Centrum** (⊠ V, Váci u. 14, ☎ 1/318–5840), a large cooperative chain that handles the production and sale of folk art by many artisans. Prices are reasonable, and selection and quality are good. **Holló Műhely** (⊠ V, Vitkovics Mihály u. 12, ☎ 1/317–8103) sells the work of László Holló, a master wood craftsman who has resurrected traditional motifs and styles of earlier centuries. There are lovely hope chests, chairs, jewelry boxes, candlesticks, and more, all hand-carved and hand-painted with cheery folk motifs—a predominance of birds and flowers in reds, blues, and greens.

Home Decor and Gifts

Bon-Bon (⊠ VIII, Baross u. 4, ☎ no phone) is a cramped little boutique near Kálvin tér packed with bohemian beads and necklaces, handpressed paper and cards, colorful ceramic mugs, hand-dipped candles, and various assorted knickknacks—all at very reasonable prices. **Hephaistos Háza** (⊠ VI, Zichy Jenő u. 20, ☎ 1/332–6329) is one of Budapest's hottest interior design stores, selling tastefully eclectic wrought-iron furniture and accessories with its signature curlicue flourishes. You can commission an entire room's decor (many local restaurants and bars do) or, more realistically, take home a creative candleholder or two.

Music

Recordings of Hungarian folk music or of pieces played by Hungarian artists are increasingly available on compact discs, though cassettes and records are much cheaper and are sold throughout the city. CDs are normally quite expensive—about 4,000 Ft.

Amadeus (⊠ V, Szende Pál u. 1, ☎ 1/318–6691), just off of the Duna korzó, has an extensive selection of classical CDs. **FOTEX Records** (⊠ V, Szervita tér 2, ☎ 1/318–3395; ⊠ V, Váci u. 13, ☎ 1/318–3128; ⊠ VI, Teréz körút 27, ☎ 1/332–7175; ⊠ XII, Alkotás út 11, ☎ 1/355–6886) is a flashy, Western-style music store with a cross section of musical types but focused on contemporary pop. **Hungaroton Hanglemez Szalon** (⊠ V, Vörösmarty tér 1, ☎ 1/338–2810) has a large selection of all types of music and is centrally located. Its separate, extensive section on Hungarian artists is great for gift- or souvenir-browsing. The **Rózsavölgyi Zenebolt** (⊠ V, Szervita tér 5, ☎ 1/318–3500) is an old, established music store crowded with sheet music and largely classical recordings, but with other selections as well.

Toys

For a step back into the world before Tickle Me Elmo and action figures, stop in at the tiny **Játékszerek Anno** (Toys Anno; ⊠ VI, Teréz krt. 54, ☎ 1/302–6234) store, where fabulous repros of antique European toy replicas are sold. From simple paper puzzles to lovely matte pastel stone building blocks from 1875 to the 1940s wind-up metal monkeys on bicycles, these "nostalgia toys" are beautifully simple and exceptionally clever. Even if you're not a collector, it's worth a stop just to browse.

Wine

Stores specializing in Hungarian wines have become a trend in Budapest over the past few years. The best of them is the store run by the **Budapest Bortársaság** (Budapest Wine Society; ✉ I, Batthyány u. 59, ☎ 1/212–0262, ☎ FAX 1/212–2569). The cellar shop at the base of Castle Hill always has an excellent selection of Hungary's finest wines, chosen by the wine society's discerning staff, who will happily help you with your purchases. Tastings are held Saturdays from 2 to 5 PM.

SIDE TRIP TO LAKE BALATON

Lake Balaton, the largest lake in Central Europe, stretches 80 km (50 mi) across Hungary. Its vast surface area is drastically contrasted with its modest depths—only 9.8 ft at the center, and just 52.5 ft at its deepest point at the Tihany Peninsula. The Balaton—the most popular playground of this landlocked nation—is just 90 km (56 mi) to the southwest of Budapest, so it is within easy reach of the capital by car, train, bus, and even bicycle. On a hot day in July or August, it'll seem the entire country and half of Germany are packed towel to towel on the lake's grassy public beaches, paddling about in the warm water and consuming fried meats and beer at the omnipresent snack bars.

On the lake's hilly northern shore, ideal for growing grapes, is Balatonfüred, Hungary's oldest spa town, famed for its natural springs that bubble out curative waters. The national park on the Tihany Peninsula is just to the south, and regular boat service links Tihany and Balatonfüred with garish, honky-tonk Siófok on the southern shore. Flatter and more crowded with resorts, cottages, and trade-union rest houses, the southern shore (beginning with Balatonszentgyörgy) is not as attractive as the northern one (north-shore locals say the only redeeming quality of the southern shore is its views back across the lake to the north), nor are there as many sights. Families with small children prefer the southern shore for its shallower, warmer waters (you can walk for almost 2 km [1 mi] before it deepens), which are ideal for youngsters and those who like to wallow—just ask one of the thousands of portly Hungarian grandmothers splashing themselves on a hot summer day. The water warms up to 25°C (77°F) in summer.

Every town along both shores has at least one *strand* (beach). The typical Balaton strand is a complex of blocky wooden changing cabanas and snack bars, fronted by a grassy flat stretch along the water for sitting and sunbathing. Most have paddleboat and other simple boat rentals. A small entrance fee is usually charged.

Those interested in exploring beyond the beach can set out by car, bicycle, or foot, on beautiful village-to-village tours—stopping to view lovely old Baroque churches, photograph a stork family perched high in its chimney-top nest, or climb a vineyard-covered hill for sweeping vistas. Since most vacationers keep close to the shore, a small amount of exploring into the roads and countryside heading away from the lake will reward you with a break from the summer crowds and picturesque scenery.

For price range information, *see* Dining *and* Lodging *in* Pleasures and Pastimes, *above.*

Numbers in the margin correspond to numbers on the Lake Balaton map.

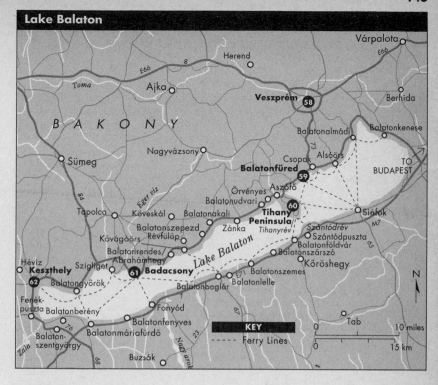

Lake Balaton

Veszprém

🔞 *116 km (72 mi) southwest of Budapest, 18 km (11 mi) north of Bal-atonfüred.*

★ Hilly Veszprém is the center of cultural life in the Balaton region. **Vár-hegy** (Castle Hill) is the most attractive part of town, north of Szabadság tér. **Hősök Kapuja** (Heroes' Gate), at the entrance to the castle, houses a small exhibit on Hungary's history. Just past the gate and down a lit-tle alley to the left is the **Tűztorony** (Fire Tower); note that the lower level is medieval, while the upper stories are Baroque. There is a good view of the town and surrounding area from the balcony. *Tower:* ☎ *88/320–485.* ⊙ *May–Oct., daily 10–6.*

Vár utca, the only street in the castle area, leads to a small square in front of the **Bishop's Palace** and the **cathedral**; outdoor concerts are held here in the summer. Vár utca continues past the square up to a terrace erected on the north staircase of the castle. Stand beside the mod-ern statues of St. Stephen and his queen, Gizella, for a far-reaching view of the old quarter of town.

OFF THE **HEREND –** Sixteen kilometers (10 miles) northwest of Veszprém on Road
BEATEN PATH 8, Herend is the home of Hungary's renowned hand-painted porcelain. The factory, founded in 1839, displays many valuable pieces in its **Herend Porcelán Művészeti Múzeum** (Herend Museum of Porcelain Arts). ✉ *Kossuth Lajos u. 144,* ☎ *88/261-144.* 🎫 *200 Ft.* ⊙ *May–Oct., Mon.-Sat. 8:30–4, Sun. 9–4:30; Nov.–mid-Dec. and Mar., weekdays 10–3; Apr., weekdays 8:30–4, Sat. 9–4:30.*

Dining

$ ✕ **Club Skorpio.** This city-center eatery might look like an alpine hut, but the menu is a cut above, with specialties such as pheasant soup and steamed wild duck. ⊠ *Virág Benedek út 1,* ☎ *88/420–319. No credit cards.*

$ ✕ **Diana.** The Diana is just a little southwest of the town center but
★ worth the trip if you want to experience the old-fashioned charm of a small provincial Hungarian restaurant. The decor is "cozy traditional," with wooden booths and tables, and the fish and game specialties are perennial favorites. There is also a 10-room pension on the premises. ⊠ *József Attila u. 22,* ☎ *88/421–061. No credit cards.*

Balatonfüred

59 *115 km (71 mi) southwest of Budapest.*

Fed by 11 medicinal springs, Balatonfüred first gained popularity as a health resort (the lake's oldest) where ailing people with heart conditions and fatigue would come to take or, more accurately, to drink a cure. The waters, said to have stimulating and beneficial effects on the heart and nerves, are still an integral part of the town's identity and consumed voraciously, but only the internationally renowned cardiac hospital has actual bathing facilities. Today Balatonfüred, also known simply as Füred, is probably the Balaton's most popular destination, with every amenity to match. Above its busy boat landing, beaches, and promenade lined with great plane and poplar trees, the twisting streets of the Old Town climb hillsides thickly planted with vines. The climate and landscape also make this one of the best wine-growing districts in Hungary. Every year in July, the most elaborate of Lake Balaton's debutante cotillions, the Anna Ball, is held here.

The center of town is **Gyógy tér** (Spa Square), where the bubbling waters from five volcanic springs rise beneath a slim, colonnaded pavilion. In the square's centerpiece, the neoclassical **Well House** of the Kossuth Spring, you can sample the water, which has a pleasant, surprisingly refreshing taste despite the sulfurous aroma; for those who can't get enough, a sign indicating a 30-liter-per-person limit is posted. All the buildings on the square are pillared like Greek temples. At No. 3 is the **Horváth Ház** (Horváth House), where the Szentgyörgyi-Horváth family arranged the first ball in 1825 in honor of their daughter Anna. It was there that she fell in love with Ernő Kiss, who became a general in the 1848–49 War of Independence and died a hero.

The Anna Ball, the event in Lake Balaton that most approximates a debutante cotillion, is now held every July in another colonnaded building on the square, the **Trade Unions' Sanatorium** (1802). Under its arcades is the **Balatoni Pantheon** (Balaton Pantheon): aesthetically interesting tablets and reliefs honoring Hungarian and foreign notables who either worked for Lake Balaton or spread the word about it. Among them is Jaroslav Hašek, the Czech author of the *Good Soldier Schweik,* who also wrote tales about Balaton. On the eastern side of the square is the **Állami Kórház** (State Hospital), where hundreds of patients from all over the world are treated. Here, too, Rabindranath Tagore, the Indian author and Nobel Prize winner, recovered from a heart attack in 1926. The tree that he planted to commemorate his stay stands in a little grove at the western end of the paths leading from the square down to the lakeside. Tagore also wrote a poem for the planting, which is memorialized beneath the tree on a strikingly animated bust of Tagore: WHEN I AM NO LONGER ON EARTH, MY TREE,/LET THE EVER-RENEWED LEAVES OF THY SPRING/MURMUR TO THE WAYFARER:/THE POET DID LOVE WHILE HE LIVED. In the same grove are trees honoring visits by another Nobel laureate, the Italian poet Salvatore Quasimodo, in 1961; and Indian prime minister Indira Gandhi, in 1972. An adjoining grove honors Soviet cosmonauts and their Hungarian partner-in-space, Bertalan Farkas.

Beginning near the boat landing, the **Tagore sétány** (Tagore Promenade) runs for nearly a kilometer (almost ½ mi) and is lined by trees, restaurants, and shops. From here, you can gaze across the water at the picturesque abbey perched high on a hill on the Tihany Peninsula.

A stroll up **Blaha Lujza utca** from Gyógy tér will take you past several landmarks, such as the **Blaha Lujza Ház** (Lujza Blaha House), a neoclassical villa built in 1867 and, later, the summer home of this famous turn-of-the-century actress, humanist, and singer (today it's a hotel); and the charming little **Kerek templom** (Round Church), consecrated in 1846, built in a classical style and with a truly rounded interior.

NEED A
BREAK?
The plush **Kedves Café** (⊠ Blaha Lujza u. 7, ☎ 87/343–229), built in 1795, was once the favorite summer haunt of well-known Hungarian writers and artists. Now more touristy than literary, it is still one of Lake Balaton's most popular and famous pastry shops.

Dining and Lodging

$$ ✕ **Baricska Csárda.** Perched on a hill overlooking wine and water— ★ its own vineyard and Lake Balaton—this rambling, reed-thatched inn is complete with wood-beamed rooms, vaulted cellars, and terraces. The food is hearty yet ambitious: roasted trout, fish *paprikás* with gnocchi to soak up the creamy sauce, and delicious desserts mixing pumpkin and poppy seed. In summer, Gypsy wedding shows are held nightly under the grape arbors. ⊠ *Baricska dülő, off Rd. 71 (Széchenyi út) behind Shell station,* ☎ *87/343–105. Reservations essential. AE, V. Closed mid-Nov.–mid-Mar.*

$$ ✕ **Tölgyfa Csárda.** Perched high on a hilltop, the Oak Tree Tavern has breathtaking views over the steeples and rooftops of Balatonfüred and the Tihany Peninsula. Its decor and menu are worthy of a first-class Budapest restaurant, and nightly live Gypsy music keeps the atmosphere festive. ⊠ *Meleghegy (up the hill at the end of Csárda utca),* ☎ *87/ 343–036. No credit cards. Closed late Oct.–mid-Apr.*

$$$$ 🏨 **Annabella.** The cool, spacious guest quarters in this large, Miami-style ★ high-rise are especially pleasant in summer heat. Overlooking the lake and Tagore Promenade, it has access to excellent swimming and watersports facilities. All rooms have balconies; for best vistas, request a room on a high floor with a view of the Tihany Peninsula. ⊠ *Deák Ferenc u. 25, H-8231,* ☎ *87/342–222, ℻ 87/483–029. 383 rooms, 5 suites. Restaurant, bar, brasserie, café, indoor pool, outdoor pool, barbershop, massage, sauna, bicycles, nightclub, baby-sitting, travel services, laundry service. AE, DC, MC, V. Closed mid-Oct.–mid-Apr.*

$$$$ 🏨 **Marina.** The Marina's central beachfront location is its main draw. Built in the mid-'80s, it it is undergoing a major overhaul, which should cheer up its dated feel. Rooms in the homely 12-story "Marina" building range from snug to small; suites have balconies but suffer from tiny bathrooms and extremely dark bedrooms. Your safest bet is to get a newly renovated, high-floor room with a lake view. Or better, stay in the "Lido" wing, which opens directly onto the water and where rooms (suites only) have pastel decor and balconies—and get plenty of sun. ⊠ *Széchenyi út 26, H-8230,* ☎ *87/343–644, ℻ 87/343–052. 291 rooms, 58 suites. Restaurant, bar, pub, indoor pool, beauty salon, massage, sauna, bowling, beach, boating, nightclub, laundry service, travel services. AE, DC, MC, V. Closed Oct.–late Apr.*

$$$ ☘ **Park.** Hidden on a side street in town but close to the lakeshore, this family-run spot is noticeably calmer than Füred's bustling main hotels. Rooms are large and bright, with high ceilings and tall windows. However, the decor is uninspired, Eastern bloc–style, with low, narrow beds and plain green and brown upholstery. Suites have large, breezy balconies but small bathrooms. ✉ *Jókai u. 24, H-8230,* ☎ FAX *87/343–203 or 87/342–005. 38 rooms, 3 suites. Restaurant, bar, exercise room, sauna, meeting room, parking. No credit cards. Closed late Oct.–late Mar.*

Outdoor Activities and Sports

Most hotels have their own private beaches, with water-sports facilities and equipment or special access to these nearby. Besides these, Balatonfüred has three public beaches, where you can rent sailboards, paddle boats, and other water toys; these are also available at Hungary's largest campground, **Füred Camping** (✉ Széchenyi u. 24, next to the Hotel Marina, ☎ 87/343–823). Although motorboats are banned from the lake, those desperate to waterski can try the campground's electric waterski machine, which tows enthusiasts around a 1-km (½-mi) circle. A two-tow ticket runs around 600 Ft.

In season you can rent **bicycles** from temporary, private outfits set up in central locations around town and near the beaches; one is usually working at the entrance to Füred Camping. Inquire at the tourist office for other current locations. Average prices for mountain-bike rentals are 500 Ft. per hour or 2,500 Ft. per day. You can also usually rent **mopeds** in front of the Halászkert restaurant (✉ Széchenyi út 2) for around 800 Ft. per hour and 3,500 Ft. per day.

Trail rides and horseback-riding lessons are available at the **Csikós Lovasudvar** (✉ Klára-puszta, Pécshely, ☎ 87/445–308), about 10 km (6 mi) away in Pécshely. Half-hour lessons cost around 1,300 Ft., hour-long trail rides about 1,500 Ft. More passive horse enthusiasts can go on a carriage ride for about 900 Ft. per person per hour.

Tihany and the Tihany Félsziget (Tihany Peninsula)

⑥⓪ *11 km (7 mi) southwest of Balatonfüred.*

The quaint town of Tihany, with its twisting, narrow cobblestone streets and hilltop abbey, is on the Tihany Félsziget (Tihany Peninsula), joined to the mainland by a narrow neck and jutting 5 km (3 mi) into the lake. Only 12 square km (less than 5 square mi), the peninsula is not only a major tourist resort but perhaps the most historic part of the Balaton area. In 1952 the entire peninsula was declared a national park, and because of its geological rarities, it became Hungary's first nature-conservation zone. On it are more than 110 geyser craters, remains of former hot springs, reminiscent of those found in Iceland, Siberia, and Wyoming's Yellowstone Park.

The smooth Belső Tó (Inner Lake), 82 ft higher than Lake Balaton, is one of the peninsula's own two lakes; around it are barren yellowish-white rocks and volcanic cones rising against the sky. Standing atop any hill in the area, you can see water in every direction. Though the hills surrounding the lake are known for their white wines, the peculiarities of this peninsula give rise to a notable Hungarian red, Tihany cabernet.

★ Tihany's crowning glory is the **Bencés Apátság** (Benedictine Abbey), with foundations laid by King Andras I in 1055. The abbey's charter—containing some 100 Hungarian words in its Latin text, thus making it the oldest written source of the Hungarian language—is kept in Pannonhalma Abbey in western Hungary. Rebuilt in Baroque style between

1719 and 1784, the abbey's church towers above the village. Its gilt-silver high altar, abbot's throne, pulpit, organ case, choir parapet, and swirling crowd of saintly and angelic faces are all the work (between 1753 and 1765) of Sebestyén Stuhlhoff. A joiner from Augsburg, Stulhoff lived and worked in the monastery as a lay brother for 25 years after the death of his Hungarian sweetheart. Local tradition says he immortalized her features as the angel who is kneeling on the right-hand side of the altar to the Virgin Mary. The magnificent Baroque organ, adorned by stucco cherubs, can be heard during evening concerts in summer.

In a Baroque house adjoining and entered through the abbey is the **Bencés Apátsági Múzeum** (Benedictine Abbey Museum). The best exhibits are in the basement lapidarium: relics from Roman colonization, including mosaic floors; a relief of David from the 2nd or 3rd century; and 1,200-year-old carved stones—all labeled in English as well as Hungarian. Three of the upstairs rooms were lived in for five days in 1921 by the last emperor of the dissolved Austro-Hungarian monarchy, Karl IV, in a futile foray to regain the throne of Hungary. Banished to Madeira, he died of pneumonia there a year later. The rooms are preserved with nostalgic relish for Franz Joseph's doomed successor. ⊠ *Első András tér 1,* ☎ *87/448–405 abbey, 87/448–650 museum.* ⊡ *180 Ft.* ☉ *May–Sept., Mon.–Sat. 9–5:30, Sun. 11–5:30; Nov.–Mar., Mon.–Sat. 10–3, Sun. 11–3; Apr. and Oct., Mon.–Sat. 10–4:30, Sun. 11–4:30.*

Visszhang domb (Echo Hill), at the end of Piski István sétány, is where as many as 16 syllables can be bounced off the abbey wall. Nowadays, with the inroads of traffic and construction, you'll have to settle for a two-second echo.

NEED A BREAK? You can practice projecting from the terraces of the **Echo Restaurant** (⊠ Visszhang út 23, ☎ 87/448–460), an inn atop Echo Hill. While you're at it, try some *fogas* (young pike perch), carp, and catfish specialties.

Dining and Lodging

$$ ✕ **Pál Csárda.** Two thatched cottages house this simple restaurant, where cold fruit soup and fish stew are the specialties. You can eat in the garden, which is decorated with gourds and strands of dried peppers. ⊠ *Visszhang u. 19,* ☎ *87/448–605. Reservations not accepted. AE, MC, V. Closed Apr.–Oct.*

$ ✕ **Halásztánya.** The relaxed atmosphere and local fish specialties— like fogas fillets with garlic—contribute to this restaurant's popularity. ⊠ *Visszhang u. 11,* ☎ *87/448–771. Reservations not accepted. AE, MC, V. Closed Nov.–Easter.*

$$$$ ⌂ **Kastély Hotel.** Lush landscaped lawns surround this stately neo-★ Baroque mansion on the water's edge, built in the 1920s for József Hapsburg and taken over by the Communist state in the '40s (it is still owned by the government). Inside, it's all understated elegance; rooms have soaring ceilings and crisp sheets. Rooms with lake-facing windows and/or balconies (slightly more expensive) are the best. Next door, a newer, unattractive concrete building houses the Kastely's sister, the Park Hotel, with 60 less expensive rooms done up in 1970s bright green upholstery. ⊠ *Fürdőtelepi út 1, H-8237,* ☎ *87/448–611,* 𝔽𝔸𝕏 *87/448–409. 25 rooms, 1 suite. Restaurant, bar, café, sauna, miniature golf, 2 tennis courts, beach. AE, DC, MC, V. Closed mid-Oct.–mid-Apr.*

$$$–$$$$ ⌂ **Club Tihany.** This 32-acre holiday village is essentially a year-round resort complex of almost Club Med proportions at the tip of the Tihany Peninsula. The list of activities is formidable—from fishing to bowl-

ing to thermal bathing at the full-service spa. The best and largest rooms in the resort's six-floor main building, the Hotel Tihany, are in its newer wing; ask for a balcony and a lake view (more expensive) on a high floor. Less fancy but more convenient for families are the 160 bungalows in various architectural styles—suburban A-frame, modern atrium, or mini-farmhouse—but all with kitchen facilities. Note: Hotel building prices include mandatory breakfast and dinner. ⊠ *Rév u. 3, H-8237, ☎ 87/448–088, FAX 87/448–110. 330 rooms, 161 bungalows. 3 restaurants, 2 bars, pool, beauty salon, spa, tennis, exercise room, beach, meeting rooms. AE, DC, MC, V.*

$$ ☷ **Kolostor.** Cozy, wood-paneled rooms are built into an attic above a popular restaurant and brewery in the heart of Tihany village. Rates include breakfast. ⊠ *Kossuth u. 14, H-8237, ☎ FAX 87/448–009. 5 rooms. Restaurant. MC, V. Closed Nov.–Mar.*

Nightlife and the Arts

The **Benedictine Abbey**'s popular summer organ-concert series runs from July to August 20 and features well-known musicians performing on the abbey's magnificent organ. Concerts are generally held weekends at 8:30 PM. Contact the abbey (☞ *above*) for information and tickets.

Outdoor Activities and Sports

BICYCLING

Bicycle rentals are available from **Tihany Tourist** (☞ Visitor Information *in* Lake Balaton A to Z, *below*); a mountain bike costs about 500 Ft. per hour.

FISHING

Belső-tó (Inner Lake) is a popular angling spot in which you can try your luck at hooking ponty, catfish, and other local fish. Fishing permits can be bought on site at the fishing warden's office (☎ 87/448–998), next door to the Tóvendéglő restaurant on the southwest side of the lake.

HIKING

Footpaths crisscross the entire peninsula, allowing visitors to climb the small hills on its west side for splendid views of the area or hike down Belső-tó (Inner Lake). If in midsummer you climb its highest hill, the **Csúcshegy** (761 ft—approximately a two-hour hike), you will find the land below carpeted with purple lavender. Introduced from France into Hungary, lavender thrives on the lime-rich soil and strong sunshine of Tihany. (The State Lavender and Medicinal Herb Farm here supplies the Hungarian pharmaceutical and cosmetics industries.)

HORSEBACK RIDING

Aszófő Lovasudvar (Aszófő Riding Center; ⊠ Aszófői út 1, ☎ 87/445–078) offers horseback-riding lessons, rides in the ring, and trail rides through the peninsula's lovely scenery; longer tours include a stop at a local wine cellar for some vintage refreshment. A two-hour trail ride costs around 1,600 Ft. The center has showers and changing rooms, as well as a snack bar.

Badacsony

★ ❻¹   *20 km (12 mi) southwest of Zánka.*

One of the northern shore's most treasured images is the slopes of Mt. Badacsony (1,437 ft high), simply called the Badacsony, rising from the lake. The mysterious, coffinlike basalt peak of the Balaton Highlands is actually an extinct volcano flanked by smaller cone-shaped hills. The masses of lava that coagulated here created bizarre and beautiful rock formations. At the upper edge, salt columns tower 180–200 ft like organ pipes in a huge semicircle. In 1965 Hungarian conservationists won a major victory that ended the quarrying of basalt from Mt. Badacsony, which is now a protected nature-preservation area.

The land below has been tilled painfully and lovingly for centuries. There are vineyards everywhere and splendid wine in every inn and tavern. In descending order of dryness, the best-loved Badacsony white wines are Rizlingszilváni, Kéknyelű, and Szürkebarát. Their proud producers claim that "no vine will produce good wine unless it can see its own reflection in the Balaton." They believe it is not enough for the sun simply to shine on a vine; the undersides of the leaves also need light, which is reflected from the lake's mirrorlike surface. Others claim the wine draws its strength from the fire of old volcanoes.

Badacsony is really an administrative name for the entire area and includes not just the mountain but also five settlements at its foot. July and August draw hoards of visitors to the wine cellars and beaches, especially on weekends, making it at times unpleasantly crowded. Spring and fall are ideal.

A good starting point for Badacsony sightseeing is the **Egry József Múzeum** (József Egry Museum), formerly the home and studio of a famous painter of Balaton landscapes. His evocative paintings beautifully depict the lake's constantly changing hues, from its angry bright green during storms to its tranquil deep blues. ⊠ *Egry sétány 12, Badacsony,* ☎ *87/431–140.* ⌷ *120 Ft.* ☉ *May–Sept., Tues.–Sun. 10–6.*

Szegedy Róza út, the steep main street climbing the mountain, is paved with basalt stones and is flanked by vineyards and villas. This is the place to get acquainted with the writer Sándor Kisfaludy and his beloved bride from Badacsony, Róza Szegedy, to whom he dedicated his love poems. At the summit of her street is **Szegedy Róza Ház** (Róza Szegedy House), a Baroque winepress house built in 1790 on a grand scale—with thatched roof, gabled wall, six semicircular arcades, and an arched and pillared balcony running the length of the four raftered upstairs rooms (it was here that the hometown girl met the visiting bard from Budapest). The house is now a memorial museum to both of them, furnished much the way it was when he was doing his best work immortalizing his two true loves, the Badacsony and his wife. ⊠ *Szegedy Róza út 87,* ☎ *no phone.* ⌷ *120 Ft.* ☉ *Apr.–Sept., Tues.–Sun. 10–6.*

The steep climb to the **Kisfaludy kilátó** (Kisfaludy Lookout Tower) on Mt. Badacsony's summit is an integral part of the Badacsony experience and a rewarding bit of exercise. Serious summitry begins behind the Kisfaludy House at the **Rózsakő** (Rose Stone), a flat, smooth basalt slab with many carved inscriptions. Local legend has it that if a boy and a girl sit on it with their backs to Lake Balaton, they will marry within a year. From here, a trail marked in yellow leads upstairs to the foot of the columns that stretch to the top. Steep flights of stone steps take you through a narrow gap between rocks and basalt walls until you reach a tree-lined plateau. You are now at the 1,391-ft level. Follow the blue triangular markings along a path to the lookout tower. Even with time out for rests and views, the ascent from Rózsakő should take less than an hour.

Wine-tasting opportunities abound in Badacsony. Many restaurants and inns have their own tastings, as do the numerous smaller, private cellars dotting the hill. Look for signs saying *bor* or *Wein* (wine, in Hungarian and German, respectively) to point the way. Most places are open mid-May to mid-September daily from around noon until 9 or 10. Just outside of town, **Rizapuzta** (⊠ Badacsonytomaj, Rizapuszta, ☎ 87/ 471–243) is a cellar and restaurant with regular tastings.

Dining and Lodging

$$ ✕ **Haláalso**. The festive Fish Garden has won numerous interna-
tional awards for its tasty Hungarian cuisine. Inside are wooden rafters
and tables draped with cheerful traditional blue-and-white *kékfestő* table-
cloths; outside is a large terrace with umbrella-shaded tables. The ex-
tensive menu has such fresh-from-the-lake dishes as the house *halászlé*
(fish stew), and *párolt harcsa* (steamed catfish) drenched with a paprika-
caper sauce. ✉ *Park u. 5,* ☎ *87/431–054. MC, V. Closed Nov.–Mar.*

$$ ✕ **Kisfaludy-ház**. Perched above the Szegedy Róza House is this Badacsony institution, once a winepress house owned by the poet's family.
Its wine cellar lies directly over a spring, but the main draw is a vast
two-tiered terrace that affords a breathtaking panoramic view of virtually the entire lake. Naturally, the wines are excellent and are incorporated into some of the cooking, such as creamy wine soup. The
grilled meats and palacsinta desserts are excellent. ✉ *Szegedy Róza u.
87,* ☎ *87/431–016. MC, V. Closed Nov.–Mar.*

$$–$$$ 🏨 **Club Tomaj**. On the shore of Lake Balaton in the Badacsonytomaj
neighborhood, this is the largest hotel in the area. It's just a step away
from the hotel to the Club's private beach. At press time it was going
under new ownership, and there were plans for renovation. ✉ *Balatoni út 14, H-8258 Badacsonytomaj,* ☎ *87/471–040,* 🖷 *87/471–059.
46 rooms, 4 suites. Restaurant, café, sauna, tennis court, bowling, beach.
MC, V. Closed mid-Oct.–Apr.*

$$–$$$ 🏨 **Hotel Volán**. This bright yellow, restored 19th-century mansion is a
cheerful, family-oriented inn with stand-out extras of a swimming pool
and a manicured yard for sunning and relaxing. Well-kept rooms are in
the main house and in four modern additions behind it. ✉ *Római út
169, H-8261 Badacsony,* ☎ *87/430–704 or 87/430–705,* ☎ 🖷 *87/431–
013. 23 rooms. Restaurant, bar, pool, tennis court. No credit cards.*

Outdoor Activities and Sports

The upper paths and roads along the slopes of Mt. Badacsony are excellent for scenic walking. Well-marked trails lead up to the summit
of Mt. Badacsony.

For beach activities, you can go to one of Badacsony's several beaches
or head 6 km (3 mi) northeast, to those at Balatonrendes and Ábrahám-
hegy, combined communities forming one of Lake Balaton's quieter
resorts.

Keszthely

㊷ *18 km (10 mi) from Szigliget.*

Keszthely, the largest town on the northern shore, lies at the western-
most end of Lake Balaton. Founded in 1404, Keszthely today offers a
rare combination of historic cultural center and restful summer resort.
With a beautifully preserved pedestrians-only avenue (Kossuth Lajos
utca) in the historic center of town, the spectacular Baroque Festetics
Kastély, and a relative absence of honky-tonk, Keszthely is far more
classically attractive and sophisticated than other large Balaton towns.
Continuing the cultural and arts tradition begun by Count György Festetics two centuries ago, Keszthely hosts numerous cultural events, including an annual summer arts festival. Just south of town is the vast
swamp called Kis-Balaton (Little Balaton), formerly part of Lake Balaton and now a protected nature area filled with birds. Water flowing
into Lake Balaton from its little sibling frequently churns up sediment,
making the water around Keszthely's beaches disconcertingly cloudy.

The **Pethő Ház**, a striking town house of medieval origins, was rebuilt
in Baroque style with a handsome arcaded gallery above its courtyard.

Hidden through its courtyard you'll find the restored 18th-century **synagogue,** in front of which stands a small memorial honoring the 829 Jewish people from the neighborhood, turned into a ghetto in 1944, who were killed during the Holocaust. ⊠ *Kossuth Lajos u. 22.*

★ Keszthely's magnificent **Festetics Kastély** (Festetics Palace) is one of the finest Baroque complexes in Hungary. Begun around 1745, it was the seat of the enlightened and philanthropic Festetics dynasty, which had acquired Keszthely six years earlier. The palace's distinctive church-like tower and more than 100 rooms were added between 1883 and 1887; the interior is exceedingly lush. The **Helikon Könyvtár** (Helikon Library) in the south wing contains some 52,000 volumes, with precious codices and documents of Festetics family history, but it can also be admired for its carved-oak furniture and collection of etchings and paintings. Chamber and orchestral concerts are held in the **Mirror Gallery** ballroom or, in summer, in the courtyard. The palace opens onto a splendid park lined with rare plants and fine sculptures. ⊠ *Kastély u. 1,* ☎ *83/312–191.* ☞ *750 Ft.* ☉ *June, Tues.–Sun. 9–5; July–Aug., daily 9–6; Sept.–May, Tues.–Sun. 10–5.*

Dining and Lodging

$–$$ ✕ **Gösser Söröző.** This centrally located beer garden keeps long hours and plenty of beer on tap for its clientele. The food is better than you might guess, judging just from the touristy atmosphere. Aside from barroom snacks, the menu includes *gulyásleves* (goulash), *gombás rostélyos* (stuffed peppers), and *töltöttpaprika* (grilled steak and mushrooms). ⊠ *Kossuth Lajos u. 35, just north of Fő tér,* ☎ *83/312–265. AE, MC, V.*

$$$$ ☐ **Danubius Hotel Helikon.** This large and comfortable lakeside hotel has plenty of sports facilities, such as an indoor swimming pool, indoor tennis courts, sailing, surfing, rowing, fishing, and, in winter, skating. The comfortable, modern rooms are on the small side, but they have soothing, cream-and-blue bedspreads and curtains. ⊠ *Balaton part 5, H-8360,* ☎ *83/311–330,* 𝔽𝔸𝕏 *83/315–403. 224 rooms, 8 suites. Restaurant, bar, indoor pool, 2 indoor tennis courts, beauty salon, sauna, bowling, health club, beach. AE, DC, MC, V.*

$$$ ☐ **Béta Hotel Hullám.** This attractive turn-of-the-century mansion with an elegant tower sits right on the Balaton shore. Rooms are clean and simply furnished with functional brown furniture; they have TVs and minibars, but no telephones. Guests can use the pool and other recreational facilities at the nearby Danubius Hotel Helikon (☞ *above*). ⊠ *Balaton part 1, H-8360,* ☎ *83/312–644,* 𝔽𝔸𝕏 *83/315–950. 44 rooms, 6 suites. Restaurant, bar, beach. AE, DC, MC, V. Closed Nov.–Mar.*

Nightlife and the Arts

The **Balaton Festival,** held annually in May, features high-caliber classical concerts and other festivities in venues around town and outdoors on Kossuth Lajos utca. In summer, classical concerts and master classes are held almost daily in the Festetics Palace's Mirror Hall.

Outdoor Activities and Sports

BALLOONING
Hot-air balloon rides in the Keszthely region have become popular with those tourists who can afford it (about 17,000 Ft. per person). Dr. Bóka György (a practicing M.D. and balloon pilot) and his friendly team will take you up in his blue-and-yellow balloon for an hour-long tour—the trip includes a postlanding champagne ritual. Flights depend strongly on wind and air-pressure conditions; in summer, they can usually fly only in early morning and early evening. Transportation to and from the sight is included. Contact **Med-Aer** (⊠ *Móricz Zsigmond u. 7,* ☎ *83/312–421)* at least one week in advance to reserve your spot.

BIRD-WATCHING

The largest river feeding Balaton, the Zala, enters the lake at its south-
western corner. On either side there is a vast swamp, formerly part of
the lake. Known as **Kis-Balaton** (Little Balaton), its almost 3,500 acres
of marshland were put under nature preservation in 1949. In 1953 a
bird-watching station was opened nearby, and ornithologists have
found some 80 species nesting among the reeds, many of them rare for
this region. The white egret is the most treasured of them. Most of the
area can be visited only by special permission. Contact Horváth Jenő
at the **Kutató-ház** (Research Station; ✉ Fenékpuszta, ☎ 83/315–341)
of the Közép Dunántúl Természetvédelmi Igazgatóság (Central Trans-
danubian Environmental Protection Directorate) to arrange a bird-watching tour (around 2,500 Ft.). The Kis-Balaton is entered near where
Highway 71 ends its trip around the lake and yields to Highway 76
continuing south.

HORSEBACK RIDING

János Lovarda (János Stable; ✉ Sömögyedüllő, ☎ 83/314–533 or 83/
312–534) offers lessons, rides in the ring, and carriage rides.

WATER SPORTS

You can rent paddleboats and other water toys at the public beach (next
to the Béta Hotel Hullám) or from the Danubius Hotel Helikon (☞
Dining and Lodging, *above*).

Lake Balaton A to Z

Arriving and Departing

BY BUS

Buses headed for the Lake Balaton region depart from Budapest's
Erzsebét tér station daily; contact **Volánbusz** (☎ 1/317–2318 in Budapest) for current schedules.

BY CAR

Highway E71/M7 is the main artery between Budapest and Lake Balaton. M7 continues down the lake's southern shore to Siófok and towns
farther west. E71 goes along the northern shore to Balatonfüred and
lakeside towns southwest. The drive from Budapest to Balatonfüred
takes about an hour and a half, except on weekends, when traffic can
be severe.

BY TRAIN

Daily express trains run from Budapest's Déli (South) Station to Balatonfüred. The two-hour trips cost about $5 each way.

Getting Around

BY BOAT

The slowest but most scenic way to travel between Lake Balaton's major
resorts is by ferry. Schedules for **MAHART** (☎ 1/318–1704 in Budapest), the national ferry company, are available from most of the tourist
offices listed in Visitor Information below.

BY BUS

Buses frequently link Lake Balaton's major resorts, but book ahead to
avoid long waits. Reservations can be made through the tourist offices
or **Volánbusz** (☎ 1/317–2318 in Budapest).

BY TRAIN

Trains from Budapest serve the resorts on the northern shore; a separate line links resorts on the southern shore. The **Balatonfüred** station
(✉ Castricum tér, ☎ 87/343–652) is very close to town center.
Veszprém's train station (✉ Jutasi út 34, ☎ 88/324–583) is about 2
km (1 mi) outside of town. There is no train service to Tihany. While

most towns are on a rail line, it's inconvenient to decipher the train schedules; trains don't run very frequently, so planning connections can be tricky. Since many towns are just a few km apart, getting stuck on a local train can feel like an endless stop-start cycle. Be sure to book tickets well in advance in high season.

Contacts and Resources

EMERGENCIES
Ambulance (☎ 104). **Fire** (☎ 105). **Police** (☎ 107).

GUIDED TOURS
IBUSZ Travel has several tours to Balaton from Budapest; inquire at the office in Budapest (✉ Rubin Aktiv Hotel, XI, Dajka Gábor u. 3, ☎ 1/319–7520, 1/319–7519). You can also arrange tours directly with the hotels in the Balaton area and with the help of Tourinform offices (see Visitor Information, *below*); these can include boat trips to vineyards, folk-music evenings, and overnight trips to local inns.

Gray Line Cityrama (☎ 1/302–4382 in Budapest) takes groups twice a week from April to October from Budapest to Balatonfüred for a walk along the promenade and then over to Tihany for a tour of the abbey. After lunch, you'll take a ferry across the Balaton, and then head back to Budapest, with a wine-tasting stop on the way.

MAHART (☎ 84/310–050) offers several boating tours and cruises on Lake Balaton. The sailboat **"Panorama Tour"** leaves Siófok Saturday at 9:30 AM and stops for guided sightseeing in Balatonfüred and Tihany. The total trip takes seven hours and is offered from early July through August. The **"Sunset Tour"** is a 1½-hour cruise on the lake during which guests can sip a glass of champagne while watching the sun sink. Departures are from Siófok from early July through August, daily at 7:30 PM. From Balatonfüred, you can board a ship for an all-day tour of the wine-growing area of Badacsony, including wine tastings, sightseeing, and enjoying lunch with live Gypsy music. This **"Wine Tasting Tour"** runs from early July through August, departing Thursday at 9:30 AM. The **"Badacsony Tour"** is also a trip to Badacsony, but it departs at 10:30 AM from Keszthely, on the same days as the tour from Balatonfüred, and returns at 4:30 PM.

VISITOR INFORMATION
Badacsony: Tourinform (✉ Római út 55, Badacsonytomaj, ☎ FAX 87/472–023). **Balatonfüred:** Tourinform (✉ Petőfi u. 8, ☎ 87/342–237); Balatontourist (✉ Tagore sétány 1, ☎ 87/342–822 or 87/343–471). **Keszthely:** Tourinform (✉ Kossuth u. 28, ☎ FAX 83/314–144). **Tihany:** Tourinform (✉ Kossuth u. 20, ☎ FAX 87/448–804); Tihany Tourist (✉ Kossuth u. 11, ☎ 87/448–481). **Veszprém:** Tourinform (✉ Rákóczi út 3, ☎ 88/404–548).

BUDAPEST A TO Z *From Vienna*

Arriving and Departing

By Boat
From early July through August, two swift hydrofoils leave Vienna daily at 8 AM and 1 PM (once-a-day trips are scheduled mid-April–early July and September–early November). After a 5½-hour journey downriver, with a stop in the Slovak capital, Bratislava, and views of Hungary's largest church, the cathedral in Esztergom, the boats make a grand entrance into Budapest via its main artery, the Danube. The upriver journey takes about an hour longer. For reservations and information in Budapest, call **MAHART Tours** (☎ 1/318–1704 or 1/318–1586, ☎ 43–1/729–2161 or 43–1/729–2162 in Vienna). The cost is 750 AS one-way.

By Bus

There is regular bus service between Budapest and selected major cities in the region. From Budapest, buses to Bratislava and Prague depart from the Erzsébet tér station (☎ 1/317–2562 for international information). Buses to Krakow, Sofia, and Brasso operate from the Népstadion station (☎ 1/252–4496). Buses to the west and south, to Austria and the former Yugoslavia, leave from the main Volán bus station at Erzsébet tér in downtown Pest (☎ 1/317–2562 for international information). Though inexpensive, these buses tend to be crowded, so reserve your seat.

By Car

At press time, Hungary was continuing a massive upgrading and reconstruction of many of its motorways, gearing up for its role as the main bridge for trade between the Balkan countries and the former Soviet Union and Western Europe. Work is scheduled to continue beyond 2000. To help fund the project, tolls on major highways were introduced for the first time in 1996. Charging 1,400 Ft. per car for the section between Győr and the border, the much-heralded M1 from Budapest to Vienna continues to be the most expensive road to travel in Europe. M1 tolls can be paid in dollars and with major credit cards, as well.

Other major routes into Budapest are the M3 from near Gyöngyös (incomplete and still free at press time), the M5 from Kecskemét, which charges about 1,100 Ft., and the M7 from the Balaton; the M3 and M5 are being upgraded over the next few years and extended to Hungary's borders with Slovakia and Serbia.

By Plane

Ferihegy (☎ 1/296–9696), Hungary's only commercial airport, is about 22 km (14 mi) southeast of Budapest. All Lufthansa and Malév flights operate from the newer Terminal 2, 4 km (2½ mi) farther from the city; other airlines use Terminal 1. For same-day **flight information,** call 1/296–7155; operators theoretically speak some English.

The most convenient way to fly between Hungary and the United States is with **Malév Hungarian Airlines** (☎ 06/80–212–121 toll free; 1/235–3804 [ticketing]; 1/296–9696 [after-hours flight information]) nonstop direct service between JFK International Airport in New York and Budapest's Ferihegy Airport—the only nonstop flight that exists. All are on roomy Boeing 767-200s and take approximately nine hours. The service runs daily most of the year.

Malév and other national airlines fly nonstop from most European capitals. **British Airways** (☎ 1/266–7790 or 1/318–3299) and Malév offer daily nonstop service between Budapest and London.

Between the Airport and Downtown: Many hotels offer their guests car or minibus transportation to and from Ferihegy, but all of them charge for the service. You should arrange for a pickup in advance. If you're taking a taxi, allow 40 minutes during nonpeak hours and at least an hour during rush hours (7 AM–9 AM from the airport, 4 PM–6 PM from the city). Official **Airport Taxis** (☎ 1/282–2222) are queued at the exit and overseen by a taxi monitor; rates are fixed according to the zone of your final destination. A taxi ride to the center of Budapest will cost around 3,500 Ft. There's also a special 1,990-Ft. rate to the airport if you call one day in advance to arrange for a pickup. Avoid taxi drivers who approach before you are out of the arrivals lounge.

LRI Centrum-Airport-Centrum (☎ 1/296–8555 or 1/296–6283) minibuses run every half hour from 5:30 AM to 9:30 PM to and from the Erzsébet tér bus station (Platform 1) in downtown Budapest. It takes almost the same time as taxis but costs only 700 Ft. from either airport terminal. The **LRI Airport Shuttle** provides convenient door-to-door service between the airport and any address in the city. To get to the airport, call to arrange a pickup (☎ 1/296–8555 or 1/296–6283); to get to the city, make arrangements at LRI's airport desk. Service to or from either terminal costs around 1,400 Ft. per person; since it normally shuttles several people at once, remember to allow time for a few other pickups or dropoffs.

By Train

There are three main *pályaudvar* (train stations) in Budapest: **Keleti** (Eastern; ✉ VII, Rákóczi út, ☎ 1/313–6835), **Nyugati** (Western; ✉ V, Nyugati tér, ☎ 1/331–5346), and **Déli** (Southern; ✉ XII, Alkotás u., ☎ 1/375–6593). Trains from Vienna usually operate from the Keleti Station, while those to Balaton depart from the Déli.

Getting Around

By Bus and Tram

Trams (*villamos*) and buses (*autóbusz*) are abundant and convenient. One fare ticket (80 Ft.; valid on all forms of public transportation) is valid for only one ride in one direction. Tickets cannot be bought on board; they are widely available in metro stations and newsstands and must be canceled on board—watch how other passengers do it—unless you've purchased a *napijegy* (day ticket, 600 Ft.; a three-day "tourist ticket" costs 1,200 Ft.), which allows unlimited travel on all services within the city limits. Hold on to whatever ticket you have; spot-checks by aggressive undercover checkers (look for the red armbands) are numerous and often targeted at tourists. Trolley-bus stops are marked with red, rectangular signs that list the route stops; regular bus stops are marked with similar light-blue signs. (The trolley-buses and regular buses themselves are red and blue, respectively.) Tram stops are marked by light-blue or yellow signs. Most lines run from 5 AM and stop operating at 11 PM, but there is all-night service on certain key lines. Consult the separate night-bus map posted in most metro stations for all-night routes.

By Car

Budapest, like any Western city, is plagued by traffic jams during the day, but motorists should have no problem later in the evening. Motorists not accustomed to sharing the city streets with trams should pay extra attention. Speed traps are numerous, so it's best to keep at the speed limit; fines are around the equivalent of $25 and must be paid on the spot. You should also be prepared to be flagged down numerous times by police conducting routine checks for drunk driving and stolen cars; police can occasionally try to take advantage of foreigners, so always have your papers at hand.

Gas stations have become plentiful in Hungary, and many on the main highways stay open all night, even on holidays. Major chains, such as MOL, Shell, and OMV, now have Western-style full-facility stations with rest rooms, brightly lit convenience stores, and 24-hour service. Lines are rarely long, and supplies are essentially stable. Unleaded gasoline (*bleifrei* or *ólommentes*) is generally available at most stations and is usually the 95-octane-level choice. If your car requires unleaded gasoline, be sure to double-check for leaded gas before you pump.

PARKING
Gone are the "anything goes" days of parking in Budapest, when cars parked for free practically anywhere in the city, straddling curbs or angled in the middle of sidewalks. Now most streets in Budapest's main

districts have restricted, fee parking; there are either parking meters that accept coins or attendants who approach your car as you park and charge you according to how many hours you intend to stay. Hourly rates average 140 Ft. In most cases, overnight parking in these areas is free. Budapest also has a number of parking lots and a few garages; two central-Pest locations are: V, Szervita tér and V, Aranykéz u. 4–6. No-parking zones are marked with the international "No Parking" sign: a white circle with a diagonal line through it.

ROAD CONDITIONS
There are three classes of roads: highways or motorways (designated by the letter M and a single digit), secondary roads (designated by a two-digit number), and minor roads (designated by a three-digit number). Highways and secondary roads are generally in good condition. The conditions of minor roads vary considerably; keep in mind that tractors and horse-drawn carts may slow your route down in rural areas.

RULES OF THE ROAD
Hungarians drive on the right and observe the usual Continental rules of the road. Unless otherwise noted, the speed limit in developed areas is 50 kph (30 mph), on main roads 80–100 kph (50–62 mph), and on highways 120 kph (75 mph). Keep alert: Speed-limit signs are few and far between. Seat belts are compulsory, and drinking alcohol is totally prohibited—there is a zero-tolerance policy, and the penalties are very severe.

By Metro
Service on Budapest's subways is cheap, fast, frequent, and comfortable; stations are easily located on maps and streets by the big letter M (for metro). Tickets—80 Ft.; valid on all forms of mass transportation—can be bought at hotels, metro stations, newsstands, and kiosks. They are valid for one ride only; you can't change lines or direction. Tickets must be canceled in the time-clock machines in station entrances and should be kept until the end of the journey, as there are frequent checks by undercover inspectors; a fine for traveling without a validated ticket is about 1,000 Ft. A *napijegy* (day ticket) costs 600 Ft. (a three-day "tourist ticket," 1,200 Ft.) and allows unlimited travel on all services within the city limits.

Line 1 (marked FÖLDALATTI), which starts downtown at Vörösmarty tér and follows Andrássy út out past Gundel restaurant and City Park, is an antique tourist attraction in itself, built in the 1890s for the Magyar Millennium; its yellow trains with tank treads still work. Lines 2 and 3 were built 90 years later. Line 2 (red) runs from the eastern suburbs, past the Keleti (Eastern) Station, through the Inner City area, and under the Danube to the Déli (Southern) Station. (One of the stations, Moszkva tér, is where the *Várbusz* [Castle Bus] can be boarded.) Line 3 (blue) runs from the southern suburbs to Deák tér, through the Inner City, and northward to the Nyugati (West) Station and the northern suburbs. On all three lines, fare tickets are canceled in machines at the station entrance. All three metro lines meet at the Deák tér station and run from 4:30 AM to shortly after 11 PM.

By Taxi
Taxis are plentiful and a good value, but make sure they have a working meter. The average initial charge is 50 Ft.–75 Ft., plus about 110 Ft. per km and 30 Ft. per minute of waiting time. Many drivers try to charge outrageous prices, especially if they sense that their passenger is a tourist. Avoid unmarked "freelance" taxis; stick with those affiliated with an established company. Your safest and most reliable bet is to do what the locals do: Order a taxi by phone; it will arrive in about

5 to 10 minutes. The best rates are with **Citytaxi** (☎ 1/211–1111) and **Fő taxi** (☎ 1/222–2222).

Contacts and Resources

Apartment Rentals

Apartments, available for short- and long-term rental, can be the most economic lodging for families or groups. A short-term rental in Budapest may cost anywhere from $30 to $60 a day.

Amadeus Apartments (✉ IX, Üllői út 197, H-1091, ☎ 06–30/422–893, FAX 1/302–8268) oversees five well-kept apartments in downtown Budapest, each consisting of two rooms plus a fully equipped kitchen and bathroom. Free transportation from the train station or airport is included; guarded parking areas are provided for a fee for those with cars. The two-person, high-season rate is approximately $40 a night.

IBUSZ Welcome Hotel Service (✉ Apáczai Csere János u. 1, ☎ 1/318–3925 or 1/318–5776, FAX 1/317–9099), open 24 hours a day, books private apartments, arranges rooms in private homes, and reserves rooms in inns and hotels. **Cooptourist** (✉ I, Attila u. 107, ☎ 1/375–2846 or 1/375–2937) arranges private apartments and rooms and makes reservations in its affiliated inns and hotels.

B&B Reservation Agencies

The rate per night for a double room in Budapest is around $23 (which usually includes the use of a bathroom but not breakfast). Two reliable resources are: **IBUSZ Welcome Hotel Service** (☞ *above*) and **Cooptourist** (☞ *above*)

Car Rentals

Avis (main office, ✉ V, Szervita tér 8, ☎ 1/318–4240; Terminal 1, ☎ 1/296–6421; Terminal 2, ☎ 1/296–7265), **Budget-Pannonia** (main office, ✉ Hotel Mercure Buda, I, Krisztina körút 41–43, ☎ 1/356–6333; Terminal 1, ☎ 1/296–8197; Terminal 2, ☎ 1/296–8481), and **Hertz** (also known in Hungary as Mercure Rent-a-Car; ✉ V, Marriott Hotel, Apáczai Csere János u. 4, ☎ 1/266–4361; Terminal 1, ☎ 1/296–7171; Terminal 2, ☎ 1/296–6988) are all here for those who prefer companies they know back home. Rates are high: Daily rates for automatics begin around $55–$60 plus 60¢ per km; personal, theft, and accident insurance (not required but recommended) runs an additional $25–$30 per day. Rates tend to be significantly lower if you arrange your rental *from home* through the American offices. Ask your travel agent for help.

Local companies offer lower rates. Inquire at **Americana Rent-a-Car** (✉ Ibis Hotel Volga, XIII, Dózsa György út 65, ☎ 1/270–2542, 1/320–8287) about unlimited-mileage weekend specials. Rates include free delivery and pickup of the car anywhere in the city. **Fötaxi** (main office, ✉ VII, Kertész u. 24–28, ☎ 1/322–1471; Terminal 1, ☎ 1/296–8629; Terminal 2, ☎ 1/296–8606) has special rates on smaller and non-Western makes, including inexpensive Russian Ladas (not a luxury make).

Embassies and Consulates

Canada (✉ XII, Zugligeti út 51–53, ☎ 1/275–1200). **U.K.** (✉ V, Harmincad u. 6, ☎ 1/266–2888, FAX 1/266–0907). **U.S.** (✉ V, Szabadság tér 12, ☎ 1/267–4400).

Emergencies

Ambulance (☎ 104), or call **Falck–SOS** (✉ II, Kapy u. 49/b, ☎ 1/200–0100 or 1/200–0122), a 24-hour private ambulance service with English-speaking personnel. **Doctor:** Ask your hotel or embassy for recommendations or visit the **R-Clinic** (✉ II, Felsőzöldmáli út 13, ☎ 1/325–9999), a private clinic staffed by English-speaking doctors offering 24-hour medical and ambulance service. The clinic accepts major credit cards and prepares full reports for your insurance company. U.S. and Canadian visitors are advised to take out full medical insurance. U.K. visitors are covered for emergencies and essential treatment. **Dentist:** Professional Dental Associates (✉ II, Sobrás u. 9, ☎ 1/200–4447 or 1/200–4448) is a private, English-speaking dental practice comprised of Western-trained dentists and hygienists; service is available 24 hours a day. **Police** (☎ 107).

English-Language Bookstores
See Books *in* Shopping, *above.*

English-Language Periodicals
Several English-language weekly newspapers have sprouted up to placate Budapest's large expatriate community. The *Budapest Sun, Budapest Week,* and the *Budapest Business Journal* are sold at major newsstands, hotels, and tourist points.

Guided Tours
Orientation Tours: IBUSZ Travel (✉ Rubin Aktiv Hotel, XI, Dajka Gábor u. 3, ☎ 1/319–7520, 1/319–7519) conducts three-hour bus tours of the city that operate all year and cost about 4,000 Ft. Starting from Erzsébet tér, they take in parts of both Buda and Pest. **Gray Line Cityrama** (✉ V, Báthori u. 22, ☎ 1/302–4382) also offers a three-hour city bus tour (about 4,000 Ft. per person). Both have commentary in English.

Special-Interest Tours: IBUSZ, Gray Line Cityrama, and **Budapest Tourist** organize a number of unusual tours, with trips to the Buda Hills, goulash parties, and visits to such traditional sites as the National Gallery and Parliament. These companies will provide English-speaking personal guides on request. Also check at your hotel.

Boat Tours: From late March through October boats leave from the dock at Vigadó tér on 1½-hour cruises between the railroad bridges north and south of the Árpád and Petőfi bridges, respectively. The trip, organized by **MAHART Tours** (☎ 1/318–1704), runs only on weekends and holidays (once a day, at noon) from March until May, then twice daily from May to October (at noon and 7 PM); the cost is about 800 Ft. From mid-June through August, the evening cruise leaves at 7:45 PM and features live music and dancing for 100 Ft. more.

Hour-long evening sightseeing cruises on the *Danube Legend* depart nightly at 8:15 in April and October, and three times nightly (at 8:15, 9, and 10) from May through September. Guests receive headphones and listen to a recorded explanation of the sights in the language of their choice. Drinks are also served. Boats depart from Pier 6–7 at Vigadó tér (☎ 1/317–2203 for reservations and information).

The *Duna-Bella* takes guests on two-hour tours on the Danube, including a one-hour walk on Margaret Island and shipboard cocktails. Recorded commentary is provided through earphones. The tour is offered July through August, six times a day; September, three times a day; and October and November, once a day. Boats depart from Pier 6–7 at Vigadó tér (☎ 1/317–2203 for reservations and information).

Jewish-Heritage Tours: The **Chosen Tours** (✉ XII, Zolyomi lépcső 27, ☎ 1/319–3427, ☎ FAX 1/319–6800) offers a three-hour combination bus and walking tour ($17) called "Budapest Through Jewish Eyes," highlighting the sights and cultural life of the city's important Jewish history. Tours run daily except Saturday and often include pick-up service from central hotels. Arrangements can also be made for un-scheduled and off-season tours, as well as custom-designed tours.

Personal Guides: The major travel agencies—**IBUSZ Travel** and **Budapest Tourist** (☞ Visitor Information, *below*)—will arrange for guides.

Late-Night Pharmacies

The state-run pharmacies close between 6 and 8 PM, but several pharmacies stay open at night and on the weekend, offering 24-hour service, with a small surcharge for items that aren't officially stamped as urgent by a physician. You must ring the buzzer next to the night window and someone will respond over the intercom. Staff is unlikely to speak English; ask for help from someone who speaks Hungarian. Central ones in Pest include those at **Teréz körút 41** (☎ 1/311–4439) in the sixth district, near the Nyugati Train Station; and the one at **Rákóczi út 39** (☎ 1/314–3695) in the 8th district, near the Keleti Train Station. In Buda, there is one across the street from the Déli train station at **Alkotás utca 1/b** (☎ 1/355–4691), in the 12th district.

Mail

Airmail letters and postcards generally take seven days to travel between Hungary and the United States, sometimes more than twice as long, however, during the Christmas season.

In Budapest, go to the main **downtown post office** branch (✉ Magyar Posta 4. sz., Városház utca 18, H-1052 Budapest). The post offices near Budapest's **Keleti** (Eastern; ✉ VII, Baross tér 11c) and **Nyugati** (Western; ✉ VI, Teréz körút 51) train stations are open 24 hours. The **American Express** office in Hungary is in Budapest (✉ Deák Ferenc u. 10 H-1052 Budapest, ☎ 1/266–8680); there are poste restante services.

POSTAL RATES

Postage for an airmail letter to the United States costs about 125 Ft.; an airmail letter to the United Kingdom and elsewhere in Western Europe costs about 115 Ft. Airmail postcards to the United States cost about 85 Ft. and to the United Kingdom and the rest of Western Europe, about 80 Ft.

RECEIVING MAIL

Although it's not recommended for urgent or valuable correspondences, a *poste restante* service, for general delivery, is available through any post office in Budapest. The envelope should have your name written on it, as well as "Posta Maradó" (*poste restante*) in big letters.

Money and Expenses

Eurocheque holders can cash personal checks in all banks and in most hotels. Many banks now also cash American Express and Visa traveler's checks. **American Express** has a full-service office in Budapest (✉ V, Deák Ferenc u. 10, ☎ 1/267–2020, 1/267–2313, or 1/266–8680; FAX 1/267–2029), which also dispenses cash to its cardholders; two smaller branches on Castle Hill—in the Budapest Hilton Hotel (☎ 1/214–6446) and the Sisi Restaurant (☎ 1/264–0118)—have a currency exchange. Budapest also has a **Citibank** (✉ V, Vörösmarty tér 4) offering full services to account holders, including a 24-hour cash machine.

Plastic has recently entered Hungary's financial scene: Most major credit cards are accepted, though don't rely on them in smaller towns or less expensive accommodations and restaurants. Twenty-four-hour cash machines have sprung up throughout Budapest; some accept Plus network bank cards and Visa credit cards, others Cirrus and MasterCard. You can withdraw forints only (automatically converted at the bank's official exchange rate) directly from your account. Most levy a 1% or

$3 service charge. Instructions are in English. For those without plastic, many cash-exchange machines, into which you feed paper currency for forints, have also sprung up. Most bank automats and cash-exchange machines are clustered around their respective bank branches throughout downtown Pest.

COSTS

The forint was significantly devalued over the last few years and continues its decline, but inflation has decreased to just under 20% from its previous annual rate of more than 25%. You'll receive more forints for your dollar but will find that prices have risen to keep up with inflation. More and more hotels now set their rates in hard currency to avoid the forint's instability. Still, even with inflation and the 25% value-added tax (VAT) in the service industry, enjoyable vacations with all the trimmings still remain less expensive than in nearby Western cities like Vienna.

CURRENCY

Hungary's unit of currency is the forint (Ft.), no longer divided into fillérs as it was a few years ago. There are bills of 50, 100, 200, 500, 1,000, 2,000, 5,000, and 10,000 forints; and coins of 1, 2, 5, 10, 20, 50, 100, and 200 forints. The exchange rate was approximately 215 Ft. to the U.S. dollar, 145 Ft. to the Canadian dollar, and 370 Ft. to the pound sterling at press time. Although cash card and Eurocheque facilities are becoming easier to find in big cities, it is probably still wise to bring traveler's checks, which can be cashed all over the country in banks and hotels. There is still a black market in hard currency, but changing money on the street is risky and illegal, and the bank rate almost always comes close. Stick with banks and official exchange offices.

SAMPLE COSTS

Cup of coffee, 100 Ft.; bottle of beer, 300 Ft.–400 Ft.; soft drinks, 100 Ft.; ham sandwich, 150 Ft.; 2-km (1-mi) taxi ride, 150 Ft.; museum admission, 100 Ft.–250 Ft.

Passports and Visas

Only a valid passport is required of U.S., British, and Canadian citizens. For additional information contact the **Hungarian Embassy** in the United States (⊠ 3910 Shoemaker St. NW, Washington, DC 20008, ☎ 202/362–6730), in Canada (⊠ 299 Waverley St. Ottawa, Ontario K2P 0V9, ☎ 613/230–9614), in London (⊠ 35b Eaton Pl., London SW1X 8BY, ☎ 0171/235–5218), or in Australia (⊠ 17 Beale Crescent Deakin Act., Canberra 2600, ☎ 6126/282–3226).

Student and Youth Travel

In Hungary, as a general rule, only Hungarian citizens and students at Hungarian institutions qualify for student discounts on domestic travel fares and admission fees. Travelers under 25, however, qualify for excellent youth rates on international airfares; those under 26 are eligible for youth rates on international train fares. The International Student Identity Card (ISIC) is accepted in Budapest, but not as widely as it is in Western countries. If you buy your Student Identity Card in Budapest at the **Express Youth and Travel Office** (⊠ V, Zoltán utca 10, ☎ 1/311–6418; ⊠ V, Szabadság tér 16, ☎ 1/311–7679; ⊠ VII, Keleti train station, ☎ 1/342–1772), which specializes in providing information on all aspects of student and youth travel throughout the country and abroad, it will cost about one-third the price of buying the card in the United States.

Telephones

Within Hungary, most towns can be dialed directly—dial 06 and wait for the buzzing tone; then dial the local number. Note that cellular phone numbers are treated like long-distance domestic calls: Dial 06 before the number (when giving their cellular phone numbers, most people include the 06 anyway).

Dial 198 for directory assistance for all of Hungary. Operators are unlikely to speak English. A safer bet is to consult *The Phone Book*, an English-language telephone directory full of important Budapest numbers as well as cultural and tourist information; it's provided in guest rooms of most major hotels, as well as at many restaurants and English-language bookstores.

Though continuously improving, the Hungarian telephone system is still antiquated, especially in the countryside. Be patient. With the slow improving of Hungary's telephone system comes the problem of numbers changing—sometimes without forewarning. Tens of thousands of phone numbers in Budapest alone will be changed over the next few years; if you're having trouble getting through, ask your concierge to check the number for you (or if the number begins with a 1, try dialing it starting with a 3 instead—many changes will be of this type).

COUNTRY CODE
The country code for Hungary is 36. When dialing from outside the country, drop the initial zero from the area code.

INTERNATIONAL CALLS
Direct calls to foreign countries can be made from Budapest by dialing 00 and waiting for the international dialing tone; on pay phones the initial charge is 60 Ft. To reach an **AT&T** long-distance operator, dial 00–800–01111; for **MCI** dial 00–800–01411; for **Sprint,** dial 00–800–01877.

LOCAL CALLS
Hungarian pay phones use 20-Ft. coins—the cost of a three-minute local call—and also accept 10-Ft. and 50-Ft.coins. Gray card-operated telephones outnumber coin-operated phones in Budapest and the Balaton region. The cards—available at post offices and most newsstands and kiosks—come in units of 50 (800 Ft.) and 120 (1,800 Ft.) calls. It is unnecessary to use the city code, 1, when dialing within Budapest. Don't be surprised if a flock of kids gathers around your pay phone while you talk—collecting and trading used phone cards is a raging fad.

Tipping
Four decades of socialism have not restrained the extended palm in Hungary—so tip when in doubt. Hairdressers and taxi drivers expect 10% to 15% tips, while porters should get a dollar or two. Coatroom attendants receive 100 to 200 Ft., as do gas-pump attendants if they wash your windows or check your tires. Gratuities are not included automatically to restaurant bills; when the waiter arrives with the bill, you should immediately add a 10% to 15% tip to the amount, as it is not customary to leave the tip on the table. If a Gypsy band plays exclusively for your table, you can leave 200 Ft. in a plate discreetly provided for that purpose.

Travel Agencies
American Express (✉ V, Déak Ferenc u. 10, ☎ 1/266–8680, FAX 1/267–2028). **Getz International** (✉ V, Falk Miksa u. 5, ☎ 1/312–0645 or 1/312–0649, FAX 1/312–1014). **Vista Travel Center** (✉ VI, Andrássy út 1, ☎ 1/269–6032 or 1/269–6033, FAX 1/269–6031).

Visitor Information
Budapest Tourist (✉ V, Roosevelt tér 5, ☎ 1/317–3555). **IBUSZ** (central branch: ✉ V, Ferenciek tere 10, ☎ 318–6866). **IBUSZ Welcome Hotel Service** (✉ Apáczai Csere János u. 1, ☎ 1/318–3925 or 1/318–

5776, FAX 1/317–9099), open 24 hours. **Tourinform** (⊠ V, Sütő u. 2, ☎ 1/317–9800). **Tourism Office of Budapest** (⊠ V, Március 15 tér 7, ☎ 1/266–0479; ⊠ VI, Nyugati pályaudvar, ☎ 1/302–8580).The Tourism Office of Budapest (☞ *above*) has developed the **Budapest Card,** which entitles holders to unlimited travel on public transportation; free admission to many museums and sights; and discounts on various entertainment events, tours, meals, and services from participating businesses. The cost (at press time) is 2,000 Ft. for two days, 2,500 Ft. for three days; one card is valid for an adult plus one child under 14.

4 Portraits of Prague and Budapest

FURTHER READING

Since the revolutions of 1989–90, a number of leading journalists have produced highly acclaimed books detailing the tumultuous changes experienced by Eastern and Central Europeans and the dramatic effects these changes have had on individual lives. Timothy Garton Ash's eyewitness account, *The Magic Lantern: The Revolution of '89 Witnessed in Warsaw, Budapest, Berlin, and Prague,* begins with Václav Havel's ringing words from his 1990 New Year's address: "People, your government has returned to you!" Winner of both a National Book Award and a Pulitzer Prize, *The Haunted Land* is Tina Rosenberg's wide-ranging, incisive look at how Poland, the Czech Republic, and Slovakia (as well as Germany) are dealing with the memories of 40 years of communism.

In *Exit into History: A Journey Through the New Eastern Europe,* Eva Hoffman returns to her Polish homeland and five other countries—Hungary, Romania, Bulgaria, the Czech Republic, and Slovakia—and captures the texture of the everyday life of a world in the midst of change. Isabel Fonseca's *Bury Me Standing: The Gypsies and Their Journey* is an unprecedented and revelatory look at the Gypsies—or Romany—of Eastern and Central Europe, the large and landless minority whose history and culture have long been obscure.

Travelogues worth reading, though less recent, include Claudio Magris's widely regarded *Danube,* which follows the river as it flows from its source in Germany to its mouth in the Black Sea; Brian Hall's *Stealing from a Deep Place,* a lively account of a solo bicycle trip through Romania and Bulgaria in 1982, followed by a stay in Budapest; Patrick Leigh Fermor's *Between the Woods and the Water,* which relates his 1934 walk through Hungary and Romania and captures life in these lands before their transformation during World War II and under the Soviets.

Forty-three writers from 16 nations of the former Soviet bloc are included in *Description of a Struggle: The Vintage Book of Contemporary Eastern European Writing,* edited by Michael March. Focusing on novels, poetry, and travel writing, the *Traveller's Literary Companion to Eastern and Central Europe* is a thorough guide to the vast array of literature from this region available in English translation. It includes country-by-country overviews, dozens of excerpts, reading lists, biographical discussions of key writers that highlight their most important works, and guides to literary landmarks.

Czech Republic

With the increased interest in the Czech Republic in recent years, English readers now have an excellent range of both fiction and nonfiction about the country at their disposal. The most widely read Czech author of fiction in English is probably Milan Kundera, whose well-crafted tales illuminate both the foibles of human nature and the unique tribulations of life in Communist Czechoslovakia. Oddly, the Czechs never really took to the novels he wrote after leaving Czechoslovakia for France in the 1970s. *The Unbearable Lightness of Being* takes a look at the 1968 invasion and its aftermath through the eyes of a strained young couple. *The Book of Laughter and Forgetting* deals in part with the importance of memory and the cruel irony of how it fades over time; Kundera was no doubt coming to terms with his own forgetting as he wrote the book from his Paris exile. *The Joke,* Kundera's earliest work available in English, takes a serious look at the dire consequences of humorlessness among Communists.

Born and raised in the German–Jewish enclave of Prague, Franz Kafka scarcely left the city his entire life. *The Trial* and *The Castle* strongly convey the dread and mystery he detected beneath the 1,000 golden spires of Prague. Kafka worked as a bureaucrat for 14 years, in a job he detested; his books are, at least in part, an indictment of the bizarre bureaucracy of the Austro-Hungarian empire, though they now seem eerily prophetic of the even crueler and more arbitrary Communist system that was to come. Until recently, most of his works could not be purchased in his native country.

The most popular Czech authors today were those banned or harassed by the communists after the Soviet invasion of 1968. Václav Havel and members of Charter 77 illegally distributed self-published manuscripts, or *samizdat* as they were called, of these authors—among them, Bohumil Hrabal, Josef Škvorecký, and Ivan Klíma. Hrabal, who died in 1997, was perhaps the most beloved of all postwar Czech writers. He spent his entire life in his homeland, and was allowed to publish regularly; many claim to have shared a table with him at his favorite pub in Prague, U Zlatéyho tygra. His books include *I Served the King of England* and the lyrical *Too Loud a Solitude,* narrated by a lonely man who spends his days in the basement compacting the world's greatest works of literature along with bloodied butcher paper into neat bundles before they get carted off for recycling and disposal. Škvorecký sought refuge and literary freedom in Toronto in the early 1970s. His book *The Engineer of Human Souls* reveals the double censorship of the writer in exile—censored in the country of his birth and unread in his adopted home. Still, Škvorecký did gain a following thanks to his translator, Paul Wilson—who lived in Prague in the 1960s and '70s until he was ousted for his assistance in dissident activities. Novelist, short story writer, and playwright Ivan Klíma is now one of the most widely read Czech writers in English; his books include the novels *Judge on Trial, Love and Garbage,* and *The Spirit of Prague,* a collection of essays about life in the Czech Republic today.

Václav Havel, one-time dissident playwright and now president of the Czech Republic, is essential nonfiction reading. The best place to start is probably *Living in Truth,* which provides an absorbing overview of his own political philosophy and of Czechoslovak politics and history over the last 30 years. Also look for *The Art of the Impossible,* a selection of Havel's speeches and articles, *Disturbing the Peace,* a collection of interviews with him, and *Letters to Olga.* Havel's plays explore the absurdities and pressures of life under the former Communist regime; the best example of his absurdist dramas is *The Memorandum,* which depicts a Communist bureaucracy more twisted than the streets of Prague's Old Town.

Many observers, Ivan Klíma among them, have bemoaned what they view as the poor quality of writing since the revolution. Among the most prominent of the young writers is Jáchym Topol, whose *A Visit to the Train Station* documents the creation of a new Prague with a sharp wit that cuts the false pretenses of American youth currently occupying Prague.

Hungary

Hungarians have played a central role in the intellectual life of the 20th century, although their literary masters are less well known in the west than those who have excelled in other arts, such as Béla Bartók in music, and Andre Kertesz and Robert and Cornell Capa in photography (the latter two founded New York City's International Center of Photography).

Novelist and poet Dezsö Kosztolányi was prominent in European intellectual circles after World War I and was greatly admired by Thomas Mann. His novels, including *Anna Édes* and *Skylark,* are known for their keen psychological insight and social commentary. Also worth discovering is novelist and essayist György Konrád, one of Hungary's leading 20th-century dissidents, whose *The Loser* is a disturbing reflection on intellectual life in a totalitarian state. The English writer Tibor Fischer's novels *Under the Frog* and *The Thought Gang* deal with life in contemporary Hungary. John Lukacs's *Budapest 1900: A Historical Portrait of a City and Its Culture* is an oversize, illustrated study of Hungary's capital as a particularly important moment in its history. For a more in-depth look at the city, András Török's *Budapest: A Critical Guide* offers detailed historical and architectural information, and is illustrated with excellent drawings.

VOCABULARY

Czech/Slovak

English	Czech/Slovak	Pronunciation
Basics		
Yes/no	Ano/ne	**Ah**-no/neh
Please	Prosím	**Pro**-seem
Thank you	Děkuji	**Dyek**-oo-yee
Pardon me	Pardon	**Par**-don
Hello.	Dobrý den	**Dob**-ree den
Do you (m/f) speak English?	Mluvíte anglicky?	**Mloo**-vit-éh ahng-**glit**-ski?
I don't speak Czech	Nemluvím česky	Nem-**luv**-eem ches-ky
I don't understand	Nerozumím	Neh-rohz-**oom**-eem
Please speak slowly	Prosím, mluvte pomalu	**Pro**-seem, **mloov**-teh poh-**mah**-lo
Please write it down.	Prosím napište	**Pro**-seem nah-**peesh**
Show me	Ukažte mně ₁	Oo-**kazh**-te mnye
I am American (m/f)	Jsem američan/američanka	Sem ah-**mer**-i-chan/Ah-mer-i-**chan**-ka
English (m/f)	Angličan/angličanka	**Ahn**-gli-chan/Ahn-gli-**chan**-ka
My name is . . .	Jmenuji se	**Ymen** weh-seh
On the right/left	Napravo/nalevo	Na-**pra**-vo/na-**leh**-vo
Arrivals	Přílety	**Pshee**-leh-tee
Where is . . . ?	Kde je	G'deh yeh
the station?	Nádraží	Nah-**drah**-zee
the train?	Vlak	Vlahk
the bus/tram?	Autobus/tramvaj	**Out**-oh-boos/**tram**-vie
the airport?	Letiště	**Leh**-tish-tyeh
the post office?	Pošta	**Po**-shta
the bank?	Banka	**Bahn**-ka
Stop here	Zastavte tady	**Zah**-stahv-teh **tah**-dee
I would like (m/f) . . .	Chtěl (chtěla) bych	Kh'tyel (**kh'tyel**-ah) bihk
How much does it cost?	Kolik to stojí?	Ko-**lik** toh **stoy**-ee?
Letter/postcard	Dopis/pohlednice	Doh-**pis**-ee/poh-**hled**-nit-seh
By airmail	Letecky	**Leh**-tet-skee
Help!	Pomoc!	**Po**-motz!
Numbers		
One	Jeden	Ye-**den**
Two	Dva	Dvah
Three	Tři	Tshree
Four	Čtyři	ch'**ti**-zhee
Five	Pět	Pyet
Six	Šest	Shest
Seven	Sedm	**Sed-oom**
Eight	Osm	**Oh**-soom
Nine	Devět	**Deh**-vyet
Ten	Deset	**Deh**-set

One hundred	Sto	Sto
Thousand	Tisíc	**Tee**-seets

Days of the Week

Sunday	Neděle	**Neh**-dyeh-leh
Monday	Pondělí	**Pon**-dye-lee
Tuesday	žterý	**Oo**-teh-ree
Wednesday	Středa	**Stshreh**-da
Thursday	Čtvrtek	Ch't'v'**r**-tek
Friday	Pátek	**Pah**-tek
Saturday	Sobota	**So**-boh-ta

Where to Sleep

A room	Pokoj	**Poh**-koy
The key	Klíč	Kleech
With bath/shower	S koupelnou/sprcha	S'**ko**-pel-noh/ sp'**r**-kho

Food

The menu	Jídelnílístek	**Yee**-dell-nee **lis**-tek
The check, please.	Učet, prosím	**Oo**-chet **pro**-seem
Breakfast	Snídaně	**Snyee**-dan-ye
Lunch	Oběd	**Ob**-yed
Dinner	Večeře	**Ve**-cher-zhe
Bread	Chléb	Khleb
Butter	Máslo	**Mah**-slo
Salt/pepper	Sůl/pepř	Sool/pepsh
Bottle	Láhev	**Lah**-hev
Red/white wine	Červené/bílé víno	**Cher**-ven-eh/**bee**-leh vee-no
Beer	Pivo	**Piv**-oh
Mineral water	Minerálka voda	Min-eh-**rahl**-ka **vo**-da
Milk	Mléko	**Mleh**-koh
Coffee	Káva	**Kah**-va
Tea (with lemon)	Čaj (s citrónem)	Tchai (se tsi-**tro**-nem)

Hungarian

English	Hungarian	Pronunciation

Basics

Yes/no	Igen/nem	**Ee**-gen/nem
Please	Kérem	**Kay**-rem
Thank you (very much)	Köszönöm (szépen)	**Kuh**-suh-num (**seh**-pen)
Excuse me	Bocsánat	**Boh**-chah-not
I'm sorry	Sajnálom	**Shahee**-nah-lome
Hello/how do you do	Szervusz	**Sair**-voose
Do you speak English?	Beszél angolul?	**Bess**-el **on**-goal-ool?
I don't speak Hungarian	Nem tudok magyarul	Nem **too**-dock **muh**-jor-ool.
I don't understand	Nem értem	Nem **air**-tem
Please speak slowly	Kérem, beszéljen lassan	**Kay**-rem, **bess**-el-yen **lush**-shun
Please write it down	Kérem, írja fel	**Kay**-rem, **eer**-yuh fell

Please show me	Megmutatná nekem	Meg-**moo**-taht-nah **neh**-kem
I am American	Amerikai vagyok	Uh-**meh**-rick-ka-ee **Vud**-yoke
I am English	Angol vagyok	**Un**-goal **vud**-yoke
My name is . . .	vagyok	**Vud**-yoke
Right/left	Bal/jobb	Buhl/yobe
Open/closed	nyitva/zárva	nit-va/**zahr-voh**
Arrival/departure	Érkezés/indulás	**Er**-keh-zesh/**In**-dool-ahsh
Where is . . . ?	Hol van	Hole vun
the train station?	a pályaudvar	uh **pah**-yo-**oot**-var
the bus station?	a buszállomás	uh **boose**-ahlo-mahsh
the bus stop?	a megálló	uh **meg**-all-oh
the airport?	a repülőtér	uh rep-ewluh-**tair**
the post office?	a pósta	uh **pohsh**-tuh
the bank?	a bank	uh bonhk
Stop here	alljon meg itt	**All**-yon meg it
I would like . . .	Szeretnék	**Sair**-et-neck
How much does it cost?	Mennyibe kerúl	**Men**-yibe **kair**-ule
Letter/postcard	Levél/képeslap	**Lev**-ehl/**kay**-pesh-lup
By airmail	Légi póstaval	**Lay**-gee **pohsh**-tuh-vol
Help!	Segitség	**Shay**-geet-shaig

Numbers

One	Egy	Edge
Two	Kettő	**Ket**-tuh
Three	Három	**Hah**-rome
Four	Négy	**Nay**-ge
Five	Öt	Ut
Six	Hat	Huht
Seven	Hét	Hate
Eight	Nyolc	Nyolts
Nine	Kilenc	**Kee**-lents
Ten	Tíz	Teez
One hundred	Száz	Sahz
One thousand	Ezer	**Eh**-zer

Days of the Week

Sunday	Vasárnap	**Vuh**-shar-nup
Monday	Hétfő	**Hate**-fuh
Tuesday	Kedd	Ked
Wednesday	Szerda	**Ser**-duh
Thursday	Csütörtök	**Chew**-tur-tuk
Friday	Péntek	**Pain**-tek
Saturday	Szombat	**Som**-but

Where to Sleep

A room	Egy szobá	Edge **soh**-bah
The key	A kulcsot	Uh **koolch**-oat
With bath/a shower	fúrdőszo-bával/egy zuhany	**Fure**-duh-soh-bah-vul/Edge **zoo**-hon

Food

A restaurant	A vendéglő/ az étterem	Uh **ven**-deh-gluh/ Uz **eht**-teh-rem
The menu	A étlap	Uh **ate**-lop
The check, please	A számlát kérem	Uh **sahm**-lot **kay**-rem
I'd like to order this	Kéem ezt	**Kay**-rem etz
Breakfast	Reggeli	**Reg**-gell-ee
Lunch	Ebéd	**Eb**-ehd
Dinner	Vacsora	**Votch**-oh-rah
Bread	Kenyér	**Ken**-yair
Butter	Vaj	Voy
Salt/pepper	Só/bors	Show/borsh
Bottle	Üveg	**Ew**-veg
Red/white wine	Vörös/fehér bor	**Vuh**-ruhsh/**feh**-hehr bore
Beer	Sör	Shur
Water/mineral water	Víz/kristályvíz	Veez/**krish**-tah-ee-veez
Milk	Tej	Tay
Coffee (with milk)	Kávé/tejeskávé	**Kah**-vay/**tey**-esh-**kah**-vay
Tea (with lemon)	Tea (citrommal)	**Tay**-oh **tsit**-rome-mol
Chocolate	Csokoládé	Chaw-kaw-**law**-day

INDEX

X = restaurant, ⊞ = hotel

176   Index

With guidebooks for every kind of travel—from weekend getaways to island hopping to adventures abroad—it's easy to understand why smart travelers go with **Fodor's**.

WHEREVER YOU TRAVEL, *H*ELP IS NEVER FAR AWAY.

From planning your trip to providing travel assistance along the way, American Express® Travel Service Offices are always there to help you do more.

Prague and Budapest

Prague
American Express TFS/Bureau de Change
Mostecka 12
(420) (2) 573 136 36

American Express Travel Service
Vaclavske Namesti 56
(420) (2) 242 199 92

Budapest
American Express Military Banking
Deak Ferenc U. 10
(36) (1) 266 8680

American Express Bureau de Change
Hotel Hilton Budapest
Hess Andras Ter1-3
(36) (1) 214 6446

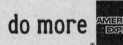

do more AMERICAN EXPRESS

Travel

www.americanexpress.com/travel